The DevOps Adoption Playbook

A Guide to Adopting DevOps in a Multi-Speed IT Enterprise

Sanjeev Sharm

WILEY   **IBM** Press™

The DevOps Adoption Playbook: A Guide to Adopting DevOps in a Multi-Speed IT Enterprise

Published by
John Wiley & Sons, Inc.
10475 Crosspoint Boulevard
Indianapolis, IN 46256
www.wiley.com

Copyright © 2017 by John Wiley & Sons, Inc., Indianapolis, Indiana

Published simultaneously in Canada

ISBN: 978-1-119-30874-4

ISBN: 978-1-119-31052-5 (ebk)

ISBN: 978-1-119-31076-1 (ebk)

Manufactured in the United States of America

10 9 8 7 6 5 4 3 2 1

Library of Congress Control Number: 2016962068

To my wife Ritika, for always motivating me to do more, be more, and never be satisfied with the status quo. And my children, Saransh and Shreya, for being the ones I am motivated to do and be more for.

About the Author

Sanjeev Sharma is an internationally known DevOps and cloud transformation thought leader, technology executive, and published author. Sanjeev's industry experience includes tenures as CTO and Worldwide Technical Sales Leader, Acquisition Integration Technical Leader, and IT Architect. As an IBM Distinguished Engineer, Sanjeev is recognized at the highest levels of the exclusive core of technical leaders at IBM.

Sanjeev provides core leadership to drive the adoption of cutting-edge solutions, architectures, and strategies for DevOps and the cloud. His experience as the Global CTO for DevOps Technical Sales at IBM, combined with his deep insight and ability to understand both business and IT needs, drives a unique perspective for any business. This perspective allows Sanjeev to advise and mentor C-level and senior technical executives on achieving DevOps and cloud transformations, across industries and geographies.

Sanjeev is a frequent speaker on the international tech scene, as a cloud and DevOps expert. He regularly publishes articles, blog posts, and videos for leading tech publications and his own blog, at http://bit.ly/sdarchitect. Sanjeev tweets as @sd_architect.

About the Technical Editor

Lee Reid has more than 30 years' experience in software engineering, architecture, product development, technology innovation, and team leadership in both manufacturing and information technology domains. Lee is an engineering graduate of General Motors Institute (BME) and the University of Michigan (MSE) and holds four U.S. patents. He has recently transitioned into higher education, where he leads IT and is introducing Lean and DevOps practices at St. Norbert College.

Credits

Project Editor
Adaobi Obi Tulton

Technical Editor
Lee Reid

Production Editor
Rebecca Anderson

Copy Editor
Marylouise Wiack

Production Manager
Katie Wisor

**Manager of Content Development
& Assembly**
Mary Beth Wakefield

Marketing Manager
Lorna Mein

**Professional Technology & Strategy
Director**
Barry Pruett

Business Manager
Amy Knies

Executive Editor
Jim Minatel

Project Coordinator, Cover
Brent Savage

Proofreader
Kim Wimpsett

Indexer
J&J Indexing

Cover Designer
Wiley

Cover Image
©traffic_analyzer/Getty Images

Acknowledgments

This book is an effort to put to paper countless conversations and (sometimes heated) discussions and debates on DevOps and IT optimization and innovation that I have had with my customers, co-workers, and peers in the DevOps community. Through these conversations and discussions, dozens of people have contributed to this book, not to mention all those whose blogs, articles, books, webinars, videos, meetings, and presentations I learned from.

The key contributors include my fellow DevOps subject matter experts and technology thought leaders at IBM. These include (in alphabetical order by first name):

- Al Wagner
- Albert Ho
- Alex Abi Khaled
- Ana Lopez-Mancisidor
- Andy Moynahan
- Ann Marie Somerville
- Anshu Kak
- Anujay Bidla
- Ava Hakim
- Bala Rajaraman
- Bernie Coyne
- Bill Higgins
- Bob Bogan
- Brian Naylor
- Chris Lazzaro
- Chris Lucca
- C. J. Paul
- Claudette Hickey
- Cliff Utstein
- Dan Berg
- David Curbishley
- David Leigh
- David Ziskind
- Dibbe Edwards
- Eric Minick
- Erik Anderson
- Greg Wunderle
- Hayden Lindsey
- Helen Dai
- Jagan Karuturi
- James Pierce
- Jeff Crume
- Jim Fieseler
- Jim Moffitt
- John Lanuti
- John Wiegand
- Kay Johnson
- Kedar Walimbe
- Kristof Kloeckner
- Kyle Brown
- Leigh Williamson
- Mahendra Pingale
- Maneesh Goyal
- Mark Borowski

- Mark Meinschein
- Mark Roberts
- Mark Tomlinson
- Meenagi Venkat
- Michael Elder
- Michael Samano
- Mike McNamee
- Mustafa Kapadia
- Paul Bahrs
- Paul Meharg
- Peter Eeles
- Peter Spung
- Randy Newell
- René Bostic
- Rick Weaver
- Rob Cuddy
- Robbie Minshall
- Roger Snook
- Rosalind Radcliffe
- Sal Vella
- Saleem Padani
- Steve Abrams
- Steve Kagan
- Steven Boone
- Sudhakar Frederick
- Swati Moran
- Tony Doyle
- Tim Hahn
- Tim Pouyer
- Varban Vassilev
- Wendy Toh

Some contributors who were formerly at IBM include the following:

- Alan Sanie
- Ashok Reddy
- Bowman Hall
- David Grimm
- David Myers
- Jan Svoboda
- Mike Lundblad
- Murray Cantor
- Steven Pogue
- Walker Royce

Several key customers, business partners, and experts also contributed, as real-life examples of leaders who led DevOps transformations at their own companies and organizations. Their stories from the trenches are the best sources of lessons learned. In many cases, they were at the other end of the conversations that led to the lessons learned and practices documented in this book. Because I met most of these people in a professional capacity as an IBM employee, I cannot list them all here. I will list the few who also co-presented at conferences, meetings, and webinars with me, or co-authored articles or blogs with me. They include the following (along with their current employers):

- Alan Shimel, DevOps.com
- Antony Morris, Monitise
- Ben Chodroff, CloudOne

- Brad Schick, Skytap
- Carmen DeArdo, Nationwide Insurance
- Chris Lepre, Wells Fargo
- Gareth Evans, Monitise
- James Governor, RedMonk
- Jayne Groll, DevOps Institute
- John Comas, NBCUniversal Media
- John Kosco, Blue Agility
- J. P. Morgenthal, CSC
- Mark Howell, Lloyds Banking Group
- Tapabrata "Topo" Pal, Capital One

I would be remiss to not acknowledge separately Gene Kim, the über-guru of DevOps, with his contributions through his books and his DevOps Enterprise Summit Conference. I personally had multiple opportunities to talk to him one-on-one, including a video interview I recorded in 2014 (`https://youtube/6QK2Mt-KPo4`).

I would also like to give a special thanks to Lee Reid. I have worked with Lee for more than a decade. He was also my "partner in crime," leading the Worldwide DevOps architect team at IBM for two years. We developed the DevOps Value Stream Mapping workshop techniques together, and I personally bounced tons of ideas off of him. It was only fitting that I had the opportunity to leverage Lee's talents and mind, despite his having left IBM for St. Norbert College, by having him be the technical editor of this book. There is no way the book would have made it to its final refined and well-structured form without Lee's insights, critique, and feedback.

Lastly, I would like to thank the wonderful editing staff at Wiley: Adaobi Obi Tulton, whose skills certainly live up to her Jedi-sounding name, and Marylouise Wiack for her complete mastery of language and prose (and yes, punctuation—my nemesis). The book is light-years ahead of what I originally put to paper because of their hard work and painstaking correction of my meek attempt to put words together into coherent sentences.

Contents at a Glance

Contents

Introduction

WHAT'S IN YOUR PLAYBOOK?

In April 2016, the Villanova Wildcats played the North Carolina Tar Heels in the 2016 NCAA Basketball National Championship Game. The game was the greatest ever, and it all came down to one last play, with just 4.7 seconds left on the clock. Joel Berry II hit a three-pointer to tie the game at 74 apiece, and Villanova Coach Jay Wright called his final timeout. In the NCAA, you have to go down the entire length of the court after a timeout. Immediately, Kris Jenkins of Villanova inbounded the ball to point guard Ryan Arcidiacono. Arcidiacono dribbled down the court past Berry, but it was the design of the play on both sides that made for the great ending. UNC played a 1-3-1 man-on-man press to Arcidiacono, to hopefully force a turnover, but if Arcidiacono got past Berry, they had Justin Jackson, Isaiah Hicks, and Brice Johnson, all who could stop the three-point shot. Villanova had designed a play to make sure that Arcidiacono got the ball off the inbound in a position in which he could get past half-court and find someone on the three-point line. Arcidiacono got past Berry, UNC collapsed, and Arcidiacono popped it back to Jenkins on the three-point line to get an almost-uncontested three-pointer to win the championship, and boy did it pay off. #Win!

—*By Saransh Sharma* (Sharma, 2016)

A Playbook for Adopting DevOps at Scale

Teams that excel do so not just because they have the best members, the best tools, the best training, the best processes, or the best leaders and coaches. They excel because they, as a team, have all of the above but also know what to do when they face various situations and challenges. They have a playbook of potential solutions (plays) for a variety of scenarios.

When faced with a unique situation or challenge, the players and coaches come together as a team to pick the right play from the playbook, and then, most importantly, they execute it. My alma mater, Villanova University, won the national championship when it came down to the final play, with seconds on the clock, because they had plays they had practiced before. They read the situation, picked the right play, and executed with precision to win. Had they not had the play that would catch North Carolina off guard, there may have been a different outcome.

In the same way, IT organizations need plays to execute. For day-to-day application delivery and operations, these so-called plays are captured in their development, delivery, and operational processes. IT organizations that succeed have good processes and execute them with excellence. However, transforming IT organizations is another story. Most organizations struggle with transformations, not having well-defined, winning plays that can overcome cultural and organizational inertia. This book captures a set of proven, repeatable plays for adopting DevOps at the enterprise scale and for transforming a large, complex, distributed IT organization to adopt DevOps.

These plays come from my experience over several years in the trenches as I helped dozens of organizations, of myriad sizes and maturity levels, in a variety of industries and geographical locations, to adopt DevOps. Since the early days of DevOps, as the Worldwide CTO of DevOps Technical Sales and Adoption at IBM, I have had a front-row seat to see the evolution and maturation of DevOps from a set of practices pioneered by startups to a cultural and technological transformation effort in large enterprises. I was a pioneer and thought leader for DevOps at IBM, and I became the face of DevOps to IBM's clients. This book distills patterns of success that I have observed among hundreds of clients working, struggling, and succeeding at adopting DevOps at organization or enterprise-wide scale.

Adopting DevOps in a small, co-located organization, without a lot of cultural memory, is not difficult. Even in large organizations, small teams— the proverbial *two-pizza*[1] teams—regularly succeed at attaining the business results promised by DevOps. In most organizations, you see many such efforts made, and most succeed. It is taking that success from an individual, isolated team level and scaling it to an enterprise that is a challenge. It is like having a series of small dance squads around the organization. However, these dance squads are all unique; some are doing the salsa, some jazz, some are ballroom dancing, while yet others are doing something my daughter tells me

---

[1] Amazon CEO Jeff Bezos claims that a team that cannot be fed with two pizzas is too big to be a productive team.

is "hip-hop." They cannot combine and grow to a massive dance ensemble that can perform at the next halftime show, filling up the entire paying field of a football stadium. For that they need to be dancing not only to the same music but also be performing the same dance form, in unison. Similarly, small unique teams cannot impact the entire organization. These teams need to make the effort to standardize practices, processes, platforms, and tools in order to allow them to be replicated in other parts of the organization.

The organization, in turn, needs to set the right environment for DevOps adoption by sponsoring transformation efforts, by enabling change to rigid legacy processes, and by a top-down push to overcome cultural inertia.

NOTE A bottom-up practitioner-led effort allows extremely productive individual teams to adopt DevOps and thrive. A top-down executive leadership-led effort enables these individual successes to scale.

The engagement of the business is imperative for these scaling efforts to succeed. IT organizations exist to deliver the capabilities a business needs in order to deliver business value to its customers. The business is asking the IT organization for *optimization*—to be more agile, to be resilient to change, to be more responsive, to do more with less, to be more productive, to increase throughput, to deliver faster, to deliver at higher quality, to be reactive to the market, to accelerate past the competition, to keep up with an ever-changing regulatory and compliance regime, and, yes, to reduce expenses.

In addition, it may also be asking for *innovation*—to allow the company to enter new markets, to enable exponential growth, to engage and grow the customer base, to be responsive to customers' needs, and, again, to reduce expenses. Delivering on these asks (hopefully not all of them at the same time) is what drives the need for change. It is what creates the motivation to work toward achieving the benefits that come from adopting DevOps.

NOTE You do not just adopt DevOps because it is cool. You need to have a business reason. The need for agility or velocity is the number-one reason that DevOps exists. The maturing and wide adoption of DevOps over the last few years is a reflection of today's dynamic marketplace, of customers' expectations.

Thus, in order for IT to undergo a transformation, this change has to improve and enhance IT's ability to deliver business capabilities in a manner that, in turn, improves and enhances the business value delivered. Proper partnering between the business and IT is imperative so that the transformation IT undergoes by adopting DevOps delivers what the business needs the most by properly balancing optimization and innovation. Business goals have to drive *why* IT transforms, which will in turn drive *how* IT transforms.

This book will categorize DevOps adoption plays as follows:

- DevOps for optimization
- DevOps for innovation
- Scaling DevOps adoption for the enterprise
- Driving DevOps transformation in the enterprise

It will include lessons learned, examples, success patterns, and anti-patterns for each adoption play. Like a sports *playbook*, this book is designed to deliver certain plays that can be executed for different scenarios and situations—depending upon your organization's current maturity and state—when it comes to transforming to a high-performance application delivery organization by adopting DevOps. An organization will need to take those plays and execute them in a tactical manner, based on the projects and teams that are adopting DevOps. Just as no battle plan ever survived contact with the enemy, these plays will need to be executed with an action plan or a broader adoption roadmap designed for each organization.

Furthermore, no organization is monolithic or homogenous in nature. Some parts of the organization may be more mature in some areas, but less mature in others. Some teams and groups may have already achieved agility and velocity, whereas others may be experiencing tremendous cultural inertia, all within the same organization, sometimes in the same building; they all need to work together in order to get scale.

An organization may have an innovation lab that is using modern agile and DevOps practices, while core systems teams may still be delivering in a rigid waterfall manner. Thus, these patterns of adoption will apply differently to different parts of the same organization and will need to be customized to suit the needs of various teams. To help with this customization effort, this book will also apply the technique of value stream mapping, used for decades as a component of *Lean* practices, that can be used to develop a custom adoption roadmap from these plays for an organization's business goals, current maturity, and capabilities.

Disrupt or Be Disrupted

We live in an era of massive change. In 1960, the average life expectancy of a Fortune 500 company was 75 years. Today, the average lifespan is just 15 years and declining further. So what gives? You only have to look as far as what is referred to as the *Uber effect* to understand why so many companies fail. A company led by a founder who is not from the taxi industry, Uber disrupted a centuries-old industry with the touch of a button on a mobile app; they have made cab service part of the on-demand, service economy, where consumers get what they want, when they want it, with no delays. New IT capabilities—accelerated by the intersection of new approaches like Agile and DevOps and technologies like cloud and microservices—are allowing startups armed with no more than services on a cloud and a mobile app to *Uber* large, established organizations with massive IT investments, valuable infrastructure, and experienced people.

NOTE   The fastest-growing transportation company in the world does not own any vehicles (Uber); the fastest-growing hospitality company providing living space for rent owns no property (Airbnb); the fastest-growing media company in the world produces no media (Facebook); the largest encyclopedia in the world has no staff writers (Wikipedia). Disruption is real.

So, ask yourself, is your organization a disruptor or a disruptee? The reality is, most organizations are the latter, putting IT organizations under more pressure today than ever before. Whether it's the fear of being Ubered by the competition or business demands to pick up the pace, IT organizations face a balancing act of ensuring the optimized operation of core applications and of being innovative. However, the truth is, innovation and maintaining the efficiencies of legacy systems can co-exist. While the prospect of competing with born-on-the-web companies like Uber and Airbnb may seem daunting, adopting DevOps at scale across your organization can enable your IT team to become more agile, efficient, and innovative. Adopting DevOps can put your IT in a position to become the enabler of change at your organization so it can fend off the disrupters; this in turn allows it to become the enabler that lets your organization become the disrupter. In today's technology-driven world, IT capabilities have become the key differentiators between the disrupter and the disrupted.

Defining DevOps

Before I begin to delve into the core capabilities and practices that you need to adopt and the various plays you need to execute in order to adopt DevOps in an organization, it is essential that you understand the definition of the term *DevOps*.

DevOps, like any new technology or tech-related movement that is adopted in industry, has become an overloaded buzzword. Everyone talks about it, not everyone knows what it is all about, and worst of all, many of those who claim to do it are really doing a terrible job. There are some excellent examples of companies that have excelled and are at the leading edge of the DevOps movement—the often-cited Etsy, Flickr, Facebook, and Netflix come to mind. But even here, there is contention and debate as to what is truly the best approach to DevOps. Netflix says what they do is *NoOps*, with developers taking over Ops responsibilities. Yet others counter that such a situation would lead to anarchy.

Such debate is to be expected as the industry refines what DevOps is as it evolves. As I will discuss at length in this book, there are different approaches to adopting DevOps, and each organization should look at adopting the right capabilities and practices of DevOps, based on their individual *risk-value* and *business drivers* balance. In fact, this adoption needs to start at a project level and then be scaled across the enterprise, leveraging techniques that will be described in this book.

As I mentioned previously, there are as many definitions of DevOps, or at least opinions of what DevOps really is, as there are blogs and tech "experts." There is the perspective of DevOps where the developer is king; DevOps where continuous delivery is the driver; DevOps where it all hinges on the cloud and one cannot have true DevOps without a cloud; and DevOps where DevOps equals microservices. So, let's start with the definition listed on a (fairly) neutral source—Wikipedia (Wikipedia, 2016):

> DevOps (a clipped compound of development and operations) is a culture, movement or practice that emphasizes the collaboration and communication of both software developers and other information-technology (IT) professionals while automating the process of software delivery and infrastructure changes. It aims at establishing a culture and environment where building, testing, and releasing software, can happen rapidly, frequently, and more reliably.

It is important to note that the Wikipedia definition has also evolved over time, as DevOps has matured. For comparison, here is the definition listed on Wikipedia in 2013:

> DevOps (a portmanteau of development and operations) is a software development method that stresses communication, collaboration and integration between software developers and Information Technology (IT) professionals. DevOps is a response to the interdependence of software development and IT operations. It aims to help an organization rapidly produce software products and services.

This evolution of the Wikipedia definition is indicative of the evolution of DevOps and how the industry views DevOps. Other than the replacement of the esoteric *portmanteau*, which had everyone looking it up on Dictionary.com, the key points to note are as follows:

- Replacement of software development method by culture, movement, or practice.
- Addition of the reference to *automation*.
- Change of the end-goal from "rapidly producing software products and services" to "building, testing, and releasing software, which can happen rapidly, frequently, and more reliably." Thus, the goal of DevOps changes from being just speed, to being speed, reliability, and quality.

Of course, I would be remiss not to mention the most concise definition of DevOps ever written; this was seen on a T-shirt at the O'Reilly Velocity Conference in 2013:

DevOps—taking the SH out of IT!

Who Is This Book For?

A sports team does not just have the players who take to the field on game day; it also has everything from coaches, assistant coaches, team management, team executives, trainers, doctors, nutritionists, physiotherapists, equipment managers, all the way to ball carriers and water servers. All are essential, and all need to excel in their roles and how they work together as a team, for the team to perform at its highest capacity. The same way, DevOps is not just about development and operations practitioners. It requires all the stakeholders in the application delivery pipeline to transform how they work, how they collaborate and communicate, how they work together like a high performance team.

This book is for all the team members in an organization who are stakeholders in the application delivery pipeline—from line of business owners, to analysts, architects, designers, developers, testers, quality assurance (QA) practitioners, automation engineers, infrastructure engineers, operations practitioners, database administrators, system administrators, documentation writers, project managers, product owners, all the way to c-suite executives. These roles may vary by organization, and many will need to evolve and transform what they do and how they do it as the organization adopts DevOps. This book is designed to benefit them all.

The application of each play discussed will impact each stakeholder role differently—some will see significant change in their role and how they interact with others, and some will see none at all. Just all the ball carriers and water servers are typically not impacted by which plays a team runs, but they are still stakeholders who can impact team performance if they do not perform as expected. The same way certain roles are supporting roles in IT too. Other roles, like key stakeholders who directly work with artifacts and processes that are a part of the application delivery pipeline, will benefit significantly from the plays in the book. They are the players and the direct supporting staff who play the game or support those who do, enabling them to perform at peak performance capacity.

Chapter 1 is an overview of DevOps. It documents the evolution of DevOps from its origins to today. It defines and describes all the common practices and capabilities that make up DevOps. It sets the stage with the broad definition of DevOps and of a DevOps transformation, which are used as the premise of this book.

Chapter 2 is focused on the leaders on the team: the coaches, the team captain, the senior players who form the core of the team. It focuses on how to assess the playing conditions and the competition to develop and select the right set of *plays*—the playbook for the team. It is for the IT management, project and program managers, product owners, team leads, senior practitioners, DevOps coaches, and anyone who aspires to be one of them.

Chapter 3 provides guidance on how to build a business case for a DevOps Transformation, allowing for the right sponsorship and investments to ensure success.

Chapters 4 through 6 are the actual plays. They are categorized as follows:

- *Chapter 4—DevOps Plays for Optimization*: Plays to optimize the application delivery pipeline to maximize efficiency, by eliminating waste

■ *Chapter 5—DevOps Plays for Innovation:* Plays to make the application delivery pipeline fast and agile to support the ability to experiment, to drive innovation

■ *Chapter 6—DevOps Plays for scaling DevOps in the enterprise:* Plays to scale DevOps adoption across the organization, an organization that is large, complex, distributed and is not homogenous in its maturity

Chapter 7 is a chapter dedicated to the executive leadership driving the DevOps adoption. Like the general managers and executives of a sports teams, executives make the executive decisions and set the direction and culture of the organization. They are the ones who need to make the decision to undertake a DevOps transformation. They need to make the necessary investment and sponsor the transformation. They will need to know how to make the business case and determine the return on investment for such a transformation. They need to drive the transformation, from the front, across the enterprise.

The book also has one appendix. It is an example of a DevOps Transformation adoption roadmap, developed for a fictitious bank by delivering a *value stream mapping* exercise.

The book purposefully has tried to remain tool and platform agnostic. While several examples of tools, platforms, and technologies—both commercial and open source—are made throughout the book, they are done to as current examples of tooling and platforms available in the market to enable automation. Tools are necessary to automate processes, making them fast, repeatable, scalable, and error free. However, tools and platforms are continuously evolving and getting replaced by newer and better ones. It is hence a futile effort to recommend or even document available tools and platforms. The goal is to highlight capabilities, while remaining as tool and platform agnostic as possible to remain relevant even as tools and platforms available evolve.

The Sports Analogies

Individual commitment to a group effort—that is what makes a team work, a company work, a society work, a civilization work.

—Vince Lombardi, legendary American football coach

There is nothing that transcends culture, language, and geographic borders than sports. If you have any doubts, just watch the reruns of the recently concluded Olympics in Rio. Analogies from sports are also very relevant to application development and delivery, as they are both team events. While developing or delivering a new application or service may not require the physical conditioning an Olympics gold medalist does, they do require the leadership, communication, collaboration, and trust that any team sport needs.

I also have a personal passion for sports. Right from my childhood I grew up in a household that had a love for sports. My maternal grandfather was an Olympian and national sports figure in India. He played for the Indian National Hockey team in his youth and later was a sports executive with the Indian National Football (Soccer) team at the 1952 Helsinki Olympic Games. He also had the opportunity to run with the Olympic torch for the 1964 Tokyo Olympics, as the torch passed through India. He remained a sports executive for domestic soccer tournaments for several decades after that, including when I was a child. Growing up with an Olympic torch in the family home gives one a high respect for sportsmen and women.

In the book I have taken examples, quotes, and players' and coaches' experiences from multiple sports and mapped them to the Plays of DevOps Adoption. The parallels are intended to make the plays more relatable and understandable and hopefully the book more interesting to read.

Major Lachhman Singh running with the '64 Tokyo Olympics Torch (Source: Singh Family Personal Collection)

Companion Website

This books comes with a companion website where I will continue to post updates and new content, including case studies, presentations, videos, and outtakes from the book. Check it out at http://devopsadoptionplaybook.com.

CHAPTER 1

DevOps: An Overview

RANT OF A DEVELOPMENT MANAGER

So, the developer completes writing code for a new service by Monday afternoon. She builds the code, runs unit tests, and delivers the code to the integration stream so it gets included in the continuous integration (CI) build. To get her service tested, before leaving for work, she opens a ticket with the Quality Assurance (QA) team.

Tuesday morning, the QA team comes in and sees the ticket assigned to them. A tester gets the ticket and emails the developer asking for the deployment instructions. As there is no deployment automation, the developer responds saying she will deploy the service to the QA environment herself. Tuesday afternoon, they get on a conference call to deploy the code. The developer discovers that test environment is not compatible with her code. They need a new environment. Tuesday evening, the tester opens a ticket with the operations (Ops) team for a new environment, with the new specs.

Wednesday morning, the Ops team assigns the ticket to an engineer who looks at the specs and sees a firewall port change. As he leaves for lunch, he opens a ticket with the security team to approve the port change. Wednesday afternoon, the security team assigns the ticket to a security engineer, who approves the change. Wednesday evening, the Ops engineer receives the approval and starts building the new environment. He needs to manually build new Virtual Machines (VMs), with an Operating System (OS), app server, database, and web server.

Thursday morning, the server build is done, and the ticket is closed. The tester emails the developer again to deploy the new service. The developer deploys the service, and the tester starts walking through the test scripts, which pass. He now needs to run a regression test but needs additional test data to re-run tests. Thursday afternoon he opens a ticket to request new test data with the production support team.

continued

continued

> Friday morning, the production support team assigns a database analyst (DBA) to extract test data from production. But now it's Friday afternoon. Everyone knows DBAs don't work on Friday afternoons. Monday morning, the tester gets the test data from the DBA. It takes him 20 minutes to run the regression tests and discover a defect. He returns the ticket to the developer—a full week after the code was written and built. A full week of coding has now been done on top of that code, not knowing it was defective. We are now another week behind.
>
> What's scary about this story is that when I tell it to my peers in other companies, they shake their heads not in empathy but in amazement as to how efficient we are compared to them!
>
> —Yet another frustrated development manager

DevOps: Origins

The DevOps movement began with a seminal talk given by John Allspaw and Paul Hammond (both at Flickr/Yahoo at that time) at the O'Reilly Velocity 2009 conference. The talk was entitled "10+ Deploys Per Day: Dev and Ops Cooperation at Flickr."[1] Ten deploys a day was considered unprecedented. Their approach was eventually referred to as *DevOps* by Patrick Debois, when he organized the first *DevOpsDays* event in Ghent, Belgium, the same year.

While the name caught on and started getting tremendous interest, the traction was initially limited to startups, more specifically, organizations delivering web applications. These applications were created by developers (the Dev) who typically delivered changes and updates to their web apps in a very rapid manner. The main hurdle they faced was that of operations (the Ops), which were slow in deploying those changes, as they had rigid and rigorous change management processes.

The goal of the DevOps movement was to address this impedance mismatch between the Dev and Ops teams; to bridge the chasm between them; and to foster more communication, collaboration, and trust. At its heart, it was a cultural movement, focused on changing the cultural differences between Dev and Ops, along with automation to make application delivery faster, more efficient,

---

[1] http://conferences.oreilly.com/velocity/velocity2009/public/schedule/detail/7641

and eventually, continuous. In 2010, Jez Humble, then at ThoughtWorks, took DevOps to practitioners throughout the industry with his book *Continuous Delivery*, codifying some of the practices that make up the core of DevOps and making DevOps adoption tangible and available to all.

Still, DevOps was seen as something done by the *unicorns*—the startups and the upstarts, organizations at the cutting edge of innovation, without large, complex legacy systems to maintain. It had not yet gone mainstream with the large enterprises. However, these large enterprises were seeing what the startups were achieving with DevOps, and were trying to determine how to adapt DevOps for their own needs. Organizations like IBM were beginning to dabble with deployment automation, and with visual architecting of environments, and even stitching these two capabilities together. At the same time, well-established companies in the build automation space, like UrbanCode, started pivoting into DevOps with the release of uDeploy, thus establishing a new category of tools to enable continuous delivery. Other companies in the automation space, like Nolio, joined in with their own competitive offerings. In parallel, coming from the Ops and *infrastructure as code* side, companies like Opscode (now called Chef) and Puppet Labs were gaining traction (Opscode with Chef, and Puppet Labs with Puppet).

The real growth for DevOps into large enterprises began in 2012, with companies like IBM jumping into the fray with their first, albeit short-lived, continuous delivery experiment with SmartCloud Continuous Delivery. Several consulting firms, like ThoughtWorks and IBM, also started to offer consulting services for organizations, especially large enterprises looking to adopt DevOps, and helping to translate what worked for the unicorns so that it could work for enterprises. IBM and CA Technologies announced their formal entrance into the DevOps world by acquiring UrbanCode and Nolio, respectively (and coincidently on the same day in April 2013). However, the biggest turning point for the DevOps movement since its inception came later, in 2013, with the publication of Gene Kim's book, *The Phoenix Project*. This book, inspired by and modeled after the historic *The Goal* by Eliyahu M. Goldratt, became the must-read book for the modern-day implementation of *Lean* practices and Goldratt's *Theory of Constraints* in the IT world, just as Goldratt's book had been a few decades earlier for the manufacturing world. Kim truly took DevOps mainstream with his book, as well as subsequent work he has done with the *State of DevOps Report* that he publishes every year, with Jez Humble and Puppet Labs.

DevOps: Roots

Where does DevOps come from? While I have already outlined its origin story, the true roots of DevOps predate Allspaw, Debois, Humble, and Kim by almost a century. You have to go way back to the 1910s and look at the origins of the Lean movement.

The Lean movement started in manufacturing with Henry Ford and his adoption of Lean for flow management in the Model T production lines. This work was further extended, refined, and codified by Kiichiro Toyoda and Taiichi Ohno at Toyota starting in the 1930s and really accelerating after World War II. Their work was both refined and influenced by Dr. William E. Deming in the 1950s, who proposed the Plan–Do–Check–Act (or Adjust) cycle (PDCA), to continuously improve manufacturing quality. Based on this core approach, the Lean manufacturing movement aimed to both continuously improve the product being manufactured and reduce waste in the manufacturing process. Lean was further refined in the works of James P. Womack and Daniel T. Jones when they published *The Machine that Changed the World* in 1990 and (required reading for everyone) *Lean Thinking* in 1996 (Lean.org, 2016).

DEMING ON LEAN THINKING AND CONTINUOUS IMPROVEMENT

Dr. W. Edwards Deming taught that by adopting appropriate principles of management, organizations can increase quality and simultaneously reduce costs (by reducing waste, rework, staff attrition and litigation while increasing customer loyalty). The key is to practice continual improvement and think of manufacturing as a system, not as bits and pieces.

—Dr. Deming's Management Training (Deming, 1998)

In 2001 came Agile, a group of 17 thought leaders, including Alistair Cockburn and Martin Fowler, who created *The Agile Manifesto*.[2] The core principles of the manifesto were to get away from the rigid, waterfall-oriented, documentation-heavy world of software development, which was resulting in most software development projects being late, over budget, or abject failures.

---

[2] http://www.agilemanifesto.org

Their goal was to move to an iterative approach where there was constant interaction with the customer, end-user, or a surrogate who represented them. They wanted to move away from measuring progress through major rigid milestones such as *Requirements Documentation*, which brought code no closer to being delivered than the day before. Other goals were to use real running code (working software) as the true measure of progress; to look at planning as being adaptive to real progress; and to create requirements that did not need to be written in stone up front, but would evolve and be refined as the applications were being developed.

Agile was refined with the development of methodologies like XP, Scrum, and, more recently, Scaled Agile Framework or SAFe. Today, Agile is used by both large and small organizations to deliver projects of all sizes and technologies.

Agile was the precursor to, and became the core driver for, the need for DevOps. As developers started delivering code faster, that code needed to be tested faster; it also needed to be deployed to Dev and test servers, and eventually to production, more often. The Ops teams were not set up for this, which resulted in a major bottleneck being created at the Dev-to-test handoff, due to lack of availability of the right test environments as and when needed and, more importantly, at the hands of production at release time. Production release remained a major undertaking, with "release weekends" that typically lasted beyond the weekend.

THE RELEASE WEEKEND

I remember when I was working as a developer at a financial services institution in the early '90s. (We called them banks back then.) On release weekends, much to my chagrin, we were asked to show up at work on Friday mornings with our sleeping bags in hand. We were expected to stay there through the weekend. There were multiple conference rooms set up with conference call bridges open to get every team in communication with each other. One conference room was set up like a war room with the project leader coordinating all the stakeholders off a massive spreadsheet. The management did their best to create a party atmosphere, but that faded right after the first few hours. We were communicating with the Ops people for the first time. We were handing off our code to people who had never

continued

continued

> seen the code before. They were deploying code into environments we had no visibility into, using scripts and tools we had no familiarity with. It would be chaos the whole weekend. Lots of delivered food and stale coffee, and nothing seemed to work as planned. And the traders we supported, they were smart. They always planned their team outing or picnics on the Monday following. They knew nothing would work. And they were right. Fortunately, we only did this twice a year. Even more fortunately for me personally, I worked there for only two releases.

The rapid development of code in short iterations amplified the need for better collaboration and coordination between Dev and Ops teams. The frequent failure of release to production exposed the need for providing developers with access to production-like environments. The major inefficiencies in the entire process were exposed by making just one part of the process—developing code—more efficient, which created major bottlenecks with test and Ops. If you think of the application development and delivery process as an assembly line in a factory, speeding up an operation of just one of the stations to increase the number of widgets it produces does not help the overall delivery speed if the downstream stations are still operating at a slower speed. It just creates more of a backlog for them. (See Figure 1-1.) This was not just a challenge for Ops, but for all the stakeholders in the delivery life cycle.

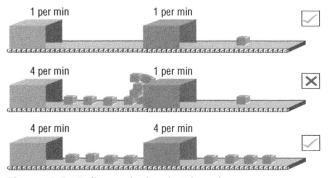

Figure 1-1: Delivery pipeline bottlenecks

The focus now turned toward minimizing *cycle time*—the time from the inception of a requirement, or *user story*, to the time that capability is in the hands of the customer, or at least is integrated, tested, and ready to be deployed to the customer. This resulted in the development of the two core capabilities of DevOps: continuous integration (already a core competency of Agile) and continuous delivery. I will discuss both capabilities in detail shortly. This extension of Agile beyond the Dev-test cycle—including the Ops team in the delivery cycle, as a part of the process, and not in a separate silo that was not engaged until the code was ready for release—became the core principle of DevOps.

Addressing Dev versus Ops

Dev and Ops have traditionally lived in different silos, with misaligned, even opposing priorities. Development (Dev) is tasked with creating innovation and getting it into the hands of users as soon as possible. Operations (Ops) is tasked with making sure that the users have access to a stable, fast, and responsive system. While Dev and Ops' ultimate goal is to make the user a satisfied (and potentially a happy, paying) customer of the systems they provide, their views of how to do it tend to be inherently antithetical. No developer wants to intentionally produce a buggy system that would cause the application to crash while a user is using it. No operations person wants developers to not produce updates with new, exciting features and capabilities. It is how they go about it that is different. This is a classic symptom of what is referred to as *water-Scrum-fall* (Forrester, 2011). Developers want, and are expected to produce, new features quickly. Operations want, and are expected to produce, a stable system, at all times.

Dev versus Ops

Before the advent of Agile, in the purely waterfall-oriented paradigm, when developers and operations lived in truly isolated worlds, these opposing priorities were not that much of an issue. Developers and operations worked on a schedule that was marked by limited interactions, only at release times. Developers knew when the release date was, and they could only release new features then. If they did not create a new feature by the release date, they would have to wait for the next *release train*. Operations knew when the train would come to town. They would have enough time to test the new features before deploying them, and they could take days (weekends) to deploy them out to customers. For large systems, they could even deploy in a phased manner spread over long periods of time. Stability was maintained.

Agile changed all that. With continuous integration (CI), developers were now deploying their features daily. There was no release train to wait for; it was a conveyer belt (pipeline) that ran all the time. The developers now wanted their features up and running—in the Dev environment, in the test environment, and finally in production (Prod)—at the same frequency at which they produced and integrated them. They wanted Ops to accommodate all these new releases.

Ops now had to deal with not one release every so often but a continuous barrage of CI builds. These builds may or may not have been deployment-ready, but they had to be managed by Ops and deployed to test, and eventually production, environments. Ops now cared more about quality. Developers and testers cared about how quickly they could get Dev and test environments and whether or not those environments were production-like. They did not want to test the code they were delivering on environments that did not function and behave like production environments. Thus, Ops could no longer take days to provision and configure new environments—for Dev, test, and eventually Prod. They had to do all of this while still maintaining stability and reliability of production systems.

> **CYCLE TIME?**
>
> If you have two-week Scrums but it takes three weeks to get a new test server, how long are your Scrums?

Dev and Ops

The solution to this battle between Dev and Ops is what DevOps addresses: to achieve the balance between innovation and stability and between speed of delivery and quality. To achieve this, both Dev and Ops need to improve how they operate and align.

The Dev View   The previous section may give the impression that Ops needs to change more than Dev, but Dev also needs to make several changes:

- Dev needs to work with Ops to understand the nature of the production systems their applications will be running on. What are the standards for the production systems (environment patterns) and how should their applications perform on them? Within what constraints do the applications need to operate? Dev now needs to understand system and enterprise architectures.

▦ Dev needs to get more involved in testing. This means not just making sure that their code is bug-free but also testing the application to see how it will perform in production. This requires Dev to work closely with Quality Assurance (QA) and to test their application in a production-like system. (I'll discuss production-like systems later in this chapter.)

▦ Dev also needs to learn how to monitor deployed applications and understand the metrics Ops cares about. They need to able to decipher how processes interact and how one process can cause another one to slow down or even crash. They need to understand how changes to their code will impact the entire production system and not just their own application.

▦ Dev needs to communicate and collaborate better with Ops.

The Ops View Ops needs to be able to provision new environments rapidly, and they need to architect their systems to absorb rapid change.

▦ Ops needs to know what code is coming and how it may impact their system. This requires them to be involved with Dev, right from understanding requirements and system specs of the applications being developed. This process is referred to in Lean and DevOps as *shift left*. They need to make sure that their systems can accommodate these applications as they are enhanced.

▦ Ops needs to automate how they manage their systems. Rapid change with stability cannot be achieved without automation. Automation will allow not only rapid change but also rapid rollbacks, if something does break.

▦ Ideally, Ops needs to version their systems. This can only be done when the infrastructure and all changes to it are captured and managed as version-controlled code. Thus, they need to leverage infrastructure as code or, even better, software-defined environments. (I'll talk more about that later in this chapter.)

▦ Ops needs to monitor everything throughout the delivery pipeline, whichever environment the Ops teams manage. They need to be able to spot potential instability as soon as it happens.

▦ Ops needs to communicate and collaborate better with Dev.

In a nutshell, Dev and Ops both need to be brought into the DevOps paradigms. They both need to know that this is not going to be easy, or something that can be achieved in a day. They need to plan for and work toward gradually adopting the changes needed to achieve the promise of DevOps. They may never get to—and in most cases should never get to—where Dev and Ops are one team, but they need to understand that their roles will change as they adopt DevOps. They need to change enough to work together and find the right alignment between Dev and Ops that their organization needs and improve from there.

That being said, the gap between Dev and Ops is not the only inhibitor to a fast cycle time in the delivery lifecycle. All the stakeholders in the delivery lifecycle need to communicate and collaborate better.

The Business View   Let's look at the *business view*. At the end of the day, it is the business's requirements that IT is delivering through the applications and services delivered. What does the business (lines of business to be more precise) need?

- Business needs visibility into the status of what is being delivered by IT. Are they on time and on budget to deliver the applications and services?
- Business needs the application delivery teams to provide feedback on how the clients and end users are utilizing the applications and services being delivered. Are they able to get the business value as expected by the business?

A more detailed analysis on the business's point of view and expectations of IT, and how DevOps helps the business will be discussed in detail in subsequent chapters.

DevOps: Practices

Much has been written in books, and even more in blog posts, about the capabilities that make up DevOps. Several thought leaders have divided these practices into various categories, and in some cases even with different names. IBM lists several such practices, which are found under the following broad categories:

- Think
- Code
- Deliver
- Run
- Manage

■ Learn
■ Culture

This taxonomy comes from the IBM Garage Method,[3] a new methodology for adopting DevOps focused on delivering Cloud Native and Hybrid Cloud hosted applications.

There are two key capabilities of DevOps at its core: *continuous integration* and *continuous delivery*. Without these two capabilities, there is no DevOps, and they should be considered essential to DevOps adoption, with all others being extensions, or supporting capabilities. These two concepts focus on minimizing *cycle time*. Let's revisit the definition of *cycle time*.

NOTE   Cycle time: The time from the inception of a requirement or user story to when that capability is in the hands of the customer, or at least is integrated, tested, and ready to be deployed to the customer.

Continuous Integration

Delivering a software application or system today involves multiple teams of developers working on separate components of the application. Typically, the completed application also needs to interact with other applications or services to perform its functions. Some of these external applications or services may be legacy applications that exist in the enterprise, or they may be external third-party services. There is, as a result, an inherent need for developers to integrate their work with components built by other development teams and with other applications and services.

This need makes integration an essential and complex task in the software development lifecycle. The process of doing this at a regular cadence is commonly referred to as *continuous integration*, and it is a key practice from Agile. In traditional development processes, integration was a secondary set of tasks conducted after the components (or sometimes the complete application) were built. This sequence was inherently costly and unpredictable, as the incompatibilities and defects that tend to be discovered only during integration were discovered late in the development process. The result was typically a significant increase in rework and risk.

The Agile movement introduced a logical step to help reduce this risk by integrating components continuously (or as continuously as possible). In this step,

---

[3] https://www.ibm.com/devops/method/

developers integrate their work with the rest of the development team regularly (at least daily) and test the integrated work. In the case of enterprise systems, which span multiple platforms, applications, or services, developers also integrate with other systems and services as often as possible. An example of Continuous Integration across multiple teams and components is shown in Figure 1-2.

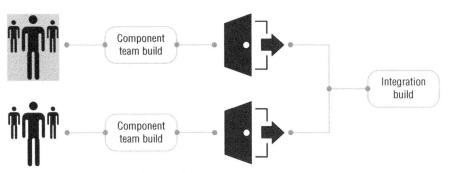

Figure 1-2: Continuous integration

These steps to integrate results can lead to early discovery and exposure of integration risks. In the case of enterprise systems, they can also expose known and unknown dependencies related to either technology or scheduling that may be at risk. As these practices have matured, some organizations have adopted continuous integration practices that developers follow every time they check in code. In the most mature organizations, continuous integration has led to capabilities for continuous delivery in which the code and components are not only integrated but are also delivered to a production-like environment for testing and verification. I'll discuss this in the next section.

The demands placed by business and customers on development organizations have driven the wide adoption by development teams of Agile development practices. These practices are aimed at reducing the gap between the business (or the customers) and the development teams. They work primarily in three ways:

- By breaking the development effort into small chunks of work that can be completed in time-bound iterations. This allows developers to identify and resolve risk earlier than when they undertake entire projects or larger portions of projects.
- By including contact with the end user or a surrogate representing the user into the development iterations. This helps give developers a better

understanding of the user's needs and allows for changing needs to be more quickly accommodated.

- By releasing software at the end of every iteration. This allows developers to demonstrate regularly what they have built in order to obtain user feedback.

As described, continuous integration is one of the tenets of such Agile development. It allows for developers to integrate their software components with components that are being developed by others—either internally or externally—on a regular basis, to allow for early identification of risks.

Practices of Continuous Integration

Martin Fowler, a signatory of what is known as the *Agile Manifesto*, is a thought leader in the development of continuous integration processes. He has broken down the concept into ten practices, which are described here.

1. **Maintain a single-source repository.** Whether managing code or any file, it is critical to use version management tools to manage the source base that allows multi-user access and streaming, or branching and merging, and that allows multiple developers in distributed locations to work on the same set of files. With any multi-platform development effort, using a common, cross-platform, single-source repository becomes even more important. If such a repository is not implemented across platforms, any platform left isolated (System z or Mobile, for example) will not be able to participate in continuous integration practices. Integration with any work conducted on the isolated platform will become an after-effort, waterfall-style integration.

   This transition to a modern source-code repository represents a significant change for legacy system development teams that may have been using the same capability for years. However, a single source code management (SCM) tool is critical to allow the management of all artifacts, help break down the silos, and remove a key bottleneck.

2. **Automate the build.** Automating the build is what makes continuous integration continuous. Additionally, it should be possible to coordinate the build across multiple platforms, when required.

3. **Make your build self-testing.** Just as builds need to be automated, so does the testing. The goal of continuous integration is not only to integrate the work of teams but also to see if the application or system being built is functioning and performing as expected. This requires

that a suite of automated test scripts be built for unit-test level and for the component and application level. In true continuous integration, developers should be able to start an integration build by kicking off the right test suite when they commit the code. This process requires that the build scripts include the capability to build the software if needed, provision the test server, provision the test environment, deploy the built software to the test server, set up the test data, and run the right test scripts.

The requirement to have the environments to do the build, deploy it, and do the automated testing at any time helps improve the quality of the final code. This requires availability of system resources, the willingness to run large numbers of automated tests on a regular basis, and the development of the automated tests.

4. **Ensure that everyone commits to the mainline every day.** The goal of having every developer, across all components and all development environments, commit their code to the mainline of their development streams every day is to help ensure that integrations remain as simple as possible. Even today, many developers work independently on their code changes until the final build, which is when they realize their work is impacted by the work of other developers. This can lead to delays in releasing functions or to last-minute changes that have not been properly tested being deployed into production. Regular integration of code can help ensure that these dependencies are identified sooner so the development team can handle them in a timely manner and without time constraints.

5. **Ensure that every commit builds the mainline on an integration machine.** This is a second part of Practice 4. Making sure that every commit is built and that automated regression tests are run can help ensure that problems are found and resolved earlier in the development cycle.

6. **Keep the build fast.** Virtually nothing impedes continuous integration more than a build that takes extremely long to run. Builds with modern tools are generally fast due to the standard practice of building only changed files.

7. **Test in a clone of the production environment.** Testing in an environment that does not accurately represent the production system leaves a lot of risk in the system. The goal of this practice, then, is to test in a clone of the production environment. It is not always possible, however, to create a clone of an entire multi-server environment just for testing.

It is even harder to create a clone environment with other workloads running on it.

Instead, this practice requires the creation of what is known as a *production-like* environment. In terms of specifications, this environment should be as close to the production environment as possible. It should also be subject to proper test data management. A test environment should not contain production data because in many cases that data needs to be masked. Proper test data management can also reduce the size and complexity of the test environment.

A complex system with multiple components—both pre-existing (such as other services and applications) and new components being developed—also creates challenges. All the components, services, and systems that applications need to access and interact with may not be available for running tests. This may occur for multiple reasons: the component, service, or system may not have been built yet; it may have been built but is available only as a production system that cannot be tested with non-production data; or it may have a cost associated with its use. For third-party services, for example, cost can become a major issue.

8. **Make it easy for anyone to get the latest executable.** Anyone associated with the project should have access to what is built and should be provided with a way to interact with it. This allows validation of what is being built against what was expected.

9. **Make sure everyone can see what is happening.** This is a communication-and-collaboration-related best practice, rather than one related to continuous integration. However, its importance to teams practicing continuous integration cannot be discounted. Visibility to the progress of continuous-integration builds via a central portal or dashboards can provide information to all practitioners.

This can boost morale and help build the sense of working as a team with a common goal. If challenges occur, visibility can provide the impetus for people to step in and help other practitioners or teams. Visibility via a common team portal is especially important for teams that are not collocated—but it is also key for collocated teams and for cross-platform teams that work on different components of a project. This visibility should extend all the way back to the Business. As described in the earlier section on the *Business View*, visibility into the current status of the applications and services being delivered is a critical need of the business.

10. **Automate deployment.** Continuous integration naturally leads to the concept and practice of continuous delivery—the process of automating the deployment of software to test, system testing, staging, and production environments.

Continuous Delivery

Continuous delivery simply involves taking the concept of continuous integration to the next step. Once the application is built, at the end of every continuous integration build, it is delivered to the next stage in the application delivery lifecycle. It is delivered to the Quality Assurance (QA) team for testing and then to the operations team for delivery to the production system. The goal of continuous delivery is to get the new features that the developers are creating out to the customers and users as soon as possible. Now, all builds that come out of a continuous integration effort do not need to go to QA; only the "good" ones with functionality that is at a stage of development where it can be tested need to go to QA.

Similarly, all the builds that go through QA do not need to go to production. Only those that are ready to be delivered to the users, in terms of functionality, stability, and other non-functional requirements (NFRs) should be delivered to production. To test whether the builds coming out are production-ready, they should be delivered to a staging or test area that is production-like. This practice of regularly delivering the application being developed to QA and operations for validation and potential release to customers is referred to as *continuous delivery*.

Continuous delivery requires the creation of a delivery pipeline (as shown in Figure 1-3), with the core capability that automates the delivery pipeline being continuous delivery. As continuous integration produces builds at a steady pace, these builds need to be rapidly progressed to other environments in the delivery pipeline. Builds need to be deployed to the test environment to perform tests, to the integration environment for integration builds and integration testing, and so on, all the way to production. Continuous delivery facilitates deployment of applications from one environment to the next, as and when deployment is needed.

Continuous delivery, however, is not as simple as just moving files around. It requires orchestrating the deployments of code, content, applications, middleware and environment configurations, and process changes, as shown in Figure 1-4.

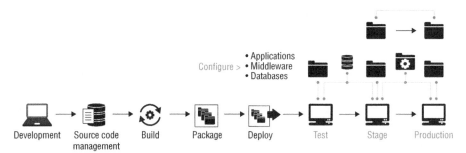

Figure 1-3: A delivery pipeline

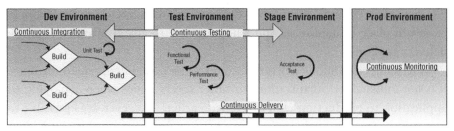

Figure 1-4: Continuous delivery

With regard to continuous delivery, there are two key points to remember:

- It does not mean deployment of every change out to production, a process commonly known as *continuous deployment*. Instead, continuous delivery is not a process but rather a capability to deploy to any environment, at any time, as needed. (I will discuss this more in the next section.)
- It does not always mean deploying a complete application. What is deployed may be the full application, one or many application components, application content, application or middleware configuration changes, or the environment to which the application is being deployed. It may also be any combination of these.

Two of the ten practices of continuous integration form the link to, and the necessity for, continuous delivery:

- Testing in a clone of the production environment
- Automating deployment

While testing in a clone of the production environment (the seventh practice) may be a testing practice, it also requires continuous delivery capabilities to deliver the new build to the clone test environment. This delivery may require provisioning the test environment and any virtualized instances of services and applications. It may also require the positioning of relevant test data, in addition to the actual deployment of the application to the right test environment.

The tenth practice of continuous integration, automating deployment, is the core practice of continuous delivery; it is not possible to achieve continuous delivery without automation of the deployment process. Whether the goal is to deploy the complete application or only one component or configuration change, continuous delivery requires having tools and processes in place to deploy, as and when needed, to any environment in the delivery pipeline.

Practicing continuous delivery also tests the actual deployment process. It is not unusual for organizations to suffer severe issues when deploying an application to production (as I discussed earlier). However, it is possible to uncover these issues early in the delivery lifecycle by automating the deployment process and validating it by deploying multiple times to production-like environments in pre-production.

Continuous Delivery versus Continuous Deployment

In the past, companies like Flickr posted on their blogs[4] how many *deploys* they had so far in a particular day or week. Looking at an organization that deploys to production 89 times in a week can be very intimidating. More importantly, it begs the question, "What do you deploy to production 89 times in a week?"

This is a scenario that may actually keep some people away from adopting DevOps practices, because they believe that they have to deploy every change to production. That is certainly not the case. First, you need to understand what is being deployed here, and second (and more importantly), you need to understand that this is not applicable, necessary, or even feasible for every organization.

What Do You Deploy 89 Times a Week?   When organizations say they are doing double-digit deploys to production every day, it does not mean that they are delivering dozens of new features or bug fixes every day! What these companies have adopted is true and full-fledged continuous deployment. This means that every change by every developer works its way out

---

[4] http://code.flickr.net

to production. These may not be complete features; several such changes by multiple developers, over a matter of days, may make up a complete usable feature. They may not be visible to a customer at all; it is only after the complete feature is available and tested that it becomes visible. Then, too, it may be a part of an A-B test effort, so only a few customers will ever see it. The deployment may also be a simple configuration or database schema change that is never seen by anyone, but that changes some performance or behavior. Yet another scenario is where the deployment involves a new environment change and not an application change at all—an operating system (OS) or middleware patch, an OS- or middleware-level configuration change, a new database schema version, an entire new architectural topology of nodes, and so on.

Such a process is not viable for many organizations. Some organizations may have some (water-Scrum-fall like) requirements and policies that require a manual approval process before deployment to production. Others may require a *segregation of duties*, which mandates that the person to deploy to production is a different person or team from the one that contributes to the development of the deployable asset.

To Continuously Deploy or Not?   There is still confusion among people between the concepts of continuous delivery and continuous deployment.

Continuous delivery doesn't mean every change is deployed to production ASAP. It means every change is proven to be deployable at any time.

—Carl Caum (Caum, 2013)

This tweet by Carl Caum, in a simple (less than 140-character) sentence, captures the essence of what *should* be done versus what *may* be done by an organization. Going by this distinction, continuous delivery is a *must*, while continuous deployment is an *option*. Having the capability to continuously deploy is more important than actually doing it in a continuous manner out to production (the key words here being *to production*). These terms are, unfortunately, still used interchangeably by most people.

What is required is the tested and validated capability to deploy to any environment in your delivery lifecycle—all the way out to production. You may only continuously deploy to an environment before *Prod* (lower environments)—for example, User Acceptance Testing (UAT), Pre-prod…, but the environments you deploy to should be *production-like*, so you know, with very high confidence, that the final deploy to production will work without issues when you actually deploy to Prod.

What you continuously deliver should be every change to Dev and QA environments and other (lower) non-production environments. What you finally choose to deploy to Prod will typically be a full feature or set of features, or a full application or service.

Supporting Practices

Other than the two core practices of DevOps—continuous integration and continuous delivery (you are not doing DevOps without both being adopted)—there are several *supporting* practices. These have been developed to support and enable the two core practices. Following are some of these practices, which are considered to be supporting but essential.

Infrastructure as Code

MASTER OF THE OPS UNIVERSE

Imagine a seasoned operations engineer (neck beard and all). Over his career, he has most certainly developed a toolkit of scripts that he can use, with minor changes, to perform all his regular tasks of provisioning and managing the plethora of environments he has seen and dealt with. When it comes to configurations, he knows all the admin consoles he deals with like the back of his hand. He can log in and make the exact tweaks to application server configs that are needed to address the issues he is facing. For database-related issues, he knows exactly who to call and that the DBA has mastered his end of the deal as well as he has his. He has things down to a routine. He knows exactly when the next application release is due. He knows when to expect the next update to the OS. He is the master of his universe.

As systems have become virtualized and as developers have started practicing continuous integration (CI), things have started to change. The number of environments, and their instances that Ops engineers have to deal with, have increased by several orders of magnitude. Developers no longer release updates and new versions every few months; they are pumping out CI builds daily—in fact, multiple builds a day. All of these builds need to be tested and validated. That requires new environment instances to be spun up, fast. These builds also often come with configuration changes. Logging into consoles to make each one of these changes individually is no longer a viable option. Furthermore, the need for speed is critical. Developers' builds are creating a backlog, as the environments to even test them on are not available as needed. *Houston, we have a problem.*

Let's start by revisiting two concepts:

1. **Cycle time.** *Cycle time* is defined as the average time taken from when a new requirement is approved, a change request is requested, or a bug that needs to be fixed via a patch is identified, to when it is delivered to production. Agile organizations want the delivery cycle time to be the bare minimum. This is what limits their ability to release new features and fixes to customers. Organizations like Etsy have cycle time down to minutes! While this is not possible for enterprise applications, the current cycle time of weeks or sometimes even months is absolutely unacceptable.

2. **Versioning environments.** The need to maintain multiple configurations and patch levels of environments that are now needed by development, on demand, requires Ops to modify how they handle change and maintain these environments. Any change Ops makes to an environment, whether it is applying a patch or making a configuration change, should be viewed as creating a new *version* of the environment, not just tweaking a config setting via a console. The only way this can be managed properly is by applying all changes via scripts. These scripts, when executed, would create a new version of the environment they are executed on. This process streamlines and simplifies change management, allowing it to scale, while keeping Ops best practices Information Technology Infrastructure Library (ITIL) and IT Service Management (ITSM) intact.

The solution to addressing both of these needs—minimizing cycle time and versioning environments—can be addressed by capturing and managing infrastructure as code. Spinning up a new virtual environment or a new version of the environment then becomes a matter of executing a script that can create and provision an image or set of images—all the way from the OS to the complete application stack being installed and configured. What took hours now takes minutes.

Versioning these scripts as you would version code in an SCM system allows for proper configuration management. Creating a new version of an environment now involves checking out the right scripts and making the necessary changes to the scripts—to patch the OS, change an app server setting, or install a new version of the application—and then checking the scripts back in as a new version of the environment, before executing it.

NOTE Without infrastructure as code, Ops can very easily become the "fall" in water-Scrum-fall.

Several automation frameworks have emerged to enable the capturing and management of infrastructure as code. The popular frameworks include Chef, Puppet, Salt, and Ansible.

With the evolution of the cloud, IT is now going to complete *software-defined environments* (SDEs). This takes the definition, versioning, and maintenance of complete environments as code. Technologies like OpenStack CloudFormation (for Amazon Web Services) are the leaders. OpenStack, for example, allows for *full stack* environments to be defined as software using Heat patterns, which can be versioned, provisioned, and configured using the likes of Chef and Salt, as needed. This also allows for the management of these environments at scale. No longer are Ops practitioners focused on managing individual servers that have long lifetimes; they are now managing large numbers of servers that are *transient* in their existence, and provisioned and de-provisioned on demand. This scale and agility can only be achieved with SDEs.

NOTE In a software-defined environment world, servers are "cattle," not "pets" (McCance, 2012) and (Bias, 2012).

Continuous Feedback

If you step back and look at *continuous feedback* in a holistic sense, it essentially means getting feedback from each functional area of the delivery pipeline to the areas to its left. So, developers provide feedback as they develop and deliver code, back to architects, analysts, and lines of business; testers provide feedback, through continuous testing to developers, architects, analysts and lines of business; and finally, Ops provides feedback to QA, testers, developers, architects, analysts, and lines of business, as well as everyone else who is a stakeholder.

The purpose of continuous feedback is to validate that the code produced and integrated with code from other developers and with other components of the application functions and performs as designed. Once the application has been deployed to a production system, it is also a goal to monitor that application to ensure that it functions and performs as designed in a production environment, as it is being used by end-users. This is essential to enable continuous improvement and quality. It is the core of Deming's PDCA cycle, as it provides the input to determine what to change and how to act.

NOTE   Continuous integration and delivery are both (almost) meaningless without continuous feedback. Not having testing and monitoring in a continuous manner, and therefore not knowing how the application is performing in production, makes the entire process of DevOps moot. What good is having a streamlined continuous delivery process if the only way you find out that your application's functionality or performance are below par is via a ticket opened by a disgruntled user?

This brings me to the two practices of DevOps that are required to enable continuous feedback: continuous testing and continuous monitoring.

Continuous Testing   *Continuous testing* is the capability for testing the application, the environment, and the delivery process at every stage of the delivery pipeline for the application being delivered. The items tested and the kinds of tests conducted can change depending on the stage of the delivery lifecycle. Continuous testing is really intertwined into the processes of continuous integration and continuous delivery, if done properly. Let's look at how this works in detail.

Individual developers work to create code. Fixing defects, adding new features, enhancing features, or making the code perform faster are some of the many tasks (work items) they may be working on. When done, they run unit tests on their own code and then deliver their code and integrate it with the work done by other developers on their team, as well as with unchanged code their team owns (*continuous integration*). Once the integration is done, they do unit tests on the integrated code. They may run other tests such as white box security tests, code performance tests, and so on. This work is then delivered to the common integration area of the team of teams—integrating the work of all the teams working on the project and all the code components that make up the service, application, or system being developed.

This is the essence of the process of continuous integration. What makes this process continuous is where an individual developer's code is integrated with that of their team, as and when they check in the code and it is delivered for integration. The important point to note here is the goal of the continuous integration process: to validate that the code integrates at all levels without error and that all tests run by developers run without error. Thus, continuous testing starts right with the developers.

After validating that the complete application (or service or system) is built without error, the application is delivered to the QA area. This delivery of code from the Dev or development environment to the QA environment is the first major step in continuous delivery. There is continuous delivery happening as the developers deliver their code to their team's integration space and to the project's integration space, but this is limited to being within the Dev space. There is no new environment to target.

When delivering to QA, I am speaking of a complete transition from one environment to another. QA has its own environment on which to run its suites of functional and performance tests. DevOps principles demand that this environment be production-like. In addition, QA may also need new data sets for each run of the suites of tests it runs. This may be one or more times every day as continuous integration leads to continuous delivery at a steady stream. This means that the continuous delivery process not only requires the processes to transition the code from Dev to QA, but also to refresh or provision new instances of QA's production-like environments, complete with the right configurations and associated test data to run the tests against. This makes continuous delivery a more complex process than just copying code over. The key point to note is that the goal of continuous delivery is to get the code ready for test, and for release, and to get the application to the right environment—continuously, so that it can be tested continuously.

If you extend the process described here to delivering the service, application, or system to a staging and eventually a production environment, the process and goal remain the same. The Ops team wants to run their own set of smoke tests, acceptance tests, and system stability tests before they deliver the application to the *must-stay-up-at-all-costs* production environment. That is done using a staging environment. This is a production-like environment that needs to be provisioned just like the QA environment. It needs to have the necessary scripts and test data for acceptance and performance tests that Ops will run. Only when this last phase of continuous testing is complete is the application delivered to production. Continuous delivery processes, hence, also perform the tasks of providing staging and production environments and delivering the application.

To delve more into this process, continuous testing is achieved by testing all aspects of the application and environment, including, but not limited to, the following:

- Unit testing
- Functional testing
- Performance testing
- Integration testing
- System integration testing
- Security testing
- User acceptance testing

In continuous testing, the biggest challenge is that some of the applications, services, and data sources that are required to perform some tests may not be available. Alternatively, even if they are available, the cost associated with using them may prohibit running tests on an ongoing basis. Furthermore, the costs of maintaining large test environments to serve all teams developing multiple applications in parallel can also be high.

The solution is to introduce the practice known as *test virtualization* (see Figure 1-5). This practice replaces actual applications, services, and data sources that the application must communicate and interact with during the test, with virtual *stubs*. These virtual instances make it possible to test applications for functionality, integration, and performance without making the entire ecosystem available. This virtualization can be utilized to perform the myriad types of testing listed earlier.

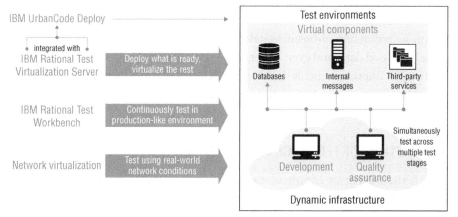

Figure 1-5: Example of test virtualization

When it comes to testing in the context of DevOps, in addition to continuous testing, there is also the practice of shift left testing, which I will examine in the "Shift Left" section, later in this chapter.

Continuous Monitoring   In production, the Ops team manages and ensures that an application is performing as desired and the environment is stable via continuous monitoring. Ops teams have their own tools to monitor their environments and running systems. Ultimately, the Ops team needs to ensure that the applications are performing, from the process level down to levels that are lower than what system-monitoring tools would allow. This requires that Ops teams use tools that can monitor application performance and issues. It may also require that they work with Dev to incorporate self-monitoring or analytics-gathering capabilities right into the applications that are being built. This would allow for true end-to-end monitoring, continuously.

As the technology in this space has grown, there has also been the emergence of tools and services that monitor application behavior and user sentiment, providing even finer-grained feedback that is useful to developers and the line of business.

In a nutshell, continuous monitoring requires the capture and analysis of metrics in four areas:

- Application performance
- System performance
- Application user behavior
- User sentiment

It is, however, essential that the Ops teams not just gather this data but also run analytics on it. Furthermore, they must make their feedback consumable by their target audience, from deep technical Ops practitioners, like performance engineers, to non-technical line-of-business stakeholders. Data is of no value unless it is consumable. Good data, and even better, good analytics on the data, can truly enable continuous improvement, as decisions at all levels of the delivery pipeline—from line of business, to developers, to testers—can now be data driven.

THE FUTURE OF FEEDBACK IS COGNITIVE

With the advent of cognitive capabilities like IBM Watson, tremendous capabilities are being brought to market in the area of predictive analytics of this feedback data. Data from user behavior, application behavior, and system behavior can now be analyzed, leveraging cognitive techniques to deliver predictive results, from predictive failure of systems, to predictive behavior of (happy or disgruntled) customers. Predictive analysis can result in businesses acting preemptively to prevent outages and disgruntlement.

Continuous Business Planning

The DevOps practice of *continuous business planning* focuses on the lines of business and their planning processes. Businesses need to be agile and able to react quickly to customer feedback. To achieve this, many businesses today employ Lean thinking techniques. These techniques involve starting small by identifying the outcomes and resources needed to test the business vision or value and then continuously adapting and adjusting based on customer feedback.

To achieve these goals, organizations measure the current baseline state, find out what customers really want, and then shift direction by updating their business plans accordingly, allowing them to make continuous trade-off decisions in a resource-constrained environment.

There has been a lot of work done in this space to leverage techniques made popular by the Lean startup movement, and described by Eric Reis in his book, *The Lean Startup*. The set of techniques, like delivering a minimum viable product, that are introduced by Reis in his book are becoming popular with businesses wanting to experiment with new markets and new business models, without having to make complete plans for delivering complex IT systems for these new areas. I will discuss this in more detail in Chapter 4.

The latest addition to the arsenal of capabilities available to ensure that you are not just building the deliverable right, but also building the right deliverables, is design thinking. Like Lean and Agile, design thinking has been used in industrial design for physical products for decades, in various levels of its evolution. It became mainstream with Peter Rowe's 1987 book, aptly named *Design Thinking*. What is new is its adaptation to IT and, specifically, application design, with a focus on user experience. Design thinking will be explored in more detail in Chapter 4.

Collaborative Development

Collaborative development was made popular by IBM, primarily as a practice supported by its *Collaborative Lifecycle Management (CLM)* tool suite. The practice is essentially in place to ensure that organizations with large, distributed teams enable visibility between, and collaboration among, cross-function practitioners and teams of teams, across silos. This is achieved by ensuring two capabilities across the delivery pipeline:

- Provision of access and visibility by practitioners not just to artifacts, work items, and metrics related to their functional area, but across all functional areas into which they need to have visibility (of course, access is managed by role and security needs).
- Seamless handoff of artifacts from one practitioner or team to another. This should be possible across functional boundaries, and should not require any translation or transformation of the artifact, in order for it to be consumed.

These capabilities can only be achieved by having a set of integrated tools utilized by practitioners and teams, across the delivery pipeline.

If you look at DevOps as a cultural movement, where the fostering of communication, collaboration, and trust are the core tenets you are striving for, then collaborative development may be seen as a core capability of DevOps. There is no better way to promote communication, collaboration, and trust than by enabling practitioners to communicate with other practitioners using a common tool (which is not email).

This can be achieved using tools such as Slack or Rational Team Concert, which are becoming popular. The collaboration can be further enhanced by leveraging in-tool collaboration around work items, enabling practitioners to move work items between each other, add notes, attach code change sets, and have visibility into what other team members have worked on, or are currently working on, that impacts their own work.

Speaking of visibility, nothing fosters trust more than full visibility. If a tester has visibility into what a developer is unit testing, the developer knows that she cannot commit code without proper unit testing.

NOTE Total visibility drives total trust.

At our company, we will no longer require filing expense claims. You can spend whatever you want and we will reimburse you. No questions asked. All we ask you to do is to post your receipt on an open Wiki page which every employee in the company can see. Trust me, you will spend wisely.

—CEO of a Silicon Valley startup

Shift Left

Shift left as a concept also has its origins in Lean. The basic idea here is to improve quality by moving tasks that can impact quality to as early in the lifecycle as possible. This is done across the lifecycle. The underlying premise is that the earlier quality issues are caught, the earlier their root cause can be identified and addressed.

> **NOTE** There is a well-known axiom in the QA space that if it takes one cent to catch and fix a defect or problem in the requirements stage, it will cost ten cents to fix the same in development, one dollar to fix in testing, and ten dollars to fix in production (Rice, 2009).

These are, of course, illustrative numbers and are not based on some statistical analysis of actual costs; however, the logic is sound. Shifting left the tasks that can identify defects and problems early saves money and improves quality.

From a DevOps culture perspective, you can also look at shift left as an approach used to improve collaboration and communication by engaging practitioners from functions that are to the right in the delivery pipeline, earlier in the lifecycle.

DEVOPS OR COUPLES' COUNSELING?

I had been asked by the architect on the account to meet with the Director of Dev and the Director of Ops for a client of his. We met for lunch, with the architect and me on one side of the table and the two directors on the other. I knew right away that all was not well on their home front. They were leaning away from each other. The Dev director complained about how Ops was not agile, and the Ops director said that Dev sent them garbage that would not even run without crashing servers. They even looked at their hands while speaking about the other. I felt I was in couples' counseling.

The solution plan I recommended to them was to begin with small steps, by shifting left when Ops was engaged. Their main challenge was a total lack of visibility between the Dev and Ops teams, till it was time to deploy to production. The suggestion I made was to pick one critical project and,

continued

continued

> once a week, have the Ops team send one resource to the Dev team's daily standup meeting and have them just listen, without needing to engage, and see if things improved. I had a follow-up meeting with the same two directors less than three months later at a conference. They were happy to report that the Ops team now had a presence at the daily standup meeting, and Ops not only listened, but actively participated, sharing their progress, plans, and blockers. Ops engagement had shifted left. They had achieved collaboration.

For maximum impact on quality improvement, there are two major areas where shift left needs to be adopted in the delivery pipeline.

Shift Left Testing

Engaging testers early, right from the requirements stage, better prepares them for what they will need to test, and in turn, they can also ensure that the requirements being written are testable. The goal, however, is to start testing earlier in the lifecycle. The practice of shift left testing, as it is gaining traction in the industry, is focused above all on ensuring integration testing earlier in the lifecycle. While other forms of testing (as described in the section, "Continuous Testing") are important to shift to earlier in the lifecycle, the value of shifting integration testing earlier is the highest.

As teams practice continuous integration, testing those integration points to identify integration and architectural deficiencies early has a significant impact on quality. What is the use of having perfectly functioning and performing services or components, if they don't work with other services and components when integrated? In order to achieve integration testing early in the lifecycle, test virtualization becomes a prerequisite, as all the services or components required in order to complete testing may not be available when needed. Test virtualization enables the stubbing out of these unavailable services with virtual instances, enabling integration—and other—testing early in the lifecycle, thus achieving shift left testing. You need to shift left to achieve the proverbial "Test Early, Test Often" goal.

Shift Left Operations Concerns

As described in the anecdote at the beginning of this section, the Ops team is usually seen as a separate silo in the delivery lifecycle. They are typically engaged at the beginning of projects, as operational requirements are determined, and then left disconnected from the Dev efforts, till it comes time to start operational readiness, before handoff to production. Engaging Ops early in the lifecycle and having them participate in the Dev-test cycle prevents challenges that manifest during deployment to production, if Ops is engaged late. Engaging Ops early makes them aware of what is being delivered and how it will result in changes to Ops environments, as the needs may have deviated from the *as designed* state.

Engaging Ops early also helps to ensure that the production-like environments Dev and test are deploying to during Dev-test, are truly still production-like and have not drifted away from real production environments. Lastly, engaging Ops early also ensures that the deployment processes and procedure being developed by Dev teams are consumable by Ops. In the pre-DevOps days, one of the biggest challenges with deployment to production on a release weekend was the fact that deployment processes had never been used or tested by Ops before. Ensuring that these processes are tested over and over again as code is deployed to non-Prod environments—early and often, using the same processes and procedures that Ops will use—ensures that they will work in production.

A significant impact of shifting left is the change that happens in the roles of the practitioners. These changes happen subtly and over time, resulting in unintended consequences when it comes to skills needed and, eventually, headcount distribution across the delivery pipeline.

As responsibilities shift left, the role of the practitioner changes from that of a *doer* to that of a *service provider*. Testers may no longer be the ones doing the tests; instead, they become providers for test automation, which can be self-served by the developers. Similarly, for Ops practitioners, they are no longer the ones running around building, provisioning, and de-provisioning servers. Instead, they build server images, manage server instances, and respond to issues. Dev, test, and other practitioners provision, configure, and de-provision instances of servers, on demand, leveraging the self-service access provided and managed by Ops teams. This raises the abstraction at which the testers and Ops now work and perform. Consequently, it impacts the skills they need, and the numbers of resources that may be needed.

Architecture and Risk Mitigation

ARCHITECTURAL THINKING

When I joined Rational Software in the mid-'90s, the focus on architecture was imbibed into my thinking. With the methodology "Three Amigos" Grady Booch, James Rumbaugh, and Ivar Jacobson developing UML

continued

continued

(Jim joined Rational Software just before I did. We still had Booch's Clouds for Objects) and Philippe Kruchten developing his 4+1 View Model of Software Architecture (Kruchten, 2002), architectural thinking was, and is, in my bloodstream.

The area of application delivery that is finally beginning to get the attention it needs, in order to get the full promise of DevOps realized, is architecture. You cannot achieve continuous delivery with large, monolithic systems. While architectural refactoring was largely ignored in the early days of DevOps, it is going mainstream now, mainly thanks to the evolution of microservices (or what are referred to as *12-factor apps*).[5]

While the debate is still ongoing over whether microservices can truly deliver the value for every kind of application, the attention that microservices have received has revived a much-needed focus on architecture. If you truly understand 12-factor apps, their focus on web apps and Software as a Service is self-evident. They may not add value to apps and systems that are large, complex, data-heavy legacy systems, without expensive refactoring of code and data. That investment is viable and necessary only if those systems are being modernized into cloud-native apps. Microservices and 12-factor apps will be discussed in more depth in Chapter 5.

The architectural transformation needed to achieve continuous delivery, irrespective of whether microservices are used, is to enable the delivery of changes in small batches—thus, reducing batch size. A *batch* is the number of changes being delivered in each cycle or sprint. These changes include any and all changes—code, configurations, infrastructure, data, data-schemas, scripts, deployment processes, and so on—that encompass a full Dev-to-Ops cycle. (Remember, not all changes are deployed to production every time.) Reducing batch size is imperative to do the following:

- Reduce risk
- Improve quality
- Enable faster delivery

These benefits are self-evident. The most effective way to manage risk and quality, while increasing speed, is to reduce the batch size in each iteration or *sprint*. This is a mind shift to deliver smaller, more frequent new versions.

---

[5] http://12factor.net

As you reduce batch size, there is less to test and validate in each cycle; there is less to deploy; and, because there is less change, there is lower risk. If challenges or issues are identified, their impact is also limited by the smaller batch size, making mitigation easier, via fixes or rollbacks.

Continuous Improvement

At the end of the day, the heart of DevOps lies in achieving continuous improvement. No matter where you start, at whatever maturity level, adopting DevOps is not a one-time project you undertake; it is an ongoing effort. The goal is to ultimately become a learning organization, as envisioned by Peter Senge in the '90s (David A. GarvinAmy C. Edmondson, 2008). In the DevOps context, a *learning organization* is constantly learning from what it just delivered, and continuously improving. What do you improve? There are three areas of improvement:

- **The application.** Are the application changes that you just delivered functioning and performing as desired? What can you learn from the continuous feedback coming in to improve the app in the next iteration?
- **The environment.** Are the environments the application is running on performing and behaving as desired? Are the service level agreements (SLAs) being met? What can you learn from the continuous feedback that is coming in to improve the environments in the next iteration?
- **The process.** What can you learn from the experiences of the practitioners and stakeholders to improve the delivery processes themselves in the next iteration?

While most organizations have efforts ongoing to continuously improve the application being delivered, fewer organizations have the same level of rigor for continuously improving the operational environments, based on real metrics. Far fewer organizations have programs in place to continuously improve delivery processes. This is the case despite movements like Lean, and their incarnations like Agile's Scrum and the broader Lean startup, which have built into them what is needed to become a learning organization or team, and to be constantly improving at a process level.

Metrics

If you can't measure it, you can't manage it.

—Attributed to Peter Drucker

Irrespective of whether Peter Drucker actually said this, or of whether it is even accurate (Kaz, 2013), the fact remains that in order to manage and consequently improve something, you need to be able to measure some critical metrics: Key Performance Indicators (KPIs). You will need both a baseline measurement of these KPIs, marking the starting point, and ongoing measurements to see if improvement is indeed occurring. Not only do you need to measure that the needle is moving—and in a positive direction—but you also need to be able to understand cause and effect: which actions result in improving KPIs. If you are making several changes to people and processes, knowing which changes are actually resulting in improvement is critical.

Business Drivers

To know which metrics to measure and improve, you have to know the business drivers. What business impact are you striving for? Change, and even improvement for the sake of improvement, does not make good business sense. If you are going to invest in transforming an organization by adopting DevOps, knowing what business drivers need to be addressed is a prerequisite. It helps to determine which metrics matter, and thus, which capabilities to focus on and invest in. Focusing on speed alone means that you are taking a very myopic view of the world.

> *As a medical device manufacturer, quality always trumps speed for us. We would rather be late in releasing a device, than ever have to issue a recall. As you can imagine, recalling installed pacemakers is not a good situation for anyone.*
>
> —Director of QA at a medical device manufacturer

What KPIs or metrics should you measure and strive to improve? As I mentioned earlier, it all depends on business drivers. What are the lines of business asking you, the IT organization, to improve? (This may vary by line of business, even within the same organization.) Is it speed, quality, agility, ability to innovate, or cost reduction? Is it something at an even higher level, such as the ability to deploy new business models or capture new markets? Is it something at a lower level, such as reducing the mean time between failures (MTBF), or improving mean time to resolve (MTTR); or is it just lowering bug density in the code? Is it being able to develop a partner ecosystem with APIs? Is it reducing the time it takes to get all the approvals IT needs to deliver a new app? Is it being able to attract more tech talent by participating in open source projects? (Everyone knows that it is the cool companies that contribute to open source projects.)

Here is a subset of core DevOps metrics that a division at IBM used to measure the impact of DevOps adoption. These metrics, shown in the following list, were all determined by the business drivers that this group needed to have an impact on (speed to market, market share, and improving profitability of the products they delivered).

- Project initiation
- Groomed backlog
- Overall time to development
- Composite build time
- Build Verification Test (BVT) availability
- Sprint test time
- Total deployment time
- Overall time to production
- Time between releases
- Time spent—innovation/maintenance (percentage)

DevOps: Culture

"Everyone is responsible for delivery to production." That is what the T-shirt says. I am giving it to everyone who is even remotely connected to my project. Of course, the analysts, designers, developers, testers, ops folk assigned to the project get it. But so do the people on the enterprise architecture team, the application architecture team, and the security guys. The people in the PMO definitely get one. I gave one to the janitor who has our floor—if the restroom is busted and an engineer wastes 20 minutes to use one on another floor, the janitor is now responsible for a delay in deployment to production. I gave one to the coffee machine maintenance guy. If the coffee machine is out of pods and we send one of the interns over to Starbucks, the coffee machine maintenance guy is now responsible for a delay. I FedEx'ed one to our CFO. If she can't manage the budget and furloughs even one of my contractors this December, like she did last year, she is now delaying deployment to production. The CIO gets it to keep my team out of email-jail. The CTO gets it for not delaying technology approvals. Heck, if my wife had not convinced me that it was a bad idea, I would have handed it to every

"significant other" who showed up at the company picnic. That, my friend, is what a DevOps culture means to me.

—VP at a large insurance company, defining DevOps culture

As I mentioned before, DevOps, at its heart, is a cultural movement. So, how do you change culture? Ultimately, even after all the process improvement and automation that can be introduced in an organization, the organization can only succeed at adopting the culture of DevOps if it is able to overcome the inherent cultural inertia. Organizations have inertia—an inherent resistance to change. Change is not easy, especially in large organizations where the cultural may have had years to develop and permeates across hundreds, if not thousands, of practitioners. These practitioners, as individuals, may appreciate the value of adopting DevOps, but as a collective, they resist change and thus have inertia. Overcoming this inertia is key. Cultural inertia can be exhibited by the following statements:

"This is the way we do things here."

"Yes, but changing X is not in my control."

"Nothing is broken in our processes. Why should we change?"

"You will need to talk to Y about that; WE cannot change how THEY work."

"Management will never allow that."

"Don't you know we are in a regulated industry?"

"DevOps is the new flavor of the month. Let's see how long this effort lasts."

Over time, organizations develop behaviors; teams and groups divide up actions and responsibilities along organizational lines; checks and balances are established in the name of governance but are not related to true governance at all; processes exist, but no one knows why—they are *just there*; reports are produced that no one reads anymore, but no one is willing to do away with them; bad things happened in the past and resulted in approval requirements to ensure they never happen again; and so on. All of these behaviors build up inertia in an organization's culture.

What kind of culture does DevOps adoption need? One of trust, communication, and collaboration. Adopting DevOps practices alone will not foster such a culture, nor will the practices take root and become ingrained in an organization's DNA unless such a culture begins to develop. It is a chicken-and-egg situation that requires a concerted effort to overcome the cultural inertia. This cultural inertia can be overcome by addressing three areas:

1. **Visibility.** I discussed this at length earlier in this chapter, and its value cannot be ignored. There is no greater cause of mistrust than not having visibility into teams or practitioners that you have to engage with, and you are not sure what they did with the artifacts they are handing off to you.

2. **Effective communication.** Email and voicemail need to be done away with as sources of communication in a DevOps environment; so do project plan and status documents, slide decks, and spreadsheets. Communication needs to be live and peer-to-peer, not via email or tickets, or done through management. One practitioner should be able to communicate with any other practitioner she needs to, without having to go through a chain of command. These live communications should replace email, status updates, and collaboration, and they should be streaming. Tools like Slack, HipChat, Yammer, and Wrike are becoming very popular as a result.

3. **Common measurements.** Out of all that I've mentioned, the area that causes the most inertia is a lack of right measurements for practitioners and teams. People will not change their behaviors, unless the way they are being measured matches the new, desired behaviors. Furthermore, to deliver true collaboration and a sense of a single team working toward a singular set of goals across silos, these measurements of success should be the same among all practitioners. Dev, test, and Ops need to have common or at least similar metrics that their success is measured on. Everyone—and I mean everyone—has to be made responsible for deploying to production.

Summary

DevOps is now mainstream. While that is a given, not everyone has come to the same understanding of what DevOps is and, more importantly, how it should be adopted. The right answer is, unfortunately, "It depends." And it does. It depends on the business goals you are striving for; it depends on what the current maturity of practices is; and it depends on the rate of change your organization is able to absorb. Change has to be adopted to achieve increased business value, but not at its expense. Any disruption results in dips in productivity, and that is also true for DevOps adoption.

Adopting DevOps is a journey that has to begin with the first step of identifying point A (your current state) and point B (your business goals). Once you have identified these points, you can develop an adoption roadmap to adopt the right practices and capabilities (the right plays) described in this chapter. How do you go about creating such an adoption roadmap? That is the topic of the next chapter.

CHAPTER 2

Adopting DevOps

continued

continued

> bowlers to put on the team, based on whose technique would be best
> suited for those pitch conditions.
>   Cricket is unique in how much a team's performance can depend on prop-
> erly studying and assessing the pitch conditions. Barring maybe baseball,
> almost all other team sports have standard playing fields and surfaces that
> do not have significant variation between locations or change as the game
> progresses. Games have been won or lost based on how well a team under-
> stood the pitch and prepared for it.

What does it mean when you say you want to adopt or implement DevOps?
What is a *DevOps solution*? DevOps is not about adopting a product or a
process. It is about adopting a philosophy, one that includes principles and
practices that affect people, processes, and tools. Adopting DevOps is not
just about adopting a product or a process; it is about undergoing transformational change.

Most organizations looking to adopt DevOps have moved on from asking
the questions, "What is DevOps?" and "Is DevOps the latest fad, or is it here
to stay?" They are now asking questions along these lines:

- Where do I start with DevOps adoption?
- Now that I have succeeded in adopting DevOps in small pockets around
  the organization, how do I scale it across the enterprise?

In either scenario, you do not just adopt DevOps. You start a journey of
adopting the capabilities that make up DevOps (introduced in Chapter 1).
Adopting DevOps is not a one-and-done project. It is adopting a mind-set, a
culture. It is a commitment to a journey of continuous improvement by adopting a set of capabilities and practices that are based on Lean principles. It is a
long-term transformation that requires a well-defined, well-planned adoption
playbook, which includes a transformation roadmap. This playbook will, of
course, need to evolve over time as the adoption progresses and other variants
present themselves. It thus needs to be a living document that is managed as
a core adoption asset. That being said, starting with a well-defined playbook
is essential to the success of the transformation.

The question then becomes, "Where do I start?" This requires knowing
Point B of your journey (where you want to go and what business goals you

want DevOps to help you achieve) and *Point A* (where you are today and how mature you are when it comes to practicing these capabilities today). Once you know Points A and B, you can chart out an adoption playbook made up of a series of plays that the teams in your IT department will need to execute in order to progress toward achieving the business goals (or arrive at Point B).

This playbook needs to include plays that touch upon the four core areas of improvement that are required for DevOps adoption:

1. **Process Improvement**—How to make the processes lean and efficient by eliminating waste
2. **Tools for Automation**—How to automate these improvement processes with tools to make them repeatable and scalable, and to reduce errors
3. **Platform and Environments**—How to make platforms and environments for the application delivery pipeline—all the way from requirements through to production—resilient, elastic, scalable, and able to manage configurations
4. **Culture**—Above all, how to foster a culture of trust, communication, and collaboration

Adopting change in all these areas is the transformation that an organization needs to take. This journey varies by organization. In fact, it varies by projects and teams within the organization. The journey takes different paths and different amounts of time, depending on various factors, the most important of which is your current state of maturity. Starting from a level of immaturity where you don't even have good source code management practices, and wanting to get to "no downtime" deployment, requires a long journey.

Developing the Playbook

I didn't believe in team motivation. I believe in getting a team prepared so it knows it will have the necessary confidence when it steps on the field and be prepared to play a good game.

—Tom Landry, American football player and coach

As in any match, irrespective of the sport, achieving success in a DevOps transformation eventually depends on the plays that you run to reach the goal. Again, as in any sport, you need a set of plays captured in a playbook that you can reference, and you need to run the right play depending on the situation—in this case, for a project, division, or organization.

Understanding the playing field is critical when developing the playbook to plan for a DevOps adoption or transformation. A playbook for a sport like basketball includes myriad plays, including the following:

- Preparatory drills
- In-bounding plays
- Press defenses
- Zone offences
- Secondary breaks
- Quick hitters
- Buzzer beaters
- Last-second plays

The coach and players call the play they will run, based on the situation: court location, score, time on the game or shot clocks, which players are on the court (their own and opposing team members), and so on. Similarly, a DevOps adoption playbook includes multiple plays that are appropriate to the situation, whether it is at a team, project, program, division, or enterprise level.

To create such a DevOps transformation playbook, you need three core ingredients:

1. A clear definition of the *target state* (business goals and drivers)
2. An understanding of the *current state* (current capability and maturity)
3. A determination of the best path to take, or *plays to run* (risk-value-investment balance)

Studying and assessing these ingredients is akin to properly understanding the field conditions on which the adoption game will be played.

Identifying the Target State (Business Goals and Drivers)

All winning teams are goal-oriented. These teams win consistently because everyone connected with them concentrates on specific objectives. They go about their business with blinders on; nothing will distract them from achieving their aims.

—Lou Holtz, American football player, coach, and analyst

Let's step back for a moment and look at the IT world through a business lens. Lines of business (LOBs) need IT departments to deliver capabilities to their customers and users that allow the customers to gain business value. In a nutshell, IT systems are nothing more than the vehicle through which business value is delivered by the LOBs to customers. Whether it is the business value of hailing a taxi, operating a weapons system, paying your taxes, or "liking" a cat video, or the business value to an organization's own employees of managing their paycheck deductions and deposits, IT is responsible for creating the systems that deliver this value.

LOBs also rely on these systems to harvest feedback on how customers and users are consuming the business capabilities and deriving value; how they are interacting with the business systems; and what new or enhanced capabilities and features they need in order to get better value. IT departments therefore need to not just align themselves to the goals of the LOBs, but also to keep transforming themselves in order to meet the changing needs of the LOBs. As an industry, IT has not done a good job at keeping up with the needs of business. This has resulted in the existence of *shadow IT*, where LOBs have bypassed their in-house IT departments and gone to outside IT vendors and service providers to satisfy their IT needs.

So, what are the LOBs asking IT departments to deliver, and how? While the exact requirements vary by organization, industry, and even geography, in general, the LOBs are asking the IT departments to deliver IT systems and applications with the following:

- Velocity
- Agility
- Innovation
- Quality
- Lower cost

Now, these requests may manifest themselves as various business requests that the LOBs may present to the IT departments, as well as technology requests that the IT departments may ask of themselves to address the LOBs' needs. Here are some examples:

- Time to value
- Speed of deployment
- Reduced cost/time to deliver
- Reduced cost/time to test

- Increased test coverage
- Increased environment utilization
- Minimized deployment-related downtime
- Minimized deployment time issues (for example, weekend-long deployment marathons)
- Minimized rollbacks of deployed apps
- Increased ability to reproduce and fix defects
- Minimized mean time to resolve (MTTR) production issues
- Reduced defect cycle time

These requirements vary by organization, and even by project or program within an organization.

Yes, Sanjeev, these are the five things the business is asking of us—lower cost, lower cost, lower cost, lower cost, and yes, lower cost.

—CIO of a major European financial services company

IT departments, especially in large organizations, are not exactly designed for velocity, agility, or innovation. They evolve over the years to deliver stability, quality, and predictability, which they achieve by focusing primarily on change management. This results in the development of change management processes, practices, and tools; overbearing governance and compliance regimes; archaic and siloed organizational structures; and cultural inertia. This has also resulted in the delivery of changes in large packages at quarterly or monthly intervals. Unfortunately, as I will discuss in Chapter 3, large "chunks" of work delivered at infrequent intervals, no matter how well the managed, are usually more complex, more likely to be interdependent, and more difficult to roll back than small change sets once discovered in production. This is further exacerbated by the lack of agility of the legacy systems and their delivery processes, which were designed before modern architectures and processes became available, but still need to be supported by the IT departments.

In some cases, this lack of ability of IT departments to deliver agility, velocity, and innovation can result in LOBs creating their own shadow IT divisions to deliver their IT needs. *Shadow IT* is a term used to describe situations where LOBs either create their own IT teams and infrastructure that are outside the enterprise IT department or use non-company resources, such as third-party development teams and public cloud services, to develop and deliver their IT needs. The challenge with shadow IT is that they are in the shadow, outside the organization's IT governance and oversight. Furthermore, shadow IT does not usually have the in-house knowledge of the business. That is, in general, they are not as good as in-house people at understanding the business of the enterprise, they are not usually in the loop, and they are not privy to or engaged with influencing the strategic direction of the enterprise. Therefore, they are not as potentially capable as your own IT people at making decisions that will add value.

The solution, of course, is to undergo a DevOps transformation that enables IT departments to adopt the necessary practices, automation tools, and organizational and cultural change to deliver applications and services with velocity and agility, and become innovative by being able to deliver rapid experimentation.

One of the core goals of DevOps is to achieve maximum efficiency with an application delivery pipeline by *optimizing* the pipeline. This *optimization* allows for agility, velocity, quality, and cost control. As I mentioned earlier in this chapter, achieving these goals requires lean and efficient processes; integrated application development and delivery tools; fast- and easy-to-provision environments; and finally, a culture of trust and communication across the cross-functional teams. Along with maximizing efficiency, most organizations need to drive innovation. This need for innovation, in turn, drives the need to adopt new technology platforms and processes that are designed for innovating at speed—for example, a Cloud-based "Platform as a Service" (PaaS) that inherently delivers all the necessary DevOps services. This need to innovate is in turn creating the realization that IT departments also need to optimize their legacy application-delivery capabilities. They need to do so to free up resources—people and money—that can be invested in innovation. They also need to do so to ensure that traditional slow delivery does not become a drag on their ability to innovate at speed.

It is important at this point to mention the models that are being used in the industry in terms of balancing *innovation* and *optimization* at multiple speeds. You can think in sports terms as balancing offense and defense. This model, commonly referred to as *Multi-Speed IT*, is discussed in depth in Chapter 3.

Assessing the Current State

NOTE I am often asked how long it will take to achieve a return on investment on a DevOps transformation. It is just like asking how long it takes me to get to Austin, TX, from Washington, DC. The flight is three hours and three minutes long. The time it takes me, however, is much longer because I do not live at the airport (although it surely feels like it). How long a journey takes depends on where exactly you start from. The same is true for your DevOps transformation.

There are many ways to look at the current state or maturity of an organization or team. Coaches and captains of sports teams need to have a very good understanding of their team's capabilities: strengths and weaknesses; individual players' skills, current form, and health; opposing teams' skills and form; and the current state of the game. This set of data allows the team coach and leaders to pick the right play to run next. Similarly, in the IT world, understanding a team, project, or organization's current maturity and state allows the leadership to run the right play from the playbook at the right time.

To start assessing current maturity, let's start with some core questions about your organization's capabilities:

1. Are you able to rapidly deliver new, innovative applications and to leverage modern architectures?
2. Are you able to modernize existing applications to allow for faster delivery and innovation?
3. Are you able to adapt culture, tools, and processes to help you succeed?

Most organizations will say that they have a challenge in at least one of these areas. Many will actually confess to all three. Properly addressing the challenges in these areas requires a three-step process:

1. Identifying the inefficiency or waste
2. Identifying the root causes of the inefficiency or waste
3. Developing a plan or *play* to address the root causes

Identifying the Inefficiency or Waste with Value Stream Mapping

Value stream mapping is a Lean-management method for analyzing the current state and designing a future state for the series of events that take a product or service from its beginning through to the customer.

—wikipedia, n.d.

You identify the inefficiency or waste by looking at the delivery pipelines for the various applications an organization delivers and looking for where there is waste. Informal surveys done by myself and others, along with anecdotal evidence, have suggested that up to 40 percent of the resources in many organizations are wasted. Because this was not a scientific survey, the margin of error in this 40-percent number is likely high. However, I have never had anyone challenge with proof to the contrary. Mary Poppendieck defines waste as "anything that depletes resources without adding customer value" (Wagner, 2009). This waste comes in several forms, most of it caused by process and governance overheads placed on the practitioners, and extra steps added to processes, all with good intentions. Examples of waste include the following:

- Unnecessary process steps
- Unnecessary rework
- Unnecessary features
- Building the wrong artifact or process
- Transforming an artifact constructed by someone else
- Waiting for someone else to act on an action or task
- Waiting for an approval
- Waiting for an environment
- Creating a ticket for a manual task
- Creating or updating an artifact that adds no value to the end user or client
- Reporting to management by manually updating databases or spreadsheets
- Status reporting

Most of the waste happens during *handoffs* between stakeholders, especially across functions, and when a practitioner waits for someone else to act. Another source of waste at the *handoffs* is the artifacts being passed on from one stakeholder to the next not being "usable as is". That is, the artifacts require the receiving stakeholder to modify or transform the artifacts before they can be used or need to return them to have them reworked. Lean methodologies refer to the metric measuring this as *%Complete and Accurate* (%C&A) (Martin, 2011).

The most effective way to identify these sources of waste and inefficiency is by conducting what is known as a *value stream mapping* exercise. Value stream mapping is not a new method; the Lean movement has been using it for years. Tom and Mary Poppendieck made it popular in the software industry as a tool to find waste in software development processes (Poppendieck, 2008).

In the context of DevOps, doing a value stream mapping exercise involves looking at the flow of requests coming in at one end of the delivery pipeline and an application running in production at the other end. These requests may include the following:

- New requirements
- Enhancement requests
- Change requests
- Bug fixes
- Policy changes
- Configuration changes
- Content updates

They include essentially anything that causes a change to the application running in production.

When a request comes in to develop or deliver a change (or something new), *stakeholders* execute *processes* that create, modify, or transform *artifacts* and move them from one environment to the next, as they are handed off from one stakeholder to the next. Requirements as artifacts come in at one end, and code running in production environments comprises the end artifacts at the other end of the *delivery pipeline*.

The end goal of DevOps is to reduce waste (or, as *Lean* methodologies call it, to *remove non-value-add work*) to make the processes more efficient (or replace them with better, more efficient processes) and then continue to do so, striving for *continuous improvement*, or what the Japanese refer to as *kaizen*. In order to do this, you need to look at all of the following:

- Artifacts
- Stakeholders
- Environments
- Processes

The goal is to identify where the waste is (see my earlier list for examples of waste) and then perform a root-cause analysis to determine the cause of the waste. Here are some examples of where waste may lie:

- The process is inefficient.
- The process is manual.
- The artifacts are not in the right form.

- Handoffs between stakeholders are inefficient.
- Stakeholders are unable to perform tasks in the processes.
- Stakeholders do not have access to the artifacts they need, when they need them.
- Stakeholders spend time on unnecessary tasks.
- Stakeholders work on unnecessary artifacts.
- Processes are overburdened by governance.

I cover root-cause analysis later in this chapter.

Using a Value Stream Map   The most effective method of identifying waste in the delivery pipeline is value stream mapping (VSM). A simple value stream map and its components are shown in Figure 2-1. Let's now explore how you identify waste using a VSM exercise.

You can visualize a process in two ways:

1. Activity-centric: The process is described by the set of operations and their order needed to carry out the process to create the work products. They are well described by flow charts or IDEF diagrams.
2. Artifact-centric: The work products and their lifecycles describe the process. The work products are treated as state machines that undergo state transitions. Taking a work product through a state transition specifies each process step (Cantor, 2014).

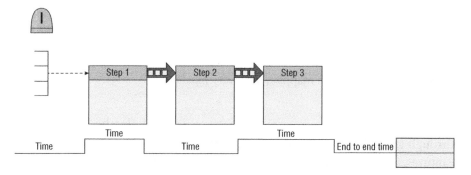

Figure 2-1: A simple value stream map

When conducting a VSM exercise, you need to look at both activities and artifacts. You do this by taking an artifact and following it through the delivery pipeline, as stakeholders perform activities on the artifact to transform (state transition) it, create more artifacts, and modify existing ones. For example, the artifact of a single enhancement request results in several code artifacts that are to be created and several that have been modified. As artifacts flow from one stakeholder to the next and are transformed and moved from one environment to the next, you need to conduct in-process analysis to determine whether there is a bottleneck or source of waste that you can address. Figure 2-2 is a picture of a value stream map developed during such an exercise.

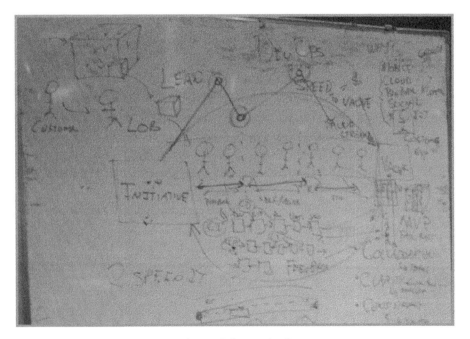

Figure 2-2: Value stream mapping a delivery pipeline

Taking this concept across the delivery pipeline, following the artifacts through the delivery pipeline results in the creation of a value map, which captures all the identified bottlenecks in the value stream.

Two sorts of measures can be found in the value map:

1. Process Time: The time it takes to actually perform the work
2. Lead Time: The elapsed time from the time work is made available until it is completed and handed off to the next stakeholder (Martin, 2011).

In addition, the quality of the work being done, as it is handed off from one stakeholder to the next, is measured using %C&A, which was introduced earlier in this chapter.

Leveraging the VSM, whether you conduct an *in-depth* VSM exercise (which generates detailed measures of process time and wait time to develop stream and in-process measures) or an *overview* VSM exercise (which focuses on just identifying bottlenecks rather than detailed measurements), you can then carry out a root-cause analysis (RCA) exercise to determine the root cause of each identified bottleneck. The root cause, in turn, is what needs to be addressed and is therefore the focus of the DevOps adoption roadmap.

As I mentioned, you can perform a value stream mapping in two general ways (there are actually as many ways to conduct a VSM as there are consulting organizations and methodologies, because everyone has their own approach):

1. In-depth VSM—This is a multi-day, or even multi-week, engagement with multiple consultants spending time with practitioners measuring wait times and process times for every task performed. With these measurements, a detailed value map can be created that identifies the exact sources of waste in the activities performed by each practitioner type. These VSM exercises are standard in manufacturing to streamline labor-intensive processes.

2. Overview VSM—This is typically a half-day to one-day workshop with the executive leadership of the organization, representing the core functional areas in the delivery pipeline, rather than practitioners. The workshop exercise draws out an exemplary delivery pipeline, for an exemplary change request or new requirement, with the goal of identifying the major bottlenecks in the delivery pipeline. These bottlenecks are then analyzed to determine root causes of waste. These VSM exercises are more common in the IT world, and I discuss them in detail later in this section.

Delivery Pipeline versus Factory Assembly Line   A common analogy that is used to explain DevOps continuous delivery is to compare it to an assembly line in a factory—or at an even broader level, to compare a software supply chain to a manufacturing supply chain. While this analogy is used across the IT industry for several reasons, and will be used in this book, it does have limitations. These limitations are significant in the context of developing a VSM. Let's examine the parallels and differences in detail.

A supply chain is a system of organizations, people, technology, activities, information and resources involved in moving a product or service from supplier to customer.

—Wikipedia, n.d.

This definition, while typically used in the context of a manufacturing supply chain, actually holds up well for a software supply chain, with some significant differences.

Manufacturing Supply Chain   A manufacturing supply chain transforms natural resources, raw materials, and components into a finished product that is delivered to the end customer (ibid). In such a supply chain, a manufacturer becomes more an integrator than a manufacturer. Be it a product as simple as a child's doll, with just a few components (plastic body, fake hair, clothes, cardboard, and plastic box) or a product as complex as a car, with more than 20,000 hardware and software components, for every component that goes into the final product, the manufacturer needs to ask a question: Can another company make the component faster or cheaper, in the quantity and with the quality they need? For every component for which they answer *yes*, the manufacturer takes on the role of an acquirer, and the company actually making the component, that of supplier. Of course, these suppliers may be internal suppliers or another group or division within the company that delivers the component.

A typical example would be the brakes of a car. They are an essential component in every car, but still, the manufacturer has to decide whether someone else can make them better and cheaper. If yes, then they should acquire the component from that supplier. Another scenario where a manufacturer becomes an acquirer is for a component where the manufacturer does not have the required expertise to manufacture it in-house—for example, traction control systems or anti-lock brakes in a car.

Another scenario may be where a supplier owns intellectual property for some components, making it necessary for the manufacturer to acquire them from that supplier—for example, high-capacity batteries in an electric car. As a result of this model, modern automobile manufacturers have become automobile designers and assemblers, acquiring most individual components from external suppliers. In reality, apart from actual physical components that go into the completed product, manufacturers may also acquire some of the design or prototyping work. For example, an aircraft manufacturer may outsource wing edge design to a boutique aeronautical engineering firm that specializes in wing edge design work.

This relationship between the acquirer and the suppliers in the supply chain subsequently becomes based entirely on communication and agreements. The acquirer communicates design specifications and quality requirements, and the supplier provides the components, typically *just in time*, with the right quality, and in the right quantity. For the acquirer, the cost benefit comes from not having to own the manufacturing plant—the facilities, equipment, and people—which creates the components that someone else can supply. For the supplier, the cost benefit comes from their ability to reduce costs as the manufacturing scales.

Software Supply Chain: A software supply chain extends this notion of a supply chain to software and systems delivery. While the underlying business logic and value of adopting a supply chain model remains the same as that for a manufacturing supply chain, the parallels do not fully apply. For a software manufacturer, it makes perfect sense to outsource parts of its software supply chain—to create a software factory. There are components of the software that others can build more cheaply, due to lower labor rates, experience in building these components, or specialized expertise (like mobile development) that the acquirer may not have, or may not want to have, in house. Here again, it is important to point out that the suppliers may be in-house software teams that are in another group or division within the company.

NOTE Here is where the parallels fall apart. The main reason for this is that factories and their assembly lines produce identical widgets and finished products, whereas software delivery does not. Widgets (components) in software are not alike; each is unique. That is what developers are paid to do: create new, unique code.

This also applies to value stream mapping. Although detailed value stream maps with granular measures of wait times and process times work well for assembly lines and manufacturing supply chains, they do not work as well for application delivery. For example, a developer taking x hours of process time to develop one component will not necessarily take the same amount of time for the next component. Wait times also tend to vary; after a developer writes code, she may be waiting for a tester to finish testing, which may vary based on how much new code went into the component that needs testing. For delivery pipelines, it is therefore better to focus on finding major bottlenecks, rather than those at a granular level. An *overview* value stream mapping exercise does just that and is the recommended approach to get started with DevOps.

Let's examine some more of the differences in detail:

- Requirements—Software specifications (that is, requirements) are never as well defined as those of physical components. Think of a set of requirements for a user interface (UI) on a software project, and compare them against the detailed engineering and design specifications that are provided for a car's main UI, the dashboard.
- Requirement stability—Software requirements are usually unstable and not well understood by even the acquirer. Requirements evolve over time as the acquirer better understands the application or system being built. (That is one of the main reasons why the industry came up with agile software development practices in the first place.)
- Change—Software products change a lot more often than physical products. A 2012 Toyota built in January is not that different from one built in May. Meanwhile, most apps on a mobile phone are updated every few weeks.
- Cost—The cost of manufacturing a software component does not decrease with scale. When you are selling over a million cars a year, each of which uses four brake assemblies, making brake assemblies becomes cheaper than it would be for one set of custom brake assemblies for, say, a Formula One race car. In software development, almost every time you write code, it is customized.
- Integration—In manufacturing, the interfaces between components are well defined. They are probably based on standards (say, fixed-size nuts and bolts); even if they are non-standard, they can be defined in exact specifications, with associated acceptable tolerances, to the supplier. Software interfaces come nowhere close to this. In fact, when it comes to the integration points between components, the line separating the responsibilities of an acquirer and a supplier is very fuzzy. Add to that the complexity of having multiple component suppliers and their various integration points, and the situation becomes really interesting. (Think, the first release of healthcare.gov.)
- Estimation—Once you have built a manufacturing facility to mass-produce a component, you can estimate with some accuracy how much material and time it will take to churn out x units of the component.

Estimating the level of effort for software development is tricky at best. Unless you are hiring the same team, with considerable experience in building just that type of component, you cannot accurately tell how long it will take to develop the component. Changes in requirements and interface specifications make estimation even more complex. Practices like Agile do allow for somewhat better estimation, but there is a reason they call it *planning poker* (Hartman, 2009).

■ Quality assurance—Quality control is another area where software deviates from manufacturing. When an automobile manufacturer receives a component, they can easily test it to see if it meets their specifications and tolerances. All they have to do is test a statistically significant sample size to validate a batch they have received. For software, every component has to be tested for all the use cases that were specified. Rigor of testing is driven by balancing the level of quality required with the cost of testing.

NOTE Defibrillator software needs to be tested more rigorously than a word processor (although enough word processor crashes may necessitate using a defibrillator).

■ Standard practices—Manufacturing practices are generally standardized and do not vary too much between suppliers with certain certifications, such as ISO. Software development practices, on the other hand, are not as well defined or standardized. Even when they are well documented, software development practices are difficult to implement and follow to the letter. The dismal success rates of waterfall projects over the past couple of decades are ample proof of that. Agile practices are still evolving and are, by definition, agile. Thus, two suppliers with Scrum-certified practitioners may practice Scrum very differently, with radically different results.

■ Incremental construction—Hardware components are not built incrementally. Although their design and even manufacturing practices may incrementally improve over time (especially for organizations following practices like *Lean* or *kaizen*-based continuous improvement), components are built from scratch for each unit. Brakes on a 2017 car may be better than those on a 2016 model, but the ones on a new 2017 car are not using any parts of an older brake. In contrast, software components are built incrementally. With every iteration, whether it is within a release or a new version of the component, new code is added to old code or old code is modified. With the evolution of re-use and of open-source libraries, even brand-new components are now typically built upon code from other components or open-source libraries.

■ Contracts—Agreements to acquire manufacturing components are based on quantity, time, and quality service level agreements (SLAs). Given known manufacturing and raw material costs, these agreements are typically easy to create and enforce. Contracts in software component acquisition, on the other hand, become very complex. Fixed-price contracts are an issue, as incorrect time-and-effort estimation may lead to missed deadlines or suppliers taking quality shortcuts to meet time-based deadlines. Time-and-effort contracts need complex SLAs and oversight, making them difficult to price and implement.

As this list demonstrates (and it is in no way exhaustive), while software and systems development, especially of large, complex software and systems, is similar to a supply chain in a factory (and at a lower level of abstraction, an application delivery pipeline is similar to an assembly line), the parallels fall apart on a closer look.

Conducting a Value Stream Mapping Workshop A value stream mapping workshop is best carried out with executives who have decision-making ability. In order to be successful, at a minimum, you want the following stakeholders:

■ VP or executive owner of the line of business
■ VP or executive owner of application development
■ VP or executive owner of Quality Assurance (QA)
■ VP or executive owners of operations

In addition, other key stakeholders can also add value to the workshop but are optional, such as executives from the following departments:

■ Security
■ Enterprise architecture
■ Program Management Office (PMO)
■ Product/offering management (if it exists)

The workshop is best done at an enterprise, division, program, or line-of-business level, rather than at a project level, because projects can become too granular to be valuable. The workshop typically takes two to four hours to run. It is essential that all the executives who are participating engage in the entire workshop. The goal is for the executives to take ownership of all the identified bottlenecks and the plan to address them.

I have never had so many of my direct reports in the same room, working towards addressing common challenges as a team, rather than focusing only on the areas they own.

—CIO of a major financial services organization after the workshop

---

The workshop is done as a series of exercises, with a facilitator driving and guiding the executives who are participating. Here is the recommended set of exercises to run:

1. Identify business goals for the customer that is driving them to adopt or consider DevOps as a practice.
2. Identify IT initiatives that are already underway or planned for DevOps. These initiatives are then mapped back to the business goals to clarify alignment.
3. Create a value stream map to identify bottlenecks and inefficiencies found by the executives that are preventing them from achieving identified business goals.
4. Identify a prioritized list of three to four capabilities that can help them address the identified bottlenecks.
5. Create a roadmap of adoption for those best practices—with milestones, time frame (dates), and identified challenges to their adoption.

The core of the workshop, of course, is the creation of the value stream map, and that is where the most time is spent during the workshop.

The best way to create a value stream map is to take one artifact, typically a new requirement, through the delivery pipeline. As I mentioned earlier in this chapter, you look at the *artifact* (new requirement) as *stakeholders* execute *processes* on it to change its *state* and then *hand off* to other stakeholders. As this happens, for each stakeholder and handoff, you need to identify any source of *waste*. Waste comes in two main forms, which are the bottlenecks in the delivery pipeline:

1. Wait times—When a stakeholder is waiting for an action or for an artifact handoff, from another stakeholder

2. Overproduction or wrong production—When a stakeholder changes the state of an artifact that is unnecessary or that does not add any value to the end deliverable

A value stream mapping exercise of a delivery pipeline may identify anywhere from 10 to 15 key bottlenecks. The next critical task is to do a root-cause analysis (RCA) to determine the cause of each bottleneck, which is typically a symptom that is exhibited to the stakeholders. I discuss doing an RCA in more detail in the section "Diagnosing the Root Cause."

Once the root cause of each bottleneck has been identified, you can then look for dependencies between them and eventually prioritize them. You need to do the dependency analysis before prioritization in order to eliminate duplicates and lower the order of bottlenecks that cannot be addressed until other bottlenecks they are dependent upon are addressed. The rest of the prioritization looks at business impact, return on investment, and effort to address. It makes sense to create a balance of high-business-impact items and *low-hanging fruit*—areas that are easy to address and can have an immediate impact and show value. A business case and quick impact obviously need to be shown to the business. This prioritized list then needs to be put in context of real timelines and budgets for the organization.

The list of prioritized bottlenecks then needs to be mapped to business goals that were initially identified. It makes no sense to work on addressing a bottleneck that does not have a direct impact on a key business objective, as provided by the lines of business. This step further refines the prioritized list of bottlenecks to be addressed. Eventually, a prioritized list of the top five to six bottlenecks is developed. This list is then used to identify the right DevOps plays that need to be run, for developing a DevOps adoption roadmap.

Diagnosing the Root Cause

Winning squads emphasize fundamentals—pick and rolls, teamwork, and defense. They play with passion and they play hard. They move the ball, and when their players don't have it, they move well without the ball. They play with sagacity by exploiting mismatches. They gauge their opponent's weaknesses and then attack them relentlessly.

—Walt Frazier, Former NBA player

As I mentioned, you need to look at the root cause of each identified bottleneck to determine which plays to include in the playbook. This is needed because the bottlenecks identified during a value stream mapping exercise are actually the symptoms of the real cause of waste or inefficiency. A root-cause analysis is needed to identify them. A typical method to carry out a *root-cause analysis* is by asking "why" five times (Ohno, 2006). This approach allows one to go past the initial symptoms and get to the source, or root cause.

Let's explore some common bottlenecks and see what their underlying root causes may be. Here is a set of symptoms of inefficiency and waste in an organization or project:

- Lack of tool integration results in wait times as artifacts move from one practitioner to the next.
- Team members lack visibility and synchronicity with other team members' work.
- It's hard to learn and contribute across team boundaries.

These symptoms are typically due to a lack of an integrated delivery pipeline. The following set of symptoms is typically due to a lack of standardization of environments:

- Multiple disconnected dev-test environments that are not similar to the production environments
- Multiple technology stacks that are maintained and managed independently
- Lack of ability to deploy to the best platform based on risk, value, and technology fit

The next set of symptoms are examples of inefficiencies that are caused by challenges with managing *multi-speed* application delivery:

- Lack of ability of lines of business' need to release *business capabilities*, rather than individual applications.
- The slowest speed delivery pipeline becomes a drag to the speed of the fastest delivery pipeline.
- Almost all IT resources are assigned to run, manage, and maintain existing applications and workloads, with minimal resources available to invest in innovation.

Choosing the Transformation Plays

NOTE   Austin, TX, may be a three-hour flight from Washington, DC, but what if I cannot fly due to budget constraints? I can drive (22 hours), take the train (17 1/2 hours), or walk (488 hours—not recommended for us mere mortals). Based on my budget, time available, fear of flying, and ability to walk for days, I have to choose a path to take.

The rest of this chapter is primarily dedicated to describing the various plays that need to be adopted and executed in order to choose the right DevOps capabilities for the identified bottlenecks. Once you identify and understand the root cause of each bottleneck, the next step is to determine which DevOps capabilities can help address the root causes. However, it is not as simple as just adopting the DevOps capability. As I alluded to in my travel analogy, you need to consider several business, technical, and organizational factors in order to decide on which DevOps capabilities to adopt and how. These factors include the following:

- Ability of the project team to consume the process and tool changes
- Ability of the broader organization to consume the organizational changes
- Investment available to fund the adoption
- Project timeline
- Time available to show results
- Executive buy-in and sponsorship
- Practitioner buy-in
- Cultural inertia

I cover all of these factors in detail in the following chapters, as I discuss particular plays and how to execute them.

Determining the right plays and the DevOps capabilities for each play requires looking at four areas for each bottleneck that is being addressed:

1. Process improvement
2. Tools for automation
3. Environments and platforms
4. Culture

Each play needs to address multiple, if not all of these, areas in order to be successful. Then, the team leading the DevOps transformation has to ensure that the right plays are executed for the right bottleneck, taking into consideration the business, technical, and organizational factors listed earlier in this section.

Adopting the Transformation Plays

Once one has selected the right DevOps transformation plays, the next set of tasks, and really the real effort, becomes driving their adoption. I will present plays dedicated to driving DevOps adoption in a large enterprise in detail in Chapter 6. However, it is important to understand and prepare for two areas that any team developing and executing a DevOps transformation roadmap needs to tackle:

1. Addressing the productivity dip
2. Overcoming cultural inertia

Let's look at how one may recognize and address them.

Minimizing the Dip

NOTE Introducing any change results in an immediate drop in productivity. I call it the dip. It is unavoidable. I experience it when I update a mobile app to a new version. Sports teams experience it when they are on the road. That's why home field advantage exists; you get to play in your comfort zone.

There will always be a dip in productivity before there is a gain. It is a natural result of introducing change, whether to processes, tools, or team structure. A good transformation effort plans for this dip and takes steps to ensure that it is minimized. Ultimately, it is a successful transformation if the productivity lost (the shaded area in Figure 2-3) is minimal compared to the productivity gained, once the productivity gain turns positive. Of course, all this is moot if the productivity after transformation is not significantly higher than that before the transformation effort.

Projects often never recover from the dip if the productivity loss becomes too significant or goes beyond what the team was prepared for. A properly planned transformation, with experienced coaches, is essential to prevent this, to minimize the dip, and get to productivity gain as soon as possible, with minimal investment of time and resources.

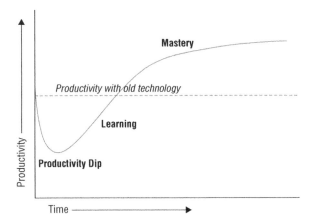

Figure 2-3: Productivity dip

The success of Agile coaches in driving Agile adoption across enterprises has similarly been extended to the role of DevOps coaches to drive DevOps adoption. Organizations from IBM to several DevOps consulting boutiques have trained DevOps coaches who are embedded in project teams and organizations adopting DevOps.

The business drivers identified for the DevOps transformation also come into play here because they are what should drive the Key Performance Indicators (KPIs) that are being used to measure productivity in the first place. These KPIs should be

- Identified before the transformation starts (measures of success)
- Taken as a baseline to know the current state
- Set as goals for what the productivity KPIs should be post-transformation (end state)

I discuss different KPIs that should be measured for different adoption plays in Chapter 3.

Just like you cannot win a game—or, for that matter, play a game—without knowing where the goals are and what constitutes a score, you cannot succeed with a transformation without knowing what the KPIs that need to be improved are, and by how much. Similarly, just as you cannot have a high-performance team that wins championships without a good coach, and a good coaching program, you cannot succeed with a DevOps transformation without an experienced DevOps coach and a well-planned transformation roadmap.

[A] perfect plan doesn't mean that it ends up the way you want it to end up.... You don't get better if you win all the time. You get better when you lose. You improve when you lose. You look at yourself more if you lose.

—Jeremy Lin, American NBA player

Initiating Adoption with Pilots

Executing on a DevOps transformation can be a very complex and large-scale effort. Starting small to refine the DevOps adoption roadmap and show success is essential to succeed at the enterprise scale. I discuss specific plays for scaling for an enterprise in Chapter 5. However, to get started, you also need to have a plan to achieve success upon which you can then build an enterprise-wide adoption. This entails picking a set of pilot projects to execute the DevOps adoption roadmap.

The way to start an enterprise-wide DevOps adoption is by starting with three to five select pilot projects and then scaling up once the adoption roadmap is proven and enhanced, based on lessons learned from the pilot projects. The goal of each project is to adopt one DevOps capability per project and measure the impact of addressing the specific bottleneck that particular capability was intended to address. The reason you adopt just one capability per pilot project is to be able to show a direct impact of the adopted capability on the bottleneck it is supposed to address. Adopting more than one capability per project does not allow for a direct assessment of impact.

The goal at the end is to show success and capture lessons learned that you can then leverage to get even better results for other projects, as adoption expands. As I have mentioned, identifying the right KPIs for the business goal being targeted, taking a baseline before starting the pilot project, and then tracking the KPIs through adoption is essential to show results—good or bad—and make adjustments to the adoption plan, as and when needed, as the project progresses.

Each pilot project should have a dedicated or shared DevOps coach assigned to it. Whether the project team needs a dedicated coach or a shared one depends on the size of the project team.

The best approach to leveraging pilots is to pick projects that are important to the business, but not mission-critical. You don't want a project that is not of any significant value to the organization, such that it does have the right team members and funding allocated. You also do not want a project that is too large in size and geographic distribution or that is so mission-critical that it can jeopardize important business functions if the project runs into issues or becomes delayed as a result. Once the pilot projects succeed and you have analyzed what worked and what didn't, you can extend adoption to any project, including large, mission-critical projects, of any size and geographical distribution.

Overcoming Cultural Inertia

Ultimately, even after all the process improvement and automation is introduced in an organization, it can only succeed at adopting the culture of DevOps if it is able to overcome its inherent *cultural inertia*. Most organizations have inertia—an inherent resistance to change. Change is not easy, especially in large organizations where the culture may have had years to develop and permeate across hundreds, if not thousands, of practitioners. These practitioners, as individuals, may appreciate the value of adopting DevOps, but as a group, they may resist change and thus have inertia. Overcoming this inertia is key.

How is this inertia exhibited? "This is the way we do things here." "Yes, but changing X is not in my control." "You will need to talk to Y about that; WE cannot change how THEY work." These are just some examples of phrases and behaviors that are symptomatic of cultural inertia. Over time, organizations develop behaviors; teams and groups divide up actions and responsibilities along organizational lines; checks and balances are established in the name of governance, which are not related to true governance at all; processes exist but no one know why—they are "just there"; reports are produced that no one reads anymore, but no one is willing to do away with them; bad things happened in the past and resulted in approval requirements to ensure they would never happen again; and so on. All these behaviors build up inertia in an organization's culture.

Overcoming cultural inertia requires a serious look at every artifact and process that may cause the organization to become inefficient—the root causes behind every bottleneck and identified waste. Addressing these bottlenecks requires change beyond just traditional DevOps practices. It requires a desire to change the culture from both the executive leadership that is sponsoring and leading the transformation and the practitioners who are executing the transformation. The leadership needs to provide cover for the practitioners who are changing how things are done, which will impact those outside the team executing the changes and potentially break legacy governance practices. The practitioners also need to break their habits; they need to break out of their functional silos, and they need to be the agents of change.

SPONSORSHIP AND ENGAGEMENT

No DevOps play can be adopted effectively, and will certainly not deliver at its full potential value, unless it is adopted with such a top-down and bottom-up approach and engagement to address cultural inertia. Top-down sponsorship is needed to initiate and drive the transformation. Bottom-up buy-in and engagement is needed to actually execute the transformation.

I will discuss how the leadership can sponsor and drive the DevOps Transformation in detail in Chapter 6.

An example roadmap, developed for a real (anonymized) client using the techniques described in this chapter, is documented in Appendix A.

Summary

To summarize, adopting DevOps is not unlike a coach and players of a sports team preparing for, playing, and (hopefully) winning a match. The coach and team's leaders need to study the playing conditions and the opposing team to understand their own strengths and weaknesses, given the conditions and competition. They then need to pick the right *plays* from their playbook and then practice. The real work is the practice of the plays till they are perfected. Till the *dip* in their paying ability due to the plays being new, or the *inertia* from previously playing different plays is overcome. Till running the plays in the actual game becomes no different from practice.

Similarly, adopting DevOps requires:

- Defining the *target state*
- Understanding the *current state*
- Picking the right *plays* to get from the current state to the target state
- Preparing to address the *dip*
- Working on top-down and bottom-up sponsorship and engagement to overcome *cultural inertia*

I will cover all of these in the rest of the chapters of this book.

CHAPTER 3

Developing a Business Case for a DevOps Transformation

THE BUSINESS CASE FOR THE GROWTH OF MAJOR LEAGUE SOCCER

If you're looking for a sporting example of an organization managing fast growth, here's an unexpected one: Major League Soccer.

As soccer's popularity continues to grow stateside, MLS has added nine new clubs since 2007 (two of which, the most recent additions, will begin play in 2015). Meanwhile, the league's average attendances now rival those of the National Hockey League and National Basketball Association, and TV ratings—though they dipped in 2013—have significantly grown from a decade ago.

This success has translated financially, too; the Columbus Crew sold for more than $60 million—a solid midmarket number that, though it pales in comparison to the valuations for Major League Baseball and National Football League teams, is a record for an MLS club.

With 18 seasons now in the books, MLS is on the verge of breaking into the pantheon of America's major league sports. But it still faces its challenges, from competing with global soccer to growing its core audience. Commissioner Don Garber spoke to *Inc.* about lessons from the league's recent growth stage and how it plans to keep it going.

With fast growth comes the capacity to run off the rails. To that end, it's important to keep measure of success—and be quick to diagnose when something might go wrong. MLS keeps tabs of its key performance indicators—which Garber listed as national and local television and media coverage, the development of soccer-specific stadiums, as well as TV ratings and stadium attendance figures.

continued

continued

> While these indicators are all way up in the last several years, the latter two—ratings and attendance—did dip during the 2013 season. To that end, Garber and MLS were quick to identify the problems for the hiccup: One team performed particularly poorly in terms of attendance, while there is room for improvement in TV broadcasting. The timing on that front is good, as the league's TV rights are currently on the open market.
>
> Garber says that with the reasons for the dips identified, the league still feels confident in its overall plan. The occasional breakage that comes with speed doesn't mean scrap everything. It means analyze and adjust where needed.
>
> "We work to create a plan for the year and then go from the top down, working with the (club) owners to make sure we have the resources to be able to achieve that plan. That approach has worked very well for us over the last number of years," Garber says. "Now and then you're going to hit some bumps in the road and you have to be smart, nimble, and focused to adjust your plan to some of the market macro-issues and micro-issues."
>
> —Vaccaro, 2014

The executives leading a *DevOps transformation* are responsible for developing the case for undertaking the DevOps transformation and then selling it to the organization (the CEO, CFO, and potentially the board). During the course of this book, several compelling reasons to act will be documented that may be the triggers or catalysts that can be leveraged to initiate a DevOps transformation. I will present an entire module on these compelling reasons to act in Chapter 7. However, you still need to make the right and compelling business case. The business case not only delivers to the organization the value proposition, in business terms, to make the necessary investments, but it also ensures that the investments are made continuously to ensure that the transformation gets the requisite time and resources required to have an impact on the business. DevOps adoption, after all, is not a one-time project, but an ongoing transformation.

Developing the Business Case

It is a given that DevOps capabilities make the *application delivery pipeline* lean and efficient by optimizing processes, tools, platforms, and culture. However, businesses require a business case with tangible numbers to show what the *return on investment* (ROI) will be for them. What *business value* can they achieve by adopting DevOps?

There are several techniques that can be leveraged to arrive at such business value numbers:

- *Case studies.* Several case studies have been done by vendors and solution providers on how their DevOps tools, platforms, and transformation services deliver business value and ROI. These can be leveraged by examining a case study of a similar organization that has adopted DevOps and the business value and ROI that they were able to achieve. It also adds value to speak with that organization, if they are open to sharing their experiences and lessons learnt, on their journey to achieving the target business value.

- *Analyst studies.* Several studies have also been done by external analyst firms. Forrester, for example, does *Total Economic Impact* (TEI) studies for tools and practices (Forrester, 2013, 2015). These can be leveraged to develop an assessment of the business value that can be gained by your own organization.

- *Value stream mapping.* I describe value stream mapping (VSM) in Chapter 2 in this book. The intent in this book has been to showcase VSM as a technique to identify areas of waste in the delivery pipeline and to develop a DevOps adoption roadmap to address them. However, you can do a much deeper VSM assessment that goes into *time and motion* type studies to not just identify areas of waste but also to quantify the actual loss in productivity that is occurring as a result and in which areas. You can then create a *value map* that maps addressing the area of waste to financial returns.

- *Business Value Assessment.* The Business Value Assessment (BVA) is a formal approach to develop a value map of the DevOps capabilities being adopted to map these capabilities to tangible financial returns. The BVA tool used by most suppliers (vendors and solution providers) has a predefined formula built in to calculate cumulative costs of current practices (using the adopted tools, platforms, and processes) and then to calculate the costs of adopting (acquiring, deploying, getting training, and using) the DevOps tools, platforms, and practices being targeted for adoption.

While all the techniques described previously can be used when adopting DevOps for projects focused on innovation (more on the distinction between DevOps for optimization vs. innovation in the next chapter), there is an additional "twist" to consider here. In most cases, the innovative solution being developed is going to be arrived at through a series of experiments. These experiments may be for innovative technology solutions or business models, or very often for both. As a result, the business case being developed cannot be very tangible. You cannot calculate true business value given all the unknowns that are driving the need for experimentation in the first place. As a result, you need to build a business case like a *venture capitalist*. This is someone who invests small amounts in several ideas via startups, with the goal of making significant returns on the one startup that goes big and succeeds. This will make a return not only on the investment on that particular startup but also on all the lost investments for all the startups that did not make it.

Several techniques have been developed to attempt to understand the business value of an idea in its early stage, before development even begins. These techniques help to define the idea, determine the investment required, and quantify the potential business value to the customers and the business.

Focusing away from the technology and just on the business model of the idea raises interesting questions for a technology organization on how to determine even the idea's viability, much less its business value. One technique that has gained traction in the *Lean startup* space is *Business Model Generation,* introduced by Alexander Osterwalder and Yves Pigneur, in their book by the same name (Osterwalder, 2013). Among other techniques, the book uses a *Business Model Canvas* to define, understand, and refine the components of a business model, including the business value to the organization.

As shown in Figure 3-1, the canvas has nine components, each of which contribute toward defining the business model, helping to refine it further, determining its viability, and understanding associated risks, required resources, and ultimately the business value. These components are as follows:

1. *Customer segments.* Who are the customers being served?
2. *Value propositions.* What are the various value propositions of each problem being addressed, for each customer segment?
3. *Channels.* What are the various modes of delivering the value propositions?
4. *Customer relationships.* What customer relationships are established as a result of engagement with each customer segment?
5. *Revenue streams.* What sources of revenue result from each value proposition?
6. *Key resources.* What are the resources required to deliver the value propositions?

7. *Key activities.* What activities need to be performed to deliver the value proposition, with the identified resources?

8. *Key partnerships.* Who are the partners, vendors, and suppliers who need to be partnered with in order to deliver the value propositions?

9. *Cost structures.* What are the costs of the investments and resources that need to be committed to deliver the value propositions?

Figure 3-1: Business Model Canvas[1] (Strategyzer, 2013)

This approach provides a comprehensive model for each *idea* being considered for investment by the organization, allowing them to make an intelligent decision as to whether to invest in it. In the context of DevOps, this canvas can also be used to develop a business model for the value proposition for undergoing a DevOps transformation.

Completing the Business Model Canvas

Next, let's fill in these components to create a business model. This will allow you to build a Business Model Canvas for a DevOps transformation, which an executive sponsoring the transformation can then leverage to develop a

---

business case. You can leverage the rest of this chapter as a guide to follow along and fill in your own Business Model Canvas and develop a DevOps Business Case for your organization.

For the purposes of this exercise, I am going to look at the Business Model Canvas from the perspective of both the line of business (LOB) and the IT organization, building in essence two separate canvases.

Because this is in the context of a DevOps transformation, only IT capabilities delivered by the organization are included. If the organization interacts with customers by delivering services that do not require IT applications or services, those services will be considered outside the scope of this exercise. For example, if a bank delivered cash to an organization for payroll, the software used to request and manage the cash would be within scope. The actual delivery service, delivering cash via a secure truck service, would not.

Customer Segments

This section captures the customers being served by the organization. As described previously, you need to look at who the customers are from the perspective of both the line of business and the IT department. Both have different customer sets.

Line of Business

For a line of business, the end goal is to deliver business capabilities to your end-users and customers. Thus, your customer segments are as follows:

1. *End-users.* An *end-user* is anyone who uses the application that is being delivered. They are different from *customers* because they may not be the ones who are generating any direct revenue for the organization (see definition 2, "Customers/clients"). For example, for social media apps like Facebook, Twitter, or Pinterest, the end-users do not pay to use the service. While these companies may monetize the data they collect as a result of these end-users utilizing their services, their real customers are the ones who pay for their services. These end-users themselves may be multiple sub-segments based on demographics, geography, usage level, and so on.

The distinction between *end-user* and *customer* is something that confuses many people. Let's look at a company like YouTube. An end-user is anyone who views or even posts videos. However, YouTube also has a segment of end-users who are power-users. These users post videos that get so many views that they are able to participate in a revenue-sharing program with YouTube. As a result, these end-users should definitely be considered a separate *customer segment*. Whether YouTube considers them end-users or customer-clients depends on their classification approach.

2. *Customers/clients*: The *customer* or *client* for an organization is someone who pays them for the services their applications deliver. In the example of social media apps, the customers are the advertisers who pay to put advertisements on the apps in order to target end-users. Here it is also important to recognize that the customers may have their own customers. This is typical for a business-to-business (B2B) application, but it may also be true for other platform offerings. The customer of the organization's primary customer is the eventual end-user. For social media sites, for example, if a customer builds an app on their platform that is used by others, then the end-users of the app are the customers of the app vendor and of the social media platform. Both the app vendor and the app end-users are also, in parallel, still the social media sites' end-users. Think of a game like FarmVille, which runs on Facebook. FarmVille users are the customers of the maker of the game, Zynga, but they are also Facebook end-users. Zynga, in turn, is a Facebook customer.

3. *Customer representatives.* In many cases there may be employees or partners who are the touchpoint between the organization and its end-users and customers. These customers interact with the organization through human representatives, who in turn consume the digital applications and services being delivered. In any non-digital customer interactions, it is these employees who are therefore the customer segment for the LOB. Examples would be tellers, customer service representatives, and agents (employees or external partners). As a customer segment, they need to be treated as surrogates for the final non-digital end-users and customers and offered appropriate business value in a manner that they can pass on to the end-users and customers.

There is no real parallel here for social media. The closest would be a celebrity, executive, or company hiring a social media manager or team that interacts with social media on their behalf. However, for social media, this user is no different from the end-user or customer they represent. But for a bank that has bank tellers in its branches or an insurance company that sells through independent franchisee insurance agents, there would be a difference in the nature of interactions that they have with the organization, requiring them to be treated as a separate customer segment.

IT Organization

For an IT organization, the *lines of business* are actually the key customer segments. Of course, all of the LOB's customer segments are indirectly the IT organization's customer segments too. In addition, the IT organization has its own internal and external customer segments:

1. *Internal end-users.* These include employees, contractors, and partners who consume IT services as end-users from within the organization. This would include the consumers of business-to-employee applications and services (e-mail, internal websites and portals, HR applications, payroll, and so on).

2. *Application delivery stakeholders.* These are all the people working as stakeholders on the application delivery pipeline: developers, QA, Ops, business analysts, architects, and security—all the people who are stakeholders in DevOps, as I discuss in previous chapters. Examples of key *application delivery stakeholders* include the following:
   - Developers
   - Testers
   - Operations
   - IT executives
   - Business owner (from the LOB)

3. *Customer IT organizations.* These would be IT organizations of customers who consume delivered IT services in order to develop and deliver their own value-added applications and services. Examples of key stakeholders for *customer IT organizations* would be the same roles as those listed in the previous definition, except that they would be employees of the customer organization.

In my earlier social media example for Facebook, this would be the IT organization at Zynga.

Value Propositions

Next, for the line of business and the IT organization, you need to determine the value proposition delivered for the multiple problems addressed, for each of the customer segments identified previously.

Line of Business

For each customer segment, the LOB needs to understand and define the myriad *value propositions* it wants to deliver.

1. *End-users:* The value propositions being delivered will vary for each subsegment of end-user identified. They will also depend on the type of business functions that are being delivered. Are these traditional functions that need to be optimized, or are they new, innovative functions, where the right requirements, business models, and delivery models are still being discovered, defined, and refined through experimentation? These value propositions for the LOB include the following:

   - Business functions need to be made available to the end-users by which they can acquire the business value the LOBs want to deliver to them.
   - Business functions need to be made available in a manner that aligns with the way the various customer segments want to consume them.
   - Updates to the business functions need to be made on a regular basis to align with the changing needs and expectations of the various customer segments.
   - Experiments need to be run to determine the user experience for the various segments.
   - Experiments need to be run to refine engagement and business models for new customer segments.
   - Business functions need to be delivered to the customer segments in a way that is superior to the competition.

   Let's continue with the example of a social media website. YouTube, as I described earlier, has regular users as well as power-users who are actually paid on a revenue-sharing basis for posting videos, based on views received. The value proposition for a regular user is simple: to be able to view videos that are available in their geographic and legal jurisdiction, with the right resolution, quality, and speed. They should also be able to subscribe to other users, leave comments on videos, share videos on other social media sites, and (the ultimate endorsement on a social media site) "like" a video. In addition, they should be able to post videos by easily uploading them in multiple supported formats and resolutions. The power-users, on the other hand, should receive the value propositions of regular users and also the value proposition of being able to generate revenue from their videos based on advertisements that are served to regular users. They should be able to upload high-quality videos, be able to access clear metrics on views and income generated, be able to control the types of advertisements served and advertisers allowed to deliver them, and, of course, be paid in an accurate and timely manner.

2. *Customers:* Customers or clients are those who actually pay for services. Thus, the core value proposition delivered to them would be to receive all the value propositions of end-users and to be able to get the business value they are paying for. The list of value propositions delivered include:

   ▪ Deliver business functions at a competitive rate, vis-à-vis the market.

   ▪ Deliver business functions at well-defined service levels, agreed upon with the customers. There may be multiple service levels, based on different pricing models and tiers.

   ▪ Make several pricing models available for various customer segments.

   ▪ Experiment with pricing and acquisition models to validate the pricing models for various customer segments.

   For customers who are developing applications and services for their own end-users and customers, by leveraging the applications and services delivered by the organization, the value propositions will also include the ability to consume the right applications and services with which to deliver their own value propositions to their end-users and customers.

3. *Customer representatives:* Because customer representatives are really surrogates for the end-users and customers engaging with them, the value propositions will generally remain the same. In addition, there will be the value proposition related to the customer service aspect of their role. They should be able to deliver business value with the highest level of customer satisfaction—higher than any tool. They also need to be able to answer questions asked by the end-users and clients, related to the organization and all it offers. The applications and services delivered to the customer representatives thus need to deliver a broader level of interaction than the direct end-user or customer applications and services.

IT Organization

From a DevOps perspective, the value propositions being delivered by the IT organization will depend on the business goals the organization has on how it intends to deliver the business value to all its customer segments. The various value propositions for end-users and customers (internal and external) can include the following:

- High-quality (defect-free) applications and services delivered
- Easy onboarding of new users
- Easy account closing and deletion of users wanting to leave
- Ability to import user data from another app
- Ability to migrate user data to another app
- Fast response to end-user issues and customer support requests
- High availability—minimal outages to service, including for maintenance (for example, the Facebook website never goes down for "scheduled maintenance," even for upgrades)
- No user data loss
- Compliance with all regulatory and legal requirements
- Access options for users with disabilities
- Globalization with support for multiple languages and currencies
- Data and privacy protection of all users and customers
- Secure services
- High customer satisfaction

The value propositions for the IT employees and suppliers who are stakeholders on the application delivery pipeline will include the following:

■ High availability, and stable and secure infrastructure and platforms
■ The right application delivery tool chain, with well-integrated tools
■ End-to-end traceability and visibility across the delivery pipeline
■ Ability to leverage the right Agile and DevOps practices and processes
■ Ability to communicate and collaborate across functional silos and delivery pipelines

Let's look at the examples of the key stakeholders listed in the previous section and identify typical examples of value propositions for each of them.

For developers:

■ Ability to use automated build, testing, and application deployment to deliver changes to an application or service into production in a two-week sprint
■ Ability to quickly assess the performance and functional characteristics of the applications or services delivered, so as to improve the same in future sprints

For testers:

■ Ability to deploy a new version of an application or service to a "production-like environment" and test it using automated tools and validated test data
■ Ability to provide feedback to developers on issues that are identified, such that they can re-create the issues in a timely manner

For operations:

■ Efficiently deliver fully automated IT processes and environments in order to balance risk and cost, with a step-change improvement in quality and speed
■ Efficiently predict and prevent production outages by exploiting analytical and cognitive operational systems that dramatically improve the quality of service and reduce the cost of operations

For IT executives:

- Access metrics dashboards to gain insight into the aggregated performance of all the applications and services being delivered, and the environments they are delivered on
- Access metrics dashboards to get detailed performance metrics on individual stakeholders and practitioners working on the application delivery pipeline
- Continuously improve application delivery processes, tools, platforms, and team culture to improve time to value

For the business owner (from the LOB):

- Experiment with new ideas in the marketplace to create differentiated client experiences and identify new business opportunities
- Access business dashboards to gain insight into the aggregated performance of their business units in order to improve business results (revenue and cost)
- Access feedback on user behavior and sentiment when consuming applications and services delivered to determine how to improve customer engagement and satisfaction and increase business value delivered

For the customer's IT organizations, the value propositions would include the following:

- Highly available, stable, and secure services via well-defined APIs and services
- Fast response to issues and customer service requests
- Fast response to new requirements and enhancement requests
- Well-defined roadmaps and visibility into future capabilities being added, modified, or removed from applications and services delivered

All of these value propositions are, of course, highly subjective and vary by application type and customer segment. They all typically manifest as *nonfunctional requirements* for the applications and services being delivered.

Channels

The channels are the various ways the organization delivers the value propositions to various customer segments.

Line of Business

For the lines of business the applications and services delivered by the IT organization are typically the sole set of channels by which they deliver the value propositions previously documented to the customer segments. These channels include:

- Applications and services being delivered that are consumed directly by the end-users and customers (web, mobile, desktop, and so on)
- Applications and services that are consumed by *representatives* who interact with end-users and customers
- Services being delivered (APIs, platforms, data sources, and so on), consumed by the customers in order to develop and deliver their own applications and services

IT Organization

The channels for the IT organization are the same as for the LOB. It is the IT organization's responsibility to deliver all the applications and services needed to enable these channels. IT is therefore responsible for all the channels.

Customer Relationships

Next you need to capture the customer relationships that get established, developed, or enhanced as these various value propositions are delivered, via the channels, to each customer segment.

Line of Business

The lines of business own the customer relationships for the three types of customer segments identified:

- Existing customers with existing relationships
- Existing customers with relationships being explored or developed
- New customers with new relationships

LOBs improve customer relationships through better customer service and improvement of the user experience.

IT Organization

The goal of the IT organization is to enable these customer relationships through their applications and services. In addition to the LOB customer relationships, the IT organization has additional customer segments with their own relationships in all three categories, as I described previously for the LOBs.

IT organizations improve customer relationships by improving the experiences of all stakeholders, across all customer segments, and empowering them to participate in *continuous improvement* of the applications and services being delivered, and the processes, tools, platforms, and organizational culture of how they are delivered.

Revenue Streams

For any business, a key result of delivering value to its customers is revenue. You will hence need to capture all the various revenue streams that can be generated from each customer segment. It is important to note here that revenue may not be the end goal of the organization. A government agency delivering value to its citizens may not be looking to generate revenue as a result (outside of taxes and fees) but will need to identify some metric(s) to measure the "return" for the value being delivered.

Line of Business

The goal here is for the LOBs to do the following:

- Improve existing revenue streams
- Develop new revenue streams by experimenting with new capabilities and new business models
- Develop new revenue streams by monetizing existing and new business capabilities through partners who develop value-added services by leveraging them

IT Organization

The goal here is for the IT organization to do the following:

- Optimize existing applications and services to maximize opportunities to improve existing revenue streams

- Enable the LOBs to experiment with new capabilities and business models, and provide them with rapid feedback on the experiments
- Deliver a platform for partners to leverage APIs and services delivered to build their own solutions by leveraging them

Key Resources

The resources leveraged by organization to develop and deliver the value proposition will need to be documented next. These resources are also a measure of investment and cost for delivering the value proposition.

Line of Business

The key resources available to the LOBs include the following:

- Human resources across the organization, including the IT organization
- Intellectual property (IP) developed and owned by the organization
- Financial resources available to invest in the development and delivery of applications and services
- Relationships and partnerships

IT Organization

The key resources available to the IT organization include the following:

- Employees and contractors working for the IT organization
- Partners and suppliers working with the IT organization, delivering services
- Intellectual property developed and owned by the IT organization
- Processes, tools, platforms, and organizational culture developed and maintained by the IT organization

Key Activities

The next step is to document the various activities the resources need to undertake to deliver the value proposition. These activities also drive the investment and cost.

Line of Business

Key activities for the LOBs include the following:

- Deliver business value to customers through existing and new applications and services (channels)
- Experiment with new applications and services, and with new business models to improve user experience, capture new markets, and develop new revenue models through partners and suppliers
- Capture and analyze feedback from customer segments to continuously improve business capabilities and user experiences that are being delivered, channels through which they are delivered, and leveraged business models

IT Organization

Key activities for the IT organization include the following:

- Develop and deliver applications and services to provide business value to customer segments
- Continuously improve the applications and services being delivered, based on feedback from users and customers and guidance from LOBs
- Provide the ability to experiment with new features, user experiences, and business models
- Deliver APIs and services to partners and suppliers
- Provide robust processes, tools, platforms, and organizational culture to stakeholders working on the application delivery pipeline
- Provide feedback to stakeholders working on the application delivery pipeline, enabling them to continuously improve the applications and services being delivered, the environments they are delivered on, and the processes, tools, platforms, and culture that are leveraged to deliver them
- Provide feedback to the LOBs on application and service functionality, performance, user experience, usage patterns, and user sentiment

Key Partnerships

Partnerships include all the business partners, vendors, and suppliers that contribute toward delivering business value. They need to be documented next.

Line of Business

The LOBs have partnerships to fill in gaps and expand reach and access to customer segments that they themselves cannot reach:

- *Partners.* These are any other organizations that may leverage the services being delivered by the organization to deliver their own value-added services. In the case of social media apps, these are organizations that leverage the services being delivered to deliver their own offerings and services. Think of any company that uses Facebook or Twitter as the way to log in to their website and that uses the Facebook or Twitter identity to identify their user, instead of using a separate username and login. Other examples include any third-party company that delivers games (FarmVille) or their own apps (Periscope) on these platforms. (Yes, there is overlap between customers and partners—many will be both. Some competitors may also be partners.)
- *Suppliers.* Suppliers also play a key role here. They fall under customer segments or under key partnerships, or both, depending upon their relationship to the organization. If it is a mutually beneficial partnership, where the supplier is delivering key services enhanced exclusively for the organization and the organization and the supplier are both benefiting from the additional value they deliver together, then you should include it as a customer segment. Again, staying with the social media examples, if a sports organization (like the NFL) is streaming its games on Twitter to gain access to new markets, then it is both a customer segment and a *key partner.*

IT Organization

The IT organization will also have partnerships to fill gaps and to expand reach and access to technology capabilities and services:

- *Suppliers and partners who are stakeholders in the application delivery pipeline.* These are third-party suppliers and partners who deliver components of the application delivery pipeline but do so externally from the organization. They include application service providers (SaaS and APIs consumed); infrastructure or platform service providers (IaaS, PaaS, and CaaS); and other technology providers and vendors.

■ *Value-added partners*. These are organizations that consume the APIs and services delivered by the organization to deliver their own value-added services. They are also a customer segment for the organization.

Cost Structures

Just like revenue generated, you need to capture all the costs and investments that go into delivering the final value to all the customer segments.

Line of Business

The cost structures for the LOBs are mapped directly to the key resources I listed previously. All human, technology, and IP resources have a cost. Some might be capital expenditures (CapEx) and some operational expenditures (OpEx). One of the goals for the LOBs is to manage these costs to maximize profitability and return on investment (ROI).

IT Organization

For the IT organization, each key resource that I identified earlier also has a cost. IT organizations typically have significant costs associated with running and maintaining existing applications and services. Today, most IT organizations are working to optimize these costs to free up resources to invest in innovation.

Summary

The example provided in this appendix can form a template to fill out a Business Model Canvas for an organization looking to build a business case for a DevOps transformation. All the key components of the business case are documented as you fill out the canvas. The canvas can also serve as a tool to validate the approach used by the organization to deliver applications and services to their customers and to validate the investments being made in the applications and services. Some of these areas to validate are listed as follows:

- Do the way the applications and services are being delivered, the associated costs, and the leveraged revenue streams justify the existing application delivery models?
- Should processes and practices be optimized to improve ROI?
- Should the organization build or buy new applications and services?
- What resources can the organization free up in order to invest in innovation?
- What investments need to be made to improve the processes, tools, platforms, and culture of the organization?

As shown in Figure 3-2, this approach of leveraging the Business Model Canvas, coupled with a *value stream mapping exercise,* across multiple delivery pipelines, as illustrated in Chapter 2, to identify areas of waste in the application delivery pipeline will allow you to fully construct a DevOps transformation roadmap, and the business case to make the investment in the transformation, for your organization.

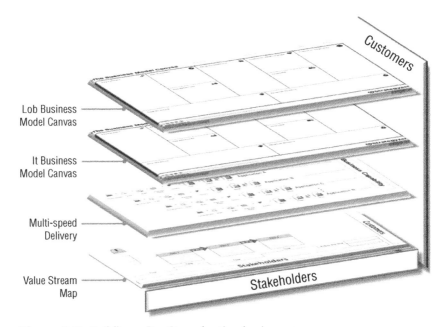

Figure 3-2: Building a DevOps adoption business case

CHAPTER 4

DevOps Plays for Optimizing the Delivery Pipeline

continued

undervalued: getting on base. The A's found relief pitcher Chad Bradford, who was unwanted because he threw the ball in an unconventional way and not very fast. But Bradford stopped opposing players from getting on base; it didn't matter to the A's how he went about doing it.

Many people have criticized *Moneyball* because of the A's focus on saber-metrics, which challenges many tenets of baseball's hallowed conventional wisdom. They argue its focus on numbers dehumanizes the game and ignores the intangibles that only trained scouts can see. Though saber-metrics is an element in the story, it's not really what *Moneyball* is about.

More broadly, *Moneyball* is a story of innovating to succeed, or as Beane puts it in the movie, "adapt or die." Beane was an entrepreneur who was innovating out of necessity.

—Bradbury, 2011

DevOps as an Optimization Exercise

It all boils down to optimizing for maximum results, in an environment of constraints. For example, you can study *Moneyball* and how the Oakland Athletics put together a winning team in an environment of significant salary constraints (the Oakland Athletics had the third-lowest team salary in the league, with only the Tampa Rays and Washington Nationals having lower team salaries in 2002); or you can read Gene Kim's *The Phoenix Project*, which is a brilliant, must-read business novel that introduces adopting DevOps in a typical IT project with all the constraints that come with it; or you can go back and study the root source in Dr. Eliyahu Goldratt's business novel *The Goal* (which actually inspired *The Phoenix Project*, and introduced the world to *continuous improvement* in a world full of real and practical constraints). Regardless of which one you choose, they all lead you to the reality of achieving success in the business world—you have to innovatively optimize how you operate to maximize productivity and to reduce waste within your operating constraints. Despite Dr. Goldratt referring to it as the *Theory of Constraints*, these sources are not examples of theory; rather, they are examples of applying optimization to achieve maximum results, from optimizing salary and skills for a sports team to optimizing within the typical constraints that exist in IT and manufacturing domains.

DevOps is the latest in a series of attempts to introduce optimization to the application delivery and broader IT domain. There have been many prior attempts to apply the practices and lessons learned from *Lean Thinking*—which had been applied successfully to manufacturing and other domains for decades—to application delivery and IT operations. DevOps succeeds where other movements have failed because all these prior attempts typically focused on optimizing one or, at most, two functional areas of the application delivery pipeline, such as Dev-test (Agile), operations (Information Technology Infrastructure Library or ITIL), or project management (Six Sigma). DevOps succeeds because it takes a holistic approach of optimizing the entire delivery pipeline, across all functional areas. In fact, it begins with the premise and intent of transforming the *culture* of communication and collaboration across functional silos and eventually eliminating the very existence of silos for all practical purposes. (They may still exist from an organizational reporting structure, which I discuss later in this and subsequent chapters.) DevOps succeeds because it puts cultural transformation, which has an impact across functional and organizational silos, above process and tools. DevOps is, before anything else, a cultural movement. In fact, in Chapter 6, I discuss why large organizations struggle with DevOps adoption, because these organizations tend to put governance and process before culture.

In this and the next two chapters, I look at DevOps through a lens of a sports team running plays to win—what DevOps *plays* can you run to adopt the cultural, process, and automation practices needed to optimize your application delivery pipeline, based on the constraints you need to operate under. I will look at both technology-agnostic plays that everyone can adopt as needed and at technology-specific plays that are tailored for specific technology-driven needs and constraints. Furthermore, I will categorize these plays into whether the business intent behind them is to achieve *optimization* or *innovation*. While every innovation-focused application delivery effort needs optimization, the reverse is not always true. When it comes to DevOps adoption, applications focused on innovation as their primary goal require special treatment. (I discuss them at length in the next chapter.) This chapter focuses on optimization. First, though, let's fully explore this distinction between application by optimization and innovation.

Business Intent: Optimization versus Innovation

Before you start looking at the various plays that you can adopt to achieve progress on a DevOps transformation, it is important to understand that which play you run depends not just on the *bottlenecks* you are working to address but also on the core business intent of the applications the play is being executed on. Organizations have two types of *business intent*: one focused on innovation (with velocity and agility) and the other focused on optimization (stability and continuity and also with velocity and agility). Classifying applications being delivered into categories based on the business intents of innovation or optimization helps you determine which DevOps play is likely to run well.

Based on these two types of business intent, applications in an organization can be divided into two categories:

1. The *industrialized core* that delivers core business capabilities—things that keep the business going. Here the primary business intent is *optimization*.
2. The *innovation edge*, where experimentation happens in order to explore and identify new business models and new customer engagement methods; in other words, the primary business intent is *innovation*.

There have been several attempts by the industry to categorize applications or IT in general as being *two-speed* or *bimodal*. These categorization efforts are based either on speed or on how much the requirements change. Two-speed IT implies that some applications go faster, and others slower. Speed, however, is not the best metric to categorize by. Bimodal, on the other hand, implies that the requirements of applications are either stable or ever changing. Both of these classification approaches are limited. Reality is more of a "normal distribution" than bimodal.

- Classifying an application just by speed does very little, as some very stable applications are able to deliver changes very quickly; mainframe applications that have been around for decades and are extremely stable, with a team of developers who know them inside-out, can deliver updates very rapidly. On the other hand, an innovative app, developed using Agile and a modern language, leveraging a Platform as a Service (PaaS), may start very slowly if the team is new to the platform or technology stack.
- How often and how much requirements change is also not a very good measure, though it is better than speed. Even well-understood business systems, like a core banking system in a bank, may have ever-changing requirements in today's environment of ever-changing banking regulations and geopolitical upheavals. On the other hand, a new social media app may have extremely well-defined requirements—for example, to get more users to post more selfies with cool filters—that change very little.

Business intent is a much better measure. Ultimately, delivering business value is what IT organizations do. What better categorization, then, than what kind of business value needs to be delivered, irrespective of speed or requirement churn?

Another way of looking at the Optimization versus Innovation categorization is to look at it from a perspective of risk. The applications that deliver core business services have a lower risk tolerance and hence need to be on the optimization track. Innovative apps, on the other hand, have a higher risk tolerance. They hence can be delivered in a manner that allows for failure in order to be able to experiment.

A good sports analogy to explore when looking at the two "optimization core" and "innovation edge" models is American football. Unlike most continuous-play sports (like soccer, basketball, volleyball, hockey, and so on), where the same set of players switches between operating in offense or defense modes, in football, there are two entirely separate rosters of players who switch being on the field, when a team switches from offense to defense, and vice versa. These are all different players who play differently, have different coaches, different training regimes, and, above all, different playbooks. Yes, there are offense and defense specialist players in most sports, but only in football are there completely separate rosters.

Industrialized Core

The applications that fall under the broad category of *industrialized core* are the *core* systems of an organization. They are what keep the business going—*keeping the lights on*, as they say. The business models being delivered here are well understood. The methods to engage with users are also well understood. Such applications are typically large and complex, as most have been around for a while. They have certain characteristics that make them similar in nature. Some examples of these characteristics include the following:

- Business models and user engagement models are well understood, even though specific requirements may keep evolving or changing.
- They are usually delivered at a steady, well-defined cadence, at the rate at which the business can consume the changes and updates.
- Success is measured by measuring their stability and uptime.
- Because they have been around for a while, they typically have monolithic architectures.

- They are diverse in the technologies they use. As technologies evolve, newer apps in the core adopt new technologies, while the older ones still remain in operation.
- These models usually have separate Dev and Ops teams, and there is a formal hand-off to Ops, beyond which the Ops owns the running of the application.
- Ops is king here. IT service management and ITIL are what drive day-to-day operations.
- If things break when in production, the Ops team owns bringing the application up again.
- Environments are hybrid in nature, with myriad technologies and platforms, including legacy systems, that the organization may want to retire.
- Optimization is the game here—to achieve agility, velocity, and efficiency.

Innovation Edge

The innovation edge is made up of applications that have been, or are being, developed to drive innovation—to experiment with new business models, to capture new markets by experimenting with new user engagement models, and to leverage new technologies and modern application delivery architectures. They are the drivers of growth for the organization. They are typically small and based on modern technologies and platforms. They use techniques from the *Lean startup* approach—like *minimum viable product* (MVP) and *A/B testing* to run these experiments with business models, and *design thinking* to develop user experience and user engagement models—to continuously innovate, based on real-time user feedback. (I discuss all these techniques at length in Chapter 5.) They also have certain characteristics that make them similar in nature, including the following:

- Business models and user engagement models are not well understood, and requirements need to be improved upon by experimentation and getting rapid user feedback.
- They are delivered in a continuous manner, to do experimentation with new features and user experiences, leveraging techniques like A/B testing.
- They are measured for their ability to deliver changes fast, in response to feedback from users.

- They are typically built using polyglot languages, picking the right one for the functionality needed.
- They use modern architecture like *cloud native* and *microservices.*
- The Dev team is king here.
- The goal is to abstract infrastructure concerns away from the developers by leveraging a PaaS, with which developers can leverage cloud services to deliver their nonfunctional requirements (NFRs).
- The developers are responsible not just for building the application but also for running the apps. If the app goes down, they bring it up.
- Innovation is the game here—organizations experiment with new ideas, features, and business models.

It should never be the technology that determines which category an application belongs to. The classification criterion should be limited to business intent alone. The *risk* versus *business value* profile of the application should also be looked at to determine this business intent. An application delivering a highly regulated system, and thus having high value and high risk, will typically lie in the industrialized core, even if it is being delivered on a PaaS using microservices and is written using modern languages like Node.js and Go. Conversely, a service written in Java can be a component of an innovative app that is designed to be a minimum viable product to validate a new business model and will typically lie on the innovation edge.

The innovation edge is referred to as an *edge* because in typical large organizations, innovation is only occurring at the "edges" of the organization. In fact, some organizations may just have an innovation *sliver.* This is because a typical IT organization spends most of its budget on running and maintaining existing systems, not on innovation. The optimization of the industrialized core is thus essential to drive innovation. It frees up resources to invest in innovation, and furthermore, the optimization ensures that slow, nonresilient systems in the industrialized core do not become a drag on the ability to innovate at speed.

Just like the sport of (American) football had to develop the understanding of how players on offense and defense rosters of the same team needed to be trained to play in different ways and coaches needed to develop different plays for offense and defense, in IT, organizations need to categorize their applications and systems being delivered into industrialized core and innovation edge and then form and organize teams based on the needs of each category of applications. The platforms and environments should also be properly matched to the type of application. As I suggested earlier, the industrialized core can have any kind of environment, from traditional IT systems to cloud and from mainframe to mobile. The goal is optimization of the environments and platforms. For the innovation edge, a platform-based environment is essential. Cloud-native applications are what give the most speed and agility to allow for the experimentation and speed of innovation that is needed. Teams that are familiar with these modern architectures, and with associated modern development practices, are essential. I discuss *Platform as a Service* (PaaS), *containers,* and cloud-native development with microservices in the next chapter.

It is important to note that these two categories of applications to deliver business capabilities are truly joined at the hip. Outside of a startup where there is no pre-existing *core system,* systems delivered on the innovation edge are dependent on the services provided by the industrialized core to deliver the innovations they are developing. As I stated before, because the industrialized core typically consumes most of the budget in typical large organizations, it needs to be optimized to free resources for innovation.

Consider a typical mobile application (say, mobile banking). To deliver that application, there is a team charged with developing the mobile front end. These kinds of applications are developed and delivered in the innovation edge. Does all of the data and business logic sit on your mobile phone when you use that application? Of course not. Most likely, the business logic and certainly the data are components of the application that are delivered by pre-existing systems or services in the industrialized core. So, the mobile application is hybrid, comprised of components running in both sides. To deliver even some experimental features of this mobile app, the company needs to release a hybrid or composite application, incorporating components delivered by both the innovation edge and the industrialized core.

Thus, the industrialized core and innovation edge are not two segregated, horizontal siloes, with completely separate teams. That would defeat the very purpose of DevOps adoption. Even in football, both offense and defense rosters are ultimately *one* team, with one goal, and they need to complement each other. They always have one head coach who leads it all, one general manager who runs the business, and one team goal: to win the next game, and the next. . . . Similarly, in the industrialized core and innovation edge models, there is really a continuum between the two sides. They are co-dependent, with the same overall business objectives, and they need to align how they operate.

Core Themes

Some people try to find things in this game that don't exist but football is only two things—blocking and tackling.

—Vince Lombardi, American football player and legendary coach

There is a set of core *themes* that have their roots in *Lean* and form the basis of most of the DevOps plays represented in this book. Before going into the plays themselves, it is essential to understand these themes and appreciate their importance as the core of DevOps. As I present the various plays, these themes will appear interwoven across them all. They are the *blocking* and *tackling* of DevOps. The themes are as follows:

- Minimizing cycle time
- Reducing batch size
- Establishing the right culture

Minimizing Cycle Time

REDUCING THE COACHING "CYCLE TIME"

The WTA can deliver deep analytics in real-time to coaches at WTA events, allowing them to interact with the athletes live, during the match, instead of waiting to discuss such deep analytics and strategy afterwards.

Coaches are armed with tablets containing the analytics needed to beat the competition; and they are able to walk this information onto the court and discuss it with their players.

The app provides tendencies; it shows the speed and direction of a serve, speed of strokes, where the stroke pattern is going, and court coverage. Coaches and players can see what's trending, the successes on the court, and the failures…all live while the match is taking place to help shape the outcome.

—Donato, 2016

For software delivery, there is no measure of true progress other than code running in production. This does not mean the full software application being delivered but rather small pieces of capability that build up toward the final product. This *continuous delivery* of software provides the opportunity to get feedback, from actual customers, or in some cases customer *surrogates* using the software and providing feedback. This feedback can then be used to improve three things (as I discuss in Chapter 2):

1. The software delivered
2. The environment to which the software was delivered
3. The process by which the software was delivered

As shown in Figure 4-1, Continuous Delivery results in *continuous feedback*. Continuous feedback results in *continuous improvement*. The focus then becomes on making the feedback cycle as short as possible, to get the feedback data and analytics back to the practitioners in the shortest time span, so they can rapidly improve the software, environments, and delivery processes.

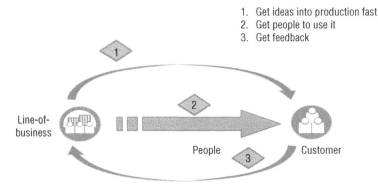

Figure 4-1: Reduced cycle time drives faster feedback.

The time it takes for each software component—whether a new component, a new enhanced version of an existing component, or a bug-fix to a set of components—to go from inception to code running in production and for the feedback from users to come back to the teams is defined as the delivery *cycle time* (also referred to as *Lead time*). This delivery cycle time has embedded within it various other cycle times.

- *Dev-test cycle time* is the time it takes developers to get test results back from the test team for a newly delivered component.
- *Deployment cycle time* is the time it takes to deploy an application to an environment and start utilizing it for testing or production.

- *Ops cycle time* is the time it takes for Ops to get a request for a new environment, to provision the environment, and to make it available to the requesting team.
- *Datacenter latency cycle time* is the time it takes to get a ping response from a remote datacenter.
- *Project approval cycle time* is the time it takes for the various approval boards and committees to approve a new project.
- *Change management cycle time* is the time it takes for the Change Control Board to approve a change.
- *Financial approval cycle time* is the time it takes the CFO to approve financial requests.
- *Acquisition cycle time* is the time it takes for the purchasing office to approve acquisition requests.
- *Management approval cycle time* is the time it takes for management to approve anything.

The goal is to reduce the delivery cycle time. This can be achieved only by reducing each embedded cycle time—the ones listed here and many more that make up the overall delivery pipeline.

Reducing cycle times is a core goal of DevOps. It is a *Lean* principle to make any interaction between stakeholders more efficient and shorter. You will see that reducing cycle time is an underlying theme across almost every DevOps play described in this book.

- How fast can you deliver an artifact?
- How quickly can a practitioner respond to a new request?
- How quickly can assigned tasks be completed?
- How quickly can applications be deployed?
- How quickly can a new practitioner be on-boarded to a project?
- How quickly can environments be provisioned and configured?
- How quickly can security changes be approved?
- How quickly can defects be replicated in a Dev environment?
- How quickly can test data be made available from production data?
- How quickly can requests be approved or disapproved?
- How quickly can reviews be done?
- How quickly can status reports be done?
- How quickly can applications be rolled back?
- How quickly can incidents be re-created?

▣ How quickly can outages be resolved?

▣ How quickly can customer feedback be incorporated into new requirements or enhancement requests?

Reducing cycle time requires all of the DevOps principles to work, making processes lean by reducing waste and improving collaboration. One key
to achieving leaner processes and reducing waste, resulting in reduced cycle
time, is reducing batch size, which I will discuss next.

Reducing Batch Size

HOW 1% PERFORMANCE IMPROVEMENTS LED TO OLYMPIC GOLD

When Sir Dave Brailsford became head of British Cycling in 2002, the team
had almost no record of success: British cycling had won only a single
gold medal in its 76-year history. That quickly changed under Sir Dave's
leadership. At the 2008 Beijing Olympics, his squad won seven out of 10
gold medals available in track cycling, and they matched the achievement
at the London Olympics four years later. Sir Dave now leads Britain's first
ever professional cycling team, which has won three of the last four Tour
de France events.

Sir Dave, a former professional cycler who holds an MBA, applied a
theory of marginal gains to cycling—he gambled that if the team broke
down everything they could think of that goes into competing on a bike
and then improved each element by 1%, they would achieve a significant
aggregated increase in performance.

—Harrell, 2015

Incremental delivery is essential to achieving lean and efficient processes.
Let's look at an assembly line in a factory (an analogy I have used before). If
you want to achieve speed and quality in the assembly line, you do this by
continuously delivering identical components. The smaller and more similar
each component is, the faster the manufacturing or assembly line can go;
the processes can also be made more efficient because they are comprised of
many small steps that are repeated over and over again. If a practitioner in
the factory or a robotic arm adds the same single rivet over and over again,
the efficiency of its actions can be maximized, as opposed to a scenario where
multiple complex sets of steps need to be carried out. The amount of work done

by each set of steps represents the *batch size*. To get maximum throughput and achieve the smallest cycle time, the batch size needs to be properly managed.

Stepping back for a second and going to the base principles of *Lean*, adopting *Lean* focuses on three areas (Reinertsen, 2009):

1. Minimizing inventory
2. Explicitly managing backlogs
3. Matching batch sizes to team capacity

These principles have been applied for years through *Lean* process adoption in traditional factory, logistics, and back-office processes. They are now being applied to software delivery by Agile and DevOps. *Minimizing inventory* and *backlog management* have been addressed by *Agile* methodologies. All Agile methodologies refer to groomed backlog, and mapping work-items (the *inventory* of software delivery) to sprints. The third area is addressed by DevOps by managing batch size, which begins with matching of the batch size to team capacity. In Agile methodologies, this is achieved by knowing the *velocity* of a team—the units of work a team can deliver in a single sprint. Based on the team size, team skills, and past historical delivery results, you can determine a team's velocity fairly accurately for a particular type of work item. The set of work items that a team can fully deliver in a fixed number of sprints will determine the ideal batch. To maximize the throughput, this batch size needs to be minimized and matched to the team velocity. Too big or too small and it reduces team productivity.

Other than team productivity improvement, reducing batch size also has other benefits:

- *Reducing cycle time*. The smaller the deliverable, the faster it can be delivered and the feedback harvested.
- *Reducing delivery risk*. The smaller the amount of change introduced, the lower its impact, and the lower the risk of introducing the change.
- *Reducing integration risk*. If small changes are continuously integrated with other small changes and then tested, integration issues can be identified faster, and mitigated faster, as they would be caused by small changes.
- *Reducing architectural complexity*. The need to deliver small batches of change forces the applications to be architected so that they can be

developed and delivered in small batches. This results in architectures that are made up of smaller, highly decoupled components, rather than large, monolithic components.

▪ *Improving testing and quality.* The quality improves as QA teams can run tests more frequently on smaller sets of changes, rather than having to run the same set of tests across large, complex sets of changes, less frequently. This results in issues and defects being identified sooner and having less impact on a smaller set of changes. This applies to all kinds of testing: functional, integration, performance, and security testing.

▪ *Reducing over-engineering.* The smaller the change delivered and the faster the feedback is received, the quicker it can be determined whether the *right* change has been delivered.

▪ *Reducing waste.* It is easier to identify and reduce waste associated with smaller changes, rather than waste in large, complex changes, which can also reduce the ability to directly identify sources of waste.

▪ *Reducing visibility complexity.* It is easier to get visibility into the real status of each team or component in the delivery pipeline. This is because each set of work items being acted on in a batch is made up of several smaller tasks that make small changes to artifacts, which, in turn, are thus easier to track and manage.

▪ *Improving environments.* Smaller changes to environments make change management of the environments easier. It is also easier to identify the root cause of issues and incidents, as their cause can be narrowed to a smaller set of changes.

▪ *Improving processes.* It is easier to make small, incremental changes to processes. This reduces the dip in productivity experienced when new processes are introduced. It also makes identifying the impact of changes more evident and easier to identify.

▪ *Improving documentation.* Documentation of large, complex changes is difficult to deliver and is typically done after all the changes have been delivered. By reducing batch size, you are now delivering a smaller set of changes in each batch, making it much easier to document changes on an ongoing basis.

▪ *Achieving continuous improvement.* Continuous improvement can only be achieved, by definition, if it involves making small, incremental improvements. These improvements need to be made to all three areas of DevOps that are the focus of improvement: the software, environments, and processes. I will discuss continuous improvement in more detail later in this chapter.

Achieving small batch sizes is not a trivial exercise. There are people, process, architectural, and tooling challenges that need to be addressed.

- *People*: The most critical aspect of addressing people, when it comes to reducing batch size, is dealing with a team's size and structure. Traditional team structures are designed for large projects with large functional teams that work on batches of work constrained within their functional area and then doing a handoff of the batch to the next functional team. To reduce the batch to its optimal size, you need to form cross-functional teams that work on a batch through its lifecycle—from requirement to production. I will discuss various team models later in this chapter and also in subsequent chapters.
- *Process*: Processes need to be handled in two ways when it comes to reducing batch size.
  - First, how can the processes be structured to handle small, frequent development, testing, and delivery of components? The process and the associated governance need to be broken down into small tasks that practitioners can perform independently and then hand them off to the next practitioner on the team who has the right skills for the next task.
  - Second, how can the processes themselves be continuously improved, incrementally? It is easier to make small improvements to processes, rather than large, radical changes. As I have already discussed, introducing change results in a drop in productivity (the *dip*). Introducing small changes results in smaller drops in productivity.
- *Architecture*: The architecture of an application has to be such that it can be broken down into small components that can be developed, tested, and deployed independently. Refactoring existing applications to such an architecture is not a trivial exercise. I discuss this in detail in the next chapter in the section on microservices. Architectures that are not based on microservices can also be worked on in small batches, but in that case you are adding incremental change to a large code base, which needs to be delivered in its entirety. Team structure and architecture are closely related to each other. I will discuss *Conway's law* (Conway, 1967), which captures this relationship, later in this chapter.
- *Tools*: Putting together the delivery pipeline tool-chain to handle rapid delivery of small batches requires that the tools be tightly integrated, with minimal nonautomated steps in the delivery processes. This is the

only way to attain the lean and efficient throughput needed. The role of the tools is to automate processes. The processes, in turn, can be made more efficient by leveraging the capabilities in the tools that are not available if performing tasks manually. Tools are best leveraged to automated, repetitive tasks, and to codify the processes.

Finally, there is the whole issue of releasing to customers. While the delivery teams might start delivering in smaller batches, resulting in continuous delivery, this mind-set shift to release smaller, more frequent new versions may not extend all the way to the end-users. The end-users may not be ready to consume changes or updates in frequent, smaller batches. Where it is not possible to release new versions that frequently to users, you need to release the small batches to a pre-production area. The deliverable in pre-production can be tested and made customer-ready and then released to the customer at formal, user-accepted, and less-frequent release dates. I will discuss release management processes in depth later in this chapter in the section "Play on Release Management."

Establishing the Right Culture

TEAM CHEMISTRY

Chemistry. To me, the most important aspect of the game. Teams with great chemistry win championships. Great teams with poor chemistry lose championships. This is why the Cavaliers have the best chance to win this year.

The Lakers are everyone's favorite. However, they have looked bad at times, due to their arrogance and lack of chemistry. The Cavaliers cannot run with the Lakers talent wise, but their chemistry will push them over the top.

—Roberts, 2009

Conway's Law: Teams and Architecture

When Melvin Conway first submitted his paper where he proposed his law, to Harvard Business Review (HBR) in 1967, they rejected it on the basis of lack of proof to make what he proposed a law. However, Fred Brooks and several other experts gave it the backing it needed to get the attention it has garnered. Whether it is a law or not depends on your definition of the weight of mathematical proof required to deem something a law. That level of mathematical proof does not exist for Conway's law. However, there is sufficient evidence in the software world to heuristically observe the nature of the architecture of software and map it to the structure of teams delivering the software to conclude that Conway's law exists.

Conway's Law: Any organization that designs a system (defined broadly) will produce a design whose structure is a copy of the organization's communication structure. (Conway, 1967)

From a DevOps teaming and organization perspective, Conway's law is regularly referenced as the basis on which to re-organize teams to make processes, and application and system architectures, more efficient. If you can make their communication and collaboration structures effective by making them lean and efficient and by removing obstacles and silos, then as per Conway's law, this change will be reflected in the design and architecture of the applications and systems being delivered by the teams. Conversely—and to most, counterintuitively—if you enforce certain architectural models that are inherently designed for delivering change in *small batches* and the teams are allowed to self-organize around the needs of delivering applications and systems with such architectures, then as per Conway's law, the resulting team models should be the right organizational models to enable the highest levels of communication and collaboration. The two emerging areas of the interlocking of team models designed for maximum collaboration and communication and the architectural models such teams can deliver to achieve maximum throughput are *squads* for team models and *12-factor apps* for architectural models. I discuss both of these areas in depth in the next chapter.

DevOps as a Cultural Movement

DevOps is first a cultural transformation. It began as a cultural movement and remains so at its heart. All the improved processes, automation with tools, and cloud-enabled environments that can be provisioned in minutes are not going to achieve the goals and the promise of DevOps if the people who are engaged do not transform how they are organized, how they communicate, and how they collaborate—not until they break down the organizational and cultural silos that hinder maximum efficiency and throughput and reduce trust. And not until they overcome the organizational *cultural inertia*.

Overcoming cultural inertia requires buy-in and a willingness to change at all levels of the organization, not just at the practitioner level.

- *Organizational*: At the organizational level, there needs to be buy-in and sponsorship from senior executives and management to change the organization. This can include setting up DevOps *Centers of Excellence,* funding DevOps enablement, creating a team of *DevOps coaches,* investing in tools, platforms, and environments for the delivery pipeline, sponsoring the transformation of legacy processes and governance, and even reorganizing the reporting structures of teams in order to facilitate the minimizing of organizational silos. I discuss how senior executives can be the lead *change agents* to allow for DevOps to be adopted at scale across large organizations in more detail in later chapters.

- *Teams:* For an application of any decent size and complexity, everything—from project plans, to requirements, to architecture and design, to Dev and test, to Ops, to security, to incident management—is done by teams. The teams have traditionally been organized into functional silos. One of the core tenets of DevOps has been to act to break down these silos; to foster a culture of trust, communication, and collaboration between all the team members, across functional areas; to have all practitioners contributing to a project or application development and delivery effort become *stakeholders* in the success of the application. They need to become stakeholders with *shared ownership and responsibility* in ensuring the application delivers the business value it was designed to deliver and not just be responsible for the completion and success of their own respective functional area or silo.

  Several team models have been proposed to accomplish this from a team organization perspective. From *NoOps*, made popular at Netflix (Cockcroft, 2012), to fully self-contained cross-functional teams called *squads,* made popular by Spotify (Kniberg, 2014), all these models are designed to break down the silos and allow teams to function as one unit. These teams are structured to include stakeholders who are responsible for each area of the application and to have fluid boundaries of functional ownership and responsibility with other teams. I discuss various team models and their strengths and weaknesses in Chapter 6. It is important to understand that, irrespective of how the teams are organized, by completely reorganizing your practitioners into cross-functional teams or creating cross-functional matrixed teams, where they retain traditional reporting structures, the goal is to remove organizational obstacles that prevent team members from collaborating and communicating and working together at maximum efficiency.

- *Individual:* Individuals can be the eventual enablers or the ultimate bottlenecks. Only individuals with the right intentions and more importantly with the willingness to change can make the necessary changes to cause a transformation. Ultimately, even if the teams are well organized to enable trust, collaboration, and communication, if one or more individuals choose not to participate and not to overcome the cultural inertia, then change will not happen.

What a coincidence! While you were off we discovered the source of the bottleneck.

—Irate boss to employee

People behave based on how they are measured (and compensated). It is thus critical to accompany any organizational change with a matching change to how individuals on the teams are measured, evaluated, and rewarded. To truly create a culture of *shared ownership and responsibility,* you need to have common measures of success for all the individual stakeholders. You cannot have an overt focus on measuring and rewarding individual performance and expect individuals to perform with the team's interest before theirs. In team sports, the trophy or gold medal goes to the whole team, not to the individual who delivered the most goals or points. Yes, there may be *MVP* (most valuable player) or *Man of the Match* awards, but those do not ever supersede the main team prize.

There are no MVPs in the Olympics and no individual contribution medals for team sports. Every player on the team gets the same medal. Brazilian soccer star and captain Neymar's gold medal for scoring the winning goal in the 2016 Olympic soccer final is the same as the gold medal of everyone else on the team. It is the same as even that of the substitute players on the team. In the Olympics, in true team spirit, the substitutes also get the medal a team won, as long as they got to come to the field and play at least once in any of the matches in the entire Olympics, even if it was just a qualifying game and not the medal game.

No matter how you arrange the entire organization, the various teams, or even how individuals behave and act, it is a combination of people (teams), processes, and automation that enables the true potential of DevOps to be achieved. Well-organized and highly collaborative teams that are following inefficient processes, are overburdened by rigid governance, don't have the right tools to enable and scale automation, or have legacy environments to deliver the application to will fail. True transformation—and that is what a DevOps adoption is, a transformation—requires transformation of all three: people, processes, and tools. None comes first. They cannot be adopted serially, and none can be ignored. Teams are the focal point of the transformation, of course—they are the ones who do the work and enable the transformation. Processes guide teams on how to do the work. Tools allow the processes to be repeatable, scalable, and error free.

The DevOps Plays

Let's begin with the plays. It is important to note that while these plays are presented in a sequential manner, they do not need to be adopted in this order. Most can be adopted in parallel. Some are dependent on others; these dependencies are self-evident, but where necessary, I'll point them out.

Play: Establishing Metrics and KPIs

A particular shot or way of moving the ball can be a player's personal signature, but efficiency of performance is what wins the game for the team.

—Pat Riley, former NBA player, coach, and team executive

As I discuss in Chapter 3, in order to identify the right DevOps plays that are needed, you need to do the following:

- Define the *target state* (business goals and drivers)
- Understand the *current state* (capability maturity)
- Identify the bottlenecks of areas of inefficiency in the delivery pipeline (by conducting a *value stream mapping* exercise)

Together, these three requirements represent the optimization goals you need to achieve and the constraints these goals need to be achieved in. Like any optimization exercise, you need to measure current *productivity* and then set a goal of target productivity. The definition of productivity and how much improvement you need to target will vary from organization to organization, and with the constraints they have. You therefore need to start with identifying the metrics that matter. What *Key Performance Indicators* (KPIs) of the business will need to be impacted? These are the KPIs that matter—the KPIs that optimizing the delivery pipeline needs to improve.

Because these KPIs will determine and measure what you improve and how you are improving, this play should be executed first. It is a prerequisite to other plays. As in any sport, you first need to know how you win that game.

Let's look at some examples of KPIs that most organizations typically measure when adopting DevOps.

Project KPIs

Never mistake activity for achievement.

—John Wooden, college basketball player and coach

There are two core project KPI areas:

- Speed
- Cost

Yes, speed and cost are probably the lowest common denominators of the KPIs every organization measures and optimizes. Speed can be measured in many ways. Here are some examples of speed-related KPIs:

- Total project duration
- Man hours (or months/years)
- Time to market/time to value
- Mean time to resolution (for fixes)
- Number of experiments run (for innovation edge projects—more in Chapter 5)
- Delivery velocity (number of features or *user stories* delivered per release)

Cost is simpler, but it can still be measured in several ways, depending on the project management and estimation practices used. Here are some examples:

- Total project cost
- Earned value

- Cost performance index
- Cost variance
- Cost ratio
- Cost per deploy (initial deploy versus re-deploy)
- Cost per issue fixed/outage
- Cost of customer acquisition versus total lifetime customer value

What typical KPI improvements do organizations that have adopted DevOps see for speed and cost? For a large communications organization that adopted DevOps, working with IBM, they saw the following (Kagan, 2015):

- Maintenance, small projects (fewer than 15 person-year)
    - 30–40% faster delivery of compete projects
    - 20–25% overall cost reduction
- Maintenance, Medium projects (fewer than 100 person-year)
    - 20–30% faster delivery of compete projects
    - 15–20% overall cost reduction
- Maintenance, Large projects (more than 100 person-year)
    - 10–15% faster delivery of compete projects
    - 4–8% overall cost reduction

Portfolio KPIs

Given the interdependence of projects with other projects and the ever-changing mix of the types of projects, most organizations should also measure KPIs related to these areas across their application portfolio. Some examples of application portfolio management KPIs include the following:

- Mix of projects in the portfolio, by application type (mainframe apps, distributed apps, mobile apps, cloud-native apps, packaged apps, SaaS applications, and so on)
- Mix of applications by *system of record* versus *system of engagement*
- Mix of applications by architecture types (monolithic, service-oriented architecture [SOA], microservices, serverless, and so on)
- Number of interdependencies between components and/or applications that are architected using APIs versus those using direct integrations
- Reuse of code and/or architectural components across portfolio
- Distribution of applications by cost, risk, and business value
- Mix of applications that are in maintenance mode, slated for retirement, versus new development

Quality KPIs

When measuring quality, and thus optimizing to improve quality, choosing the right measure of quality is essential. Here again, the right KPI will vary from project to project and also from industry to industry. An organization building a medical device will have a much higher set of quality goals than an organization building a photo sharing app, even one with cool filters.

There are two functional areas where quality KPIs are measured: *Quality Assurance* (QA), which is a part of application development process; and *operations*, which measures quality in production.

For Quality Assurance KPIs, the typical DevOps-related questions that need to be asked are as follows:

- What percentage of tests (unit, functional, integration, performance, and security tests) are automated?
- What percentage of services and applications can be automatically "virtualized," or stubbed out, for testing?
- What percentage of testing is done on *production-like* environments, using *production-like* data?
- What percentage of QA practitioner time is spent in test environment provisioning, configuration, and application deployment (nontesting-related tasks)?
- What percentage of developer time is spent re-creating defects found by QA?

Typical Quality Assurance KPIs involve measuring effort and duration in multiple areas. Here are some examples:

- Testing preparation discussion
- Test data preparation
- Test environment checks (smoke tests)
- Test readiness review
- Test case selection
- Test case execution
- Test result analysis
- Defect creation
- Defect re-testing
- Test summary report preparation
- Test summary report communication

After adopting DevOps, it is not uncommon to see a 40 to 50 percent reduction in both duration and effort for most of these areas (Kagan, 2015).

The core metrics that the business would be focused on, typically measured by operations teams, are as follows:

- Number of Severity (Sev) 1 and Sev 2 incidents
- Average resolution time of Sev 1 and Sev 2 incidents
- Average cost of Sev 1 and Sev 2 incidents

DevOps focuses on reducing these Sev 1 and Sev 2 incidents and reducing the average resolution time when they do happen, eventually resulting in reduction of the cost of such incidents (Quirk, 2004). DevOps does so through *continuous monitoring* to observe the types and causes of errors and issues in production. Examples of such KPIs include the following:

- Software failure
- Application failure
- Data error
- Data transmission error
- Infrastructure induced issues
- Services alert state/stopped
- High space utilization
- Configuration error

Improvements for IBM clients in the area of quality in operations, upon adopting quality, have included the following (Kagan, 2015):

- 50% reduction in outages and application performance slowdowns
- 60–90% improvement in availability
- 90% faster diagnosis of root causes of application problems

Delivery Pipeline Optimization KPIs

MUDA

Muda is a Japanese term for wastefulness of valuable resources. According to Taiichi Ohno, father of the Toyota Production System, these are Seven Wastes or sources of Muda:

- Transportation
- Inventory

- Motion
- Waiting
- Overproduction
- Over-processing
- Defects

—Pereira, 2009

The ultimate goal of DevOps is to reduce waste to optimize the entire delivery pipeline—from *ideation* (idea stage) to *production*. To achieve this, you need to have KPIs that measure how complex the application delivery process is and work on simplifying it. Following are some good examples of KPIs to measure delivery pipeline complexity. These KPIs should be measured both for initial deploy and re-deploys of the application:

- Cost per delivery cycle
- Duration of the delivery cycle (lead time)
- Number of approval steps in the delivery cycle
- Number of management or governance reviews (gates) in the delivery cycle
- Number of nonproject team stakeholders who have to approve at different review steps (security, legal, and compliance; enterprise architecture; change control boards; standards boards, and so on)

Here are some other examples of KPIs that can be measured at a project level to determine process improvement, at that level:

- Project initiation time
- Groomed backlog (for Agile projects)
- Overall time to development
- Composite build time
- Sprint test time
- Build Verification Test (BVT) availability
- Total deployment time
- Overall time to production
- Time between releases
- Percentage of practitioner time spent on new development versus maintenance

Culture KPIs

One man can be a crucial ingredient on a team, but one man cannot make a team.

—Kareem Abdul-Jabbar, former NBA player

It has been suggested that anyone who finds the right KPIs to measure *culture* deserves the Nobel Prize, for both Economics and Peace (for stopping all the metrics of culture wars). How do you measure cultural inertia? How do you measure whether culture is improving? One common way is to measure morale. Is it improving? But tracing a direct line from cultural change to an uplift in morale is difficult to achieve. You can actually be in an organization that has great *organizational culture* and still ultimately have low morale. Think of a cool startup with open floor plans, beer (and) pong, massages during lunch, and ludicrous stock options. However, if the company has technology that fails to get the promised results, no amount of culture can save it; morale goes down along with the stock option prices.

Looking at first principles of DevOps—developing a culture of trust, collaboration, and communication—you can measure if these are improving. If pre-DevOps cross-silo communication was only through tickets or practitioners spent more than an average of one hour each day in status meetings, or spent any time updating status reports, and today they don't, then you have achieved *improvement of culture.* To measure culture, any metrics you choose should measure how much teaming and communication within teams and across teams are occurring.

Here are some examples of KPIs that can be measured, which indirectly indicate the maturity of the culture:

- Percentage of artifacts that could be consumed by the practitioners receiving them without need to modification or rework (*%Complete and Accurate*)
- Percentage of practitioner time spent in meetings versus doing productive work
- Percentage of practitioner *wait-time*, waiting for someone to respond to a request, with no visibility into their status
- Percentage of communication between practitioners that is not real-time (think e-mail versus messaging)
- Number of artifacts created and updated by practitioners that add no value to the final deliverable

- Number of people from other functional areas that practitioners interact with on a weekly basis, outside status meetings
- Level of decisions that a team can make on their own, without involving management (team empowerment)
- Percentage of reporting done via meetings or status reports versus dashboards
- Visibility of project metrics and KPIs across practitioners via dashboards
- How well team members feel their individual contribution is aligned with the broader business and organizational goals
- Practitioner turnover
- Practitioner contribution to company intellectual property (IP) and/or open source projects (giveback)

Some key points here that are very interesting are *team empowerment* and *contribution to IP or open source projects*. Both of these measures are critical in today's world, especially with teams that have Millennials. Both of these metrics are good measures of how much *self-worth* and *confidence* practitioners feel and are able to build upon.

If you look at culture purely as being how people behave and interact, then making sure you have the right people on the team is eventually the most important measure and cause of *right* culture. Are the people on the team productive team members? Are they happy? Do they go above and beyond the call of duty, so to speak, to make the team successful? Do they have a positive impact on the team morale and culture, or are they the cause of cultural inertia? Probably the most extreme example of steps companies take to ensure they have the right people on their teams comes from Amazon and its subsidiary Zappos. These companies actually pay people who are unhappy to leave. Amazon makes an offer, once a year, to its fulfillment-center employees, paying them anywhere from $2,000 to $5,000 to leave if they are not happy. Zappos does the same after its aggressive, deep-dive training program for new employees. They would rather pay people to quit than keep them on the team, hurting it and the company culture (Taylor, 2014).

Play: Agile Adoption

Before the start of a game I thought it was a good idea to motivate the team with phrases like: "we really need to win, otherwise we're out." The effect was rather the contrary, it did not help them to perform better. Initially I was wondering why. Now

I know. The problem is that the individual player has no chance to influence the outcome of the game by himself. Even though she does [her] very best there are too many other factors she cannot control and which can be decisive for the outcome. This lack of control made them tensed and nervous hindering them to function optimally. I realized that winning or losing is merely the result of the way we play. The good news is that each individual player CAN influence the way she plays. So instead of talking about winning or losing before a game we carefully repeat our strategy before a game as well as the personal things each player has to pay attention to. That's concrete and much better controllable. Through this approach they are much more relaxed and in a condition to bring the very best out of them. Our results proved that.

—Marc Lammers, field hockey player and head coach, Netherlands (Peter, 2008)

Most organizations begin DevOps adoption with projects that have already adopted Agile. It is in essence a prerequisite to DevOps adoption. Some have even argued that DevOps extends adoption of Agile *left* towards the project management, project initiation, and design phase of a project, and *right* towards operations.

One question that goes hand-in-hand with this assertion that DevOps begins with Agile is whether DevOps can be adopted by teams practicing waterfall development processes. Of course, you cannot have practices like *continuous integration* and *continuous delivery* in a waterfall approach, as there is nothing *continuous* about it. If one delivers just once, then by definition one cannot be *continuous*. While this is true, that you cannot adopt all DevOps practices and can certainly not get all the benefits of DevOps when using a waterfall application delivery process, you can, however, benefit from several individual DevOps practices that can make even a waterfall-based delivery pipeline more efficient. Such practices include the following:

- *Deployment automation.* Manual deployments are a waste of time and effort and are error prone. Even if you are not continuously deploying, automating deployments adds tremendous value in time saved and improved quality of deployments.
- *Access to production-like environments.* Having developers and testers work with Dev-test environments that are not like the production environments lowers quality and creates re-work. It can be easily addressed by providing access to production-like environments through all states of application delivery.

■ *Test automation.* Here again, automation drives speed and reduces errors.

■ *Monitoring and feedback.* Providing access to production performance metrics to the lines of business and developers adds value to their ability to improve the application and production environments.

These and several other practices included in the DevOps framework, and discussed in this book, are agnostic to whether the application delivery processes are Agile or waterfall and can be adopted by any project.

Other than the fact that from a process perspective Agile projects are the most suitable for DevOps adoption, such projects become the breeding ground for grassroots DevOps adoption because of the limitations of Agile. The key limitation of Agile is that its scope is limited to Dev-test. Yes, Agile includes the business in the Dev-test cycle, but the role of business is limited to engaging with Dev-test at every sprint to ensure that they are developing the right things. Agile approaches like Scrum and Scaled Agile Framework (SAFe) do not extend to transforming how the lines of business operate to make them more agile, nor do they extend to Ops to make it more agile. With the rest of the delivery pipeline operating in a waterfall-like manner, with defined, fixed-date *gates*, or Ops engaging with Dev-test through a manual ticket-based system, this approach results in what I refer to in Chapter 2 as *water-Scrum-fall.*

Agile teams hit the limit of their productivity pretty soon in such a water-Scrum-fall environment. As they speed up, if the inputs are coming in to them from stakeholders who don't match the speed or if the stakeholders who consume their outputs are unable to match their speed, then the *impedance mismatch* limits their speed and agility, as shown in Figure 4-2. This becomes a compelling reason for them to adopt DevOps to take their speed and agility across the delivery pipeline, eliminating the mismatch.

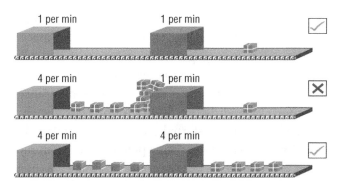

Figure 4-2: Addressing the impedance mismatch caused by "water-Scrum-fall"

It is not uncommon to see the efforts to eliminate the impedance mismatch result in the removal of a series of obstacles, or as I call them earlier in the book, *bottlenecks*. Here are some examples:

- If developers are practicing *continuous integration*, ending each day with a build ready to test, and if the test organization is unable to test at that rate, then it needs to be addressed.
- If Dev-test is running two-week sprints but the Ops team takes three weeks to provision a new test server, it needs to be addressed.
- If Dev-test teams are able to operate continuously, delivering code with a high velocity through two-week sprints, but the business analysts are providing new user stories in large blocks once a quarter, which is slower than the delivery velocity, it needs to be addressed.
- If the security team is only able to run their security tests on new apps, only once per release cycle, and take 5 to 10 days to run their tests, it needs to be addressed.
- If integration builds are taking hours to complete because they build every component and module, even those that did not change, it needs to be addressed.
- If the lines of business expect projects to operate on project plans with fixed, gate-based schedules but in reality their requirements are not well understood, the project plans need to be addressed.

Such bottlenecks can be pre-emptively identified and a mitigation plan made to address them through the *value stream mapping exercise* mentioned in Chapter 2.

As Agile teams hit these walls, this makes a case for DevOps adoption to maximize the full potential of what these teams can achieve and maximize the full potential of Agile itself. They need to do so by introducing DevOps practices to extend the "agility" *left* and *right* in the delivery lifecycle. DevOps extends the agility *left* by bringing DevOps practices to the stakeholders in the front end of the lifecycle, leveraging techniques and practices like *Agile product management*, design thinking, and *Lean* startup (all discussed more in the next chapter). Extending this agility to the *right* goes to the soul of DevOps. That is where DevOps started (and got its name), by bringing Dev and Ops closer. Doing so leads to adopting practices like continuous delivery, *Infrastructure as Code*, *software-defined environments*, and continuous feedback. I will discuss all of these practices and techniques in the coming plays. You will see how they drive agility and efficiency in the entire delivery pipeline, from ideation to production.

So, from a DevOps plays perspective, there are two ways the *Agile adoption* play can be adopted:

1. *Agile teams:* If you have teams or projects that have already adopted Agile, find the teams that have matured enough to start hitting the limit of their productivity due to the constraints water-Scrum-fall puts on them. These teams are ripe for progressing up to DevOps adoption, as shown in Figure 4-3.
2. *Non-agile teams:* As discussed earlier in this chapter, these teams can certainly benefit from adopting certain DevOps practices, even if they are not going to change to an Agile development methodology.

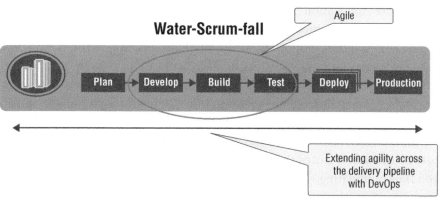

Figure 4-3: Achieving agility across the delivery pipeline

Play: Integrated Delivery Pipeline

In order to maximize the efficiency across the entire delivery pipeline, you need to eliminate or minimize the bottlenecks and inefficiencies across the pipeline, impacting every stakeholder. Most of the bottlenecks happen at the touchpoints between stakeholders—where they interact with each other—across their functional areas and where they hand off artifacts from one to another. Manual tasks are the number-one reason for these inefficiencies. Tools are necessary to automate processes, reducing wait-times and manual errors. That being said, tools can add to the complexity and inefficiencies if the tools are not integrated. Pre-DevOps, the focus was to optimize individual functional areas in the delivery pipeline. Individual functional teams sourced *best-of-breed* tools for their functional areas. However, tools, like stakeholders, do not operate in a vacuum. Artifacts are either created in the tool or need to be input from tools used by another stakeholder team. Artifacts that are created or modified need to be handed off to another stakeholder team, with their own chosen toolset. If these tools are not integrated, creating a seamless *tool-chain*, they can create significant inefficiencies at these handoff touchpoints.

It is not uncommon to see a practitioner get an artifact from another stakeholder team in a format that her tool cannot consume. She may get a file that then needs a manual *import* into the tool she and her team use—for example, getting a data model from a data analyst team, which needs to be converted to XML or CVS (comma-separated values) before it can be imported into an application architecture tool. Or developers may be creating code using a Jetty or Tomcat servlet container, which then needs to be deployed to a WebSphere Application Server. All these situations require additional steps, whether manual or automated, causing inefficiencies.

The real solution is an integrated tool-chain, one where there is a *single source of truth*—a single repository for each artifact type that any stakeholder with the right permissions can access. It is a tool-chain where artifacts can be passed seamlessly from one tool to another, either through well-developed point-to-point tool integrations or, even better, using a standardized format for the artifacts. A lot of work has also been done to build data-level linkage between tool data stores themselves, providing data store-level integrations, and thus eliminating the need for moving artifacts from one tool to the next. The Open Services for Lifecycle Collaboration (OSLC) open-standards community effort is dedicated to address standards for this data-level linkage.

Figure 4-4 shows an example of a delivery pipeline. In reality, the delivery pipeline will be much broader, including additional stakeholders and the tools they use, such as requirements management, architecture, application design, project management, security, release managers, and so on. The actual stakeholders will, of course, vary by organization and even by project. The environments shown will also vary. There may be multiple test and QA environments for functional, integration, performance, stress, system integration testing (SIT), user acceptance testing (UAT), and security testing, to name a few. There may be multiple staging environments. Some organizations also have both pre-production and post-production environments. There will also be monitoring and administration tools for all these environments. The number of tools and environments needs to be within reason, but more importantly, the tools should be in an integrated tool-chain, as discussed earlier.

Development   SCM   Build   Package Repo   Deploy   Test   Stage   Prod

Figure 4-4: Integrated delivery pipeline

Achieving End-to-End Traceability

One of the core benefits of having an integrated delivery pipeline is end-to-end traceability, across artifacts, across the delivery pipeline. This end-to-end traceability enables the existence of a single source of truth for all practitioners and stakeholders, across functional areas. The most significant benefit of end-to-end traceability is that it gives the practitioners and stakeholders the ability to have *visibility* into the relationships between the artifacts and access to the right version of the right artifact that they need for the task they are working on.

Take a look at Figure 4-5, which shows an example of end-to-end traceability for a *defect* related to a *change request*. Let's take a typical situation: a developer has worked to make code changes to satisfy a new change request. She delivers the *change set* to the *integration stream* and a CI build is created. The CI build is *delivered* to the testers. They run a *test suite* and one of the *test scripts* fails. A defect is opened to capture the failure. In the absence of end-to-end traceability, it is not uncommon for multiple developers and testers working on resolving such a defect to have to go back and forth multiple times to identify which change set which test was run on and to properly isolate the root cause of the defect in the code. It is even more cumbersome to do proper *impact analysis* and estimate the effort required to mitigate such a defect. With end-to-end traceability, all the artifacts can be traced to one another, making defect identification, impact analysis, and the actual resolution much more efficient.

Let's walk through the traceability diagram. (*Note: this diagram represents just a subset of a full end-to-end traceability model.*)

- The *defect* is found by running a *test script*.
- The test script is a part of a *test suite*.
- The test suite represents a *test plan*.
- The test plan is created to validate a set of *requirements*.
- The failed test script has an associated *test execution record*.
- The failed test script has a *test result*.
- The test result is used to create the *defect*.

- The defect can be traced to a code *change set,* which was the last set of code changes in the CI build.
- The change set is made to satisfy a *change request.*
- The change request impacts a set of *requirements.*

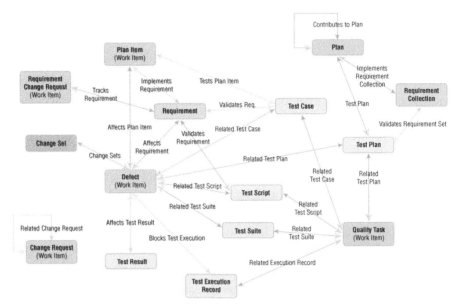

Figure 4-5: End-to-end traceability of a defect

This level of traceability is virtually impossible to achieve without an integrated tool-chain, across the delivery pipeline.

Other than visibility, additional benefits of having end-to-end traceability include the following:

- *Impact analysis.* Stakeholders are able to reduce risk by assessing the impact analysis of changes, open defects, and so on.
- *Change management.* Traceability allows for proper change management of artifacts, by allowing all changes across all artifacts to be traced, by change set and by *work item.*
- *Reduce overproduction.* Traceability allows for the identification of dead code, code that does not trace to active requirements, test cases that do not trace to requirements, and so on.
- *Practitioner efficiency.* Practitioners can ensure that they are working on the right artifacts and can trace their work upstream and downstream, without manual tasks.

- *Test coverage.* This ensures that all requirements are tested and all tests are testing active requirements.
- *Status reporting.* End-to-end traceability allows for status reporting to become automated. No more spreadsheets are required to correlate status reports across functional teams.
- *Compliance and auditability.* End-to-end traceability allows for the creation of *audit trails*—who, what, why, and when of each and every change, across artifacts, across stakeholders, and across the delivery pipeline.

End-to-end traceability is not easy to achieve. As you build an integrated delivery pipeline, you should strive to ensure that proper traceability is maintained across the artifacts that were not traceable before the new integrations were added.

Multi-Speed IT with Multiple Delivery Pipelines

There has been a lot of discussion and back and forth in the industry about the term *Multi-Speed IT*. The classification of the application in an organization originated as *two-speed IT* in papers by Gartner, the analyst firm. This quickly gave way to *bimodal IT*, to get away from the notion of having everything categorized as *fast* or *slow*. Bimodal IT was designed to classify applications based on how stable their requirements were and whether the applications were *evolutionary* or *experimental* in their development. Bimodal also does not appear to fully satisfy the classification models the industry needed and is now being replaced by the notion of *multi-speed*, as it is impossible to have just two *modes* in which to categorize all IT efforts and projects. What exists is really a continuum, especially when it comes to the factor of speed.

Today, the consensus in the industry is that all these models (bimodal, multi-speed, and any new one that may present itself) are statements in time. Carmen DeArdo of Nationwide Insurance has long been proposing that the future will be *variable-speed*. Each application will choose its speed and mode based on business intent and goals alone.

Just as lanes in a highway are not designated by speed or whether the driver is on her daily commute or driving to a new destination for the first time, speed or mode in application delivery will also not need to be designated. They will be chosen by the delivery team based on business need and team maturity. A teenager with a new driver's license will not (and should not) be driving at the maximum allowable speed on the freeway. Similarly, an ambulance getting to an emergency will not need to heed the posted speed limits.

The core driver behind multi-speed is the fact that you will never have just one delivery pipeline (unless you are at a startup, which has just one app). As shown in Figure 4-6, there will be multiple pipelines. These delivery pipelines will vary by technology stack, development languages used, environments delivered to, practitioner maturity, geographic distribution of various practitioners, *industrialized core* versus *innovation edge* business intent, risk-value profile of the application to the business, and, of course, the need for speed by the business. All these factors, and many more, result in these delivery pipelines moving at different speeds. This existence of delivery pipelines operating at multiple speeds is referred to as *Multi-Speed IT*. These delivery pipelines do not operate in isolation; they are dependent upon each other, creating challenges that adopting Multi-Speed IT needs to address. In Chapter 6, I give a detailed discussion of this interdependence and how handling Multi-Speed IT is essential to scaling DevOps adoption across an enterprise.

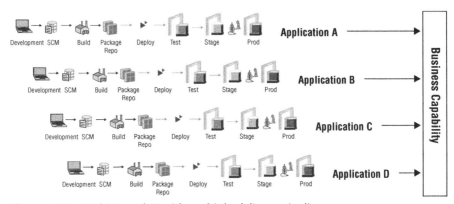

Figure 4-6: Multi-Speed IT with multiple delivery pipelines

From a perspective of building an integrated delivery pipeline, what Multi-Speed IT implies is that you need multiple such integrated delivery pipelines. These may all have different tools, best suited for the delivery pipeline's platform, technology, and delivery speed. What is important is that they are integrated across horizontally. This does not mean that there can be anarchy and every delivery pipeline can have its own unique combination of tools, even though they may be integrated. Standardization is essential. Standardization of tools allows for the standardization of processes and of practitioner enablement, making them *fungible* across several delivery pipelines that have the same tool-chain. Standardization also enables the creation of a well-defined metrics regime allowing for continuous improvement. The goal of this play is to eventually get to one or, at the most, two integrated delivery pipelines for each technology area. COBOL/CICS, Java, .NET, iOS/Android mobile apps, cognitive apps, big data, blockchain apps—each may have one or two standardized tool-chains. There cannot be dozens of such delivery pipeline tool-chains in an organization without it resulting in chaos.

Where there is no standard, there can be no kaizen.[1]

—Taiichi Ohno, father of the Toyota Production System

In addition to integration needs across a delivery pipeline, vertical integrations need to exist across multiple delivery pipelines. There are five specific areas where these integrations, and the accompanying standardization of tooling, are imperative.

1. *Planning*: Coordination between the planning of work and projects, across delivery pipelines, with an analysis of the dependencies between them

2. *Architecture and APIs*: Decoupling of the dependencies as much as possible, by establishing well-architected application touchpoints, implemented using APIs

3. *Deployment automation and orchestration*: Ability to provision, orchestrate, and deploy environments, middleware, and applications, as and when needed

4. *Virtualization of services and environments for testing*: Ability to test any application or service when the full environments, services, and application it is dependent on are not available

5. *Release management*: Executing on the release plans—preempting and addressing any resource contention, delays, and integration challenges

These integrations also enable *traceability* across multiple delivery pipelines. I will discuss these integration points across multiple delivery pipelines in more detail in later plays.

Play: Continuous Integration

A *sprint* is the Scrum term for an iteration. Of the many unfortunate names chosen in IT, this is one. A sprint in track or swimming implies a short, fast run (swim) that an athlete runs (swims) to finish at their maximum speed

---

[1] Kaizen: A Japanese business philosophy of continuous improvement of working practices, personal efficiency, and so on.

possible—think Usain Bolt or Michael Phelps putting it all on the line to win a 100-meter race. Furthermore, a sprint in a race has a fixed distance that runners are trying to run at faster times than their competitors. A sprint in Scrum, on the other hand, is typically structured to be for a fixed time-period iteration—like a two or three-week sprint, in which the team works to complete as many units of work as possible, based on their velocity. *Velocity* is a term used in Agile methodologies like Scrum to measure how many units of work a team can typically deliver in one sprint.

In reality, developing and delivering applications is more like a marathon than a sprint. Just like marathon runners, the team needs to develop a *cadence*—a regular rhythm at which they are able to complete and deliver units of work. The teams then continuously work on optimizing this cadence to maximize their velocity. Just like a marathon runner during training works to find her optimal *runner's cadence*—typically between 160 and 180 steps per minute in order to be able sustain the complete length of running the marathon—members of an application delivery team adopting continuous integration and continuous delivery need to find their delivery cadence. They don't need *death marches* and heroic efforts to push projects to completion, with team members *burning out* along the way. They need to be able to sustain the team for the entire duration of the project, with a workable, sustainable cadence.

Continuous integration (CI) as a practice is introduced in detail in Chapter 2. I not only present CI but also go into its core characteristics. Establishing a continuous integration practice is essential. However, once it is set up, it is essential for each team to establish a cadence or *rhythm* for CI. This CI cadence or rhythm is the regular frequency of builds that the developers will deliver for testing and eventually for potential release to Ops. This cadence sets expectations for all teams. A typical CI cadence is a daily build that is delivered for continuous delivery to start moving toward production. This does not mean that there should be daily deliveries to production—that is unreasonable for most enterprises—but they should go at least as far as the test environment daily.

The CI cadence will be different for each organization. Daily is not the only option, but there needs to be a steady cadence, even if it is over longer time periods. Furthermore, there may be a different CI cadence for different project teams in the organization. The cadence should be determined by the team itself, based on their comfort level with the processes, tools, and working together as a team, which in turn will determine their velocity. At a minimum, a team should do a daily build to enable CI. To enable CI, the build should be automated and fast, and the cycle time of feedback from integration tests should be short. If builds take hours and cycle time from testing takes days, a CI cadence cannot be sustained. There will be no rhythm.

Enabling CI is every developer's responsibility. Each developer needs to be disciplined to deliver their code to the integration stream, in accordance with the CI cadence the team has adopted. If they do not deliver their code at least once a day to be included in the daily build (at a minimum), then their code will not be included in the CI build, breaking CI for the whole team.

Successful daily builds are the heartbeat of a software project. If you do not have successful daily builds, then you have no heartbeat, and your project is dead!

—Jim McCarthy, Microsoft Visual C++ product manager

Enabling CI requires that teams and projects have good branching schemes that allow developers to work in isolation, on multiple work items, that create multiple versions of their code, in parallel, and allow them to easily deliver code into the integration stream. There are many philosophies on branching schemes, whether developers should deliver to the *mainline* or to a dedicated *integration branch* (referred to as the *integration stream* in this book). Teams need to pick which is most appropriate for their needs of component size per developer, team size, and team velocity. Any branching scheme or source code management tool that limits developers' ability to develop code across multiple versions in parallel and deliver code to the integration stream from any branch should be avoided.

CI tools are built to enable a team-wide CI cadence. Modern CI tools like Jenkins, UrbanCode Build, TeamCity, and Travis CI have the capability to regularly query the source code management (SCM) system for developers *checking in* their code to the integration stream. Once the developer delivers the code, the tool goes into action and builds the code and integrates it into the rest of the pre-existing code in the integration stream. Of course, if the build breaks, the developer whose code was added needs to be notified immediately—enabling a short feedback cycle time. If the build succeeds, it needs to be promoted to run appropriate unit and integration tests. These tests should be automated. The key tests that are critical to run every time are the integration tests to validate and identify integration errors. If integration tests pass, key builds such as that at the end of the day (daily build) should be promoted and deployed to a test environment to run other tests—functional, security, performance, and so on—and then deployed onward to higher environments. CI tools thus need to be integrated with deployment automation tools to enable continuous delivery, which I will discuss in the next play.

As I described in the previous play on *integrated delivery pipeline*, a typical organization does not have just one delivery pipeline. There are several pipelines, and they are interdependent. In the same way, most project teams do not develop and deliver code in isolation. Multiple teams may be working on code that comes together to deliver a single component. The components they are developing, in turn, are interdependent with other components. Furthermore, several such components come together to deliver a service or application. Continuous integration thus needs to happen on at least two levels (see Figure 4-7):

1. *Component-level CI.* Where multiple individuals or teams working on the same component need to deliver their individual code developed to an integration stream and initiate an integration build, continuously. Such a build should ideally be done every time a team member delivers new code to the integration stream or, at the minimum, once a day.

2. *Application-level CI.* Where all the components that deliver an application are integrated together by an integration build. Such builds are done less frequently than a component-level build. Still, at least one daily build should be a bare minimum.

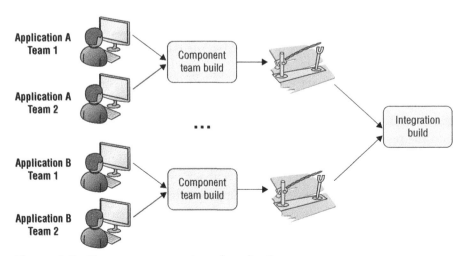

Figure 4-7: CI across components and applications

There is also system-level integration, where multiple services or applications come together for integration. At this scale, it is not continuous integration, but it is still done as frequently as possible. There is also no real *build* because these services and applications are free standing and running independently. They do not need to be rebuilt to integrate with other services and applications. That integration should be at an API level. (I will discuss APIs more in later plays.)

At all levels, each CI build should be followed by an integration test to identify integration errors and defects as soon as the build completes. Doing a CI build and not doing integration testing to validate it and identify any defects just tells you that you can do a CI build, nothing more about what you have actually built.

As organizations adopt CI across teams, projects, and applications, the governance of the build processes starts to become essential to enable scaling across the enterprise. Most CI tools can scale to fairly large projects and applications, with hundreds of components. However, it is not uncommon to see build and CI tool sprawl in organizations, with each project implementing their own instance of the tools. This creates a standardization challenge and can result in high variance in build quality. Standardization is essential to getting to enterprise scale. I discuss this in detail in Chapter 6.

Continuous integration is a critical play for DevOps adoption. It drives several other plays. It is what *pushes* code into continuous delivery and other stages in the delivery pipeline (Figure 4-8). The CI cadence sets the pace at which code flows through the entire delivery pipeline. Doing CI right sets up DevOps for success.

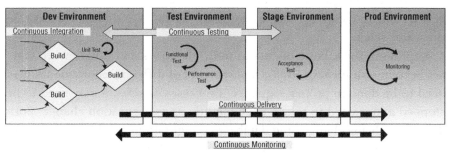

Figure 4-8: Continuous integration drives the delivery pipeline.

Play: Continuous Delivery

It is a gently progressive program involving four days of running a week. The long run in the first week of training is a relatively easy 6-miler. Each weekend, the long run gets longer, peaking at 20 miles three weeks before the marathon. A tapering period allows runners to gather energy for the race. Stepback weeks allow runners to avoid overtraining. Cross-training and ample amounts of rest complete the mix.

—Hal Higdon, American writer, runner, and trainer (Higdon, 2011)

Like continuous integration, continuous delivery is also introduced in Chapter 2. The difference between the often-misused terms continuous *delivery* and continuous *deployment* is also defined. To recap, continuous delivery is the ability to deploy applications to various environments in the delivery pipeline, on a continuous basis. This requires that the deployment process be automated in order to be repeatable, reliable, and scalable.

Deployment Automation

As developers develop code, they need to deploy it to a Dev server to make sure it works. Once they are done writing code, they then deliver it for continuous integration. The CI build needs to be deployed to a test server for testing and promoted to other test and QA environments, all the way out to production. Continuous delivery thus involves multiple deployments to multiple environments. These may range from simple deployments of a module of code, *built* into a deployable binary by a developer, to much more complex deployments that are essentially complex orchestrations. As code becomes integrated and built into components, services, and applications, it is not just a simple binary that needs to be deployed to a server. What you deploy may be anything, from simple configuration changes to incremental code changes toward a new feature, to database schema changes, to changes to the environment, to the whole stack.

Deploying these components to multiple nodes and middleware servers becomes an *orchestration*. Deployments of different components may need to be done in proper sequence. Processes or servers may need to be stopped and started to take a code module or configuration change. Both database schema changes and database configurations need to be managed. Middleware components always come with configuration changes, which need to be updated and applied across all instances of the clusters of servers.

This requires that the deployment automation tool be able to create complex deployment processes and orchestrate and update multiple middleware servers and processes, as shown in Figure 4-9.

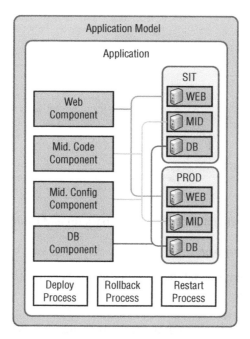

Figure 4-9: Deploying application components

In addition to deployment processes, creating proper rollback processes is also essential, as shown in Figure 4-10. Rollbacks may be needed for multiple reasons. To begin with, if the deployment itself fails, whatever has been partially deployed needs to be rolled back. Fully deployed applications may need to be rolled back due to critical defects being identified. Rollback processes can be complex, both for partially deployed applications (tracking what was deployed and what was not) and for completely rolling back full applications—database changes being one of the biggest sticking points. One approach states that applications are never rolled back at all, just forward. Rollback in such an approach is rolling forward by deploying an older working version of the application and replacing the application that needs to be rolled back. State and data changes to the database still remain an issue here and need to be handled with care.

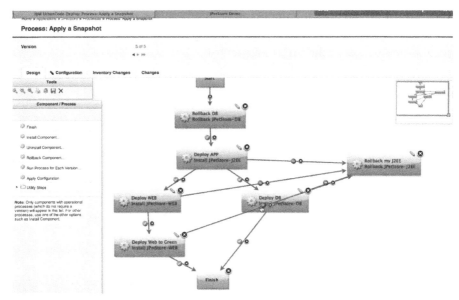

Figure 4-10: Deployment process, with rollback (in IBM UrbanCode Deploy)

Database Deployment

Automation of deploying database components comes with very specific challenges that are unique to databases:

- Updates to a database have to be incremental. While an application component can be replaced entirely by a brand new version, this is not viable for databases.
- Database updates have to be done in an orderly manner. Each change builds upon the previous change. Updates of multiple application WAR files to an application server, for example, can be done in parallel or in any order. For a database, updates need to be done in the prescribed order to guarantee the final datasets in tables.
- If you deploy an application component twice by error, it is a non-issue. However, adding the same database record twice results in duplicate records, which is not acceptable.
- Database changes are irreversible. Application deployments can be rolled back or overwritten. Databases can be rolled back only by replacing the entire database from a backup.

Tools have been developed to handle database deployments, given their special handling needs. Traditionally DBAs have used scripts, which need to be manually managed and are error prone. To attain the scale and speed needed for DevOps, automation is essential. Open-source tools like *Liquibase* and *dbdeploy*, and commercial tools from *Datical* and *DBmaestro*, enable database deployment automation for continuous delivery.

There are also the cultural challenges related to database deployment. Updates to databases are controlled by DBAs. In traditional, non-DevOps-enabled teams, the DBAs are in a separate silo from Dev-test. They are disconnected from developers and may not appreciate the rapid rate of change to databases the developers need to enable continuous delivery. Furthermore, they push back on automation where they don't control the tools. This creates challenges with establishing an integrated delivery pipeline, which includes database deployment tools in the tool-chain for CD. To address these challenges, DBAs should be equal stakeholders in the squads, eliminating the existence of a separate DBA silo.

The What, How, and Where of Deployment

THE ALL-ROUNDER

In the history of cricket there have been few that have been gifted enough to be considered weapons with both the ball and bat.

Only a handful of players can claim to be amongst this exclusive group, while only a sprinkling of these will go down in the history books as being an all-time great.

Even rarer still is a true all-rounder, someone who is equally adept with both the bat and ball and has the ability to make a team as either a bowler or a batter.

—Cheshire, 2012

When it comes to looking at the actual deployments, which need to be automated and made continuous, you need to understand all three aspects of deployments:

1. *What* is deployed?
2. *How* is it deployed?
3. *Where* is it deployed?

The model in Figure 4-11, in UML notation (UML, 2005), shows the relationship between these three aspects of deployments. This model represents how these three aspects of a deployment are captured in IBM UrbanCode Deploy Blueprint. Other deployment tools use similar concepts.

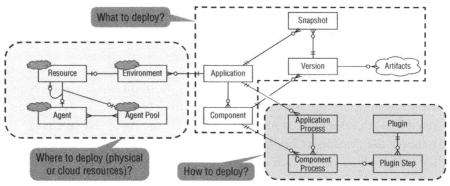

Figure 4-11: Deployment automation "blueprints"

The *What?* The *what* includes the artifacts that need to be deployed. These may include code, configurations, database schema, data, content, web pages, and so on. As the model describes:

- *Artifacts* are all the assets that can be deployed, versioned, and stored in an artifact repository.
- *Components* are collections of versions of artifacts.
- An *application* is made up of components.
- Versions of components go together to form a *snapshot*—a set of version components that need to be deployed with each other.
- All applications, snapshots, components, and artifacts have *versions*.

Thus, when deploying, you can deploy an entire application, just some components, or a snapshot (which captures a set of versions of components, representing the entire application, or just a part of it).

The *How?* To deploy anything from the *what*, you need to carry out a series of steps, which constitute a deployment *process*, or the *how*. These steps may be technology specific. They may need to be *orchestrated*—done in a particular order, with logic between the steps. Certain steps may be capable of being carried out in parallel with other steps. Others may have dependencies and prerequisites. Furthermore, the process may have steps to handle failures in individual steps or the overall process. As the model describes:

- The *application* has a deployment *process*.
- Each *component* making up the application also has a deployment process.
- The application deployment process calls the individual component deployment processes.

- Each component process is made up of multiple steps, several or all of which may be technology-specific steps that are executed by a technology-specific *plug-in*.
- The deployment process may also be dependent upon the target environment you are deploying to (the *Where*): is the component deployed to an application server or a database, or is it an executable that needs to be installed at the OS level?
- The deployment process may also include steps that *configure* the application itself, or the middleware, or the environment, to which it is being deployed.

The entire application deployment process is executed, or only a component deployment process is executed, depending on whether you are deploying the full application, or just a few components.

The *Where?*   The *where* is the target environments you are deploying to. Each environment you deploy to may be made up of several servers, each having various application servers and other middleware installed on them. These servers and middleware may need to have their configurations updated, as a part of the deployment processes. As the model describes:

- The *environments* are composed of nodes or *resources*.
- Each resource has an *agent* that runs on it, which does the actual deployment, and manages inventory.
- Sets of nodes may belong to *agent pools*—sets of nodes that are identical, need to have the same sets of components deployed to them, and have the same configurations.
- There is mapping between the application *components* and the *resources*. This mapping tells the deployment process which application component needs to be deployed to which node.
- The deployment process also specifies which configuration settings need to be managed on each node.

There are two types of environments that you may be deploying applications to:

1. *Static. Static* environments are steady-state environments. They have a fixed number of nodes (servers), with predefined and static network connections between them, forming a static *topology*.

   When deploying an application to a static environment, the only thing the deployment processes do with the environment is to manage the configurations of the various servers, and then deploy the right application components across the right servers.

2. *Dynamic.* As the name suggests, *dynamic* environments are not static. The number of nodes changes over time, depending on various factors that govern their state. Nodes are provisioned and de-provisioned, as needed. While the network between the nodes is predefined, the topologies are more dynamic in nature.

When deploying to a dynamic environment, there will be scenarios where nodes are provisioned independent of the deployment process, and the application components just need to be deployed to the nodes once they are provisioned. Alternatively, the application deployment process itself may provide the nodes, based on rules and conditions embedded in the deployment processes. The *full stack* is thus deployed—the node and the application. I'll talk more about this in the next section.

The advent of cloud-hosted environments is resulting in dynamic environments becoming the norm. These dynamic environments are designed as cloud *patterns.* There are various cloud pattern definitions and standards, including *OpenStack Heat Orchestration Template* (HOT), IBM *Virtual System Pattern* (vSys), Amazon *AWS CloudFormation template,* and Docker *Swarm.* Other than the definition of the virtual machine images (nodes) and their network connectivity (topology), patterns also capture the behavior of the environments—how they are orchestrated, based on process flows and rules included in the patterns. Figure 4-12 shows such a pattern as an OpenStack HEAT template, designed with IBM UrbanCode Deploy. I discuss cloud environments and the role patterns play in continuous delivery more in the next chapter.

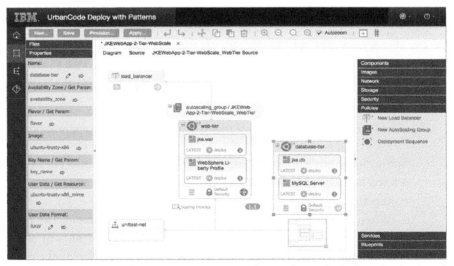

Figure 4-12: OpenStack Heat pattern (in IBM UrbanCode Deploy's Blueprint Designer)

From a perspective of mapping application components (the *what*) to the environments (the *where*), this is a simple process for static environments. For dynamic environments, the applications need to be architected to scale *horizontally* in order to support the dynamic nature of the environments that scale up and down elastically, based on scale and functional needs.

Production-Like Environments   One of the core tenets of DevOps is providing Dev-test practitioners with *production-like environments*. One of the key challenges and sources of inefficiency in the delivery pipeline is that developers and testers do not have access to environments that even remotely resemble the actual production environments. This can result in applications being developed and tested in environments that function and behave very differently in production environments, when they are eventually deployed there. The actual deployment process can be fraught with errors if it has never been tested on an environment that is like the production environment.

The ideal scenario would be that Dev, test, and other preproduction environments be exact clones of the production environment. That is not viable from an economic perspective as the infrastructure required could be cost-prohibitive. The next best solution is to provide environments that closely resemble the production environment in terms of functionality and performance. You may not have the same scalability or the same number of compute nodes, memory, storage, or network bandwidth as production. However, you should ensure that the same general node topology exists, the same version of OS and middleware is used, and the OS and middleware use similar configuration settings.

Typical anti-patterns would be scenarios like the following:

- Leveraging an open-source application server for Dev-test and a commercial application server for production
- Using different versions of server OS for different environments
- Using custom, self-developed *stubs* to replace expensive-to-use services for testing purposes, rather than *service virtualization*, which can properly emulate such services
- Using test data that does not resemble production data schema
- Not managing middleware configurations to match them to production configurations, across the lower environments
- Sharing test environments across multiple applications, resulting in configuration and behavior *drift*

Full Stack Deployment   What does a full stack deployment process actually deploy? Let's look at what makes up the full stack (Figure 4-13).

- Application (including application code and application configuration)
- Data
- Middleware configuration
- Middleware
- Operating system (OS)
- Virtualization
- Servers (compute nodes)
- Storage
- Networking

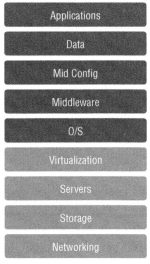

Figure 4-13: The full stack

When it comes to deploying the full stack, this means deploying all these layers. In non-full stack deployment, all you deploy is the higher layers—application data, application configurations, the application, and middleware configuration. The rest of the lower layers are considered a part of the environment and are provisioned prior to the application deployment. The exact demarcation between what is deployed with the application deployment process and what is provisioned with the environment is subjective and is dependent upon the application being deployed. There are multiple scenarios where the application deployment process includes deploying the middleware itself and the environments being provisioned with only the bare OS on the nodes.

Continuous Integration to Continuous Delivery

The 4x100 relay race is just as much a skill event as a speed event. A team with four decent sprinters can out-race a team with four better sprinters by beating the faster team in the exchange zones. The key to this event is how much time the baton spends in those exchange zones.

—Rosenbaum, n.d.

As you look at building a delivery pipeline tool-chain, one of the key points of integration is the handoff of the deployable assets from the build and continuous integration tool to the continuous delivery tool. The continuous integration cadence should drive the continuous delivery cadence. Furthermore, if the goal is to minimize the cycle time, then both build and delivery processes should be fast. CI to CD should ideally be a continuous, seamless process, with minimal cycle time (see Figure 4-14).

Build   Package   Deploy
         Repo

Figure 4-14: Continuous integration to continuous delivery

In most cases, it is recommended that there be a *package* or *artifact repository,* in addition to the build tool and the delivery automation tool, in the delivery pipeline. This artifact repository acts as the repository for all the deployable assets, configurations, and their dependencies. It becomes the *single source of truth*—the one repository where any stakeholder can go to in order to get the right sets of assets needed to deploy an application or component. This repository can be in *series,* or in *parallel* to the build tool, making it a delivery tool integration point. That is, it may be between the two tools, where the build tool pushes the assets to the repository, and the deployment tool picks it up from there (serial path), or it may be to the side, where the build tool publishes the assets to the repository every time it hands them off to the deployment automation tool (in parallel).

The artifact repository remains just a *pass through* when in a continuous delivery cycle. However, when a deployment is needed out of cycle—to re-create a defect, for example—the artifact repository becomes essential in ensuring that the right versions of the right sets of assets are deployed. The repository also becomes an essential enabler of *end-to-end-traceability,* as it has all version sets of all the deployable assets.

From a tooling perspective, there are myriad artifact repositories. There are general-purpose repository managers like JFrog Artifactory, or Nexus from Sonatype. Most deployment automation tools come with their own embedded artifact repositories, which store only deployable assets. IBM UrbanCode Deploy has a repository called *CodeStation* embedded in it. When using an embedded repository, it is not uncommon to also see a general-purpose repository in use. The embedded deployment automation repository stores copies of assets that have been deployed.

Push versus Pull Handoff

THREE WAYS TO PASS THE BATON

Each of the three ways to pass the baton has pros and cons. Drummond prefers the push-in method, which is often considered the safest, although not always the fastest.

Push-In: Receiver's palm faces toward the incoming runner, who holds the baton vertically and pushes it straight in.

Upsweep: Receiver's palm faces down; the incoming runner swings the baton up between the thumb and fingers.

Overhand pass: Receiver's palm faces up, and the incoming runner places the baton in the crease of the hand.

—Jon Drummond, United States Olympic 4x100 relay gold medalist (2000) and coach (2012) (Ward, 2012)

There are two approaches to hand off from CI to CD:

1. A *pull* mechanism. In this approach, the deployment automation tool *pulls* the deliverable assets from the build tool or artifact repository.
2. A *push* mechanism. In this approach, the build tool or artifact repository *pushes* the assets into the deployment automation tool.

When practicing continuous delivery, *push* is the preferred method of operation. The build tool completes a build and then pushes it on, triggering a deployment. In a *pull* approach, there can be issues because there is no way for the deployment automation tool to know if the build has completed or if all the deployable assets needed to deploy the component are available. It may result in deployments of a partial set of assets. Pull works just fine when deploying assets that have been built beforehand and may have even been deployed previously (that is, not in a continuous delivery cycle). Because only the build tool knows when it is all done with the build process, it is better to let it trigger the deployment, once done.

Adopting Continuous Delivery

One of the biggest reasons for challenges during *release to production* is that for projects not practicing continuous delivery, the first time the application is deployed to the production environment is during release to production. When it comes to the actual deployment of the application, the deployments of various components often fail, or they have challenges because this is the first time the deployment processes, even those that are automated, are being executed in the production environment. They have never really been tested and validated. This, along with several other challenges discussed in this chapter, is why traditional projects have a *release weekend* when software is released, with the entire team on hand for the entire weekend (or longer) to fix things as they break during deployments of various components.

When practicing continuous delivery of applications, you are validating not only the functionality and performance of the components being delivered and the environments they are being delivered to but also the processes of deploying the components. Deployment of the software is not as simple as copying some binaries over FTP. It involves file transfers to multiple locations on a potentially complex set of nodes, but it also involves configuration changes to the OS, databases, and middleware. It also involves an orchestration of steps. You cannot simply carry out deployment steps in a mechanical, linear manner. Middleware processes may need to be restarted after configuration changes. Services may need to be stopped before file transfers and then restarted, all in a coordinated, orchestrated manner. Continuous delivery allows for these processes to be tested and refined to ensure that when it comes to the final deployment to production, it is not the first time the team is executing the processes. As multiple deployments happen through multiple cycles or sprints, the processes are tested and debugged continuously and are thus proven to work at all times. Furthermore, these deployment processes should also include the processes to deploy the environments, not just the applications.

The key here is to start continuous delivery right from the start of the project—from sprint zero—all the way through the project. In the beginning, the deployments may be simple, but they will become much more complex, orchestrated deployments later in the project. Continuously delivering changes—application, middleware, configuration, data, and environment—in small pieces, using the right automation tools, reduces risk by validating the automation, the deployment processes, the configuration changes, the environments being deployed to, and, of course, the application being deployed.

Deploy right from sprint zero. What do you deploy in sprint zero? There is no code yet. That's easy: you deploy the environment. Get the Linux (or if you really have to, Windows) distribution and install it—somewhere... get started.

The Continuous Delivery Platform

Give me a platform. Let's rock, let's rock, today.

—Dewey Finn (Jack Black, perf.), in School of Rock. Paramount Pictures, 2003.

Eventually the goal is to deliver a platform to the practitioners, a platform on which they can continuously and efficiently deploy the application to Dev, test, SIT, UAT, and eventually production environments. The goal of the platform is to introduce a *layer of abstraction* between the infrastructure and the application delivery pipeline capabilities. A practitioner should not need to worry about the nuances of the infrastructure; the hardware, the hypervisor, the virtual machines, the datacenter, and the network should all be abstracted away from the practitioners. They need to focus on their goal of developing, testing, and delivering the applications and services, without any concern about what is being provisioned on what kind of infrastructure and where. The environments should appear to them as well-defined, well-architected, seamless, always-available, resilient, scalable environments, fine-tuned for their application's and service's specific needs. This *abstraction* can be provided either at the infrastructure layer, delivering the *Infrastructure as a Service* (IaaS), or at the platform layer, delivering the Platform as a Service (PaaS), or by leveraging containers that create an API-based segregation between the application or service being delivered and the infrastructure services. All three options have their strengths and weaknesses. I discuss them in detail in the next chapter.

Whatever the level of the abstraction may be, creating a platform for the application delivery practitioners is essential. This platform will need to span the various environments that make up the delivery pipeline. Such a platform is constructed by building a *tool stack* that provides the various services or capabilities needed to enable the delivery pipeline. The tool stack typically includes tools or services that provide the following capabilities:

1. Source code management
2. Build
3. Continuous integration
4. Deployment automation
5. Middleware configuration
6. Environment configuration
7. Environment provisioning

Several other services can be added to this list to form a fully functional platform, but these are the bare minimum required to create a functional platform. If you are doing *full stack deployment,* capabilities 4 to 7 are included in a single environment pattern, which includes the complete stack—application to compute nodes—and is provisioned as one process. If you are not doing full stack deployment, then each capability is a separate service, and the environments are not provisioned every time the application is deployed. The middleware and environment may still need to be configured every time a new version of the application is deployed.

A tool stack to enable such a platform would include the following:

- A source code management tool, like Git, GitHub, Subversion, or Rational Team Concert
- A build and continuous integration tool, like Jenkins or IBM UrbanCode Build
- A deployment automation and middleware configuration tool, like IBM UrbanCode Build or XebiaLabs Deployit
- An environment configuration tool, like Chef, Puppet, or Salt
- An environment management tool, or provider, like VMware vRealize, IBM Cloud Orchestrator, or Amazon Web Services EC2

Leveraging a standardized, integrated tool stack is essential. To ensure portability and prevent vendor lock-in, these tools should be based on open standards.

Play: Shift Left—Testing

In the DevOps delivery pipeline, *shift left testing* involves enabling the testing to happen as early (left) in the delivery pipeline as possible. This applies to all types of testing: unit, functional, regression, integration, performance, stress, security, and so on. Typically, other than unit testing, this is done by developers; all other forms of testing happen later in the delivery pipeline. Some forms of testing—like performance testing, load and stress testing, or security testing—typically do not happen till just before the final release. In large multi-vendor projects, it is not uncommon to see even integration testing left till the last phases of the project. This late testing prevents the discovery of defects and issues till too late in the project, resulting in high risk and high cost of fixing the defects and issues. I am sure most people remember the issues with the U.S. healthcare.gov website when it was launched in October 2013. Most of the issues were attributed to testing happening too late in the release cycle, allowing critical defects to go undetected when the website was released (Pollock, 2013).

Shifting testing to earlier in the lifecycle offers two benefits:

1. Early testing means early discovery of defects and issues, lowering their cost of mitigation and lowering the overall project risk.
2. Early testing means that it happens more often and addresses smaller change sets (smaller batches). This more frequent testing of smaller sets of changes significantly lowers the associated risk and raises the overall quality of the deliverables, as they are tested more often.

Shift left testing requires creating production-like environments where more realistic tests can be done earlier in the delivery lifecycle. Techniques such as service virtualization, emulation of production data, and production-like simulated load are used to create environments with low overhead. I will discuss service virtualization in more detail later in this module.

Test Automation and Continuous Testing

Obstacles don't have to stop you. If you run into a wall, don't turn around and give up. Figure out how to climb it, go through it, or work around it.

—Michael Jordan, basketball icon

What is the goal of continuous integration? Is it to enable continuous delivery of the developers' code out to production? Yes, eventually. But before that, it is to enable ongoing testing and verification of the code. It is to enable the testing needed to validate that the code produced and integrated with that from other developers and with other components of the application functions and performs as designed. Continuous integration and delivery are both (almost) meaningless without continuous testing. What good is having a streamlined continuous delivery process if the only way you find out about your applications' functionality or performance being below par is via a ticket opened by a disgruntled user?

As developers create code to add new functionality, enhance existing functionality, or address defects, they are continuously integrating their code with that of other components being developed and delivered to the integration stream. Along the way, they run unit tests on their own code. Once the integration is done, they do *integration testing* on the integrated code. They may run other tests such as *white box* or code-level security tests, code performance tests, and so on. This work is then delivered to the common integration area of the team of teams—integrating the work of all the teams working on the project and all the code components that make up the service, application, or system being developed. The important point to note here is the immediate step after the continuous integration process is always to validate that the code integrates at all levels without error and that all tests run by developers run without error. Continuous testing therefore starts right with the developers as a part and parcel of continuous integration.

After validating that the complete application (or service or system) is built without error, the application is delivered to the QA area. This delivering of code from the Dev or development environment to the QA environment is the first major step in continuous delivery. Continuous delivery is happening as the developers deliver their code to their teams' integration space and to the project's integration space, but this is limited to being within the Dev space. No new environment is being targeted. When delivering to QA, I am speaking of a complete transition from one environment to another. QA would have its own production-like environments on which to run its suites of functional and performance tests. In addition, QA would potentially also need new data sets for each run of the suites of tests it runs. This means that the continuous delivery process would not only require the processes to transition the code from Dev to QA but may also include steps to provision new instances of QA's production-like environments, complete with the right configurations and associated test data to run the tests against. This makes continuous delivery a more complex process than just FTPing code over. The key point is that the goal of continuous delivery is to get the code ready for testing, and to get the application to the right environment—continuously, so that it can be tested continuously.

If you extend the process described here to delivering the service, application, or system to a staging and eventually a production environment, the process and goal remain the same. Traditionally, despite all the testing done earlier in the delivery lifecycle, the Ops team wants to run their own set of smoke tests, acceptance tests, and system stability tests before they deliver the application to the *must-stay-up-at-all-costs* production environment. The security team wants to run their own set of security and compliance tests, again in a production-like environment. These are production-like environments that need to be provisioned just like the QA environments. They need to have the necessary test automation and test data for the various tests that will be run. Only when this last phase of continuous testing is complete will the application be delivered to production.

In a nutshell, if you need to *shift left* all these various tests and run them early and often, four key capabilities need to exist:

1. Ability to provision production-like environments, as and when needed
2. Ability to *automate* the tests, to make them fast and repeatable
3. Ability to *virtualize* services and environments that are not available, or those that would significantly increase the cost of testing
4. Ability to provide (continuously) new sets of *test data* required for the multiple sets of myriad types of tests being run, early and often

The concept of production-like environments has been already covered. The need for automating tests is self-evident. It is not possible to scale testing staff to meet the needs of the rapid and repeated testing needed to enable shift left testing. What good is an efficient cycle of two-week sprints, if running functional tests takes up three to four days of the sprint? What good is efficiently delivering the application, only to be held up for the three weeks that the security team needs to run all its tests and validations? It is thus essential that all tests be automated. Automation allows the testing to be fast, modularized, repeatable, and included as a part of the continuous integration and continuous delivery processes. Automation tools exist for all forms of testing: unit, integration, functional, performance, load and stress, security, policy testing, and so on. These tools should be included in the integrated delivery pipeline to ensure continuous delivery of components, applications, and services that are thoroughly tested, early and often.

I will now discuss the last two capabilities—service virtualization and *test data management*—needed to enable shift left testing.

Test Service and Environment Virtualization

Deploy what is ready, virtualize the rest.

—IBM testing practice

When you are ready to deploy a component, service, or complete application to a test environment, in order to run some tests, all the services, applications, environments, and data sources that are needed to test the application under test will not be available. Others may be available, but utilizing them for testing purposes, especially when testing repeatedly small sets of changes, may be cost prohibitive. It is not practical to wait for all of the services to become available in time to run the tests. This can become a major bottleneck in the delivery pipeline. In any of these cases, these applications, services, environments, or data sources that are consumed or utilized by the application under test to function, need to be virtualized. Traditionally, developers have written stubs to replace applications or services that are not available for testing. Writing and maintaining such stubs is time-consuming, expensive, and error prone. Utilizing service virtualization tools resolves this problem by introducing automation and scalability to the process. Such tools include IBM Rational Test Virtualization Server (previously Green Hat) and CA Service Virtualization (previously ITKO LISA). These tools allow for applications, services, and data stores to be simulated by virtual representations running on a test virtualization server. See Figure 4-15 below.

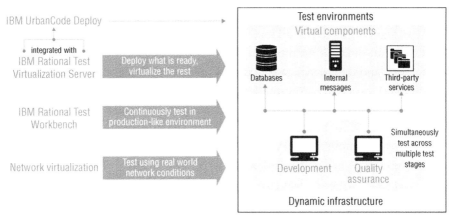

Figure 4-15: Test service virtualization

You begin by running tests with several of the required applications, services, and data stores being virtualized. As the project matures, more and more of these applications, services, and data stores become available. The virtual instances are then progressively replaced by actual instances, as they become available and usable. Eventually, tests need to be done with all real instances, before the application under test can be released to production.

In addition to application, services, and data stores, environment availability can also become a bottleneck. In mainframe environments, for example, it is not uncommon for a logical partition (LPAR) to be dedicated for testing and shared by multiple applications. In contrast, in distributed environments, it is not uncommon to see servers dedicated to test labs running at utilizations in the single digits. This happens because the process of acquiring, provisioning, and configuring the test environments is so cumbersome, that once a project gets an environment, they reserve it and keep it idle for most of the time, just so that they have it whenever they need it for testing. The mainframe challenges are unique, and I will discuss them later in this chapter, in a play dedicated to the mainframe. Introducing cloud-hosted environments in the test lab is essential to address these availability and utilization issues. These environments can be on a private or public cloud. Cloud-hosted environments allow for test environments to be made available on demand and to be de-provisioned when they are not needed.

A new class of cloud offerings in the continuous testing space are *test-environment-as-service* features. These features offer scalable cloud-hosted environments that can fully clone an existing on-premises or cloud-hosted environment for Dev-test purposes, by importing all the existing environment's virtual machines. Some of these environments that are built for DevOps also have the capability to create complete *clones* of an environment, including state and network (Internet Protocol or IP addresses). The use case is ideal for enabling continuous testing. If a tester finds a defect, she can create a complete clone of the environment, capturing the state at which the defect was found. She can then send the developer a URL pointing to the clone, and it is then re-provisioned for the developer on an appropriate cloud datacenter, creating a clone with the right environment, tools, state, and network addresses. This eliminates the bottleneck of developers struggling to re-create a defect identified by a tester. IBM Development and Test Environment Services (IDTES), provided with technology from a company called Skytap, is a good example of such a service.

Test Data Management

Test data management is about easily creating targeted, right-sized test databases rather than cloning entire production environments. Without the need to manually create and maintain test data, development and test environments are more manageable for continuous testing. Simply stated, test data management is the process of quickly creating realistic test data at the time it is required for testing.

So, how does test data management fit with DevOps? As discussed before, DevOps requires that developers and testers deploy applications regularly in order to validate their integrations, functionality, and performance. The goal of testing in DevOps is to perform these validations by carrying out appropriate integration, functional, and performance tests. This implies that applications should be tested every time they are integrated and deployed, requiring sets of test data each time. Providing good sets of test data is inherently challenging. This is further exacerbated by the need to test the application with new and refreshed test data each time developers deploy a new version of the application. In order to address these challenges, test data management thus becomes a prerequisite to the very existence of DevOps.

The following is a list of best practices for test data management that enable continuous integration and delivery for DevOps (Moran, 2013):

- *Discover test data.* Test cases need to be associated with the appropriate test data, and finding the right test data for each of the test cases is critical. In some cases, this data may exist across several production databases. For example, an application might use data from a customer record from a customer relationship management (CRM) database along with related details on purchased items from a separate inventory management system database. The goal is to capture the end-to-end business process and associated test data, wherever it may reside. This will enable teams to extract the appropriate data into the subset needed for the test cases.
- *Automate creation of realistic "right-sized" test data.* Organizations are creating test data either manually or by just cloning their entire production system to obtain their test data, instead of extracting only the subset of test data needed to support the test case. These manual processes do not provide the agility needed for continuous integration and delivery for DevOps. Automated test data generation allows for rapid creation of test databases for various types of testing on demand.
- *Mask sensitive information for compliance and protection.* Protecting data privacy is no longer optional—it's the law! Organizations must have procedures in place to de-identify data across non-production environments to comply with data privacy regulations and avoid data breaches. Data masking provides development teams with meaningful test data, without exposing sensitive private information such as personally identifiable information (PII) and protected health information (PHI). Masking takes real data and makes it realistic but fictional so that no sensitive data is compromised.
- *Refresh test data for continuous delivery.* To enable continuous delivery, testers and developers need access to test data continuously in order to run tests each time a new version of the application is delivered and run them again for the next version. Organizations can streamline test data delivery by enabling testers and developers with tools and processes to refresh test data without the need to involve DBAs. This improves operational efficiency, provides more time for testing, and enables releases to be delivered more quickly and continuously.
- *Analyze test data results.* While functional testing confirms the behavior of the application, test data management enables organizations to assess

changes in test data for success or failure. Analyzing test data results by comparing pre-test data against post-test data helps to assess whether the test passed or failed. This best practice addresses any hidden errors, allowing organizations to quickly identify and resolve defects for continuous integration and delivery.

Play: Shift Left—Ops Engagement

PULLING THE GOALIE

The most exciting 90 seconds in sports are created by a man who isn't there. A hockey team is down a goal or two with the clock ticking toward double digits, and the coach pulls the goaltender and sends an extra skater over the dasher for an all-or-nothing gamble. More often than not the puck bounces off sticks, bodies, and walls or ends up in the empty cage. But the six-on-five gamble works often enough that it's worth the risk, especially when the alternative is extinction.

—Powers, 2013

There has always been a healthy tension between development and operations teams. In most enterprises they are in separate reporting structures, typically under different executives, keeping them organizationally apart. The reasoning behind the "tension" is justified and not really negative in nature. Dev wants be able to take the new or updated applications and services they have developed and deploy them in stable and fast environments provided by Ops, in a continuous manner. Ops, on the other hand, wants stability and control. They want all the applications they run to co-exist and not affect each other or the systems they run on. They want the Dev team to build applications whose system needs to conform to their specifications and require minimal attention, once deployed.

Developers view operations as the people who just run the ferries that carry their precious cargo. Operations view developers as the providers of the payload their precious ships are designed to carry. (Any resemblance to jokes about how the United States Navy and Marines view each other is entirely coincidental...)

—Overheard at a DevOps conference

As mentioned in "Play: Agile Adoption," the advent of Agile development practices has increased this tension by an order of magnitude. Developers who are practicing continuous integration want Ops to be able to provide environments capable of continuous delivery. The QA teams want the test environments to be provisioned on demand, to the specifications of the QA team, and the QA environments to be built ideally to mirror the production (Prod) environment. Once QA has tested and approved the application, preferably using automated tests, the continuous delivery process then delivers the application to a higher environment for further testing and eventual deployment to production. All these environments should also be provisioned automatically and mirror the production environment.

In an ideal world, all of this happens automatically and continuously. Environments (Dev, test, and so on, all the way to production) are provisioned and configured for the application in question, as and when needed. They are also destroyed automatically, once the application is promoted to the next environment.

This is obviously a major cultural and technological shift for operations. They suddenly don't just do one deployment of a new version of an application every few months but now have to deal with potentially hundreds of builds that the developers produce weekly or even daily. This is further complicated if these are builds that they little have little or no confidence in. Furthermore, they are now expected to spin up new environments to test and validate most of these builds!

They therefore need to change how they engage with Dev-test, how they handle change, how they manage their environments, and how they automate. To fully adopt DevOps, Ops needs to be on board and willing to change. Most importantly, trust needs to develop between Ops and Dev. This trust can be enhanced by taking the following steps:

- *Shift-left engagement*: One critical goal of DevOps is to engage Ops earlier in the delivery lifecycle and keep them engaged throughout. In traditional waterfall projects, Ops engagement is primarily limited to when there is something to deploy. Ops may be involved in developing system design and defining specifications and requirements during the requirements phase but then remain disengaged till Dev teams start deploying working code (builds). For DevOps adoption, Ops teams need to be engaged regularly, as an integral part of the team, all through the process. Shifting left can begin with a step as simple as having an Ops team member participating in the Dev teams' *daily standup meeting* (a Scrum and extreme programming concept). Different teaming models that are employed to include Ops in the team are discussed later in this book.

▨ *Get Agile*: Ops needs to adopt (some of) the Agile practices that Dev has already adopted. They need to start using their sprint structures, work item management strategies, work burn down charts and dashboards, which capture the work backlog, and so on. Preferably, they will do this using the same tools and repositories as the developers. This does not mean that Ops starts adopting a methodology like Scrum, with two-week sprints, but that they become more agile to align their ability to make changes with the speed of the Dev-test teams. This reduces the impedance mismatch between them.

▨ *Virtualization and automation*: Adopting software-defined environments provides the ultimate level of agility for Ops. I discuss these environments in detail in later plays.

▨ *Change management*: Operations need to adapt their change management practices. This does not mean abandoning proven practices like ITIL but extending and adapting them to handle the order-of-magnitudes-higher number of change management tasks that now need to be performed for all these environments being provisioned and de-commissioned and builds being deployed. This requires the automation of all Ops tasks, from provisioning and orchestrating environments, to implementing policies; to leveraging software-defined environments; and to standardized dashboards capturing all relevant metrics and operational KPIs.

Changing of Ops Roles

As with most transformations, the role of the Ops teams changes with a DevOps transformation. Engineers who are responsible for the infrastructure or platform are the ones most impacted by these role changes. Before the DevOps transformation, they are responsible for doing all the management tasks on servers, such as provisioning and de-provisioning of servers, orchestrating and configuring server behavior, and installing and patching OS and middleware. With DevOps, they no longer perform lower-level tasks; their role changes to a higher level of abstraction where they design, create, and manage patterns and also manage running environments provisioned by these patterns.

The Ops teams provide these patterns, making them available to practitioners, from Dev to test to production, via a self-service catalog. The patterns themselves are environment topologies, with pre-built images, with associated policies for their governance, pre-defined process flows for their orchestration, and scripts for their configuration. Practitioners can provision these patterns to get environments on-demand, configure them within the constraints of the defined policies, orchestrate their deployments using the process flows, configure them using the configuration automation scripts, and deploy applications and data to them, as needed. When the environments are no longer needed, they de-provision them. All of this happens with no direct manual engagement from the Ops team.

If the practitioners need to make a change that lies outside what is permitted by policy, which is defined by practitioner role, they put in a request for a change to the Ops team, who will create a new pattern or a new version of an existing pattern for them.

This is the next level of working for Ops, delivering a much higher-leverage productivity and, at the same time, making working with environments much leaner and more efficient for practitioners working with Dev-test-prod environments.

Such a mechanism is, of course, best enabled in a cloud-based environment. However, the level of abstraction at which Ops works can also be elevated for non-cloud environments. How much control the Ops team hands off to practitioners in Dev-test is also technology dependent, as there are restrictions when not using a cloud-based environment. For example, only when using a cloud-based environment, leveraging technologies like OpenStack Heat Orchestration Templates, can you achieve the design and provisioning of patterns capturing *full stack* environments—that is, environments that include all the layers of the environment, from compute, memory, storage, and network, to OS and middleware, and the eventual application and data, all in one pattern, delivering full software-defined environments.

When operating in a legacy environment like a mainframe where Dev-test environments are typically on dedicated *logical partitions* (LPARs), the Ops teams are not going to relinquish any control of the environments to developers and testers. Allowing someone outside the Ops team to provision middleware on a test- or production-dedicated LPAR, for example, would be a no-no. They would do that themselves and allow Dev-test practitioners only to deploy applications to the LPAR or to the middleware servers.

On the other end of the spectrum, if using containers, the Ops team would not care about what Dev-test practitioners deploy or configure inside a set of containers, as long as the containers themselves are coming from an image from an Ops team-approved image registry. Isolating Ops from what's inside a container, of course, is the very premise of the value containers.

As you move to a model that is based on delivering applications on a Platform as a Service, the role of the Ops teams changes even further. The platform may be vendor managed altogether (like IBM Bluemix PaaS), and furthermore there may be third-party services from multiple vendors that are being consumed by the applications being delivered. The role of Ops here becomes one of a service broker and orchestrator, who is managing the internal and vendor-delivered services, dealing with their contracts, metering, security, and SLAs. They ensure that all the application services and PaaS-provided cloud services are available and are functioning and performing as desired to keep the organization's own developed applications and services up and running. If the organization is also delivering services to its clients and partners and they in turn are consuming to develop their own applications, the role of Ops also includes managing these outgoing services—their contracts, metering, security, and SLAs—ensuring the consumers of the services are able to consume them as desired.

This change in the role of Ops requires that a good, comprehensive, cross-platform monitoring and continuous feedback practice be put in place. That is the only way Ops teams can ensure that environments and systems are behaving and performing as desired, without having to be hands-on with each one.

IT Service Management and DevOps

A common discussion, and often pushback, that occurs when adopting DevOps is regarding how DevOps aligns with IT service management (ITSM) frameworks like Information Technology Infrastructure Library (ITIL), Business Process Framework (eTOM), or Control Objectives for Information and Related Technology (COBIT). Of these, over the years ITIL has become the go-to framework for most IT organizations to build a set of documented, repeatable processes to manage and govern the IT services delivered to the organization, upon which the applications delivering business value to the customers and users are deployed, run, and managed. The quality, scalability, stability, and predictability of these IT services are essential for the applications to run in a scalable, stable, and predictable manner. ITIL practices provide the framework that IT organizations can adopt in order to support these needs. Introducing

DevOps practices like continuous delivery appears to be at odds with ITIL practices, which are geared toward rigorous change management and service management processes. In reality, DevOps practices, which are geared to provide efficient, repeatable, automated, scalable processes, align fully with the goals of ITIL. While the increased frequency of deployments may appear to add to the complexity that the change management and service management processes have to handle, the reduced batch size and shorter cycle times actually reduce the risk associated with each deployment. The same ITSM practices are now handling smaller changes more frequently, rather than large, complex changes less frequently.

ITSM practices, from frameworks like ITIL, provide capabilities that support DevOps in four core areas (Hodges, 2015):

- *Configuration management,* ensuring consistent production-like environments across Dev, Test, and Prod.
- *Incident management,* enabling timely corrective actions to issues and incidents identified in any environment.
- *Infrastructure and application performance management*, providing the continuous monitoring required for sustained application quality. I will discuss this more in the section "Play: Continuous Monitoring and Feedback."
- *Business service management,* providing business dashboards powered by analytics, giving all stakeholders continuous business feedback, and allowing them to adjust their plans if necessary.

IT service management practices and tools thus enable and ensure consistent and reliable operation and feedback to all the stakeholders in the delivery pipeline. They enable the shift left of Ops engagement to earlier phases of the lifecycle and also provide capabilities for continuous feedback, which enables continuous improvement of the application, environments, and delivery processes.

The critical component of the play of aligning ITIL practices with DevOps is twofold:

- Make the ITIL practices leaner and more efficient in order to make the cycle time of addressing requests coming to IT—change management, or incident management related, for example—shorter.
- Reduce the manual steps in approval processes for IT by introducing policy- and rule-based automation.

■ Automatically capture metrics and audit trail data across the integrated delivery pipeline as evidence of compliance to ITIL controls.

Areas where automation can add significant value for ITSM processes are as follows:

■ Orchestration automation for services and environments using a business process management (BPM) based orchestration tool, such as IBM Cloud Orchestrator (ICO) or VMware vRealize

■ Automation of logging and alerting, and associated analytics leveraging tools like Splunk or IBM Operations Analytics

■ Operationalization of processes for incident management, using tools like ServiceNow or IBM Control Desk

Play: Continuous Monitoring and Feedback

SOCCER PERFORMANCE FEEDBACK

In September 2008, when the [Manchester City Football Club] was acquired by the Abu Dhabi United Group for Development and Investment, a private-equity outfit owned by a member of the Abu Dhabi royal family, the team suddenly found itself with the resources necessary to mount a challenge for the Premier League....

After each match, they compile exhaustive reports about the team's performance data, focusing on statistics that they think most relevant. The list is extensive. They analyze, for instance, the number of line breaks, a term borrowed from rugby which means a forward pass that goes through the opposition's midfielders or, more crucially, its line of defenders. They look at what happens in the 20 seconds after the team wins or loses the ball. They pay attention to City's ball possession in the last third of the pitch, a measure that they found to be strongly correlated with winning matches.

—Medeiros, 2014

Because one of the goals of DevOps is the rapid feedback of metrics and analytics back to all stakeholders in the delivery pipeline, establishing *continuous monitoring and feedback* capabilities is essential. DevOps guru Gene Kim, in his blog post *Three ways of DevOps*, describes this under the goal of *amplifying feedback loops* (Kim, 2013). He states that "the goal of almost any process improvement initiative is to shorten and amplify feedback loops so necessary corrections can be continually made." Feedback is the input that is essential to make improvements to the applications and environments that are delivered and the processes being utilized to deliver them.

When someone mentions continuous monitoring, the tendency is to focus on, monitoring of production environments alone. However, continuous monitoring includes monitoring of every environment in the delivery pipeline: Dev, test, and prod. Similarly, continuous feedback means feedback from every process in the delivery pipeline, including tests run, defects found, work items backlogged or deferred, requirements changed, and incidents in production.

What is essential is to ensure that the feedback be provided in a form that is consumable by the stakeholders it is being provided to. Providing logs to business analysts does not provide much value to them. However, analytics related to the root causes of spikes in the usage of particular features, or changes in user behavior based on a configuration or UI change, are very relevant to the business analysts.

Providing Monitoring and Feedback

When talking of monitoring and feedback, one does not just mean monitoring in production but across the entire delivery pipeline. Monitoring and gathering feedback from nonproduction environments can identify potential issues related to performance early in the lifecycle, long before the application or service is deployed to production, allowing for the issue to be identified and addressed. Across the delivery pipeline, monitoring comes from five areas:

1. *Application monitoring.* Gather metrics and analytics to see if the application is functioning and performing as desired. If not, under what conditions are there issues, and what types of issues?

2. *System monitoring.* Is the entire system, including the underlying infrastructure, functioning and performing as desired? If not, what workload or infrastructure (compute, memory, storage, network, and so on) conditions are the issues caused by?

    This also includes incident management.

3. *Application user behavior.* How is the application being used? Are certain features and capabilities used more or not at all? Where do users spend their time in the application? What are they doing—using features or struggling to get things to work?

    This also includes doing A/B testing, where multiple variants of the application are delivered to different sets of users to test new features and capabilities. I discuss A/B testing in more detail in the next chapter.

4. *User sentiment.* Ensuring that the *user experience* (UX) is a positive and productive one has become the core of most *system of engagement* applications. These are applications that deliver business value directly to the end-user. Several techniques and frameworks have recently been developed to deliver this high-quality user experience, including design thinking, *Lean UX,* and so on. Measuring the user's experience to determine how user-friendly their user experience actually is thus becomes an essential measurement and source of feedback to the UX designers. This has led to the development entire sets of practices and tools to measure and capture *user sentiment*— how the users are feeling. Tools are available to measure a user's actual interaction with the app—which parts are they using, are they struggling in some areas, are they productive, or do they seem lost in the app? There are also tools that actually capture direct user interactions. A good example is the IBM Mobile Quality Assurance (MQA) tool.

    Another critical source of feedback on user sentiment is social media. It should not be ignored, given the tendency of many consumers to make decisions based on what they see and hear on social media. Tools and services like IBM Watson Analytics for Social Media can capture social media postings across myriad channels and analyze them to provide a holistic view of the user base's sentiment.

5. *Delivery pipeline metrics.* All metrics gathering and analytics capabilities need not be limited to end-users and systems in production. The delivery pipeline and all the stakeholders working on artifacts through it is a rich source of metrics. These metrics can deliver an accurate status of projects, tools, environments, artifacts, and work being delivered. I'll discuss this next.

Delivery Pipeline Metrics

INTRODUCING HYGIEIA

At Capital One, we believe that while tools, automation and collaboration are very important, a continuous feedback loop is critical to DevOps success....

So after evaluating many such dashboard products, we decided it was time to create our own because Capital One needed one single dashboard to visualize the full delivery pipeline at any given point in time.

When designing and building the dashboard, we focused on making it simple to configure and easy to use. Plus, since we knew it would be useful to others, we built it with the intention of sharing it with the world and offering an open source version.

Our DevOps dashboard, now known as Hygieia^{SM} (Figure 4-16), is used extensively across Capital One, and we're pleased to now offer it to you....

The main purpose of this dashboard is to make any clog in the pipeline easily visible so that a member of the team can take immediate action to remove it.

—Tapabrata "Topo" Pal, Director, Next Generation Infrastructure,
Capital One (Pal, 2015)

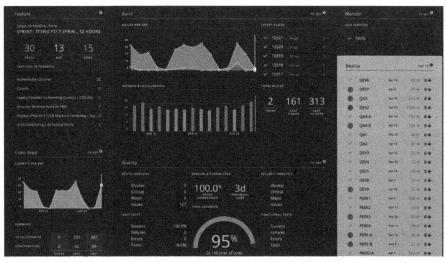

Figure 4-16: Hygieia, from Capital One

There is no one better to introduce the value of providing a single dashboard to present and visualize the metrics from the end-to-end delivery pipeline than (my friend) "Topo" Pal from Capital One. Reading the introduction of Hygieia (and the more complete version on the original web page), you can see the core business value points that are delivered by having such a dashboard enabling continuous feedback of delivery pipeline metrics and analytics:

- A *continuous feedback* loop is essential for DevOps. Every practitioner in the delivery pipeline should have visibility into metrics related to the delivery pipeline, providing them feedback on their work, and downstream work related to their artifacts.
- A single *dashboard* to visualize the entire delivery pipeline is the ideal solution. The dashboard needs to be able to consume metrics and data from every tool in the delivery pipeline.
- The dashboard should continuously expose bottlenecks. If the goal of a value stream mapping exercise is to find pre-existing bottlenecks in the delivery pipeline, the dashboard then acts as a real-time *bottleneck detection system*.
- Such a dashboard should be easy to configure and use. Setting up and configuring the dashboard should not introduce a new bottleneck in the delivery pipeline. Furthermore, the metrics and analytics should be easily consumable, as visual representations.

Hygieia is an open source project started by Capital One to create a dashboard to visualize the delivery pipeline metrics in one place. Figure 4-16 and 4-17 show screenshots of the Hygieia dashboards. Several vendors, from IBM to HP to XebiaLabs to Jenkins, have contributed code to Hygieia, allowing metrics from their tools to be exposed in the dashboard (Capital One GitHub, 2015).

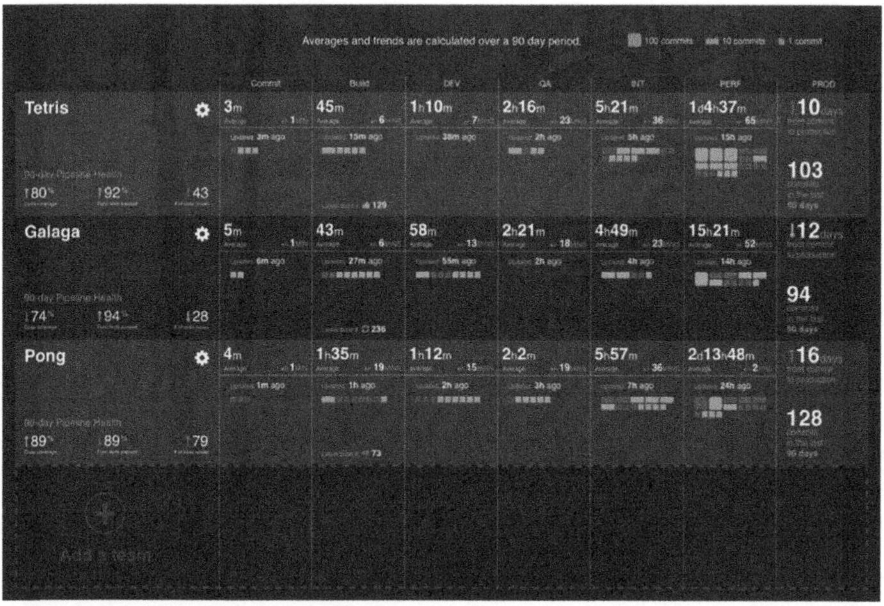

Figure 4-17: Hygieia—pipeline view

Continuous Improvement

Today, in sports, what you are is what you make yourself into. Innate athletic ability matters, but it's taken to be the base from which you have to ascend. Training efforts that forty years ago would have seemed unimaginably sophisticated and obsessive are now what it takes to stay in the game. Athletes don't merely work harder than they once did. As Mark McClusky documents in his fascinating new book, Faster, Higher, Stronger *[Hudson Street], they also work smarter, using science and technology to enhance the way they train and perform. It isn't enough to eat right and put in the hours.*

—Surowiecki, 2014

The '72 Miami Dolphins notwithstanding, records are meant to be broken. What Surowiecki is implying is that, in sports, the players are getting better every season. They are getting stronger, training more, using better equipment, receiving better coaching, and leveraging better technology to continuously learn what and how to improve. They are striving to be better not only than those who came before them, or than their current competition, but than they themselves were the day before.

A DevOps adoption effort needs to introduce this culture of continuous improvement in the project teams.

- How can they improve the application or service of which they just delivered the latest version?
- How can they improve the infrastructure and environments on which they just delivered the application or service?
- How can they be better than they were in the last sprint so they can deliver a higher-quality product, at lower cost, faster, and more efficiently?

This improvement can only come in the same manner as it comes for Olympic-level or world-class players: by instrumenting every aspect of their training routine, by providing visibility into detailed and myriad metrics about productivity and performance, and by looking for where they can improve, even ever so slightly. After all, even a thousandth of a second can make the difference between a gold medal or not in some Olympic sports.

THIS IS WHY THERE ARE SO MANY TIES IN SWIMMING

In a 50-meter Olympic pool, at the current men's world record 50m pace, a thousandth-of-a-second constitutes 2.39 millimeters of travel. FINA pool dimension regulations allow a tolerance of 3 centimeters in each lane, more than ten times that amount. Could you time swimmers to a thousandth-of-a-second? Sure, but you couldn't guarantee the winning swimmer didn't have a thousandth-of-a-second-shorter course to swim. (Attempting to construct a concrete pool to any tighter a tolerance is nearly impossible; the effective length of a pool can change depending on the ambient temperature, the water temperature, and even whether or not there are people in the pool itself.)

Sports that subject athletes to an identical course—bobsled, for example—can use thousandths because this question doesn't matter. Speed skating uses thousandths, though given how start commands are issued in that sport and the incredibly slow speed of sound, maybe they shouldn't.

—Burke, 2016

Knowing where to invest when it comes to continuous improvement is also critical. Just like in swimming, shaving off a thousandth of a second may not make a significant enough difference to win a higher medal; a competitor needs to shave off in the hundreds of a second. In the same way, focusing and investing the Dev-test cycle to improve the velocity will not have a significant impact if the real bottlenecks are in the project change approval or requirement elicitation processes. Similarly, knowing what to focus on when improving the application and environments delivered is essential to ensuring you are focusing on and investing in the right areas. An efficient and complete metrics regime enables continuous monitoring and feedback of the entire delivery pipeline—from project inception to maintenance. It also captures the KPIs for the application delivery processes for the application delivery pipeline.

Play: Release Management

You don't show up on game day and expect to be great. Greatness happens in practice. You have to expect things of yourself before you can do them.

—Michael Jordan, basketball legend

Release day is *game day*. Everything the team has done and worked hard for culminates in the software being released to production. Only then do users start using the application to get business value.

This is old-school thinking. It is big-batch, full-application-release thinking. By adopting DevOps practices, release day should not be an event that lasts long or is significant enough because it happens only once in a project's release cycle. With DevOps, release to production should be as simple as switching configuration settings to expose a new version of the application that has already been delivered to a pre-production or even the production environment or switching a feature flag in the application to start exposing new feature sets in an application already delivered. The delivery processes should also be trivial, as they have delivered small batches of the application though the delivery pipeline to various environments dozens, if not hundreds, of times. The *release to users* may remain an infrequent event, but delivery to production (or pre-production) should be continuous.

The Release Management Process

Let's step back and look at why organizations have such cumbersome and complex *release management* processes. It all boils down to managing the quality and success of a release.

What is the definition of a release? A *release* is a collection of new or changed configuration items or components that are tested and introduced into production together. It may include a combination of *application* software, *system* software, and *hardware* together with associated *documentation*. Because various versions of these components may be coming together from various teams, they need to go through formal Quality Assurance and *governance* steps that have well-defined gates in order to ensure that the right versions of the right components, which have passed the right QA checks and are integrated properly, are successfully deployed. Release management processes may thus be fairly rigorous, depending upon the mission-critical nature of the application and the regulatory and compliance requirements they may operate under. The release management process to release a *payment processing system,* for example, needs to be more rigorous than that to release the next version of a virtual monster-hunting game (no matter how mission-critical your teenager may feel the virtual monster-hunting game is).

Release management becomes more complex when it involves multiple components and services, from multiple application delivery pipelines. This was introduced earlier on as Multi-Speed IT. Here the coordination of the flow of artifacts needs to be coordinated across these multiple delivery pipelines. The dependencies between the various components and services need to be well understood and documented to fully understand the impact of changes to the components and services and that of any delays in their release schedules.

- Can components be released independently, or do they need to be released together?
- What dependencies are there that require components or services to be released in a particular order?
- Are new versions of some components or services compatible with older versions of others that may not yet have been updated?
- What quality gates are there for each component?
- Do some components and services have special QA or security/compliance requirements?
- Are there certain high-severity defects that can block a component from being released? And conversely, are there low-impact defects that do not block a release?
- How are changes to release plans handled?
- How is version management of assets and artifacts dealt with in order to ensure that the right versions of components and services are being released?
- How are deployment failures, which stop a release from being completed, triaged, and addressed?
- How is the inventory of releases managed and documented?
- How are rollbacks of release handled?
- What are the audit requirements for a release? What level of release records need to be maintained, and for how long?
- What are the criteria to mark a release completed?
- Is there a *warranty* period for a release, during which the release is not marked as *closed*?

These and many more questions go into a comprehensive release management process.

Given this level of complexity in the requirements of a release plan, it is essential that the processes behind them be automated and have visual dashboards to provide visibility into the process and any issues and bottlenecks that may occur during a release process. IBM UrbanCode Release (shown in Figure 4-18) and XebiaLabs XL Release are two good examples of such release management tools.

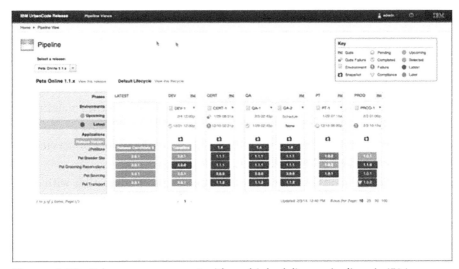

Figure 4-18: Release management with multiple delivery pipelines in IBM UrbanCode Release

Continuous Delivery for Non-continuous Release Cycles

While the formal releases may remain at a fixed cadence—monthly, quarterly, yearly, and so on—DevOps practices can still be employed to have continuous delivery to *pre-production* environments. All the release management processes are now applied to get the components and services to the pre-production environments. During the continuous delivery to pre-production, the release management processes may remain just as rigorous as before, but the automation makes them faster. Furthermore, the fact that small batches are being deployed to the pre-production environments, at a high frequency, reduces the time required to go through all the gates and makes the process less cumbersome. At the time of actual release to the users, the release becomes an almost trivial set of steps to deploy from the pre-production to production environments. Some organizations have pre-production environments that are actually identical to production. At the time of release, they just switch the network (Domain Name Server or DNS) settings to swap the two environments, making pre-production the new production. The old production is rebuilt as the next pre-production environment, for the next release.

Specializing Core Plays

It is not uncommon for swimmers to participate in multiple events in swim meets—Michael Phelps alone has won medals in as many as eight separate events each in multiple Olympics. In swimming, there are multiple types of events that not only vary by distance (100m, 200m, and so on) but also by the swimming stroke (freestyle, breaststroke, backstroke, butterfly, and medley, which includes all four). While the basics of swimming remain the same, the swimmers need to practice differently to prepare for each race. In essence, they take their *core plays* and *tweak* or enhance them for each race, given its distance and stroke type.

The next few plays are technology-specific. The plays presented in the book so far have been generic, technology-agnostic plays that can and should be adopted by any organization undergoing a DevOps transformation. These are the *core plays* that need to be included in any DevOps transformation *playbook*. However, the nuances of certain technologies require that specific *tweaks* or enhancements be made to certain plays when adopting them, for projects and teams working in such technology platforms. The rest of this chapter presents these technology-specific plays.

Play: DevOps for Mobile

There is really no such thing as a separate *DevOps for mobile*. DevOps as an approach works for all applications and components, from front-end mobile apps, to middleware, to back-end server components and data stores. The goal is to apply the practices and principles of DevOps across all Dev and Ops teams in the enterprise to enable continuous delivery of all of these components, including mobile apps.

Mobile apps do have specific needs and challenges that must be addressed. In this play, I will present best practices for adopting DevOps capabilities, as applied for mobile app delivery, to address these mobile-specific needs. The goal of these best practices is to bring mobile app development, Quality Assurance, and operational practices in line with other enterprise applications adopting DevOps. Adopting these best practices thus allows enterprises to adopt DevOps across their mobile development teams, deliver higher-quality mobile apps, and enable continuous improvement and innovation.

Mobile-Specific DevOps Challenges

While the basic principles of DevOps are the same for enterprise and mobile apps, mobile apps do present specific challenges to DevOps. These challenges include the following (Williamson, 2014):

- *Multi-platform support.* Most mobile apps target multiple devices, which means dealing with various technical specifications, OS versions, and form factors. Android is well known for being fragmented, as each device vendor has forked the operating system for its own devices. (Examples include Android for Nexus, Android for Kindle Fire, and Android for Nook.) Other players like BlackBerry, Windows, Ubuntu, and Firefox are now further fragmenting the mobile OS market. Even with iOS, which was once standard across all Apple mobile devices, today there are multiple variants. An iOS application needs to support different versions of iOS: the iPhone 4S and below form factors; the regular iPhone and Plus form factors; and the iPad, iPad Pro, and iPad mini form factors.
- *Mobile apps as an enterprise front end.* Mobile apps, especially enterprise business-to-consumer (B2C) or business-to-employee (B2E) mobile apps, typically have little business logic code that runs on the mobile device itself. Instead, a B2C or B2E mobile app serves as a front end to multiple enterprise applications and services delivering business functions for the organization, such as transaction processing systems, employee HR systems, or customer acquisition systems. Figure 4-19 highlights such an app with limited business logic in the app itself. The example is that of the popular LinkedIn mobile app (LinkedIn, Engineering Blog, 2011).

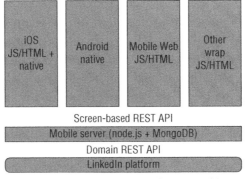

Figure 4-19: LinkedIn mobile app architecture

The LinkedIn mobile app is really a front end to the back-end LinkedIn platform, which delivers the core business services of LinkedIn to its users. The mobile app, which is delivered to multiple platforms as a native or hybrid app, needs to be developed and delivered in conjunction with the back-end LinkedIn platform services. As discussed before, for DevOps adoption the challenge is to think holistically of all of the applications and services in the enterprise that deliver functionality and capabilities to the mobile app and coordinate their build and release processes and cycles.

- *Speed of delivery and cycle time.* Because of the strong business motivation to deliver mobile applications to market quickly, get feedback, and iterate rapidly, mobile development projects typically have extremely aggressive timelines. An inception-to-delivery period of a few months, or even weeks, is common. The pressure to deliver mobile apps quickly results in the adoption of Agile development methods for successful mobile projects. It results in the need for continuous integration and continuous delivery, with extremely short cycle times.

  For CI and CD to work with mobile app delivery, application changes delivered by developers need to be integrated and built for all of the targeted mobile platforms. If the mobile application is a hybrid or native implementation, several different builds of the application need to be triggered, in parallel, each time a change set for the application is delivered by a developer. The build setup and configuration for each supported mobile environment is different from the others. To speed this up, a small farm of build servers may need to be provisioned and made available to handle these multiple mobile target operating system CI builds.

- *The app store.* Typically, a mobile app cannot be directly deployed to a device. It has to go through an app store. Apple introduced this app distribution model and locked its devices to prevent direct installation of apps by app developers or vendors. All mobile platform vendors have followed suit. The app store adds an additional asynchronous step to the deployment process because developers are unable to deploy app updates on demand. Even for critical bug fixes, new app versions go through an app store submission-and-review process. Continuous delivery becomes *submit and wait*.

- *"Pull" not "push" deployment.* Traditional deployment operates on a *push* model whereby operations can push out a new version of an application on demand, be it a web application or any other server-based application. The process for updating mobile apps is a *pull* process, however, where, in most cases, users must choose to update their apps themselves. Mobile application developers have little control over which version of the app an established user keeps on his or her device. From a DevOps perspective, this means that the deployed back-end services that an app interacts with must provide continuous support for multiple—current and previous—releases of the mobile app.

- *Long-term impact of negative ratings.* Nothing is more hurtful to a brand than an app with a one-star rating, particularly when that rating is broadcast through the medium of an app store. Unsatisfied users of consumer mobile apps can become public and visible quickly, regardless of whether the app is purchased or free. While complaints about issues with a website are communicated to a technical support desk, complaints about mobile apps are broadcasted via the app store for everyone to see. Mobile apps must undergo extensive functional, usability, and performance testing to ensure their quality. User experience begins to trump functionality.

DevOps Plays Applied to Mobile App Delivery

Based on the challenges that are specific to mobile apps, the following DevOps plays have been tweaked and enhanced for mobile apps.

Continuous Integration and Continuous Delivery   How CI and CD are implemented is impacted by the very nature of Mobile App development and delivery.

- *End-to-end traceability across all assets:* I discussed the value of traceability across all artifacts earlier in this chapter. A mobile app development team must ensure end-to-end traceability across all development assets, such as code, configurations, scripts, infrastructure as code, test scripts, and design documents. It is also imperative that traceability not be limited to mobile development assets; it must extend to enterprise applications and services that mobile apps integrate with, connect to, or access.
- *Continuous integration:* Continuous integration should not only be performed for the mobile app components but also periodically with the mobile back-end and server-side components and services that are accessed by the mobile app under development.

■ *Build server farms:* To enable continuous integration for mobile apps, the development teams may share central build and integration servers for the mobile app code that serves all mobile platforms that are targeted. Setting up build server farms automating the build and deployment process ensures fast and reliable continuous integration builds that can be performed in parallel for all supported mobile platforms and targeted form factors.

■ *Separate integration streams by SDK:* Developers should maintain separate build and integration areas for each native mobile OS SDK version that is supported. Fragmentation in the mobile device space extends beyond just the four major mobile operating systems of iOS, Android, BlackBerry, and Windows; each of these operating systems is also internally fragmented. Several new mobile platforms are also emerging, including ones from Ubuntu, Chrome, and Firefox. As a result, mobile app developers must write multiple app variants to support each targeted platform and its variants, even if they are targeting just one platform. Every mobile app requires multiple versions of its SDK.

To ensure separation of code and the specific capabilities of each targeted platform, developers must maintain separate *streams* of development and integration for each platform-specific version of a mobile app.

■ *Automated deployments*: Mobile developers are accustomed to using an IDE to manually run builds and deploy the app to the appropriate device. As the complexity and number of builds increases, developers should set up automated builds and deployments. This not only ensures a higher quality of builds and deployments, but it also ensures that each build can be reproduced and deployed at any time and by any developer or tester, on demand.

Testing and Monitoring   Testing and monitoring become exponentially complex based on the myriad mobile platforms and devices, each with their own form factors, that you may need to support.

■ *Automated testing on simulated and physical devices:* Test automation is an area where mobile app development lagged behind enterprise apps. Most mobile developers test extensively on a simulator but not on physical devices. Even the testing done on a simulator is mostly manual. Given the speed of development and the inherently agile nature of mobile development, automated functional regression testing is the only real way to ensure quality. Due to the myriad of platforms and form factors that are supported, it is not possible to manually do enough testing. The solution is to test all apps with automated testing tools, on simulators that are provided by the SDKs and then also on all actual supported physical devices. Service providers are available to provide multi-device testing.

- *Test virtualization:* This approach allows you to virtualize and simulate mobile back-end services that are not available during mobile app testing. Mobile apps follow a rapid development process, which can result in many more releases when compared to back-end enterprise applications and services. Such rapid development can keep mobile apps technically ahead of the curve of the back-end applications and services, meaning that they have newer features that aren't yet supported by back-end enterprise applications and services. As mentioned earlier, even when back-end services are available, they might cost money or resources to test against. Development teams can solve this problem by virtualizing (simulating) back-end services. The entire ecosystem of applications, services, and data stores that the mobile app needs to interact with can be made available as virtual instances, simulating the behavior of the actual capabilities the mobile app needs to interact with. This arrangement allows for rapid testing of the mobile app and its interactions. It also saves hardware resources that would be needed to run actual instances of these services and applications for testing purposes.

- *Application and system performance monitoring*: Mobile app developers face no bigger challenge than an app that performs well in the test environment but fails in the wild. Unreliable network conditions, low memory, low power, and data loss are some underlying causes of poor mobile application performance. Not all of these conditions can be predicted and tested in a lab, so it is imperative that developers enable continuous performance monitoring as apps are used. Such monitoring should be done to monitor the entire stack—not just the mobile app but also the applications and systems that are delivering the mobile back-end services.

- *User sentiment feedback:* The ultimate failure is when a mobile app does not function or perform while in a user's hands out in the field. Adding capabilities to the app that captures context information in the case of issues, including location data and device characteristics, can provide the developer with sufficient data to find the root cause of the issue and correct it. Embedded crash capture and analysis logic is an essential component of mobile apps. Newer services like IBM *Mobile Quality Assurance* can capture user sentiment, allowing for not just capture of app crashes but also the user's feedback when an app does not function or perform as desired, directly from within the app.

Mobile App Delivery Mobile apps are at the forefront of continuous delivery. It is not uncommon to look at one's mobile device and find tens of apps that have new updates on a weekly basis. However, delivering mobile apps is not as straightforward as delivering web apps or SaaS offerings.

- *Centralized governance for mobile provisioning profiles, certificates, and API keys:* Whether to submit an app to an app store or to use an API provided by an internal or external application, a developer or organization identifies the authenticity and ownership of an app via a vendor-issued provisioning or profile key. These keys serve as the authorization pass to the store or API. Typically, individual developers get their own keys that they use for development purposes. However, when the final app is released, steps need to be taken to remove all these personal keys and replace them with the official organizational keys. There have been instances where organizations have had major issues, and even had to withdraw apps, either because official apps were released without replacing personal developer keys with organizational keys or because the organizational keys or profiles were released publicly, or for both reasons.

  The organizational keys and profiles need to be protected and only used for official app releases. Mobile governance processes for key and profile management must be well defined and tightly controlled. Above all, restricting access to organizational keys and profiles is critical, as it is both a security and a privacy issue that requires strict governance.

- *Using a virtual app store to test end-user device app provisioning:* A mobile app can only be provisioned to a mobile device via a vendor's app store. Usually the app goes through a manual approval process before it gets into the app store. Once it's in the store, a user needs to *get* the app, which is then pushed to her device. To test this entire process, development teams can use a *private development app store.* These virtual app stores simulate the behavior of a real app store, enabling developers to effectively test the process of submitting an app and provisioning it to a device.

▪ *Capturing user feedback:* Mobile apps have a unique feedback mechanism via app stores that allows users to provide *ratings* and written feedback about them. A well-liked app is likely to receive a four- or five-star rating. A less popular app usually receives a one- or two-star rating, possibly accompanied by negative feedback. This direct feedback from users for mobile apps is not available as a formal centralized mechanism for any other platform. Developers typically find out about problems with traditional apps only if a user calls tech support or leaves a comment on a forum that is monitored by the developers. Mobile development teams should therefore closely monitor app store feedback and ratings and incorporate the feedback into future user stories, enhancements, and software improvements. Making the most of this valuable feedback is imperative to continuously improving mobile apps.

Culture and Teams　In most organizations, mobile app teams have traditionally been small teams with their own development and delivery tools and practices.

▪ *Collaboration across mobile and back-end teams:* It is not uncommon for the mobile app development teams to be separate groups within an organization—be they vendors or employees. For DevOps adoption, it is essential to include mobile development teams when adopting DevOps across the organization, even if the mobile team is a small part of the organization or follows a different software development process. Mobile apps that interact directly with enterprise applications and services need to be first-class citizens in the DevOps lifecycle. As new features are added to the enterprise application or service, the teams can seamlessly integrate them into the mobile app.

▪ *Learning agility from mobile app teams:* It is also common to see these mobile development teams be extremely agile with rapid development and delivery capabilities. Their skills and agile processes can actually be leveraged by the rest of the organization, adding significant value.

Play: DevOps for Mainframe

The world's businesses still run on the mainframe. For the past 50-plus years, even since the first distributed systems started gaining popularity, the pundits have been predicting the demise of the mainframe. However, it is still growing strong, despite the emergence of the cloud and mobile computing. Here are some *myth busters* about the mainframe—specifically IBM System z—that, while being a few years old, still hold true (Sun, 2013):

■ Ninety-six of the world's top 100 banks, 23 of the top 25 U.S. retailers, and 9 out of 10 of the world's largest insurance companies run System z.

■ Seventy-one percent of global Fortune 500 companies are System z clients.

■ Nine out of the top 10 global life and health insurance providers process their high-volume transactions on a System z mainframe.

■ Mainframes process roughly 30 billion business transactions per day, including most major credit card transactions and stock trades, money transfers, manufacturing processes, and ERP systems.

Mainframes therefore deserve a section in this book. Moreover, they do have some *nuances* that require that the DevOps plays be enhanced or tweaked for adoption on the mainframe.

Organizations that have significant workloads running on the mainframe share a few common patterns of concern:

■ The processes and tools used by mainframe teams have not kept pace with those for teams delivering applications on distributed or cloud-hosted systems.

■ Most mainframe-hosted workloads have been in production for a long time—decades in some cases—with little new development being done. While these systems are extremely stable and well understood, they have legacy architectures and are difficult to transform to modern architectures for better consumption.

■ The total cost of running and maintaining systems on the mainframe is fairly significant. This is due to their cost models and because the tools and processes have not been transformed to become more efficient.

■ While it is politically incorrect to say so, the reality is that practitioners who work on the mainframe are aging and retiring. It is becoming more and more difficult for organizations to find replacements as younger engineers are not familiar with the legacy processes and tools or are unwilling to work with tools that do not have modern user interfaces.

At the end of the day, most mainframe systems are the ones delivering the core business services. They exemplify the *core* in *industrialized core*. However, they might not be very *industrialized*. Their old tools and processes, non-modern architectures, and lack of lean delivery pipelines result in these systems being unable to deliver changes at speed. These systems can thus become a *drag* on the organization's ability to innovate at speed. It does not matter how fast an *innovation edge* application can be delivered. If it is dependent on a back-end service that runs on the mainframe and will not be updated for another six weeks, the new app cannot be released till then.

Also, from an investment perspective, if the greatest inefficiency is in the delivery capability of applications on the mainframe, then making these systems more efficient will have the greatest impact on freeing up resources—money and human—which can then be invested into innovation.

Optimization needs to come first in order to allow innovation to even happen and to happen unhindered.

DevOps Plays Applied to the Mainframe

Based on the challenges that are specific to application delivery on the mainframe, the following DevOps plays have been tweaked and enhanced for the mainframe (Radcliffe, 2014).

- *Maintain a single-source repository:* With any multi-platform development effort, using a common, cross-platform, single-source repository is critical to enable CI. However, it is not uncommon to see mainframe teams using legacy source code repositories that are different from, and disconnected from, those used by other non-mainframe teams. If such a singular repository is not implemented across platforms, the System z teams end up being left isolated and not able to participate in continuous integration practices. Integration with any work conducted on the mainframe becomes an after-effort, waterfall-style integration.

    This transition to a modern source-code repository represents a significant change for mainframe development teams that may have been using the same capability for years. However, a single source code management (SCM) tool is critical to allow the management of all artifacts, help break down the silos, and remove a key bottleneck.

■ *Ensure that everyone commits to the mainline every day:* CI requires having every developer, across all components and all development environments, commit their code to the integration streams every day to help ensure that integrations remain as continuous as possible. For System z/OS development today, many users work independently on their code changes until the final audit, which is when they realize their work is impacted by the work of other developers. This can lead to delays in releasing functions or to last-minute changes that have not been properly tested being deployed into production. Regular integration of code can help ensure that these dependencies are identified sooner so the development team can handle them in a timely manner and without time constraints.

■ *Automate the build:* Automating the build is what makes continuous integration continuous. For System z builds, automation can become a challenge, as the availability of the System z environment and the cost of accessing it can both become issues. Availability certainly becomes an issue during production and business operation hours.

■ *Test automation:* Just as builds need to be automated, so does the testing. The goal of continuous integration is not only to integrate the work of teams but also to see if the application or system being built is functioning and performing as expected. As described earlier, *continuous testing* requires that the automation include the capability to build the software if needed, provision the test server, provision the test environment, deploy the built software to the test server, set up the test data, and run the right test scripts.

All of this can be a particular challenge for System z/OS development, but it must be addressed. The requirement to have the environments to do the build, deploy it, and do the automated testing at any time helps improve the quality of the final code. This requires availability of system resources, the willingness to run large numbers of automated tests on a regular basis, and the development of the automated tests.

■ *Keep the build fast:* Fast builds are essential, as virtually nothing impedes continuous integration more than a build that takes extremely long to run. System z/OS builds are generally fast due to the standard practice of building only changed files. However, these builds do need to be coordinated with builds on other platforms, and scheduling the appropriate time when System z/OS resources are available can be an issue.

■ *Test in production-like environments:* Testing in an environment that does not accurately represent the production system leaves a lot of risk in the system. It is not always possible, however, to create a clone of an entire System z or non-System z environment just for testing. It is even harder to create a clone environment with other workloads running on it. For systems hosted on System z, the cost of maintaining such test environments can become a major issue. Generally, a limited number of development and test LPARs must be shared across teams. In addition, many organizations carefully control the MIPS utilization of their test teams in order to develop capacity for production.

Organizations looking to limit utilization and maximize availability of System z test environments can utilize tooling that allows for non-production instances of System z/OS to run on distributed systems for development and testing. One example of such a solution is IBM Rational Development and Test Environment (RD&T) for System z. It provides non-production System z/OS environments such as development or Quality Assurance on Intel-based Linux systems. This environment includes a System z/OS hardware emulation that enables running the true System z/OS platform, with necessary middleware. In such a scenario, the continuous delivery process would deliver the application to these Dev-test environments and eventually to production back on System z. Other than providing easy access to multiple production-like environments, such a solution to offload Dev-test environments from the mainframe also frees the System z mainframes exclusively for production use.

■ *Adopt deployment automation:* Continuous integration naturally leads to the concept and practice of continuous delivery—the process of automating the deployment of software to test, system test, staging, and production environments.

Automated deployments are common in System z/OS environments because SCM systems generally include build and deployment. However, most projects do not have enough System z/OS resources for each team to deploy into a test environment at all times. Deployments also need to be coordinated with the distributed side of the infrastructure, which can present a challenge due to the lack of common tooling. An effective practice to meet these needs is that of continuous release and deployment.

For System z applications, there are two common mechanisms or paths to continuous delivery:

1. For organizations with a mature set of deployment tools and practices in place, deployment to the target logical partition (LPAR) may be carried out leveraging a legacy configuration management tool. While limited in their ability to deliver the full capability of continuous delivery, these tools can automate deployment to z/OS systems.

2. Alternatively, an organization can utilize a specialized deployment automation tool that has full support for multi-platform deployments including System z/OS. Deployment automation tools, such as IBM UrbanCode Deploy, have a System z/OS agent that can install natively on the target LPARs to enable continuous delivery.

- *Collaborate and communicate:* This is a culture-focused play, as presented earlier. Just like DevOps for mobile adoption, it is essential to include the mainframe development teams when adopting DevOps across the organization, even if the mainframe teams may still utilize different tools and process. While they modernize the tools and practices, they should be included in the DevOps team and also in the organizational transformation to become leaner and more efficient. If the organization does have a significant percentage of their workloads and applications running on the mainframe, doing so will result in a significant overall return on investment of the DevOps transformation.

Play: DevOps for Internet of Things

One of the most significant shifts in how technology has penetrated the daily lives of humans—our homes, our transports, our workplace, our factories, our health—has been the advent of *smart* or *connected devices*, collectively known as the *Internet of Things* (IoT). Technology has existed in all these areas for decades, but the advent of IoT has allowed the devices we use to be connected, in real time, to all other devices, and to back-end services via the Internet. It is no longer just our smartphones and tablets that can communicate with, and deliver services from, service providers; it is our thermostats, refrigerators, weighing scales, cars and trucks, commercial HVAC systems, security systems, watches, exercise tracking devices, televisions, and even street corners.

While all these devices have always had software on them, the software was embedded in the device as *firmware*, at the time of manufacturing. Updating to a new version meant replacing a physical component—a chip, a board, or the entire device—with a new version of the component that had the new software (firmware) version. Updating in place, what is referred to as *over the air* (OTA), was not an option because the devices had no connectivity nor were they designed to be updated when in the possession of the user. Firmware, even when it could be updated, was updated by *flashing* it on to the device chip that ran it, something that could be done only with specialized equipment.

The application delivery process of the devices had two separate and distinct cycles. During the development stage of such devices, both the hardware and software are being developed, typically disconnected from each other. The design and manufacturing of the physical hardware, and development of the firmware that runs on this hardware both need to be synchronized just before the release of the devices. The devices, of course, cannot be delivered without the firmware running on them, and the software development cannot be finalized if the hardware engineering is still evolving and iterating. As the device hardware design approaches completion, the firmware team can start finalizing the software and testing it on a prototype or a simulator, if a real device is not yet available. Once the device becomes available, there is a *handoff* of the firmware to the engineering team that owns the device, and they then own testing of the final device—hardware and firmware. They iterate with the software development teams to address changes and defects, till release. The diagram in Figure 4-20 refers to these teams as the software development lifecycle (SDLC) and product lifecycle management (PLM) teams, respectively—terms commonly used by organizations. Once delivered, the next challenge is related to the updating of the firmware to newer versions. As I've mentioned, in pre-IoT devices, the only mechanism was to replace all or part of the hardware components that had the firmware embedded.

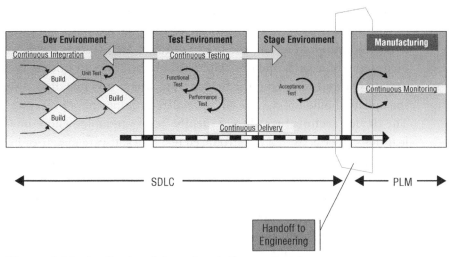

Figure 4-20: Application delivery handoff to engineering

With IoT creating a surge in such devices, DevOps is being adopted by organizations delivering IoT devices to make their entire delivery process leaner and more agile. Here are some key DevOps practices that need to be tweaked for IoT when adopted:

- *Continuous integration and testing.* These progress as in traditional software delivery. However, the availability of simulators or device prototypes that resemble the final device as much as possible (production-like system) is essential. The development cycles of the firmware and hardware need to be better synchronized.
- *Continuous delivery challenges.* Once in production, even connected devices may not be in a state to be updated when an update is made available. They may not have continuous connectivity to the network—for example, devices that are connected only when docked or only when connected to another device is brought into their proximity. This behavior may necessitate that firmware updates be done only when the device is idle and not in a state that needs to be maintained (for example, a suspended state). Furthermore, they may only have a "pull" mode of receiving updates, rather than a "push" mode, which necessitates that the user initiate the update process.
- *Hardware design for CD.* Traditionally, hardware for devices was not designed to have its firmware continuously updated like a mobile app.

If the device manufacturer intends to have a CD mechanism in place to continuously update the firmware of their devices once they are deployed into production, then the hardware architecture needs to be designed for such updates. There should be a way to initiate the update without removing the device from where it is installed, and the update should not require any specialized equipment or processes. The device architecture should ideally be expandable, where new features can be activated or introduced just by a software update or by turning on a software feature that is already installed but only turned on for certain paying customers or in certain special situations. It is not uncommon for such devices to have two layers of firmware: a core operational firmware (an OS), which operates the device and is infrequently updated; and the *app*, which provides specific features and services to the user and is more frequently updated.

- *Teaming and culture.* The alignment between the hardware and firmware teams during the development stage of the device is essential. The hardware and software designs—architecture, requirements, and delivery cycles—are mutually dependent, requiring that the two teams (SDLC and PLM) operate in sync. The *Ops* in DevOps for IoT is, after all, the device hardware team.

Play: DevOps for Big Data and Analytics

Big data and analytics solutions are an entire category of applications and services that are driving demand for new, faster, and more frequent approaches to software delivery. In the past, basic tasks such as delivering a simple code change could take four to six weeks; yet waiting weeks or even months to get an update to clients is no longer acceptable. The traditional lifecycle for delivering new or enhanced big data and analytics solutions took months or even years as features and functions were collectively designed, developed, tested, and deployed. Increasingly, development organizations are looking toward DevOps for ways to implement continuous delivery as a means to improve business agility, speed up delivery, capitalize on new marketplace opportunities, and respond to changing landscapes. The goal of continuous delivery is to constantly design, test, and deploy incremental enhancements in production to more rapidly provide value to customers as well as to roll back those changes if any problems are detected.

Adopting DevOps plays results in these big data and analytics solutions being delivered in a more efficient and effective manner, with continuous process improvement, while ensuring that the changes and enhancements to the software are based on real customer feedback.

Figure 4-21 shows a big data and analytics reference architecture, highlighting the complexity of delivering such applications and services. The architecture describes a set of components that facilitate data ingestion, staging, exploration, analytics, and reporting to achieve desired business outcomes balancing requirements related to quality, relevance, and flexibility.

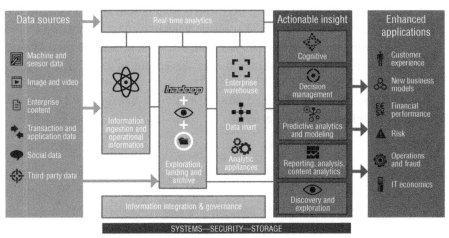

Figure 4-21: A big data and analytics reference architecture

Analytics Solutions Unified Method

Fortunately, unlike mainframe development, the big data and analytics space is not alien to Agile practices. IBM Analytics Solutions Unified Method (ASUM) (ASUM, 2016), for example, is a step-by-step guide to conducting a complete implementation lifecycle for big data and analytics solutions. ASUM uses a hybrid of Agile and traditional implementation principles to achieve your solution objectives and provide an optimal result to your organization. These principles are listed here, and their alignment with DevOps plays presented in this chapter is evident, making DevOps adoption easier for projects following ASUM:

- The project is assessed for the application of Agile principles.
- The project is scoped, and initial business requirements are gathered.

- Both business and IT personnel form an integral part of the project implementation team.
- Requirements are clarified and fine-tuned through a number of iterative prototyping sprints. Based on the number and priority of requirements, timeline, and available resources, a staged implementation approach is adopted to achieve the objectives.
- Prototyping results are then compared to total requirements to assess achievements and determine further iterations.
- Iterative and incremental development is used to finalize configuration and build.
- Following adequate testing performed throughout the lifecycle of the project, the first stage of the solution goes live.
- Remaining stages of the project follow the same path of prototyping sprints and iterative and incremental development as the first stage.

ASUM follows five fully defined phases, as shown in Figure 4-22, with an umbrella area of project management.

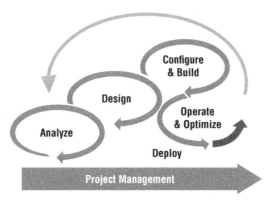

Figure 4-22: Analytics Solutions Unified Method (ASUM) phases

1. *Analyze:* Define what the solution needs to accomplish, both in terms of features and non-functional attributes (performance, usability, and so on). Obtain agreement between all parties about these requirements.
2. *Design:* Define all solution components and their dependencies, identify resources, and install a development environment. Iterative prototyping sprints are used when applicable to clarify requirements.

3. *Configure and build:* Configure, build, and integrate components based on an iterative and incremental approach. Utilize multi-environment testing and validation plans.

4. *Deploy:* Create a plan to run and maintain the solution, including a support schedule. Migrate to a production environment, configure as necessary, and communicate the deployment to the business user audience.

5. *Operate and optimize:* Operate includes the maintenance tasks and checkpoints after rollout that facilitate a successful application of the solution and preserve its health. And continuously optimize these operational tasks.

6. *Project management:* Consists of processes that assist with managing and monitoring the progress and maintenance of the project.

Next, using ASUM as an exemplar process by which to deliver big data and analytics applications and services, I will map these stages to DevOps plays that can be adopted for a DevOps adoption effort.

Analyze and Design   For any big data and analytics solution, it is essential to understand the sources, producers, and consumers of the data. As described in the big data and analytics reference architecture shown in Figure 4-21, these include multiple data types, spread across multiple sources, utilizing multiple technologies. Furthermore, the data and analytics produced may also need to be in different data types and to be delivered to multiple consumers, across multiple technologies. An *enterprise architecture* documents the IT systems (data stores, applications, infrastructure, and networks) and technologies that define these big data and analytics sources, producers, and consumers, as shown in the reference architecture earlier in this section (Figure 4-21).

Configure and Build   Let's look at the configuration and testing related processes, in context of Big Data and Analytics applications.

- *End-to-end traceability:* It is imperative that traceability exist across the software development lifecycle and the data management lifecycle. These lifecycles typically happen in parallel, but the teams have limited interactions, and the artifacts limited traceability.
- *Test early and often:* The creation of realistic, big data test datasets can add significant extra time to projects due to the volume and variety of the datasets needed to test big data and analytics applications and services. Test data management tools like IBM InfoSphere Optim

streamline the creation and management of test data sets, mask sensitive data, automate test result comparisons, and eliminate the expense and effort of maintaining multiple data clones for testing.

■ *Data and service virtualization for testing*: As organizations develop applications and services against big data stores that these applications need in order to be fully tested, this may pose a challenge where

   ■ *testing needs to be done against a data store that does not yet exist.* For example, this may involve a test against a social media application where the social interactions have not yet taken place.

   ■ *testing needs to be done against a data store that is unavailable.* For example, the data may be in an external source that is not yet available, or that is too expensive to access for testing purposes.

   ■ *testing needs to access data that cannot be accessed in its raw form.* This may involve medical or financial data that includes private information.

In such cases, in order to perform continuous testing, the test data needs to be virtualized or simulated. This can be achieved by simulating test data stores using service virtualization tools like IBM Rational Test Virtualization Server (previously Green Hat) or CA Service Virtualization (previously ITKO LISA). These tools allow for data stores to be simulated by virtual representation running on a test virtualization server. The testing is then performed against these virtual instances of the data stores, without requiring the actual data stores to be utilized or even present.

Deploy, Operate, and Optimize Deploying Big Data and Analytics applications and services, operating them, and optimizing the operations has its nuances, given the nature of these applications and services.

■ *Continuous delivery:* For big data and analytics applications, an incremental development approach is recommended. Incremental development means a staging and scheduling strategy in which the various parts of the systems are developed at different times or rates and integrated as they are completed. Adopting the practice of automated and continuous delivery enables incremental development by allowing components developed at different velocities to be deployed and tested as they become ready for deployment, as opposed to a big bang approach of deploying all components together.

■ *Data store configuration management:* Data store configuration management is becoming a challenge for organizations with dynamic data stores and analytics needs at scale. This is compounded by the proliferation of multiple types of data stores—relational databases, object stores, NoSQL databases, Hadoop DFS, graph databases, data warehouse, and data marts, to name a few. Configurations of data stores need to be managed, versioned, and governed. These configurations change with changes to the underlying data schema version and with changes to the applications accessing the data.

Data store configuration management across multiple data stores is a practice that needs to be adopted to manage the inventory of configuration settings across multiple instances of data stores and to prevent configuration "drift." While for some data store technologies these configurations are stored in separate XML files, for others they need to be programmatically accessed and managed via an API. Deployment automation tools like IBM UrbanCode Deploy have plug-ins for most popular data stores, provide a central tool that can manage and store multiple versions of these configurations, and also manage the inventory of which data store instance is at which configuration setting version, addressing these challenges.

■ *Teams and culture:* As with every set of technology-specific variants of the DevOps plays, the teaming and culture aspects are essential. In the case of big data and analytics applications and services, other than the traditional stakeholders and practitioners, there are also the big data-specific stakeholders and practitioners: data store administrators; data store developers (MapReduce, Spark, R, and so on); ETL specialists; and business intelligence (BI) specialists, to name a few. All these stakeholders and practitioners need to be included in the DevOps adoption and enabled with the processes being adopted, and their tools need to be integrated into the delivery pipeline tool-chain.

Given the rapidly evolving nature of Cloud and Cloud services, and their impact on driving innovation, the plays related to Cloud are covered in the next chapter, which is dedicated to DevOps plays for the Innovation Edge.

Summary

This is a very long chapter. If I had put in all the content I could on the topics covered in this chapter, it could be a book by itself. And that is not without reason. The practices and capabilities covered here are the core of DevOps. If you are a large organization looking to adopt DevOps across your organization, this chapter needs to be the starting point for you. Now, a quick reminder—all the plays in the chapter will not apply to you. The intent of this "playbook" is to present to you all the potential plays. You need to use the information presented in this and Chapter 3 to build your organizational playbook, selecting the plays that you need. As no large organization is monolithic or homogenous, you may need multiple variants of the playbook for various divisions, programs, and even projects. Lastly, we are not done yet. These are just the plays focused on *optimization*. Chapter 5 has plays focused on *innovation*. Chapter 6 has plays for scaling DevOps, and Chapter 7 has plays for the leadership on how to lead a DevOps transformation. All these chapters will contribute plays to your playbook.

So, let's review what I covered in this chapter. I began, and I will begin the following chapters, too, with some themes. These themes provide the core capabilities or shifts in thinking and working you want to introduce in your organization. The three themes I introduced were:

- Minimizing cycle time
- Reducing batch size
- Establishing the right culture

These three teams are interrelated. Your goal for your organization, each project in your organization, and even for each phase in your project is to reduce *Cycle Time* (or as Lean practitioners like to call it, *Lead Time)*. Reducing batch size goes hand in hand as it drives reducing cycle time. It also reduces risk and facilitates better planning and change management. And last but not the least, all this is for naught, if one does not change the culture in the organization. I will talk much more about culture in Chapter 6 and 7.

The plays I introduced all have these themes interwoven through them. They are the sets of actions and changes that need to be adopted to achieve the results these three themes promise.

- Establishing metrics and KPIs
- Agile adoption

- Integrated delivery pipeline
- Continuous integration
- Continuous delivery
- Shift left—testing
- Shift left—Ops engagement
- Continuous monitoring and feedback
- Release management

For anyone who has been engaged in adopting DevOps for some time, these terms and practices included in these plays should not be unique. I have presented them here with a focus on adopting them at enterprise scale for large, distributed organizations, with significant *Cultural Inertia*, and existing rigid processes and governance mechanisms.

Lastly, in the chapter I looked at certain technology-specific areas, presenting how various DevOps practices and capabilities may need to be *tweaked* for the needs and nuances of these technologies.

- DevOps for mobile
- DevOps for mainframe
- DevOps for Internet of Things
- DevOps for big data and analytics

In the next chapter, I will continue to add on to the list of themes and plays with themes and plays focused on driving innovation.

CHAPTER 5

DevOps Plays for Driving Innovation

FEDERER'S NEW SABR MOVE

Turns out you can teach an old dog new tricks.

This summer, tennis fans were treated to a new maneuver by the 34-year-old tennis legend Roger Federer. It's called the SABR and features Federer moving way up on an opponent's second serve to hit a half-volley in an attempt to dictate pace and frustrate opponents. Whenever anyone hears about it, the first question is: What does SABR mean?

It's an acronym:

- Sneak
- Attack
- By
- Roger

Federer used it in his dominating win in Cincinnati and utilized it during his other U.S. Open matches, with the exception of his fourth-round win over the mega-serving John Isner. The move helps him position himself after he hits a deep, chipped return and puts his opponents, like Richard Gasquet, off balance.

—Chase, 2015

The sport of cricket has evolved and innovated more than probably any other sport that exists. While other sports have evolved by changing rules or equipment, or introducing new, innovative plays like Federer's *SABR move*, none has created completely new formats for the game. Cricket in its original form was called a *test match* and is (still) played with each match lasting five days! Both teams bat for two innings each, and the game seems to go on forever. With time, however, radical innovations were brought to the game to capture an audience that did not have time or patience to watch a game for five days at a time. This resulted in the creation of the *one-day match* format, back in 1971. The entire match is over in a day, with each side batting just one inning each. The number of *overs* (a set of six balls by the same bowler) is limited to between 50 and 60 per side, thus capping how long the game can last. With the latest generation of TV-centric audiences demanding an even more exciting format, 2003 brought yet another innovation to the game: the 20-over format, called Twenty20 or the *T20*. These games are over in around three hours and can therefore be completed in an evening.

These innovations, especially the T20 format, have resulted in a massive growth of the audience in the cricket-playing world. One of the largest, most watched, and most expensive sports tournaments in the world is the *Indian Premier League* (IPL) annual T20 tournament. Its broadcast rights alone sold for an unprecedented US\$1.63 billion in 2009 for an eight-year deal (Kalavalapalli, 2016)! The market drove the need for innovation, and the market paid dividends for what resulted.

The advent of these new formats also changed how teams were formed to suit each format. Professional cricket clubs today are almost solely focused on the T20 format, although national teams do still play all three formats. The cricketing bodies of countries like England have recognized the need for different teams for each of the formats. The shorter T20 and one-day formats require younger, more aggressive players; here, fitness and agility trump everything. The longer five-day format (with test matches played less frequently nowadays) requires more experienced players with strategic knowledge and the ability to stay the course over five days; in this case, strategic and defensive skills trump everything. The shorter format is more tactical in its plays; the longer format is more strategic. In each case, players with different skills, and different *plays*, are needed to win.

Optimize to Innovate

While this chapter is dedicated to plays for innovation, the need to optimize must not be ignored. As I discuss in Chapter 4, most *innovation*-focused applications are designed to deliver innovative, new technology-driven capabilities for the organizations. Examples include the following:

- *New business services.* These are completely new services and capabilities that, up to now, were not delivered by the organization to its users—for example, a bank offering a peer-to-peer money transfer service to its clients.

- *New business models.* These are new business models for the organization to introduce monetization of services they may not have monetized up to now—for example, a trading desk of an investment bank offering a *Greek calculation* service to its partners, by exposing APIs to an internally used service.
- *New models or platforms to engage with users.* This is new technology to interact with users. A good example is digital banking, where clients can consume almost all their banking services via a mobile phone—from bill payments to check deposits to applying for a loan.
- *New markets.* This involves reaching completely new markets for the organization. One example is banks introducing a peer-to-peer money transfer service to capture new customers, such as Millennials who need banking services but do not use traditional banks.

If you were applying the need to innovate to a startup, a new company with no existing or legacy systems delivering business functions or services, then the conversation would be limited to just the innovation-focused application. However, most organizations, from large enterprises to small companies, have existing software systems that are already delivering core business services and, thus, business value to customers. In such organizations, the innovative applications are almost always dependent upon the core business services being delivered by these pre-existing, legacy systems. An innovative peer-to-peer money transfer app offered by a bank needs the existing legacy systems to deliver core services like identity management, fraud detection, anti-money laundering services, and so on. If those services are already being delivered to the rest of the banking application by these core systems, why would the bank create new services to deliver them to the new innovation-centric apps? The dependence is not negotiable. It is thus an architectural dependency in each innovative app.

These back-end systems can potentially become a drag on the innovation-centric apps' need for speed. If the innovative app requires a back-end service to make a change to fulfill its needs, then if the legacy app has a slower cycle time to deliver the change, it can slow down the innovative app's delivery time. Optimizing the delivery pipeline and capabilities to deliver changes to the back-end systems in a leaner and more efficient manner becomes a necessity in order to innovate and remove the *impedance mismatch* in the speed of delivery of the innovation-focused app and that of the legacy apps. *Optimization* becomes a prerequisite of innovation.

Another reason why the back-end systems need to optimize is resources. In most large organizations, a majority of the IT resources are being spent on *running and maintaining* systems. If all the available resources—people and money—are fully utilized with running and maintaining existing applications, none will be available to invest in innovation. *Optimizing* the back-end system to free up resources to invest in innovation becomes imperative.

The Uber Syndrome

There is a new phenomenon that is driving the need to innovate across the business world. It is known as the *Uber syndrome*. This is the urgent need for most organizations, large and small, to act against the perceived threat of a competitor coming from nowhere into their space, just like Uber, the ride-hailing app, did in the taxi industry. The founder of Uber, Travis Kalanick, is not from the taxi industry. Before he founded Uber, he started a peer-to-peer file sharing company called Red Swoosh, which he sold to Akamai in 2007 (Roettgers, 2008).

This fear of being *Ubered* is not limited to industries that seem vulnerable to disruption. A recent IBM Institute for Business Value survey found that 60 percent of global CEOs expect their next competitor will come from outside their industry (IBM Institute for Business Value, 2016), with a new, innovative business model, armed with maybe no more than a mobile app—like Uber did. This is a compelling reason to act for most organizations—from financial service to retail to the public sector. This need for innovation is based on a theme: *disrupt or be disrupted!*

This need for innovation is actually driving the need to adopt new technology platforms and processes that are designed for innovating at speed. DevOps and cloud-based Platform as a Service are certainly two examples. This need to innovate is in turn driving the realization that these organizations need to optimize their legacy application delivery capabilities. They need to do so to free up resources—people and money—that can be invested in innovation. They also need to do so to ensure that traditional slow delivery does not become a drag on their ability to innovate with speed. DevOps again is the answer.

Innovation and the Role of Technology

A common misconception in today's world, where most innovation is startup-driven, is the role of technology in driving innovation. The innovation is rarely in the technology itself. Yes, there are technology innovators like Apple, IBM,

Netflix, Salesforce.com, and, of course, Tesla, where the core of their business is new, innovative, disruptive technology. But for the vast majority of innovative companies—from pharmaceutical companies like Regeneron, to clothing companies like Under Armour, to eCommerce vendors like Alibaba, to hotels like Marriott International, to government agencies like the UK's HM Revenue and Customs—the technology is the platform on which they deliver business services to their users. The role of IT becomes not to deliver disruptive and innovative technologies but to deliver a lean, efficient, predictable, stable platform on which the disruptive and innovative business services can be delivered. If the business services require the development of innovative and disruptive technologies, then that is what IT needs to deliver. They should not deliver innovative technology for the sake of delivering innovative technology but to enable innovation for the business.

Innovating for New Business Models

WHO IS YOUR CUSTOMER?

They had built an awesome app. A game changer. An app the whole world could be a customer of. The app solved a major problem: customer service phone hold times. Almost every adult in the country has experienced being on hold on the phone for minutes, if not hours, with customer service. You call a customer service and have to go through a series of menu options to get to the right department, and then the wait begins. FastCustomer did the waiting for you. You picked the company and department you wanted to get to, in the app, and then you could go on with your life. The app called you when a human being was at the other end and connected you! (Martin, 2014)

The problem was that after the initial burst of purchases, the app stopped selling. Whenever the app was covered by a media outlet or blogger, it sold, but at other times, there were virtually no sales. They could not understand why this happened. The problem was identified, the market was identified, the app solved the problem in a simple-to-use, effective manner. What was wrong?

The answer was that they were selling to the wrong people. The end consumers of the app were users. They had wrongly identified them as customers. Customers are the people willing to pay for the problem to be

continued

continued

> solved. Individual customers did not feel the pain enough to be willing seek
> out a solution and pay for it! The real customers were the companies who
> wanted to improve their customer experience and who were willing to pay
> for a service to reduce customer hold times. FastCustomer made a change
> in their business model. They made the app free to consumers (users) and
> started selling the service to companies. These companies would pay to have
> the app's back end integrate right into their call center systems or even pay
> to have a *Call me back* button right on their website! No more hold times.
> FastCustomer had arrived.

Business Model Experimentation

Experimentation for innovation is done not just to determine which are the
right features in an application or which web page will get more clicks, but
also to discover the right business model. As in the previous examples, the
same product, with a different, innovative business model, can be the difference maker between success and failure. Let's examine how to discover new
business models.

As presented in Chapter 3, in their innovative book *Business Model
Generation,* Alexander Osterwalder and Yves Pigneur give several examples
of companies—like Nespresso, the home espresso machine vendor—who,
like the previous example, FastCustomer, had to experiment with various
business models to get to one that worked for them. The model would have to
allow them to take their product to market in a manner that provided the best
business value for the customers and thus allowed the company to establish
themselves in the market and become a successful business. They did not
change their product. They experimented with various business models to
find one that was the right product-market fit.

The business model of how the book was written is also innovative. The
authors, instead of interviewing dozens of business leaders from around the
world to develop, refine, and validate their ideas and propositions, set up a
community on Ning.com, a community building site, and started collecting
a fee for people to join the book as co-creators. They kept raising the price
till it went from 24 to 243 dollars. At this point, they had 470 people from
45 countries who were willing to contribute to the book, by reviewing and

rewriting content, contributing case studies, and helping design the heavily illustrated book. The result was a best-seller that has become a must-read for startups and innovators around the world, and a completely new book-writing model (Wilson, 2010).

From the IT perspective, when people think of innovation, they think of an app with cool, new features, one that, with its sophisticated technology and fine-tuned user experience design, disrupts the industry it targets. However, more innovation happens through the disruption of the business model, not the technology. For example, although Uber has a really good, easy-to-use mobile app, it did not succeed because of the features or ease of use of its app. Having an easy-to-use app is the fee of admission into the mobile app world. Where Uber innovated was in its business model, and to get there, Kalanick and his team had to experiment with various business models (and they still are). They started by providing a ride-hailing app that found idle limos that could be hired at a much lower cost, between their scheduled rides. This still exists within Uber as *UberBLACK*. The core business, though, evolved through experimentation to become Uber as you know it today: non-professional drivers providing rides for a fee in their personal cars.

Here, the role of IT becomes that of the platform with which experimentation with the business model can occur. Several business models can be introduced and rolled back, as needed. Rapid feedback can be gathered and analyzed to assess the results of each experiment to decide whether to roll forward or roll back. This feedback can be used to see which model works with what user profile and which does not. The innovation is not the technology itself. When a customer who has hailed a taxi is standing at a street corner, on a rainy night, waiting for their ride, they are not concerned with what technology is used. They don't care which mapping API is displaying the location of their ride on the map or whether some of the services on the mobile back-end are *containerized*. The goal of IT becomes that of a *service provider* of a lean, efficient platform on which business models can be delivered and rapidly changed for experimentation.

Innovating for New User Engagement Models

Another common path of innovation is to explore new user engagement models. These new models may be to deliver new business capabilities to existing customers or to capture new markets for existing capabilities. Experimentation again plays a key role here to discover new engagement models.

Consider another real-world example. McDonald's, the fast food franchising company, was trying a new approach to engage with its customers, by expanding to selling groceries (The Movie Network, 2014). They developed a fully automated convenience store, directly in the path of consumers who were heading home from work. The automated store, shown in Figure 5-1, had vending machines selling everything a convenience store sells: from fresh food to milk to snacks to DVDs. The stores were even made to be portable; this allowed them to easily move the stores and experiment with locations. Unfortunately, the experiment was a failure. Apparently, not everything can be sold through an automated vending machine—not milk or fresh foods, for sure.

Instead of abandoning the entire concept, the executives looked at what worked. DVD sales and rentals were working. No one hesitated to rent a DVD from a vending machine. Who needed a human to check out a DVD? The company decided to get rid of all the other automated vending machines and just keep the DVD vending machine. Thus Redbox, the DVD, Blu-ray, and video game rental kiosk company, was born!

Figure 5-1: Redbox grocery kiosk in Washington, DC, 2002 (Imgur, 2013)

In this example, the actual business model, at its core, remained unchanged—providing a self-serve kiosk to sell products to customers. What did change was the technology platform on which the business services were being delivered. It was enhanced with experimentation, changing how the customers engaged with it, and was reduced from a full-scale kiosk delivering groceries for sale to a smaller kiosk delivering just DVDs. That platform has since been enhanced to also include Blu-ray and video game discs. The platform delivery team needed to be agile and to be able to transform (in this case, significantly reduce) the platform in order to follow the direction the business was taking and how it engaged with its clients to deliver business services to them.

The IT team was responsible for the technology behind the platform, ensuring it was agile and resilient to change. It was also responsible for ensuring that there was detailed instrumentation embedded into the platform to provide *continuous feedback* to the business. That was how the business saw that while overall their kiosks were not succeeding, the DVD rental part of the business was making money. They therefore chose to scuttle all but the DVD rental part of the kiosk and focused on the narrow, but more successful, experiment that worked.

In reality, as in the case of the original Redbox kiosk, the instrumentation required to see which experiment is succeeding may be as trivial as being able to measure which products are bringing in revenue and which are not. In more complex scenarios where an app may be running multiple experiments, a significant amount of instrumentation may be required to gather data for the various experiments, followed by potentially intensive analysis of the data to assess the result of every experiment individually, to provide the right feedback to the business. I will discuss this in more detail in the next section when I discuss the need to run experiments.

INNOVATION AND THE SPORTS CUSTOMER EXPERIENCE

Customer eXperience, or CX, is among the hottest issues facing CMOs and all marketers today. The need to provide the most optimal CX at all times is essential for success.

It is no different when it comes to professional sports. Long gone are the days when the experience with fans was based entirely on what transpired on the field. Today, the need is inherent for sports teams, as it is for any

continued

continued

business, to put the customer front and center and deliver the best experience possible.

Over the past year or so ... two NFL teams are upping their CX game. The Indianapolis Colts utilize a mobile app to keep the in-game experience engaging. And the Philadelphia Eagles partnered with Panasonic to provide its fans with the highest resolution display end zone video boards in the entire NFL along with a series of highly interactive HD boards around the stadium.

—Olenski, 2015

Core Themes

Just as I look at some core themes that weave through the various plays in Chapter 4, I will now introduce some core themes that form the basis of multiple innovation-centric plays. These are as follows:

- Achieving Multi-Speed IT
- Building the *right* thing
- Enabling experimentation
- Delivering *Antifragile* systems

Achieving Multi-Speed IT

MULTI-SPORT ATHLETES

Football players who participated in additional sports while in high school dominated the first round of the 2016 NFL Draft on Thursday night.

Twenty-eight of the 31 players selected were multi-sport athletes in their prep days, including No. 1 overall pick Jared Goff, who played both baseball and basketball at Marin Catholic High School in Greenbrae, Calif.

Goff is one of 12 former three-sport athletes. He's joined by the likes of fellow quarterback Carson Wentz (baseball, basketball), receiver Corey Coleman (basketball, track), and lineman Jack Conklin (basketball, track).

—Spiewak, 2016

Without stepping into the debate over whether or not young athletes should play multiple sports to develop multi-disciplinary skills, in the IT world, the ability to support multiple delivery pipelines, with varying cycle times and delivery velocities, resulting in *Multi-Speed IT*, is not an option—it is a reality. As I discuss in Chapter 4, the real world requires DevOps to be adopted across multiple delivery pipelines to support the various speeds and technology platforms that different delivery teams may adopt. Because most business systems require services from multiple applications, coordination across these delivery pipelines is essential. Identifying and understanding the *architectural dependencies* between the various services delivered by different delivery pipelines is essential to ensure that the delivery and release of each application is coordinated with that of other services and applications the application is dependent upon, or which are dependent upon it. In addition, ensuring *traceability* across these delivery pipelines is essential to effectively capture and analyze the status of each delivery pipeline and proactively identify the impact of any issues, delays, or changes in delivery and release plans of any application or service.

As I also introduced in Chapter 4 and shown here in Figure 5-2, there are five specific areas where these multi-speed delivery pipelines need integration and the accompanying standardization of tooling across all the delivery pipelines. Having a set of standardized or integrated tools, across the delivery pipelines, ensures proper planning, architectural design, traceability, and status reporting across multiple, *multi-speed* delivery pipelines. Let's look at these five *touchpoints* in detail.

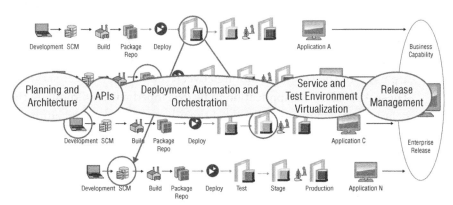

Figure 5-2: Multi-Speed IT touchpoints

1. *Planning and Architecture.* The delivery and release plans for these applications should not exist independently. You need to document

and understand the architectural dependencies between the various applications. Only when these dependencies are identified will you be able to assess properly which application and service are dependent upon which one. Once you know these dependencies, you can properly plan for the development, delivery, and release of each application and service, in coordination with the plans of others that it is dependent upon and those that are dependent on it. It is of no use for a particular application to utilize all the resources available in order to be released by a particular date, only to discover that a service it is dependent upon will not be available for several more weeks. Those resources could have been better utilized elsewhere, and more time could have been given to releasing the application. Once plans are made, it is essential that a standardized tool set be used to manage the project tasks and work-items. All the practitioners, across all delivery pipelines, should have access and visibility to the delivery plans, work-items assigned to their team, and the project backlogs. The level of visibility that practitioners need to have across projects should be determined by the dependencies between their projects and others.

2. *APIs.* The development and release cycle of various applications is dependent upon that of other applications because of the architectural dependencies one application has on another. To make things more complex, these architectural dependencies may even be version-dependent. That is, a particular version of one application can only communicate with certain versions of another application. The point-to-point integration between the applications changes with every new version of each application. The architectural dependency can be reduced by de-coupling the applications. This is achieved by introducing well-defined APIs that are used for the communication between the applications or services. These APIs allow an application to be developed without knowing the detailed implementation details of the other application and eliminating point-to-point integrations that change with each new version of the application. The APIs typically do not change much over time, allowing the architectural interfaces between the applications to remain unchanged. Designing and implementing good APIs is the topic of a play that I discuss later in this chapter.

3. *Deployment automation and orchestration.* I discuss *deployment automation* in detail in Chapter 4. This is an area that needs to be standardized across all delivery pipelines. The ability to deploy any application to the

right environment, as and when needed, is essential. When different delivery pipelines have different deployment tools, this creates complexities when deployments need to be coordinated across delivery pipelines. Standardizing deployment processes and tools allows for a single deployment process to be created to deploy all the components, applications, and services across multiple delivery pipelines and environments, if needed. The same holds true for provisioning and orchestrating environments. Having a single platform to provision and orchestrate allows for simplification of the provisioning and orchestration processes and allows multiple environments to be provisioned as needed.

Now, it is not always practical to standardize on just a single technology or tool for deployment automation or for environment provisioning and orchestration. However, the goal should be to minimize the number of tools. Having just one or at the most two standardized tools for each technology stack is a good goal to strive for.

4. *Virtualization of services and environments for testing.* As various applications and services become ready for testing, other applications and services they are dependent upon may not be ready, as they are likely to have different cycle times and release plans. Availability cannot always be coordinated. In addition, test environments and test data may not be available as and when needed by each application or service. Virtualizing services, applications, environments, and data sources addresses this problem, allowing each application and service to be tested, independent of other applications and services. I discuss these solutions in detail in Chapter 4.

5. *Release management.* The release of a business system, comprised of multiple applications and services and delivered via multiple delivery pipelines, needs to be a coordinated effort of executing the delivery and releasing plans across all the involved delivery pipelines. Traditionally, organizations have relied on massive spreadsheets with data on each component that is being developed and delivered, the dependencies between them, and their status in their respective delivery pipelines. This involves tracking and managing the applications and services as they progress through the various quality gates that need to be validated before release to production. They need to track and manage all the integration points and their testing, across all the dependent applications and services. It is essential to leverage a standardized tool that tracks and manages the release of each application and service, across

all delivery pipelines and technology stacks. An added benefit would be if this tool could extract status information for each delivery pipeline automatically from the project and work-item management and also extract the status information for deployment automation tools being utilized by each delivery pipeline.

Enabling the capability to support Multi-Speed IT is essential to foster innovation. When delivering new innovation, you need speed. You need to be able to deliver products as and when needed and to be able to run multiple experiments (as I will discuss next). You need to be unencumbered by the dependencies of other delivery pipelines. You cannot be restricted by the speed of the slowest delivery pipeline.

Building the Right Thing

OVERTRAINING SYNDROME

It is no secret among athletes that in order to improve performance you've got to work hard. However, hard training breaks you down and makes you weaker. It is rest that makes you stronger. Physiologic improvement in sports occurs only during the rest period following hard training. This adaptation is in response to maximal loading of the cardiovascular and muscular systems and is accomplished by improving efficiency of the heart, increasing capillaries in the muscles, and increasing glycogen stores and mitochondrial enzyme systems within the muscle cells. During recovery periods these systems build to greater levels to compensate for the stress that you have applied. The result is that you are now at a higher level of performance.

If sufficient rest is not included in a training program, then regeneration cannot occur and performance plateaus. If this imbalance between excess training and inadequate rest persists, then performance will decline. Overtraining can best be defined as the state where the athlete has been repeatedly stressed by training to the point where rest is no longer adequate to allow for recovery. The "overtraining syndrome" is the name given to the collection of emotional, behavioral, and physical symptoms due to overtraining that has persisted for weeks to months. Athletes and coaches also know it as "burnout" or "staleness." This is different from the day-to-day variation in performance and post exercise tiredness that is common in conditioned athletes. Overtraining is marked by cumulative exhaustion that persists even after recovery periods.

The most common symptom is fatigue. This may limit workouts and may be present at rest. The athlete may also become moody, easily irritated, have altered sleep patterns, become depressed, or lose the competitive desire and enthusiasm for the sport. Some will report decreased appetite and weight loss. Physical symptoms include persistent muscular soreness, increased frequency of viral illnesses, and increased incidence of injuries.

—Jenkins, 1998

While overtraining may cause athletes to become "moody, easily irritated, have altered sleep patterns, and become depressed," one thing that certainly causes any IT professional, especially developers, to have the same emotional experience is to passionately work on a project, putting in hours of work and sweat equity to deliver the project, only to discover that they have built the wrong thing. Whether it be a full project or just a module of code, it is a complete waste of resources and individual contributions of time, energy, and problem solving to deliver something, only to have it never be used because it was solving the wrong problem. Entire companies have gone under because they invested their future, or in some cases even their very existence, in a product that the market did not want or accept. Think of any dotcom startup failure—from Pets.com, to eToys.com, to Webvan.com. The large corporation IT space is full of such projects that never saw the light of day or were shelved soon after they were launched due to a lack of customer interest and traction. In most cases, this mismatch between the product capabilities and customer expectations was not discovered till the product was fully developed and delivered, only to be shunned by users.

Lean Startup

The *Lean startup* movement, launched by Eric Ries (Ries, 2011) in his seminal book by the same name, presents an alternate approach to delivering products (IT or otherwise). In his approach, the goal is not to build a full product but to ensure that you are building the right product by *continuously validating* the product's vision with users. This validation is done by developing a cycle that allows you to keep ensuring that you are building the *right* thing as you deliver small steps of new capability (think *small batches*) and rapidly get feedback on what you just built from actual users (think *minimized cycle time*). As you can see, these principles are completely in alignment with the DevOps principles I introduce in Chapter 4.

The four core pillars of the Lean startup are as follows:

1. *Eliminate uncertainty.* Have a well-defined methodology around delivering a product. The goal is not to put in heroic efforts to get a product out the door, no matter what, but to do so in a well-organized, disciplined manner. Once again, this is in line with the DevOps plays presented in this book.
2. *Work smarter, not harder.* The most important question to ask is not "Can this product be built?" but "Should this product be built?" Engaging users and potential customers early to validate the premise of the product, before even a line of code is written, and working with them through the development lifecycle is the only way to ensure that the right product is being delivered.
3. *Develop an MVP.* A *minimum viable product* (MVP), or in some cases *minimum viable feature*, is the bare minimum capability you can take to a user to see if it fulfills their needs and delivers business value. An MVP is the pathway to *learning* with the least possible investment made.
4. *Validated learning.* The unit of progress in the Lean startup method is *validated learning.* When teams spend their time continuously figuring out whether they are building the *right* thing for their users, it ensures that they are able to change paths—what the Lean startup movement calls *pivot*—as soon as they discover that they have deviated from the user's needs.

THE MINIMUM VIABLE PRODUCT

[A] minimum viable product in the world of apps is the absolute bare minimum set of features and functionality that you need to develop in order to meet the need of your customers and test your idea in market. In less technical terms, putting together an MVP is sort of like building a sports team. Your minimum viable product is like your set of star players—your incredibly talented quarterback (or your playmaking number ten, if soccer is more your thing). With that player signed to a contract (or equivalently that killer app feature developed), then you can start to think about the rest of the roster/ other app extras that will help improve your likelihood of success over time.

—Blue Label Labs, 2016

The *Lean startup movement*—and it has become a movement—has become the approach, not just to use to deliver new products in the startup world but also to deliver quality IT systems in the enterprise IT world. Whether the end-user is a Millennial looking for the next "change-the-world-of-networking" app, an employee looking to better understand his employer-provided health benefits, or a sales rep looking for the right product for his longtime, loyal customer, the Lean startup approach can ensure that there is no over-production of features and capabilities that no one uses. It ensures that the delivery teams build the *right* things.

Design Thinking

Design as a professional discipline has undergone a tremendous evolution in the last generation from a practice focused mainly on aesthetic style to one with a clear and explicit focus on the "user" (aka: person or group of people who use a product or service) and their hopes, desires, challenges, and needs.

By establishing empathy with the user, designers are able to work toward outcomes that meet those needs more successfully.

This user-centered approach known as "design thinking" enables designers and others to address a wide range of complex business and social issues.

—IBM Design, 2016

The three principles that are the pillars of *design thinking* are presented here. These principles exist to ensure that you are building the *right thing*.

1. *A Focus on User Outcomes: Our users rely on our solutions to get their jobs done everyday. Success isn't measured by the features and functions we ship—it's measured by how well we fulfill our users' needs.*
2. *Diverse Empowered Teams: Diverse teams generate more ideas than homogeneous ones, increasing your chance of a breakthrough. Empower them with the expertise and authority to turn those ideas into outcomes.*
3. *Restless Reinvention: Everything is a prototype. Everything—even in-market solutions. When you think of everything as just another iteration, you're empowered to bring new thinking to even the oldest problems.*

—IBM Design, 2016

Organizations like IBM have incorporated both Lean startup and design thinking principles into their product offering management processes. They have further operationalized the development and delivery of the *right* thing by adopting DevOps practices. The result: they build the *right* thing, *correctly*.

Enabling Experimentation

EXPERIMENTATION IN COACHING

Many coaches develop their skills and expertise through their experiences and by watching other coaches. However, simply acquiring experiences does not guarantee coaching competence. It is the integration of experience and knowledge in a meaningful way that promotes learning and in turn develops expertise. Coaches need to know how to best learn through their experiences. Reflective practice is a major learning tool in this regard....

Once coaches are armed with a few solutions, they then need to explore the likely consequences of each and select the most appropriate response. In some cases this experimentation may be hypothetical. They may present their ideas to their peer coaches for feedback. Hypothetical experimentation can be a practical way to reflect after a season is over and coaches are preparing for a new season. Real-world experimentation occurs in the sport domain where coaches can carry out their envisioned solution and review its impact.

It is important to note that experimentation within reflective practice is different than trial-and-error practice. Trial and error simply involves doing something and when it fails, doing something else until something works. The approach is random and unpredictable in comparison to reflective experimentation. In reflective experimentation, the idea is to build upon existing knowledge by drawing from experiences and learning to make educated selections based on the relevant information. This approach is more predictable and thoughtful and promotes a more effective learning environment for athletes.

—Farres, 2004

Coaches need to prepare for the next game by experimenting with new plays to address the challenges of playing against a particular team or to address deficiencies in plays observed in the last game or practice. Similarly, an organization driving innovation needs to be able to experiment with new ideas, new features, new user experiences, new user interfaces, new business models, and new technologies. As I will present in the first play I discuss in this chapter, there are two concepts in driving innovation, made popular by the Lean startup movement:

- Minimum viable product
- Fail fast

The goal of experimentation is to prevent the development of fully functional products to see if they are the right product and instead to experiment with an MVP and fail fast with it so you can eventually get to the right product that succeeds.

This approach of delivering minimum viable products and *failing* them *fast* is all designed for rapid experimentation. The speed of innovation is driven by the speed with which you can run multiple experiments and rapidly fail with those that should fail in order to discover the ones that succeed.

A/B Testing

A/B testing is a common technique used to enable this rapid experimentation by running tests of multiple variants of a feature in parallel. The goal of A/B testing is to present two versions of a web page, feature, or app randomly to users to see which works better or is more productive. The process requires instrumentation built into the app to ensure you can measure various details of how the users interacted with the two versions and compare them. Such testing allows developers and business teams to make decisions on which versions of features to keep and continue developing and which to drop.

Here are some core practices for implementing A/B testing to get maximum results and implement fail fast for the features whose versions are being tested:

- *Define measures of success.* What metrics and measures will determine which version has succeeded? Items sold, registrations made, number of clicks, time spent, items browsed, exits away from page (bounce rate), shopping carts abandoned—measures of success or failure should be determines beforehand, and instrumentation put in place to measure them.
- *Simultaneous testing.* For A/B testing to work, both versions need to be presented to an equal number of unique users for the same period of time.

- *Consistent versions across the app.* The same version of the feature should show up across the app, and not just be limited to a few areas, for the approach to work and produce consistent results.
- *Monitoring over time.* Statistically significant data sets need to be collected to ensure proper analysis of the test results from both versions. The tests should therefore be run for a long enough time to get enough users to use the feature. This also allows you to capture trends and eliminate the impact of outliers.
- *Multiple A/B tests.* The idea is to continuously produce small changes (small batches) and rapidly do A/B testing to determine which sets of changes work. This allows for failing fast with minimal waste.

To be able to run A/B tests, you require certain key capabilities in the delivery platform and the production environments:

- The ability to deploy the two versions of the apps to two sets of servers to allow half of the users coming in to be routed to each of the two versions. This requires deployments to be targeted to sets of servers. An all-or-nothing deployment model, which deploys an app to all the servers, will not work.
- Routing capability to randomly route users to each set of servers with an equal number of users going to each set.
- The ability to roll deployments forward to replace the version that failed with the version that succeeded.

Rapid experimentation therefore needs a technology platform—an application delivery pipeline—that is designed to enable experimentation. It must be able to deliver new capabilities and features fast to targeted sets of servers, to be able to monitor application and user behavior, and to be able to capture the right test data and analyze it to fail fast.

Delivering Antifragile Systems

BUILDING THE ANTIFRAGILE ATHLETE

I just came back from the Seattle Sounders 2014 Sports Science Weekend on Building the Anti-Fragile Athlete. . . . The first [session], by Sounders Performance Manager Dave Tenney, presented a general overview of where the concept of Building an Anti-Fragile athlete came from (too many games lost to injury), what lessons we can learn from the most anti-fragile industries (airlines and nuclear power), and if we can in fact take a fragile athlete and change him into one that is injury resistant (it appears so).

In the field, the Sounders [are] recognized for being at the forefront of obtaining and analyzing sport and performance data on recovery, nervous system readiness, relationships between injuries and compliance with certain initiatives, sleep, distances travelled by athletes, and the types of loads the athletes' experience. Two metrics jumped out at me.

One was that they are able to measure what is termed "velocity load" vs. "body load." This is where the technology available is again astounding me. Not only are they using GPS to measure the distance that each athlete is covering during games and practices, but they are also measuring the *nature* of those distances. "Velocity load" represents linear movement (sprinting downfield, for example), is extensor dominant, and is more common during a regular game situation. Body loads represent changes in direction. They tend to underload the posterior chain and occur with greater frequency during small-sided games. Once they have this data, they can analyze it to gain insight into the musculoskeletal stresses on individual athletes.

Another interesting metric was sleep data. They use monitors to track what time their athletes go to bed each night, when they get up, and how much tossing and turning they do. Dave noted that the most consistently high performers in their club are the ones that sleep the best, not only in terms of number of hours and regularity but in quality as well. The average times two of their best athletes went to bed? 9:44 and 10:15 pm.

—Cavin, 2014

The greatest challenge to an athlete is injury. However, athletes cannot avoid injury. Being exposed to situations that can cause an injury is a part of what an athlete does. And I don't just mean a contact sport like American football or high-risk sports like the vault in gymnastics, which are by their very nature high-velocity impact sports, but also seemingly "safe" sports like golf or tennis where injury can come from athletes over-extending or over-stressing their muscles. Athletes can be impacted by an injury anywhere, from missing a few minutes of a game to a career-ending injury, to even permanent disability or death. A tremendous amount of research has been done to help athletes train and condition to make them thrive in these high-stress environments, to make them resilient, to make them recover faster and be even stronger, to make their bodies Antifragile. This also applies to IT systems, especially IT systems designed for continuous change, for continuous experimentation, that need to be able to thrive in chaos, in stressful conditions where servers go down, and new ones come online all the time—to be Antifragile.

The term *Antifragile* was coined by Nassim Nicholas Taleb, an options trader who has written a series of books on randomness, on probability and their impacts on the markets, and on life. He introduced the term for the first time in his book *The Black Swan* (Taleb, 2007), where he discusses rare events, which he contends are not as random and rare as people think—like stock market crashes. He then wrote a book named *Antifragile* (Taleb, 2012), where he expanded on the concept of *antifragility* to describe things that are neither fragile nor robust, but that, in fact, benefit from chaos.

If you are reading this book in a printed format, it is a robust artifact. You can drop it, and it will not break. On the other hand, if you are reading this on an e-reader or tablet, the device is fragile by nature. Dropping it on a hard surface is very likely to damage it. These are both examples of systems you are very familiar with. Taleb challenges us to think of Antifragile systems—those that are neither fragile nor robust but are such that they become stronger when put in stressful situations. All living, and really most organic, systems are Antifragile in nature. An example Taleb gives is that of a bone. When broken, if allowed to heal properly, the resulting healed spot on the bone is actually denser and thus stronger than the undamaged bone was. Vaccines inherently work on leveraging the antifragility of animal immune systems. A human or animal injected with a small quantity of a germ produces antibodies that can protect it from an actual infection of the germ.

The human brain is the ultimate example of an Antifragile system. As you read this book—in print or on your tablet—if you happen to find parts of the book interesting enough to commit to memory, a stress situation of trying to forget them actually makes the memory imprinted in your neurons stronger. You can't ever consciously try to forget something; it only makes you remember more—ask any heartbroken teenager. Let's try an experiment: if I ask you to *not* think of a "dancing monkey eating a banana" as you read the rest of this book, I have created a stress situation for you by asking you to *not* think of something, which is an impossibility. As you continue to read this book, your Antifragile brain neurons are going to randomly show you an image of a monkey doing the *whip nae nae* while devouring a banana. You have no way to prevent it from happening. You can thank me later…

To summarize:

- *Fragile* things break or get damaged under stress.
- *Robust* things are unaffected by stress; they grow neither stronger nor weaker.
- *Antifragile* systems become stronger under stress conditions.

IT Systems and Antifragility

Ops teams have traditionally always been striving to make their systems robust. They want systems that don't go down. They want systems that are unaffected by any stress situations they may encounter. They want systems that are predictable in their behavior so that they can mitigate every stress situation if it happens, which may cause systems to go down or even just degrade in performance. In order to make a truly robust system, you need to be able to predict and build into the system and to mitigate each and every source of failure in the system. In today's world of multiple unknowns, this is literally impossible. Systems today are not static. They are dynamic with servers being provisioned and de-provisioned in real time. They are leveraging multiple services from multiple providers, several of which may be owned by other supplier teams, including third-party suppliers outside their organization. The sheer number of potential failure points makes it impossible to predict failures and make mitigation plans for them. Add to this the additional stresses of the change caused by continuous delivery of new versions of applications and services being delivered by development teams that are constantly creating new innovations, and the failure points increase exponentially. To truly architect systems to enable DevOps, especially DevOps for applications focused on innovation and thus experimentation, you must avoid this approach, which is destined for failure.

The alternative approach is to use Antifragile systems. These systems assume that failures will happen. Servers will go down. Discs will fail. Networks will deliver traffic with high latency. Network switches will fail. Third-party network connectivity providers will go offline. Memory allocated will not be sufficient. Data sets will exceed the capacity of the queues handling them. Entire sources of data streams will go down or deliver the streams too slowly. Third-party services will not conform to the service level agreements (SLAs) of the providers and suppliers. Applications being delivered will have defects. Too many users will want to access a hot, new application feature. Middleware configurations will be incorrectly set up or not fine-tuned for the app in question. Hackers will try to compromise services. Bots will overload the app with useless traffic. An app completely separate from yours will cause a service you need to go down. An app in another system will crash, creating a domino effect in the systems, which will impact your app. Humans will intentionally cause disruption. Humans will insert malicious backdoors in services. Humans will insert benign *Easter eggs* in their code. Humans will make errors.

You need to build systems that thrive in this chaos. These systems must be built to handle situations where you assume beforehand that something will go down and the system will need to stay up anyway, by finding an alternate way to get the services it needs to stay up. Here are some key characteristics of such an Antifragile system:

- *Fail fast.* In line with the principle of fail fast, Antifragile systems need to be built to handle any failure—fast. One popular approach is to build systems that never fix a server instance that has a fault or is not functioning or performing as desired. You just kill that server instance and replace it with a new instance, and you do so without allowing the rest of the system to be impacted.

  The goal is to have systems that never go down, even for maintenance or upgrades. Facebook never shows a message stating it will be "down for maintenance this Sunday night from 2 a.m. to 4 a.m."; the next time you log in, you just get the upgraded version of the site. I will discuss techniques like *blue-green deployments* later in this chapter.

- *Fail often.* How do you prepare to handle failure and to handle it fast? You fail often.

CHAOS MONKEY AND NETFLIX SIMIAN ARMY

Imagine getting a flat tire. Even if you have a spare tire in your trunk, do you know if it is inflated? Do you have the tools to change it? And, most importantly, do you remember how to do it right? One way to make sure you can deal with a flat tire on the freeway, in the rain, in the middle of the night is to poke a hole in your tire once a week in your driveway on a Sunday afternoon and go through the drill of replacing it. This is expensive and time-consuming in the real world but can be (almost) free and automated in the cloud.

This was our philosophy when we built Chaos Monkey (Figure 5-3), a tool that randomly disables our production instances to make sure we can survive this common type of failure without any customer impact. The

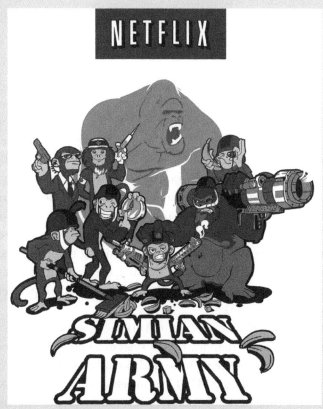

Figure 5-3: Netflix Simian Army (image source: github .com/Netflix)

continued

continued

name comes from the idea of unleashing a wild monkey with a weapon in your data center (or cloud region) to randomly shoot down instances and chew through cables—all the while we continue serving our customers without interruption. By running Chaos Monkey in the middle of a business day, in a carefully monitored environment with engineers standing by to address any problems, we can still learn the lessons about the weaknesses of our system and build automatic recovery mechanisms to deal with them. So next time an instance fails at 3 am on a Sunday, we won't even notice.

Inspired by the success of the Chaos Monkey, we've started creating new simians that induce various kinds of failures, or detect abnormal conditions, and test our ability to survive them; a virtual Simian Army to keep our cloud safe, secure, and highly available.

—Tseitlin, 2011

Antifragile systems need to be able to address failures continuously. Unfortunately, while all IT Ops organizations have plans and protocols to handle incidents, they are rarely tested. A sports team has to practice continuously, through pre-season and the season, to perfect the plays they want to run. This may be a standard set of plays they run all the time, or a game-changing play they want to run as a surprise tactic to win a critical game. The New Orleans Saints football team won Super Bowl XLIV in 2010 by running a surprise "on-side" kick against the Indianapolis Colts. However, they succeeded in the play not because they caught the opposing team off-guard with an ambush (which they did) but because they practiced it several times and only added it to their playbook after it worked perfectly in practice (Triplett, 2014).

■ *MTBF to MTTR.* The success of Antifragile systems needs to be measured differently than for robust systems, and so it requires different metrics. Robust systems have traditionally used a metric called *mean time between failures* (MTBF) to measure their stability. MTBF measures the time period between failures or incidents. An Antifragile IT system should not focus on MTBF. The goal is to fail fast and fail often, making that metric counter-productive. Antifragile systems assume that failures will happen and that there is no way to avoid them. As a result, an Antifragile system focuses its architecture and operational models on *mean time to resolve* (MTTR). How quickly can a failure be repaired and a service that has gone down be brought up? How can it minimize MTTR and also minimize the impact of a service being down on other services and the overall system? How can it go to an operational state where, although servers may go "red," services are always "green"?

■ *Cattle not pets. Fragility* in systems actually comes from a desire to make them too robust. System administrators who maintain individual servers to keep them always up take steps to provide all the care and feeding the servers need to handle any issue or stress situation they may face and manually handle the situation when it does occur. The servers are inherently unique, so they treat them like *pets.* This would be fine in a world of physical servers with static instances running on them. However, in today's dynamic world, this is not scalable. Automation is needed both to manage the servers at scale and to monitor them and mitigate challenges in real time. They need to be treated like *cattle.* Cattle do not have names. For all intents and purposes, they are inherently identical to each other. They are *tagged* using a scalable naming convention (CattleTags.com, 2016). They are culled if they get sick. They are fed in bulk. They are managed and maintained in bulk. And they have a finite, pre-determined lifespan, which ends with them being steak or hamburger or sausage.[1] In a similar manner, server instances need to be named using a scalable naming convention, not individual names. They need to be identical to each other. They need to be monitored and managed in bulk. They need to be killed and replaced with new instances when they have issues. And, they need to have a predetermined, finite lifecycle that manages how they are provisioned and de-provisioned (McCance, 2012, Bias, 2012). Sorry, no more cows named "Daisy" live on the cattle ranch. (If they do, they are the rancher's pet.) Similarly, no more servers named *midnight.rational .com* should live in your datacenter.

I will discuss leveraging cloud technologies to architect and deliver Antifragile systems later in this chapter.

Next, I will discuss some of the plays dedicated to driving adoption of DevOps for the business intent of driving innovation: DevOps for applications and services focused on the *innovation edge.*

---

[1] My apologies to vegetarians and vegans for this analogy. Sports analogies really did not work here. I tried.

Play: Build a DevOps Platform

AMERICA'S SCHOOLS: A PLATFORM FOR OVER 1,000 OLYMPIANS

For many NCAA student-athletes, dreams of Olympic medals are just within their reach.

There are 1,018 incoming, current, and former NCAA student-athletes set to compete in the 2016 Summer Olympics in Brazil, representing 107 countries and 223 NCAA member institutions across all three divisions.

Of the 1,018 athletes competing, 168 are current student-athletes competing in 15 sports, with swimming and athletics as the most represented events with 64 and 42 athletes, respectively.

California will send 13 *current* student-athletes to the summer games, the most by any university. The Bears also rank second amongst all NCAA programs with a combined 40 athletes competing in the summer games. Southern California edges out its fellow Pac-12 member with an impressive 42 athletes that will represent the Trojans in Rio. Stanford rounds out the top three with 39 athletes.

—Martinez, 2016

The key points in this article are as follows:

- 1,018 athletes were current and former students.
- They were representing 107 countries (a total of 206 countries competed in the 2016 Rio Olympics).
- They were from 223 American colleges and universities.

The colleges and universities in the United States have thus developed a platform for sports and athletics that is truly world class. It is a platform that is broad enough to support almost every Olympic sport (and more—think American football, which is not an Olympic sport, and the Winter Olympics sports, which are not included in this count). It is also a platform that has attracted, through scholarships and world-class training facilities, the world's best emerging athletes (Farrell, 2008). It is a truly agile, resilient, scalable, reliable platform.

What would delivering such an agile, resilient, scalable, reliable DevOps platform entail? In Chapter 4, I present multiple approaches to building an application delivery pipeline. These include both a technology-agnostic point of view and approaches that are technology specific. Let's merge those ideas of building an integrated delivery pipeline with the need for Antifragile systems that I presented earlier in this chapter. Because the focus of this chapter is on DevOps plays for innovation, the need for a DevOps platform that supports the themes I presented earlier (and which are repeated here for ease of consumption) is the priority:

- Achieving Multi-Speed IT
- Building the *right* thing
- Enabling experimentation
- Delivering Antifragile systems

While such a platform can be delivered on any underlying infrastructure, leveraging cloud technology to deliver it is imperative. Only a cloud platform can provide the agility, flexibility, resilience, scale, and speed needed to deliver on the requirements of these themes.

Chapter 4 contains the following list of capabilities that go into a delivery pipeline tool stack:

- Source code management
- Build
- Continuous integration
- Deployment automation
- Middleware configuration
- Environment configuration
- Environment provisioning

To better understand how all of these capabilities fit together to set up a delivery pipeline, let's revisit the figure of an application delivery pipeline from Chapter 4 (Figure 5-4).

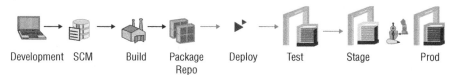

Development   SCM   Build   Package   Deploy   Test   Stage   Prod
                            Repo

Figure 5-4: Integrated delivery pipeline

As you can see in the figure, there are application development, testing, and delivery tools, and there are environments (Dev, test, stage, and production, for example) to which the application is *continuously delivered*. When building a DevOps platform, where the application development, testing, and delivery tools are installed is not the critical decision. They can be installed on-premises on traditional hardware, or they can be installed in the cloud platform; it does not make a significant difference to the capability of the platform. It certainly makes a difference to the performance of the tools, but not their functionality. There is the alternative scenario, where these tools are not installed and managed by the organization at all, but are consumed as a *Software as a Service* (SaaS) offering, delivered as managed, hosted tools, by a tool vendor. Most popular DevOps application delivery tools, like Git, Jenkins, IBM Rational Team Concert, IBM UrbanCode Deploy, and so on, are all available as SaaS offerings, with pay-as-you-go subscription models.

The critical decision for the DevOps platform is the target deployment environments—Dev, various test environments, various staging environments, and production. When I speak of delivering Antifragile environments, these are the environments that need to be Antifragile, especially production.

Application Delivery and Antifragile Systems

One of the core requirements of Antifragile environments is the elimination of downtime for standard planned operations like maintenance and application deployments. The environment services and the applications running on the environments should also not go down, outside of outages due to incidents.

Building such *high-availability* environments requires several capabilities:

- Redundancy built into the environment services
- Redundancy built into the application architecture
- Blue-green deployments as a part of the continuous delivery process
- *Continuous monitoring* of the environments and applications to identify issues in real time and mitigate them if possible

From a DevOps perspective, the key focus needs to be on implementing blue-green deployments to ensure no downtime happens due to application deployments to production.

HIGH AVAILABILITY WITH BLUE-GREEN DEPLOYMENTS

The Bluemix Garage Method website is continuously delivered—as often as daily. To ensure that the transition to the upgraded version of the website has zero downtime, the team implemented blue-green deployment. As a new function is pushed to production, it is deployed to an instance that isn't the actual running instance. After the new application instance is validated, the public URL is mapped to the new instance of the application.

Blue-green deployment involves these steps:

- If the blue app exists, manually delete it before you restart.
- Push a new version of the blue app.
- Set environment variables for the blue app.
- Create and bind services for the blue app.
- Start the blue app.
- Test the blue app.
- Map traffic to the new version of the blue app by binding it to the public host.
- Delete the temporary route for the blue app that was used for testing.
- Rename the green app to "green app backup." The backup application continues to run so that active sessions are not terminated.
- Rename the blue app to "green" app.

The team completes the blue-green deployment steps by using the Cloud Foundry command-line interface that is built into the DevOps Services runtime.

—Joe Loewengruber, 2016

Environment Abstraction

The first and foremost goal of building the right DevOps platform, especially one that is Antifragile, is to abstract the environment and infrastructure concerns from the practitioners developing and testing the applications and services. To them, the environment should appear as an abstract set of infrastructure or platform services that they can leverage and utilize to develop and deliver. This allows them to achieve delivery of multiple applications through multiple delivery pipelines, performing at multiple speeds; to achieve rapid experimentation, using techniques like A/B testing, of business ideas and new features; to fail fast and fail often; and to not be concerned with the environment's stability due to the experiments that fail or apps and services delivered that do not behave or perform as desired.

Software-Defined Environments

The way to introduce a layer of abstraction above the infrastructure is to leverage software-defined environments (SDEs). An SDE allows the Ops team delivering the Infrastructure as a Service—whether an internal Ops team or a cloud vendor—to expose the infrastructure as a set of services that any practitioner in the application delivery lifecycle can access and utilize via a well-defined set of APIs. SDEs can be delivered by just having a layer virtualization, running on a hypervisor, or a fully functional cloud.

SDEs provide different levels of abstraction by allowing various components of the environments to be defined and managed as software (Li, 2014). These include the following:

- Software-defined storage (SDS)
- Software-defined networks (SDNs)
- Software-defined compute (SDC)
- Software-defined management (SDM)
- Orchestration and workload automation

Companies like VMware and IBM are now providing software solutions to manage entire datacenters, not just environments, referring to their solutions as software-defined datacenters (SDDCs).

Software-defined environments, while delivering a layer of abstraction and access to environments via APIs to the environment consumers, also deliver the capability to automate via software the management of the environments to the environment providers. Environment providers can do the following:

- Version environments by versioning the software defining the environments.
- Store the environment versions in a repository, allowing for prior versions of environments to be easily accessible in case they need to be re-created for defect assessment.
- Change management of the environments. This becomes easier as each change that Ops makes to an environment—whether it is applying a

patch or making a configuration change—becomes software driven, by creating a new version of the environment. The changes are applied via scripts (no logging into admin consoles—it does not scale and cannot be easily managed). These scripts are versioned with the code and other artifacts of the application stack being delivered.

- Perform traditional software engineering practices like software configuration management, which can be applied to the code representing the environments.

- Perform inventory management of the software-defined environments. This becomes easier as the latest versions of the code representing the SDE provide the inventory.

- Perform configuration management of the environments. This becomes easier to manage because here too, all configuration management is done via versioned code.

Cloud-hosted environments are by definition software-defined. However, the level of software definition and management may vary by cloud vendor and the cloud management software stack that is utilized. For example, bare-metal servers in a cloud may not have fully functional software-defined networks as they utilize physical hardware (bare metal) on which to provision the server instances. Similarly, software-defined storage will determine whether the vendor provides object storage or not.

Cloud-Hosted DevOps Platform

A cloud-hosted environment, whether delivered as *Infrastructure as a Service* (IaaS), *Platform as a Service* (PaaS), or *containers*, delivers this level of abstraction, allowing an Antifragile DevOps platform to be delivered. I will compare and contrast IaaS and PaaS models, as well as how to deliver a DevOps platform on either model, later in this chapter.

Cloud Consumption Models

Before I start delving into how a DevOps platform can be built on a cloud platform, let's make sure we are on the same page when it comes to cloud technology. *Cloud* has become yet another overloaded and misused term. Most people's vision of the cloud is still of a public, multi-tenant cloud, offering infrastructure as a service, allowing organizations to utilize a supplier's datacenter to get infrastructure services without owning the hardware. First of all, the cloud is more than just virtualized infrastructure. In fact, the real value of the cloud lies in the ability of organizations to leverage cloud services, beyond the infrastructure; to deliver innovative business services, fast, and at scale; to not only lower costs, but to also be able to deliver services that they could not before these cloud services were available. Cloud consumption models have also evolved beyond the traditional off-premises infrastructure model. Let's start with these consumption models.

ESPN AND SPORTS CONSUMPTION

Children today will never know the feeling of forcing your eyes to stay open hoping that John Tudor could finish off the Astros or that Lee Smith could record a save and notch a win for the original Chris Carpenter. They will never have to risk getting briars or stickers in their feet fetching the Arkansas Democrat-Gazette to review the box score of an extra inning Cardinals-Reds game. The reason they will never know these feelings of anticipation is thanks, in large part, to the Entertainment and Sports Programming Network—better known as ESPN.

I will spare readers the birth and history of ESPN, I'm gonna focus instead on its effect on how we view, consume, and devour sports 24/7. Today there are hundreds—probably thousands—of ESPN platforms across every imaginable medium. For starters there are their multiple television channels such as ESPN, ESPN2, ESPNews, and ESPN Classic. Then there are their websites, espn.com, espn360.com, and espnradio.com and of course their wildly popular radio network. Each offers us never-ending coverage of scores, transactions, rumors, opinions, insight, and analysis. If those options were not enough, they have multiple apps such as the Score Center, Sports Center, and ESPN Radio apps, just to name a few. With the advent of Twitter, you can even follow your favorite ESPN personality there so that you really never have to do without sports if you don't want to. The reality is most of us do not want to do without sports. It is a simple matter of supply and demand. ESPN and other sports networks—supply us with endless selections on a sports buffet because we demand it. I am not saying this is a bad thing—as a sports fan I enjoy it—I am just in awe of how far the marriage of sports and technology has come from the days when I was adjusting the antenna on my sometimes-color television, before we had cable and when only the wealthy could afford satellite T.V.

—Antonio Lopez (Lopez, 2014)

Given how new the cloud is, you can't even say, "This is not your father's cloud," or (like the author of this article) talk about how "children today will never experience" the feeling of provisioning a server instance on the cloud of yesteryear. The rate of change in cloud technology is moving at such breakneck speed and acceleration that it is becoming almost impossible for many organizations to keep up. The ever-evolving nature of cloud technology has also resulted in a significant evolution in the consumption models of the cloud. No longer is choosing how you want to consume the cloud as simple as choosing between "Private" and "Public," like it was in the good not-so-old-days. There is a myriad of options to choose from today, and the decision is not just about cost or location, but many other factors. Choosing the right model, or in most cases, all the models to create what is referred to as a *hybrid cloud*, will determine what components of the environments your DevOps platform will exist on and will need to support.

Private versus Public   This is probably the first significant change in how organizations consume the cloud. When the cloud began, there was only the *public* cloud—located in the vendor's datacenter, managed by the vendor, and multi-tenant. This was the only model offered by early cloud providers like Salesforce.com (launched in 1999) and Amazon Web Services (launched in 2002). Even today, the general assumption is that when you mention the word *cloud*, you mean a public cloud. As cloud technology evolved, cloud management software became available that allowed organizations to set up a *private* cloud in their own datacenters. This was a self-managed cloud, located within the organization's firewall, in their own datacenter. It was on-premises (*on-prem* for short), running on their own hardware, and it was, of course, single tenant. As a result, *private* was always thought of as on-premises.

Private and public became the two available choices. A decision on which one to choose was based on many factors: cost, data location, single or multi-tenant, ability to support and self-manage an in-house cloud, and so on. Most organizations chose the private cloud for mission-critical applications that were highly regulated and had strict data residency and privacy concerns, which required data to be kept on-premises. Other applications were deployed leveraging the public cloud, which offered a lower cost and no need for new hardware in their own datacenter. Most large organizations ended up with a hybrid cloud model that had both public and private cloud hosting and traditional, on-premises hardware-hosted applications.

A recent evolution in consumption models has evolved to completely disrupt the notion that mapped public to off-premises and private to on-premises. This evolution has resulted in two new types of consumption: *dedicated* and *local*. There are hence three options available now–Public, Dedicated and Local (see Figure 5-5).

Dedicated Cloud   Cloud technology has reached a state where cloud vendors are able to provide a single-tenant, managed cloud in their datacenters. IBM, a pioneer in delivering this model, refers to it as a *dedicated* cloud. So, now you have a cloud that is "dedicated" to your organization, but still vendor managed, and remaining in a vendor's datacenter (off-premises), running on the vendor's hardware, but single-tenant. It is thus a private cloud, but located off-premises, and vendor managed. Thus, you can think of dedicated as *private, managed, off-premises cloud*-as-a-service.

Local Cloud   The next evolution in how organizations can consume the cloud is even more disruptive. Organizations, especially those with highly regulated applications or with strict privacy concerns, have typically wanted the luxury and comfort of having the cloud on-premises. With an on-premises cloud, there are no issues with where the client data is; no issues with managing compliance related to running critical applications in someone else's datacenter; no issues with having to "tunnel" into another network to access applications and infrastructure. However, the challenge with having an on-premises cloud has always been the skills needed and risk associated with self-managing the cloud. I am talking about IT organizations that have excelled in managing hardware infrastructure, now managing the cloud and the constantly evolving technology stacks that need to be managed and maintained. I am talking about running and managing an efficient cloud with all the relevant cloud services with their own SLAs, which are required to have an on-premises cloud deliver the promise of a public cloud.

Such a consumption model delivering the best of both worlds is now available through what is known as a *local* cloud. This is a cloud that is in a client's own datacenter (on-premises); it is, however, managed by the vendor who is delivering the cloud; and, it is, of course, single-tenant. In such a model, the organization consuming the cloud continues to just manage the hardware infrastructure on which the cloud is delivered. The cloud, though, is managed by the vendor. This is achieved by a *tether* that allows the vendor to initially deploy the cloud itself remotely and continue to periodically monitor and update the cloud software stack, as and when needed. (IBM, which has also pioneered this model, calls their tether technology a *relay*.) The client organization coordinates the timeframe for when updates will be done, allowing them to control outage windows, if any. It is thus a vendor-managed private cloud, which is, however, on-premises. You can therefore think of local as being a *private, managed, on-premises cloud*-as-a-service.

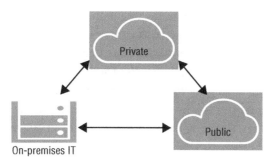

Figure 5-5: Cloud consumption models

Choosing the right consumption model is not trivial. Consuming a public cloud is by definition *non-sticky*—it is (relatively) easy-on/easy-off from a public cloud. Dedicated is also the same way, because you are essentially leveraging a public cloud that has now been dedicated to your organization. It is similar to renting a stand-alone building, as opposed to an apartment in a multi-tenant building. Local, on the other hand, is different. Understanding the division of duties between your organization and the vendor is critical. Understanding the change management processes is essential. You are forming a partnership with the vendor that is more complex and, in turn, much more valuable than using a public cloud.

Self-Managed versus Vendor-Managed   As you choose which model is the best for your DevOps platform, the first decision point to be made is the most critical: Are you looking for a vendor-managed cloud environment, or will you self-manage? If you prefer the latter, then the right model is a traditional, on-premises private cloud. The organization buys the cloud platform technology from a vendor, trains its people, prepares its infrastructure in the datacenter, and builds the platform leveraging the delivered cloud.

If you prefer the vendor-managed model, then the organization needs to next choose between an on-premises and off-premises cloud platform. This decision of a managed versus self-managed cloud has to be made first. It impacts not only which cloud is selected but also IT staffing. If an organization is challenged by its ability to manage a cloud with its own IT staff, due to skills or headcount, or it is unsure of its ability and desire to be able to deliver the services and associated SLAs its clients are expecting from a cloud, then it should consider a managed cloud. This decision was not an option until now because all managed cloud options were available only on an off-premises cloud. With the advent of local cloud offerings, both for IaaS and PaaS, this is no longer the case. An organization can get an on-premises cloud, as a managed service, and build a DevOps platform on it.

Once the cloud consumption model has been chosen, the next decision set is to determine whether the right cloud adoption model is Infrastructure as a Service, Platform as a Service, or containers. When you make this decision, you are beginning to choose the services that make up the DevOps platform. How does the organization want those services delivered? Will they be services built with DevOps tools running on top of the IaaS cloud, or is it better that they be a part of the actual platform being delivered? Let's examine these options next.

Infrastructure as a Service

INFRASTRUCTURE AS A SERVICE

The capability provided to the consumer is to provision processing, storage, networks, and other fundamental computing resources where the consumer is able to deploy and run arbitrary software, which can include operating systems and applications. The consumer does not manage or control the underlying cloud infrastructure but has control over operating systems, storage, deployed applications, and possibly limited control of select networking components (e.g., host firewalls).

—NIST, U.S. Department of Commerce, 2011

Figure 5-6 best illustrates the definition described by the U.S. National Institute of Standards and Technology (NIST). It shows the components that are cloud provider-managed in an IaaS offering, compared to those that are not. The cloud provider here may be the cloud vendor, or the organization's own Ops team, depending upon whether the cloud is vendor-managed or self-managed.

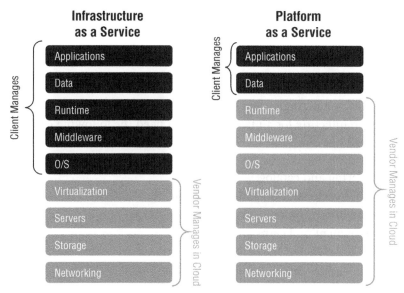

Figure 5-6: IaaS versus PaaS

Figure 5-6 also visually describes what distinguishes the two cloud adoption models—IaaS and PaaS—that is, how much of the stack is managed by the user (or client) versus how much is managed by the cloud platform provider, which again can be a vendor or an organization's own Ops team. I will discuss delivering a DevOps leveraging a PaaS later in this chapter, in the section on PaaS.

The goal of leveraging an IaaS cloud platform for these environments is to add the layer of abstraction that I discussed before between the practitioners delivering software and the infrastructure. They see one simplified view of the infrastructure, while under the surface it may have all the classic challenges and need the same levels of maintenance that any hardware infrastructure needs.

It is important to note that it is not uncommon to see organizations take a hybrid approach to adopting a cloud platform. While they may leverage a public or dedicated off-premises cloud for Dev-test environments, due to lower costs, and no data-residency (where the data is stored) needs, no real production data is needed for Dev-test, so organizations may choose to keep production environments on-premises. (See the section "Test Data Management" in Chapter 4 for more information.) This brings the applications running in production closer to the data sources and also allows for better management of compliance requirements related to data residency. With the evolution of models like dedicated clouds, these concerns are becoming less of an obstacle to adopting off-premises clouds, even for production.

IaaS Capability Stack

Creating and managing an IaaS offering requires that you first create the necessary architecture for an IaaS cloud. You need the following capabilities, also captured in Figure 5-7:

- Brokering and catalog
- Service orchestration and integration
- Cloud orchestration
- Deployment orchestration

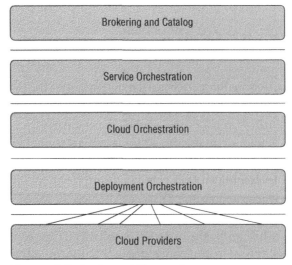

Figure 5-7: IaaS capability stack

Brokerage and Catalog The proliferation of cloud vendors, and the acceptance of hybrid cloud adoption, leveraging multiple vendors and multiple cloud adoption models, has given rise to a new capability area in the cloud stack: *cloud brokerage*. A football coach may have multiple quarterbacks,[2] running backs, and receivers on his bench, whom he can choose from to best match the play he is running—say, a heavier quarterback, running back, and full back for a "third and goal" play. Similarly, cloud brokerage tools like IBM cloudMatrix and

---

[2] Multiple first-string quarterbacks are more common in college football than the NFL.

RightScale Cloud Comparison allow organizations to choose the right cloud for the application being deployed, from a catalog of available options. This decision can be made in real time, based on the application's needs for computing, storage, network, and memory, and the capability and pricing available from each cloud option, in-house or through an external vendor.

Service Orchestration and Integration   Service orchestration, or service integration, is the set of capabilities needed to integrate services being delivered by the various clouds and the applications running across multiple clouds. It is thus the cloud service integration layer. The core component in this layer is *business process management* tooling for managing the orchestration and business workflows of the services being integrated and delivered to meet the business requirements. The tools for service orchestration and integration fall into the broad category of business process management tools, which utilize workflows to capture the orchestration and business rules of managing the various services and their interactions. Languages such as *Business Process Execution Language* (BPEL) and *Business Process Modeling Notation* (BPMN) are standards used to capture these orchestration workflows and business rules.

Tools for API and service management—for monitoring, security, metering and billing, and so on, of APIs and services—also fall into this space.

Cloud Orchestration

COACHES ORCHESTRATING THE BIG GAME

Fandom has a perception of coaches preparing for the big game. It involves emotion and energy. This is true, but emotion and energy are mere factors, such as two bees in a hive. Much more is involved. How a coaching staff chooses to prepare a team for a monster and epic rivalry game that has taken on a grudge match exterior is important, very important. Just like conductors decide on how to play the bizarre *Symphonie Fantastique* by Berlioz, coaches must set a total tone for preparing a team for a game such as Michigan and Notre Dame. Note this: the preparation began long before Monday, when exactly is anyone's guess....

There is no tolerance for any distractions in the game preparation period, excepting an occasional "boys will be boys" disagreement on the field. Even

continued

continued

these episodes can be manipulated by the staff and used for further motivation. There is no need to worry about a lack of focus if everyone buys into the mission. The orchestrators (coaches) go bonkers when a player strays off the path and causes some sort of unnecessary distraction, typically an overactive mouth. The coaches do not want the opponents to have further motivation; there is already an ample supply.

—Wolverine, 2014

Cloud orchestration involves the management of the automation of various components and services being delivered by the cloud environments. The goal of orchestration is to manage the provisioning and de-provisioning, resource allocation, configuration, and workflow of all the components in the cloud technology stack and all the infrastructure services being delivered by the cloud. One way of defining orchestration is to look at it as the codification of the best practices and workflows for managing the IaaS cloud.

Capabilities of cloud orchestration include the following (Peranandam, 2012):

- Integration of cloud capabilities across heterogeneous environments and infrastructures to simplify, automate, and optimize service deployment
- Automation to allow a lower ratio of administrators to physical and virtual servers
- Automated high-scale provisioning and de-provisioning of resources with policy-based tools to manage virtual machine sprawl by reclaiming resources automatically
- Ability to integrate workflows and approval chains across technology silos to improve collaboration and reduce delays
- Real-time monitoring of physical and virtual cloud resources, as well as usage and accounting chargeback capabilities to track and optimize system usage
- Prepackaged automation templates and workflows for the most common resource types to ease adoption of best practices and minimize transition time

IBM Cloud Orchestrator and VMware vRealize are two examples of market leaders in the cloud orchestration space.

CLOUD COMPUTING PATTERN

[A] repeatable solution that is based on specific sets of virtual images, middleware, applications, and runtime configurations. The result of deploying a pattern is a configured, tuned, and optimized application environment.

—Chiara Brandle, 2014

Orchestration, along with the architectural definition, may be captured in *cloud patterns*. A common standard of patterns is OpenStack Heat patterns, called *Heat Orchestration Templates* (HOTs).

While they have matured significantly in the last couple of years, patterns for defining and codifying the cloud are not new. IBM was a pioneer in this space when its proprietary cloud patterns made their first appearance with the creation of the CloudBurst appliance in 2009, which in 2011 evolved into IBM Workload Deployer (IWD). These patterns, called Virtual System Patterns (vSys), have also evolved and are today supported primarily by the IBM PureApplication Systems (PureAS) offerings. The vSys patterns at IBM are being gradually phased out and replaced with OpenStack Heat as the standard. Outside IBM, other patterns also evolved. Of these, Amazon Web Services (AWS) CloudFormation, released in 2011, is the most popular, given the expansive footprint of Amazon.

From a standards perspective, AWS CloudFormation inspired the development of a community standard in the OpenStack HOT templates, supporting the OpenStack Heat provisioning engine. Most cloud vendors today support OpenStack Heat directly or provide support for OpenStack APIs, allowing for Heat to provision environments on these non-OpenStack clouds.

Here are some examples of components of the Cloud that are defined and included in a pattern:

- Pre-installation on an operating system
- Pre-integration across components
- Pre-configured and tuned middleware
- Pre-configured monitoring
- Pre-configured security
- Lifecycle management

As a result, patterns are, at a bare minimum, composed of the following:

- Base images of operating systems
- Binary files to deliver applications
- Automation scripts (for example, Chef, Puppet, SaltStack, or Ansible)
- Orchestration templates (for example, OpenStack Heat or Amazon CloudFormation)

The future of patterns as you know them is itself being challenged with the evolution of containers. While containers are not an Infrastructure as a Service in the classic sense of the definition, their lightweight and portability are resulting in their acceptance as an alternative to the traditional approach to IaaS, and even more so as an alternative to PaaS. While several container technologies are emerging, the leader in the container space is, of course, Docker. I will discuss containers in more detail later in this chapter.

Deployment Orchestration I discuss deployment orchestration at length in Chapter 4. The key thing to note is whether the cloud environment is being provisioned independently of the applications and the applications are deployed on top of those environments or whether you are deploying the applications and the environments as one *full-stack deployment* process. The *pattern* in each case will be defined differently, as environment patterns and application patterns, or one *full-stack pattern*. As I describe in Chapter 4, tools like IBM UrbanCode Deploy have capabilities to design and provision full-stack environments using OpenStack Heat patterns, defined as *application blueprints*.

OpenStack Heat as an Abstraction Layer

One of the benefits of leveraging OpenStack Heat is that it can be used as an abstraction layer allowing for the environments to be *cloud agnostic*—that is, the ability for a single environment, captured in a Heat template, to be provisioned on multiple clouds. In fact, complex environments composed of multiple templates can be provisioned across multiple clouds from multiple vendors, as shown in Figure 5-8. This support also allows for cloud portability—a holy grail of the Cloud. An environment provisioned on one cloud today can be provisioned on another cloud tomorrow, if that is deemed better (see the section "Brokerage and Catalog").

IBM UrbanCode Deploy is an example of a tool that supports such a paradigm. Using UrbanCode Deploy's Designer, a single Heat document (HOT) can be created to target any of the multiple clouds supported by the Heat engine included in UrbanCode Deploy (Frederick, 2016).

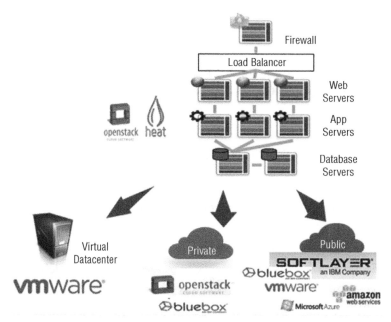

Figure 5-8: OpenStack Heat supporting multiple clouds

As my friend Sudhakar "Freddie" Frederick mentions in the blog post that I cited here, portability across clouds is not fully addressed yet, even with OpenStack. Some things in some clouds will simply not have an equivalent in other clouds, so the more special, cloud-specific services that are used, the less portable the HOT document becomes.

Platform as a Service

PLATFORM AS A SERVICE

The capability provided to the consumer is to deploy onto the cloud infrastructure consumer-created or acquired applications created using programming languages and tools supported by the provider. The consumer does not manage or control the underlying cloud infrastructure including network, servers, operating systems, or storage, but has control over the deployed applications and possibly application hosting environment configurations.

—NIST, U.S. Department of Commerce, 2011

Like most terms in the IT industry (or to really generalize, in the human communication medium known as *language*), PaaS is overloaded, overused, and misunderstood. A quick web search or even a visit to the Wikipedia page on PaaS proves this point.

Defining PaaS

The most critical section of the NIST definition of PaaS, which differentiates PaaS from an "Infrastructure as a service" consumption model for the cloud, is as follows:

> ... *The consumer does not manage or control the underlying cloud infrastructure including network, servers, operating systems, or storage, but has control over the deployed applications and possibly application hosting environment configurations.*

Figure 5-6 best illustrates the differences between IaaS and PaaS. As you can see in the figure, what distinguishes the two cloud adoption models—IaaS and PaaS—is how much of the stack is managed by the user (or client) versus how much is managed by the cloud platform provider (which might be an internal Ops team or an external cloud vendor). It is important to highlight two things:

- Every capability in the stack is available as a managed service; this would be a shared, multi-tenant service available to users, with the underlying implementation abstracted from the user.
- The client/user only has to be concerned about managing their own applications, data, and user access, leveraging the services available on the platform, which manages the rest.

Platforms as a service may be either public (IBM Bluemix, Pivotal, Salesforce Heroku, Google App Engine, and so on) or private (hosted Cloud Foundry; a self-built and hosted platform). Organizations may also build their own hosted and managed environments leveraging multiple technologies and self-hosted on a private cloud. For a private instance, of course, the organization hosting it in their own datacenter would be responsible for managing all the services hosted on the platform. Building a PaaS leveraging self-managed Cloud Foundry from Pivotal would be a good example.

DevOps Services on PaaS

When you look at DevOps on PaaS, you have to look at the services that need to be hosted on the platform in order to implement a DevOps application delivery pipeline on the platform. If you look at a DevOps application delivery pipeline and the core components that make up the delivery pipeline, each of the components needs to be available as a service in order to provide a complete *DevOps on PaaS* solution.

Revisiting the list of capabilities that make up a delivery pipeline, these all need to be made available as services on the PaaS:

- Source code management
- Build
- Continuous integration
- Deployment automation
- Middleware configuration
- Automated Testing

These are what you refer to as DevOps services, shown in Figure 5-9. If you pay attention, you will notice that this is a subset of the list presented in the IaaS section. That is because a PaaS includes the capabilities related to the environment's provisioning and configuration management as core services of the PaaS. The entire goal of the PaaS is to make environments that are abstracted away from the platform consumers.

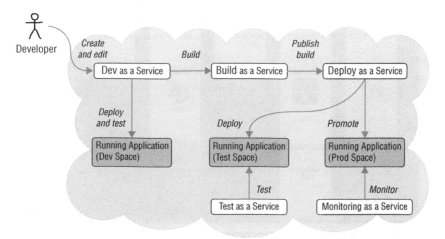

Figure 5-9: DevOps services

Fully functional, managed PaaS offerings like IBM Bluemix include the DevOps services as an inherent part of the platform. Here are some of the DevOps services on Bluemix:

- Git as a service, and GitHub Enterprise as a service
- Web-based IDE
- Agile planning and tracking, team collaboration as a service
- Delivery pipeline as a service
- Globalization as a service
- Deployment automation as a service
- Auto scaling as a service
- Performance monitoring as a service
- Alert notification as a service

These capabilities, working in concert, provide a continuous delivery pipeline on IBM Bluemix PaaS, as shown in Figure 5-10.

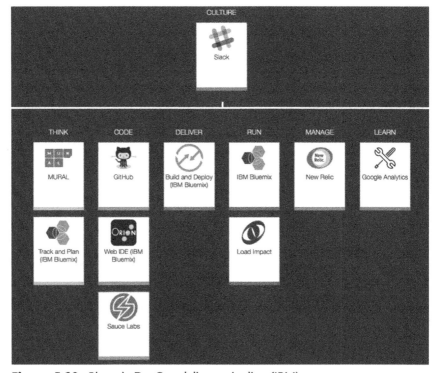

Figure 5-10: Bluemix DevOps delivery pipeline (IBM)

DevOps as a Service

The value proposition for adopting a PaaS platform is self-evident. For any organization looking to adopt DevOps, a PaaS offering that includes DevOps services allows you to adopt DevOps at a very low cost of entry. You do not need to craft a delivery pipeline and implement the entire continuous delivery tool chain. Integrations, hosting, servicing—these are not your problem. Pay-as-you-go, and allow for scale.

PaaS with Cloud Foundry

You cannot leave the topic of PaaS without mentioning Cloud Foundry, which has without a doubt become the standard for delivering a PaaS. Cloud Foundry is an open source PaaS that is now managed by the Cloud Foundry Foundation. The foundation's board is made up of representatives from major Cloud Foundry adopters and vendors like IBM, Pivotal, HP, EMC, SAP, and VMware, who support or provide PaaS platforms based on Cloud Foundry. IBM Bluemix Public PaaS, as of the writing of this book, is the largest instance of a Cloud Foundry–based PaaS.

The true value of Cloud Foundry, other than being open source, is in the variety of choices it provides to empower developers, and PaaS providers:

- *Development frameworks and languages.* Cloud Foundry is truly poly-glot in nature, supporting all major languages, either intrinsically or through community-added *buildpacks.*
- *Application services.* In addition to the core application services included in Cloud Foundry (like MySQL, MongoDB, PostgreSQL, Redis, and RabbitMQ), vendors such as IBM have added several others, including WebSphere Application Server, DB2, Blockchain, MQ Light, and so on.
- *Multiple clouds.* Organizations can choose which cloud to deploy Cloud Foundry on. Vendors like Pivotal allow deployment on multiple clouds, including AWS and Microsoft Azure. IBM, which offers only managed PaaS, deploys Bluemix on SoftLayer (the IBM public cloud), VMware, and OpenStack.

Containers

DEION SANDERS: HOME RUNS AND TOUCHDOWNS

Nicknamed "Prime Time" and "Neon Deion," Sanders played nine years in baseball, and will probably be a Hall of Fame football player when he becomes eligible.[3] While he was a great football player—an eight-time Pro Bowl player who won two Super Bowls—he was also an above-average baseball player and probably would have been better had he played the sport full-time.

Sanders is the only man ever to play in both the Super Bowl and the World Series, and he is the only man ever to hit a home run and score a touchdown in the same week.

—Timmons, 2008

Athletes like Deion Sanders are unique. They can excel in pretty much any sports arena. Their athleticism is agnostic of the sport being played. Teach them the rules and the basics of how to play, and coach them on which plays to execute, and they are good to go.

Like these unique athletes, who appear to be "portable" across sports, containers too are agnostic to where they run, and are portable across environments. The idea of containers itself is not new. Linux has had containers since 2008. Linux containers allow isolation at the CPU, memory, block I/O, and network resource level, while sharing the operating system (OS) kernel. This allows processes to run independently, while not having the overhead that virtual machines (VMs) have, where each instance has a full local OS. This allows containers to be much more lightweight than VMs, allowing them to run on a server at a much higher scale than VMs. Docker was started as an open source project to make Linux containers much more portable, allowing them to be moved across any Linux instance, on any physical server, or in the Cloud. Since their release in 2013, Docker has become one of the most successful open source projects ever, with over 100 million downloads of the Docker engine (Martin N., 2015).

In a nutshell, the key benefit of containers is that they provide a standard way to package an application, its configurations, and all its dependencies, so

---

[3] Deion Sanders was inducted into the Football Hall of Fame in 2011, three years after the quoted article was written.

that it becomes portable across environments. The unique application code inside the container is isolated from the environment outside the container. It is almost *DevOps nirvana*. The developers do not need to be concerned with what the environment is outside the container. They focus on packaging their application in the standardized container image that is best for their application. Similarly, the Ops team does not need to worry about the changing code, configurations, and dependencies of the applications inside the container. They just need to focus on running the standardized, approved containers on their environment.

DevOps Platform with Containers

The tools that organizations use to build their application delivery pipeline can be deployed in containers, making them available as services to leverage the delivery of the application delivery pipeline capabilities, as I have discussed previously. Alternatively, the tools of the application delivery pipeline can be deployed anywhere outside of containers in a traditional manner to develop the applications and services, and just packaged in containers when they need to be deployed to test, pre-production, and production environments. In either scenario, the key benefit of containers is to provide a standardized set of dev-test-prod and other environments where the application can be deployed in portable containers and promoted from one environment to another without any compatibility concerns or configuration management to be done.

When it comes to the application delivery pipeline, the only change that needs to be made is to the build process, which now includes the step of packaging the application in the container. Modern build tools, like Jenkins and IBM UrbanCode Deploy, all support the following capabilities:

- Building a Docker image from a *Dockerfile*
- Publishing a Docker image to a registry

Once built, the Docker container can be deployed to the desired environment, leveraging the Docker tooling or, if a higher level of deployment capability is needed, a deployment automation tool like IBM UrbanCode Deploy.

It is important to note that there are several container technologies in the market, like CoreOS Rocket and VMware Photon containers. However, Docker is by far the market leader, with significant market adoption over the alternatives. In April 2016, the Open Container Initiative was launched by dozens of vendors, to standardize container formats and runtimes.

Container Orchestration

The sheer scalability of containers results in multiple instances of multiple containers being deployed. Managing these containers, across their lifecycle, involves several types of tasks and capabilities, including the following:

- Deployment
- Updates to containers
- Provisioning
- Container discovery
- Monitoring
- Scheduling
- Clustering and scaling
- Failover
- Policy management
- Constraint management

As a result of the challenges presented to provide these capabilities, several technologies have emerged to manage orchestration of containers:

- *Docker Swarm*. Docker is beginning to provide support for large-scale clusters of Docker containers with Docker Swarm, leveraging the core Docker APIs to manage a pool of Docker engines, rather than one at a time.
- *Kubernetes*. The orchestration technology in the container space getting the most traction is Kubernetes for Google. Google claims that it manages over two billion containers on a daily basis using Kubernetes, which provides some serious credibility. Kubernetes architecture is that of a *master* managing multiple *minions*. The master runs the management and orchestration processes to manage all the minions. These *minions* in turn has multiple collections of containers called *pods* deployed to it.
- *Mesos*: Mesos is an open source project that existed independent of Docker to manage running complex tasks on a shared pool of servers. It has since added support for Docker, allowing for container management. Similar to Kubernetes, Mesos has a *master-slave* model. The master runs the high-level tasks and delegates tasks to the *slaves*, which manage the containers. Higher-level control, scale, and high availability

are provided by software called ZooKeeper, which can coordinate a collection of master nodes. ZooKeeper informs all masters and slaves which master is the current leading master.

Container as a Service

As an alternative to PaaS, *Container as a Service* (CaaS) offerings have become popular. Here, like a PaaS, the environments are available as a service and managed by internal Ops teams or by a vendor. Developers just need to run the containers they build on the service, without any concerns for the environment setup, management, or configuration to be done. Unlike a PaaS, a CaaS does not inherently provide any application or middleware services. If the application needs any such services, beyond the CaaS, they need to deploy a container that runs the service on the CaaS or leverage an externally running service, directly from the application that needs to consume it.

Popular CaaS services include Docker Cloud (previously Tutum), IBM Bluemix Containers, Amazon ECS, CoreOS Tectonic, Rancher from Rancher Labs, and Google Container Engine.

Play: Deliver Microservices Architectures

REGULAR TEAMS VERSUS SPECIAL TEAMS

Former NFL safety and linebacker Coy Wire played nine seasons in the league and contributed as a core guy on special teams. He acknowledged that covering kicks isn't high on everyone's list when they come into the NFL but talked about the importance of adapting to a new role as a pro.

"Most of the guys who star on special teams in the NFL never played a down of it in their college career. So, you have to be like a chameleon and adapt to the new circumstance," Wire said. "Every special teams player wishes they were a full-time starter in the NFL. But to truly buy into the special teams units and excel on them, you have to put your ego aside and embrace the new role that you play for your team."

—Bowen, 2015

From a DevOps perspective, *delivering small batches* is a core theme—as presented in Chapter 4. The value proposition of small batches is self-evident: small changes delivered frequently, reducing the *cycle time* to feedback, and minimizing the impact of change. Testing and security validation becomes easier, as you validate small changes more frequently. Deployment becomes easier as you are deploying smaller sets of changes. Change management, similarly, becomes less complex. DevOps nirvana.

From an architectural perspective, though, delivering small batches is not always viable. Most enterprise applications are *monolithic* in nature. They have a few large components, each of which are delivered as one deployable asset:

- *User interface* (UI), which is typically one component for each UI type—web page, mobile app, API for third-party apps, and so on
- *Database,* which is typically spread across multiple databases running on servers
- *Server-side* components, which may be multiple executable components, although if it is more than one component, the components are large and few in number

So, from a deployment perspective, you have a minimum of three large *monoliths* to deploy. All of these components may be developed by multiple teams, potentially using short *sprints* that deliver small batches of changes to code with each sprint. However, all these changes need to be integrated and built into the single large deployable component. This defeats the purpose of delivering small batches. While each delivery cycle delivers small, incremental changes to the deployable component, the component itself has to be delivered as an *all-or-nothing* deployment of the monolithic component.

The next challenge from a deployment orchestration perspective is deploying multiple instances of the components. If any component is to be scaled, it can only be scaled *horizontally* by deploying multiple instances on multiple servers. Here again, even if just a part of the functionality needs to be scaled—say, the shopping cart of an eCommerce website—the monolithic architecture requires that multiple instances of the entire component be deployed. The monolithic component is the lowest atomic deployable asset.

Microservices Architecture

THE MICROSERVICES ARCHITECTURAL STYLE

[T]he microservice architectural style is an approach to developing a single application as a suite of small services, each running in its own process and communicating with lightweight mechanisms, often an HTTP resource API. These services are built around business capabilities and independently deployable by fully automated deployment machinery. There is a bare minimum of centralized management of these services, which may be written in different programming languages and use different data storage technologies.

—Fowler, 2014

The solutions to both delivering small batches and scalability (Figure 5-11) are effectively addressed by a microservices approach. The key characteristics of microservices are defined by Martin Fowler as follows:

- *Componentization via services.* Microservices allow for the development and delivery of *componentized* services, with well-defined APIs, which can be *composed* together to deliver complex services.

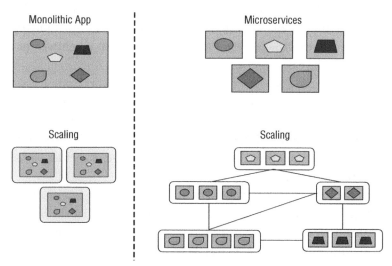

Figure 5-11: Scaling with microservices

- *Organized around business capabilities.* The goal of microservices is to decompose the monolithic architectures into smaller services by business function. As per *Conway's law,* discussed in Chapter 4, teams tend to put business logic into architectural components that they are responsible for, even if they are not architecturally the right places to put it. Each business capability that needs to be delivered is architected as independent services, which can be developed and delivered independently.

   Developing microservices around business capabilities also addresses the scalability challenge. The need for scale typically comes around certain business capabilities, just like the shopping cart I mentioned before, or, say, the *check balance* capability for a bank around the end of the month. Having distinct microservices, or a set of microservices for individual business capabilities, allows only those microservices that are needed to be scaled horizontally when the need arises, without impacting the deployment of other microservices.

- *Products not projects.* Products are not transient, but projects are. The same team should own the microservices through their lifecycle, rather than there being a series of projects executed by different teams, on a set of components, with no ownership from the project team through the component's lifecycle.

- *Smart endpoints and dumb pipes.* Microservices are built using simple REST APIs or a lightweight message bus, as their architectural interfaces. This allows for microservices to communicate with other microservices, as well as external services and applications, in a lightweight manner that can be easily orchestrated and managed.

- *Decentralized governance.* This allows for teams developing and delivering microservices to utilize the best platform and tools for the technology they need to deliver. Microservices are independent from each other, communicating through a well-defined API. They do not need to have a standardized development language or technology stack for their implementation.

- *Decentralized data management.* If the application layer is being architected into small components, it is only logical that the data schemas of the persistence layer need to match the requirements of this architectural model. You no longer need a data store that supports one single monolith accessing the data.

- *Infrastructure automation.* Orchestrating *continuous delivery* of a large number of microservices requires tooling to support their scale and delivery and their lifecycle management needs. Leveraging a PaaS or containers to manage their deployment is imperative.
- *Design for failure.* Designed for antifragility from the ground up, microservices, through their ability to be small, independently running services, facilitate the design of Antifragile systems.
- *Evolutionary design.* Architecting an application leveraging microservices has the additional impact of not locking the developers into an application architecture from the beginning, as is typically the case with monolithic apps. The architecture and design can evolve, as microservices can be changed, replaced, and removed to enhance the architectures on the rapid feedback cycle time, which comes from delivering small batches.

12-Factor App

The microservices approach, while being focused on architectural styles for modern application design and development, has also spawned methodologies on how to develop and deliver such applications. Of these, the most popular, called the *12-Factor App,* was developed by the folks at Heroku, a PaaS service provider now owned by Salesforce.com. The 12-Factor App methodology was developed by Heroku to help organizations develop and deliver *cloud-native* apps, which are apps designed exclusively for the cloud. (I will discuss these in more detail later in this section.) However, the microservices architecture and the 12-Factor App methodology are extremely well aligned, resulting in the 12-Factor App methodology becoming a common approach to develop and deliver microservices.

Let's take a quick look at the 12-Factor App concepts and best practices, of which there are obviously twelve (Koffel, 2014):

1. *Codebase.* Have all your code in a single source code management (SCM) system. It can, of course, be a federated and distributed SCM system like Git.
2. *Dependencies.* From application source code to infrastructure code, ensure that all dependencies are declared and isolated.
3. *Config.* Configuration variables change from environment to environment, or may change with time, independent from the application itself. Store these variables in the environment and not in the application.

4. *Backing services.* Applications utilize external *backing* services that they consume in order to run—from databases to caches to queuing systems. Address these via simple endpoints, which abstract the app from the service.

5. *Build, release, run.* Make build-release-run independent stages in the application delivery pipeline, with automation to *promote* the app from one stage to the other.

6. *Processes.* Build services in the application to run as stateless processes. All *stateful* content of the app should be stored in a data store that is external to the actual service. This allows the app to become Antifragile. If one service instance dies, another instance can replace it without losing any state-related information.

7. *Port binding.* Make all application services addressable by applications and services that consume the service as a URL. This, in a way, extends Factor 4.

8. *Concurrency.* This factor is completely in line with the scalability challenge presented when introducing *microservices.* Ensure that services in the app are capable of having multiple instances running concurrently. This allows the individual granular services to be scaled without scaling the entire app.

9. *Disposability.* Maximize making the app Antifragile by designing services for "fast startup and graceful shutdown." In simpler terms, allow services to start up and shut down rapidly, independent of other services. This requires that all the services that a service in the app consumes, and needs to be present in order to start up fast, are highly available and optimized for speed.

10. *Dev/production parity.* Quite simply, provide *production-like environments* through all stages of the application delivery pipeline.

11. *Logs.* Treat *logs* as event streams that can be actively monitored in real time and analyzed to provide rapid *feedback* to all stakeholders who need the data and information.

12. *Admin processes.* Ensure that admin processes that are run to monitor and gather information about the app—such as managing A/B testing results, data cleanup, and running analytics—all run as processes in the production environment to ensure accuracy of the gathered data.

If you look at these 12 Factors, they appear to be just another version of several of the DevOps plays presented in this book. They are just a methodology to reach the same end results that DevOps does, while being specialized for what are called cloud-native applications. Adopting the 12-Factor App is ideally suited for developing apps using a *microservices architecture.*

Cloud Native

Before moving on, it is essential to better define the term *cloud-native app* that I introduced in this section. Cloud-native apps are the culmination of the coming together of the following concepts:

- DevOps
- Microservices
- Containers

These concepts—merging with the sole intent of delivering applications that are built for the cloud and that need a new development, delivery, and operations paradigm to run at cloud scale—have the capability to manage the orchestration needed for that scale and to deliver an Antifragile environment capable of handling that scale.

CLOUD-NATIVE SYSTEM PROPERTIES

a. Container packaged. Running applications and processes in software containers as an isolated unit of application deployment and as a mechanism to achieve high levels of resource isolation. Improves overall developer experience, fosters code and component reuse, and simplif[ies] operations for cloud native applications.

b. Dynamically managed. Actively scheduled and actively managed by a central orchestrating process. Radically improve machine efficiency and resource utilization while reducing the cost associated with maintenance and operations.

c. Micro-services oriented. Loosely coupled with dependencies explicitly described (e.g., through service endpoints). Significantly increase the overall agility and maintainability of applications. The foundation will shape the evolution of the technology to advance the state of the art for application management and to make the technology ubiquitous and easily available through reliable interfaces.

—Cloud Native Computing Foundation, 2015

Cloud-native applications, by definition, require a PaaS or CaaS in order to run—leveraging containers to deploy and run in either cloud model. They are designed using a microservices architecture. They are developed and delivered using a 12-Factor App methodology. Small batches, rapid delivery, scalability, and antifragility are some of their core themes.

Developing and delivering *cloud-native applications* requires that the Dev and Ops teams have a good understanding of how such apps differ from traditional apps in several core assumptions that the Dev and Ops teams make about an app (Brown, 2016):

- In a cloud-native app, it is the application and services themselves that provide any non-functional requirements (NFRs), as opposed to traditional apps where the NFRs are provided by the infrastructure. Examples include load-balancing, high availability, and application monitoring.
- The infrastructure is constantly changing (it is *elastic* in nature), as opposed to traditional apps, which run on infrastructure that is static, with a fixed topology.
- The application components may be globally distributed, across multiple cloud environments, running as services, as opposed to a traditional app where components are typically co-located in the same environment, made of co-located servers.
- The DevOps team members control the production servers, as opposed to a traditional app where the *Ops* team is responsible for running the production servers. For a cloud-native app, the Ops team runs the platform or containers service. It becomes the DevOps team that owns the app to run their own production instances on the platform—whether they are individual server instances or containers.
- If a disaster happens, it is the DevOps team's responsibility to make sure the app stays up, as opposed to traditional apps where there is a formal hand-off from Dev to production and from that point onwards, the Ops team runs the application with minimal Dev engagement, if any. Again, for cloud-native apps, the Ops team runs the platform or containers service. As long as their core platform services are available, they are good. If an app running on the platform crashes, it is the responsibility of the DevOps team that owns the app to bring it back up.

Developing and delivering cloud-native apps is not just an architectural or methodology shift. The entire composition of the team, the roles of team members, and the skills they need in order to effectively and efficiently develop and deliver these apps, all need to change.

Microservices and Containers

Microservices and containers are gaining traction in tandem, and for good reason. While neither has a dependency on the other—containers don't need what is packaged inside to be microservices, and microservices don't need containers to be deployed—the value proposition of leveraging containers to enable the build, deployment, and running of microservices is tremendous. There are three main benefits:

1. *Environment abstraction.* By definition, containers cause what is running inside them to be abstracted from the environments on which the containers are running. Portability of the containers is the whole idea. To the microservice, they always leverage the environment's services in the same way, irrespective of which environment the containers are deployed to.

2. *Granular execution.* Because containers are much lighter than full virtual machines, they can be scaled at a much lower cost. Thus, the microservices they are running can be scaled horizontally more easily without needing the underlying infrastructure to be taxed inefficiently.

3. *Isolation.* Microservices in containers can be run as isolated, independent processes, unencumbered by where and how other services they are consuming or interacting with are running. Multiple microservices can be run on the same server instance, or be distributed across multiple server instances, without being concerned about interference between multiple microservices. Load balancing can thus be much better planned and managed to maximize server utilization, and redundancy for a microservice can be better achieved by running multiple instances of the same microservice across multiple server instances.

Migrating to Microservices

SIMPLIFYING FOOTBALL PLAY CALLING

The backbone of the Erhardt-Perkins system is that plays—pass plays in particular—are not organized by a route tree or by calling a single receiver's route but by what coaches refer to as "concepts." Each play has a name, and

continued

continued

that name conjures up an image for both the quarterback and the other players on offense. And, most importantly, the concept can be called from almost any formation or set. Who does what changes, but the theory and tactics driving the play do not. "In essence, you're running the same play," said Perkins. "You're just giving them some window-dressing to make it look different."

The biggest advantage of the concept-based system is that it operates from the perspective of the most critical player on offense: the quarterback. In other systems, even if the underlying principles are the exact same, the play and its name might be very different. Rather than juggling all this information in real time, an Erhardt-Perkins quarterback only has to read a given arrangement of receivers. "You can cut down on the plays and get different looks from your formations and who's in them. It's easier for the players to learn. It's easier for the quarterback to learn," former Patriots offensive coordinator Charlie Weis said back in 2000. "You get different looks without changing his reads. You don't need an open-ended number of plays."

—Brown C., 2013

To close this play to deliver microservices architectures, let's return to the core topic of the play: developing and delivering microservices architectures. There are two scenarios here:

- Develop and deliver new cloud-native apps
- Migrate existing *monolithic apps* to microservices

The first scenario can be achieved using the microservices, 12-Factor App, and cloud-native app principles and guidance provided earlier. This is a new application, which, while it may consume existing applications and services, is being built from the ground up and will not be encumbered by existing architectures and constraints due to existing code and data.

In the second scenario, it is like developing a new football *play calling system*. The goal is to simplify the existing architecture—code and data—into architectural components that can be migrated to components that can each map to a microservice. However, the architectural decisions made for the monolithic app and the existing data stored in databases become a source of major challenges. The application and the data need to be refactored, as shown in Figure 5-12. In addition, Conway's law comes into play with the existing team structures, which may need to be broken down to properly re-architect the app.

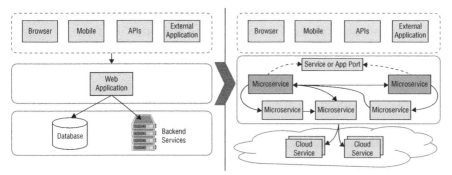

Figure 5-12: Re-architecting to a microservices architecture

Here are the core steps to refactor a traditional monolithic app to microservices (Brown, 2016):

■ *Repackaging the application.* Let's take a Java app as an example. Most Java apps are deployed as a large EAR file deployed to an app server like IBM WebSphere, Oracle WebLogic, or Apache Tomcat. These EAR files are typically composed of multiple WAR files that were developed by different development teams and "integrated" into the EAR file. As shown in Figure 5-13, decomposing the EAR files into individually deployable WAR files, each becoming a microservice, is a good start. While it does not address the architectural complexities by *decoupling* the underlying components (in other words, it does not address the architectural dependencies added due to Conway's law), it does address the need to make each component capable of being built, deployed, and managed independently of others, a key requirement of microservices.

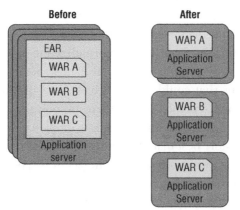

Figure 5-13: Repackaging Java apps into microservices

- *Refactoring the code.* Now you are looking at taking the architectural dependencies that do not make sense and breaking them down into microservices that are truly granular in nature. This effort requires looking at the code to determine where there are granular *service-like* behaviors embedded in the existing components and then refactoring the code into its own component. This component will then need to be given a well-defined RESTful interface, if it does not exist, in order to make a complete microservice. Depending upon the design patterns used, this refactoring can be a fairly complex effort and should be treated as such.

- *Refactoring the data.* The toughest challenge to migrating existing applications to microservices is not related to the code at all, but the data. Over the years, existing applications with large and often multiple data sources and complex data flows between the databases and application components make even understanding what is stored and why a complex task. However, when it comes to refactoring the applications into microservices, refactoring the data structure models becomes critical. For microservices to behave and operate independently of other microservices, they need to be able to interact with the right data structure, stored in the right data store. In order to achieve this, all the data models and data storage decisions need to be revisited:

  - Is the right data structure being used?
  - Is the right data store being used?
  - Is the right approach being used to query the data?

  In the past, a relational database was the only option. This resulted in all data formats, from binary data to structured Java objects to graph data models, all being stored in relational databases. Furthermore, these relational databases were heavily normalized to save space. All these resulted in overly complex relational data structures, binaries being stored as blobs that could not effectively have queried, or extremely complex queries of graphs. Today there are polyglot data stores—from object storage to JSON document stores to graph databases—to store the data in a data store best matched for its format and query requirements. Again, this refactoring is not trivial. In fact, it is typically an even more complex undertaking than refactoring code, given the complexity of the data structure types, data models, and data stores that may be involved. However, to get a true microservices architecture, there is no calling for a *punt* to get around it.

Play: Develop an API Economy

IT'S THE ECONOMY, STUPID!

World soccer clubs, constrained by their inability to increase their income from their traditional businesses, have begun to adopt strategies to transform themselves into modern sports and media companies. Under the recent presidency of Florentino Pérez, the Spanish football club Real Madrid presents a good example of the application of this expanded vision. One of the fundamental pillars of this model has involved designing and implementing a new marketing strategy aimed at strengthening the value of the club's brand. The adoption of this model has resulted in a significant increase in income from marketing. Undeniably, in this area, Real Madrid has become the leader in world soccer.

—Fordacell, 2006

Just like soccer clubs looking for innovative ways to develop new monetization models to increase their brand's value, APIs can help organizations looking to innovate with business models beyond their core competencies and capabilities.

APIs allow applications and services to expose their functionality and capabilities outside their team to other applications and services, both inside and outside their organizations. APIs are sometimes also referred to as such—*inner* APIs are those that are leveraged internally within the organization, and *outer* APIs are leveraged externally. The security, management, and metering requirements are, of course, different based on the intended target audience of the API.

APIs should be the default mechanism by which applications and services communicate with each other. If you have developed a microservices-based architecture, that is the default mode. In legacy apps, there may be scenarios where there are point-to-point custom integrations between applications. These should be replaced with well-defined APIs.

APIs are not new. The concept has been around for a long time, especially gaining traction with the popularity of service-oriented architecture (SOA). In fact, there is often debate about the differences between SOA and APIs. In their purest form, both provide a mechanism to decouple applications into services, which have a well-defined architectural interface with which to communicate and connect with other services. By definition, this architectural interface is an API. The main difference between what is today referred to as an API and the traditional SOA interfaces is that APIs are associated with REST/JSON interfaces, whereas SOA is associated with XML and SOAP. This enables APIs to be extremely lightweight, flexible, and easy to manage and to consume, compared to SOA.

APIs have become a mechanism for driving innovation by allowing developers to create new applications leveraging internal and external APIs to add more services to their applications. They do so in two ways:

- *Leveraging the ecosystem.* Organizations can do this by developing new, innovative applications leveraging APIs from external third-party services. Why build your own mapping service if there is a third-party public API that delivers the service? Why build a user identity management service if another team in the organization has already built one and has exposed it via an API? Figure 5-14 shows the sports network ESPN's public APIs, which allow any developer to include sports data in their apps.
- *Scaling through the ecosystem.* Organizations can now monetize their own business capabilities beyond the monetization capabilities of their own business models by exposing them to a broader ecosystem via APIs. If a bank has developed a service that efficiently and accurately calculates the "Greeks" or risk profile of a derivatives trade, why not monetize it by allowing external partners to consume that service and pay for it via an API?

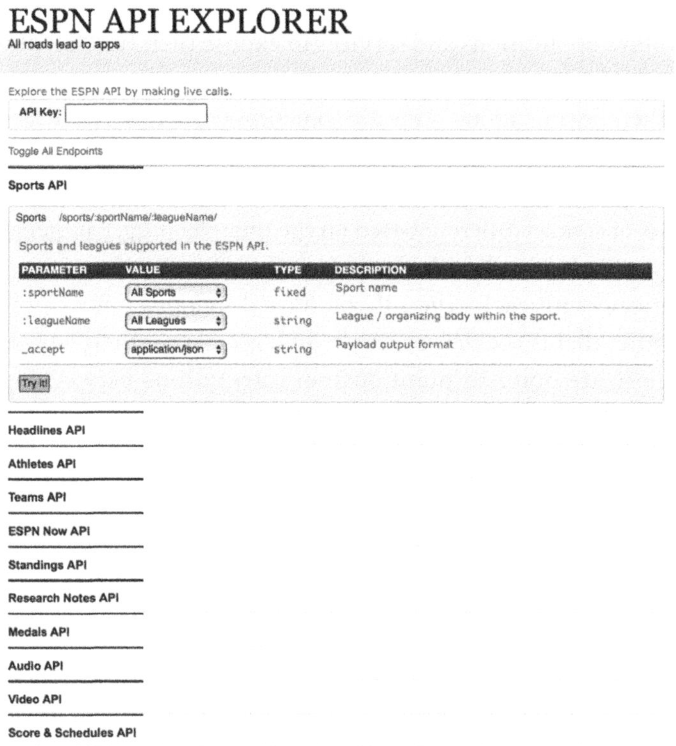

Figure 5-14: ESPN public APIs (ESPN Developer Center, 2015)

Deployment Automation and APIs

From a DevOps perspective, APIs are the same as a service. Organizations need to treat APIs as a product. This is especially true for "outer" APIs, whether they are monetized or not. Even internally, though, an API is a *contract* between the provider and the consumer and needs to be treated as such. For application delivery purposes, delivering an API is providing the service that the API exposes. The lifecycle of the service, however, now also includes steps that address the APIs. For example:

- *Testing* the app or services' functionality, performance, and security is not enough. You need to do the same to the APIs, leveraging use cases of how the APIs would be consumed.
- *Configuration management* of the app and services typically also includes managing the configuration of the associated middleware. Now, configuration management of the API and any API management software that is utilized should also be addressed.
- For *release management,* the release of a business capability is the release of all the applications and services that go into delivering the business capability. With APIs included, the release will also need to include all the third-party APIs consumed by the applications and services being released. Managing the SLAs of these APIs becomes a concern of the release management team.

I have already discussed the core value proposition of APIs for continuous delivery at length in the section on microservices architecture. APIs allow applications and services to be de-coupled. They can thus be built, deployed, and run independently of each other, without being concerned about the deployment location of the other services they consume. All that matters is the availability of the APIs. Applications and services can also be scaled by deploying more instances of the service that needs to be scaled, without having to scale other services that are not impacted by the scale of the service being requested for scaling. APIs thus allow for true continuous delivery, by allowing for the delivery of small batches of change, with rapid feedback cycle times.

DevOps Platform and APIs

The role of APIs is also a crucial component because the DevOps platform itself is also accessible via APIs, whether it is implemented using IaaS, PaaS, or CaaS. Let's look at the role of APIs for each of these variants.

▓ If the platform is implemented leveraging an IaaS cloud, then the IaaS services are all exposed as APIs. These services and the resources they deliver are all consumed by the applications being delivered and run on the platform via APIs. In the scenario I described earlier in the section "Cloud Orchestration" of full stack provisioning across multiple clouds using portable Heat patterns, leveraging OpenStack APIs to provision the HEAT patterns on multiple clouds. Figure 5-15 shows an example of the networking API available for OpenStack.

POST   /v2.0/networks
        Create network

Creates a network.

A request body is optional. An administrative user can specify another tenant UUID, which is the tenant who owns the network, in the request body.

Error response codes: 201,401,400

Request

Request Example

```
{
    "network": {
        "name": "sample_network",
        "admin_state_up": true
    }
}
```

Response Parameters

Name	In	Type	Description
status	body	string	The network status.
router:external (Optional)	body	boolean	Indicates whether this network is externally accessible.
availability_zone_hints	body	array	The availability zone candidate for the network.
availability_zones	body	array	The availability zone for the network.
name	body	string	Human-readable name of the resource.
admin_state_up	body	boolean	The administrative state of the resource, which is up (true) or down (false).
tenant_id	body	string	The ID of the tenant who owns the resource.
mtu	body	integer	The MTU of a network resource.
qos_policy_id (Optional)	body	string	The UUID of the QoS policy.
subnets	body	array	The associated subnets.
shared (Optional)	body	boolean	Admin-only. Indicates whether this network is shared across all tenants.
id	body	string	The UUID of the network.
network	body	object	A network object.

Figure 5-15: OpenStack networking API (OpenStack.org, 2016)

▓ If the platform is being implemented using a PaaS or a CaaS, the tooling also becomes accessible by leveraging APIs. The DevOps tooling in these scenarios are services running on the PaaS or in containers. These services are connected and orchestrated to implement the application delivery pipeline using their APIs.

Play: Organizing for Innovation

DEVELOPING PROS

The Dominican Republic and Nicaragua are roughly comparable in population and share an equally deep passion for baseball. But the Dominican Republic has sent well over 100 players to Major League Baseball (MLB) teams, while Nicaragua counts only three big-time players.

Nicaragua is looking to change that disparity. And the first step in achieving that may have come early this year with the opening of the Nicaraguan Baseball Academy. Dennis Martínez, who in 1976 became the first Nicaraguan to make it to the majors, is helping to lead this effort to train aspiring major leaguers with the skills necessary to attract attention from scouts.

Success will not only boost a new generation of Nicaraguan players but inject some needed cash into the country's economy—judging by the example of the Dominican Republic.

In the Dominican Republic, pitchers, hitters, and fielders are major export commodities, earning serious foreign exchange for the country and massive remittances for the athletes' families. The fame of Dominican superstars like David Ortiz, Robinson Canó, and Sammy Sosa (before his steroids scandal) fill MLB stadiums and also help boost tourism—a major growth industry—to their homeland.

Just as important, baseball has been the path out of poverty for thousands of Dominican youth—a healthy and lucrative alternative to dangerous careers in gangs and crime.

Nicaragua's Martínez, who in 1991 became the only Latin American-born pitcher to throw a perfect game, is betting that Nicaraguan youth—like their Dominican counterparts—have the talent and ambition to succeed in MLB. The challenge had been developing the proper business model.

—Feinberg, 2011

How do you identify and develop professional players? The *Moneyball* model only works when the player already has a statistically significant track record to base a selection decision on. How do you go through the thousands of young players who are striving for stardom to identify the emerging prospects and invest in them?

Innovation is the same. For every startup that became Uber and Airbnb, and before them Facebook and PayPal, and even before them Microsoft and Apple, there are thousands of startups that failed. Some never got past the formation of the founder team, while others even exited via an IPO, or by being acquired, only to die despite the prospects. You, of course, do not hear of all those that didn't make it.

Within large organizations, the situation is even worse. There are very few large companies like Google, which never lost its innovation culture and has several mechanisms in place to encourage new ideas from its employees (He, 2013). Most large organizations are not designed for innovation. They do not have a culture of innovation; in fact, most have the exact opposite. Employees are stifled by strict governance and performance management measures that encourage them to do their prescribed job, to remain "in the box," and to do their work to the best of their ability, and new ideas are not encouraged. This, of course, is not a viable business model for today's competitive and rapidly changing world. Having the best DevOps platform and efficient technology platforms designed for innovation is not of any value if there are no innovative ideas being developed and experimented with.

> *The story of innovation has not changed. It has always been a small team of people who have a new idea, typically not understood by people around them and their executives.*
>
> —Eric Schmidt, Chairman, Google

From a DevOps adoption perspective, this culture is critical, and creating it trumps all the technology and process improvement that can be adopted by the IT teams. All the themes and plays discussed in this chapter are designed to enable the teams Eric Schmidt talks about. These are the teams that come up with the innovative ideas and work hard to experiment with them to see if a business opportunity exists and if the innovative idea is viable. All this is moot if the culture at the organization does not even allow the team to work on the idea with the freedom and the resources they need, if the people around them and the executives that Eric mentions do not enable a culture that allows ideas to evolve and thrive and fail without consequences. That culture is not easy to establish in a large organization with significant *cultural inertia*, but it is essential. Large organizations are often able to do this in small teams that are able to fly under the radar but that works only for small projects in isolation. To achieve an organization-wide innovation culture requires the ability to innovate across the organization, at enterprise scale.

Developing an Innovation Culture in Large Organizations

Many sports, not just football, have kind of the macho meathead mentality where innovation is almost frowned upon.

—Lawrence Jackson, former American football player

McKinsey and company have presented four proven approaches on how to establish and scale this innovation culture. They speak in the context of a *digital disruption* (Edelman, 2015):

1. *Organizational pivot.* The organization puts the innovation leaders in charge of the entire organization, not just of driving innovation. This allows the organization to develop an *innovation first* culture, which also accelerates the optimization of the legacy systems.

2. *Reverse takeover.* This is a more aggressive option where the innovation leaders take over the legacy apps and systems and transform their processes, technology, and teams to be the same as those of the innovation teams, enabling organization-wide innovation processes, technology, and culture.

3. *Spinoff.* This is a slice-and-dice approach where the innovation-focused teams are grouped into a separate, independent division to allow them all to grow, thrive, and develop the right processes, IT platforms, and culture on their own, unencumbered by the rest of the organization's cultural inertia. In some extreme cases, these divisions have also been spun off as separate companies either independent or as a subsidiary.

4. *The piggyback.* This is a partnership approach where the organization teams up with another firm that has the necessary innovation-focused skills, know-how, and culture. The partner then starts delivering innovation systems to complement the legacy systems from the base organization, without the organization needing to transform itself.

I will be discussing specific team models for adopting a DevOps culture, both for optimization and for innovation, in the next chapter.

Summary

In this chapter I focused on DevOps plays that are patterns of success seen when adopting DevOps for projects and programs that have the goal of innovation. It is important to note that outside of startups, most organizations rarely have innovative projects that operate in isolation. Hence, each innovative product will dependencies on existing applications and services that are not innovative in nature but deliver core business services. Real DevOps adoption in large organizations will hence always include both plays for optimization and innovation.

The four plays I introduced in this chapter are:

- Build a DevOps Platform
- Deliver Microservices Architectures
- Develop an API Economy
- Organizing for Innovation

These plays help achieve the four *themes* highlighted at the beginning of this chapter:

- Achieving Multi-Speed IT
- Building the right thing
- Enabling experimentation
- Delivering Antifragile systems

At the end of the day, it is achieving these themes are what is critical to success. These are the goals one is trying to achieve.

Multi-speed is reality. In most large organization there is a wide spread of technology stacks, practices, team maturity, regulatory and compliance needs, and business drivers that result in multiple speeds across applications and services being delivered.

A very significant percentage projects fail because they built the wrong thing, despite building it right. Unfortunately, more investment is made in most organizations on improving development and delivery processes, rather than on design practices, and on leveraging techniques like those from the *Lean startup* movement. Leveraging *experimentation* to discover this *right* thing to build it and the *right* way to deliver it, goes hand in hand.

And finally, as one builds systems that can handle rapid experimentation, handle variable usage and loads, and be able to scale in real-time, one needs to deliver *Antifragile* systems, systems that thrive in chaos.

CHAPTER 6

Scaling DevOps for the Enterprise

BUILDING A CULTURE OF WINNING

The prospect of going from a team that's at the bottom of the standings to one that's on top is daunting. When you've done a lot of losing, it gets hard to imagine yourself winning. So even as I'm confronting players about their weaknesses, I'm also always trying to build a culture of success. That's not something you can do overnight. You have to go one step at a time, the same way you move the ball down the field, yard by yard.

Here's my philosophy: to win games, you need to believe as a team that you have the ability to win games. That is, confidence is born only of demonstrated ability. This may sound like a catch-22, but it's important to remember that even small successes can be extremely powerful in helping people believe in themselves.

In training camp, therefore, we don't focus on the ultimate goal—getting to the Super Bowl. We establish a clear set of goals that are within immediate reach: we're going to be a smart team; we're going to be a well-conditioned team; we're going to be a team that plays hard; we're going to be a team that has pride; we're going to be a team that wants to win collectively; we're going to be a team that doesn't criticize one another.

When we start acting in ways that fulfill these goals, I make sure everybody knows it. I accentuate the positive at every possible opportunity, and at the same time I emphasize the next goal that we need to fulfill. If we have a particularly good practice, then I call the team together and say, "We got something done today; we executed real well. I'm very pleased with your work. But here's what I want to do tomorrow: I want to see flawless special

continued

continued

teams work. If you accomplish that, then we'll be ready for the game on Sunday."

When you set small, visible goals and people achieve them, they start to get it into their heads that they can succeed. They break the habit of losing and begin to get into the habit of winning. It's extremely satisfying to see that kind of shift take place in the way a team thinks about itself.

—Parcells, 2000

The set of *plays* presented in this chapter examine how DevOps can be scaled across a large organization. Large organizations are not monolithic in nature. They have several smaller divisions and business units within them, each with its own platforms, processes, maturity, politics, and culture. These organizations may have grown through acquisitions and mergers. It is not uncommon to see these acquired or merged organizations continue to exist within the parent organization almost as independently operating suborganizations. In some cases, this may be intentional, where the parent organization just operates the acquired company as a wholly owned subsidiary with no intent to integrate it into the parent organization. In other cases, it is mostly the result of an integration effort gone bad; this effort may have failed either because of bad planning or execution or most likely due to a lack of full buy-in from the leadership of the merging organization to truly integrate—to truly change its culture. Integrating or standardizing technology is relatively easy. Standardizing culture is not.

Furthermore, as I discuss in Chapters 3 and 4, large organizations typically have rigid and complex governance practices that stifle speed and innovation. These practices are designed to manage and control a sprawling organization with many moving parts, not to enable agility and creativity. As a result, such organizations see success with DevOps adoption within small teams, working on small projects. These projects are able to "fly under the radar" or are protected by the executives sponsoring them, which allows them to operate outside the traditional governance and processes. They are allowed to be agile and innovative. However, without changing the governance models or changing the culture at an organizational level, this success cannot be scaled. The plays in this chapter are designed to achieve the scaling.

Core Themes

Just like the previous two chapters, I'll begin by looking at a few core themes. These themes are woven through the plays presented in this chapter, which are designed to scale DevOps adoption across a large, potentially distributed organization.

Organizational Culture

The culture precedes positive results. It doesn't get tacked on as an afterthought on your way to the victory stand. Champions behave like champions before they're champions; they have a winning standard of performance before they are winners.

—Bill Walsh, American football coach

I have repeated this statement several times through this book: *DevOps is at its core a cultural movement.* The first goal of DevOps is to build up trust, communication, and collaboration between the different stakeholders in the application delivery pipeline. All other goals are secondary, or enablers of this primary goal. If you have a fully automated, integrated delivery pipeline, with a push-button self-serve environment, and highly optimized processes, but the developers and testers never collaborate with the Ops practitioners; never give them guidance on changes they will be deploying and that will impact their dev-test-prod environments; and never receive feedback from the Ops teams, then the application being delivered will not meet the business goals to its fullest potential.

This becomes a major challenge in large organizations. Such organizations have inherent *cultural inertia,* as I discuss in Chapter 2. They are organized with complex, bureaucratic organizational structures and governance processes. These structures were designed over time to manage and maintain oversight over a large organization. Organizations are broken down along *divisions* representing *lines of business,* or an arbitrary separation along parochial organizational lines, such as those representing acquired or merged businesses. These divisions may be further organized along functional silos. There may also be some other operational silos representing *shared services*—service providers who are shared across multiple lines of business.

Creating a *culture* that permeates across all these boundaries and silos is not a trivial task. It requires leadership and sponsorship from the highest levels of the organization. That is the only level that can influence and promote change across all organizational divisions and silos. Only the highest leadership level can overcome cultural inertia by providing the "air cover" necessary to allow teams adopting DevOps processes and practices to operate outside the traditional organizational governance controls and inherent culture.

Probably the most important caveat to remember here is that cultural transformation is not a one-time effort. It is not a project that has a beginning and an end. Cultural inertia also develops in a new culture, resulting in the challenges of rigid processes and people becoming set in their ways, leading to inefficiencies in even the best of DevOps cultures. True cultural transformation needs to come with a culture of *continuous improvement*—to be better today than you were yesterday.

Standardization of Tools and Practices

It is impossible to improve any process until it is standardized. If the process is shifting from here to there, then any improvement will just be one more variation that is occasionally used and mostly ignored. One must standardize, and thus stabilize the process, before continuous improvement can be made.

—Masaaki Imai, Japanese organizational theorist and founder of the Kaizen Institute

Continuous improvement requires standardization to be in place before it can be executed. As Imai-san states here, if a process has variations as it is executed each time, it cannot be improved upon. It will not be possible to determine what needs to be improved in order to maximize the efficiency of the process. Also, if an improvement has been made to a process but the process is executed in a manner different than it was before the improvement was made, it will not be possible to measure whether the improvement had an impact and at what level. Now multiply this by the number of teams and whether each team executes the processes with its own variations and flavors, and you can see that determining what to improve becomes almost impossible. I need to state here that I don't mean that processes should be followed rigidly, because that itself defeats the principle of *Agility*; however, variations should be within reason and for a reason, one that customizes the process for a specific need the team or project may have.

Overall, processes need to be standardized to a bare minimum set from which the team can choose the standardized processes that are best for their needs. Organizations need to determine how many "sets" of standardized processes need to be in place based on the *risk-value profiles* of various projects. The thinking on processes described here applies equally to the tools implementing and automating these processes, and these tools also need to be standardized.

Furthermore, people need to be *fungible*.[1] While calling people fungible seems cold and certainly politically incorrect, it is a necessity in *Agile* organizations with multiple projects and deliverables with staffing needs that change over time. Consider a practitioner with a particular skill set. If one team no longer needs those skills but another team does, what level of effort is required to transition the practitioner from the first team to the next? Will training on processes be required? Will training on tools be required? How much time will be needed to *onboard* the practitioner to her new team? Standardization of processes and tools makes this transition seamless. It makes the practitioner fungible across teams and projects.

Organized Adoption

Champions do not become champions when they win the event, but in the hours, weeks, months, and years they spend preparing for it. The victorious performance itself is merely the demonstration of their championship character.

—T. Alan Armstrong, American author

As I mentioned earlier, adopting DevOps is not a one-time project, but an ongoing effort. When adopting across a large organization, it is imperative to do so in an organized manner to ensure proper standardization of processes and tooling and to ensure minimization of any loss of productivity. As I discuss in previous chapters, introducing any change, even one for the positive, results in a drop in productivity as practitioners adjust to the changes and get comfortable with the new way of working. Having an organized approach to change, with proper enablement and coaching, ensures minimization of this *dip* in productivity.

Another reason to do so in an organized manner is to invest the minimum resources in driving change. There will be only so many leaders available to provide coaching and only so many processes and tool specialists to help drive process and tool adoption. There is only so much capacity in an organization

---

[1] Fungible: Being of such a nature that one part or quantity may be replaced by another equal part or quantity in the satisfaction of an obligation. (*The Merriam-Webster Dictionary*)

to absorb change and the associated loss of productivity. Change should thus be made in a *rolling adoption* across the enterprise, as sets of projects and teams are onboarded one set at a time. The size of each set will depend on the coaching and enablement resources available.

Because organizations may have significant variations in practitioner and process maturity across teams, divisions, and geographies, it is also imperative to plan for handling these variations. There may be a need to run sets of pilot projects in different divisions and geographies to prove that the adoption of the new processes and tools will work for the local variants, and if they do not work, what changes and enhancements need to be made to accommodate these variations. For example, an offshore team with more junior practitioners and larger team sizes may need more coaching and enablement than a smaller team with highly experienced practitioners. Teams working on an older toolset due to the needs of their projects may need to do an upgrade to an intermediate level of tools, before going to the highest level of automation. For example, you would want to move COBOL programmers working on "green screens" to an Eclipse-based desktop IDE, before moving them to a web-based IDE.

Breaking Down Organizational Silos

Breaking down organizational silos in large organizations is extremely difficult. There are political powers that resist change. There are executives and senior managers whose power structures, influences, and "fiefdoms" are threatened when exploring organizational change. Very few organizations have leadership with the political will to reorganize entire reporting structures from the top down. Creating a new senior executive role with all the functional teams in the application delivery pipeline reporting to her would be extremely unusual, and it would be even more unusual for this implementation to succeed.

The breaking down of organizational silos is essential, but in large organizations it needs to be done without disrupting existing reporting structures. Leveraging *matrixed* teams where practitioners remain in their existing reporting lines but functionally work on a team with matrixed reporting into that team's leadership is an alternative that works. It really doesn't matter which vice president the Ops practitioner reports to, as long as she knows, and is able to freely work with, her project teams and to get direction from the team's leadership. If communication has to go through "proper management chains," then such a matrixed model will not work. Practitioners need to be able to communicate freely and collaborate with their team. Free communication and visibility into all the team's practitioners' work builds trust.

Play: DevOps Center of Competency

INDIA'S BADMINTON CENTER OF COMPETENCY

If there is one person and one academy that helped India produce world-class shuttlers[2] and emerge as a badminton hotbed, it's Pullela Gopichand and his badminton academy [in Hyderabad]. Sixteen years after his heart-breaking defeat at the Sydney Olympics, Gopichand came close to realizing his Olympic dream—albeit in a different role.

The amazing run of P.V. Sindhu at the Rio Olympics has brought the focus on her celebrated coach and his academy here. Sindhu, who created history by bagging silver in the women's singles event, is one of the products of Pullela Gopichand Badminton Academy.

Sindhu is the second woman shuttler after Saina Nehwal to take the badminton world by storm and bring laurels to the academy set up by former All England Open Champion.

Analysts say the credit of turning India into a formidable force in the world of badminton goes to the 42-year-old, who has groomed world-class talents....

Gopichand always had dreams of producing Olympic medalists. His efforts started yielding results with Saina bagging bronze in the 2012 London Olympics.

She became the first Indian woman shuttler to achieve the feat. Four years later, Gopichand's dream again came true with Sindhu reaching the final and losing there only to World No. 1 Carolina Marin.

—TheSportsCampus, 2016

Probably the most significant investment that can be made in driving the adoption of a *DevOps culture* across a large organization is the setting up of a *DevOps Center of Competency* (CoC). India has produced two Olympic women's badminton medalists in successive Olympics, in a country with no major legacy in the sport, all because of one coach named Pullela Gopichand and his Gopichand Badminton Academy, a badminton Center of Competency. Coach Gopichand, himself a world-class badminton player, missed out on an Olympic medal in his own career but has created a central source of expertise, enablement, and coaching for budding badminton players to follow a proven

---

[2] Badminton players are referred to as *shuttlers*.

methodology to develop into world-class, Olympic medal-winning players. Similarly, a DevOps Center of Competency can serve the purpose of being a source of expertise, enablement, and coaching for teams in an organization looking to adopt DevOps.

Let's begin by first defining what a Center of Competency is.

COMPETENCY CENTER

An organizational structure used to coordinate IT skills with an enterprise. Competency centers provide expertise for project or program support, acting both as repositories of knowledge and resource pools for multiple business areas. Skills-based competency centers, the most common type in an information services organization, are used for application development, software language skills, data management, Internet development, and network design. Within the enterprise, it is increasingly common to find competency centers (or shared services) for travel, finance, and human resources. Repository-based competencies act exclusively as sources of information.

—Gartner, 2016

This Center of Competency is not an administrative organization or a "tools/ enablement group," but a place where DevOps adoptees come to learn from experts and from each other and to share expertise and lessons learnt. As organizations adopt and scale DevOps practices, this CoC also becomes a source of DevOps expertise, enablement, tooling guidance, and even hosting, as well as DevOps coaches who can help teams and programs to adopt DevOps. The CoC also owns the organization's DevOps framework or methodology—their own flavor of DevOps.

Capabilities and Goals of a DevOps CoC

The CoC needs to have a well-defined charter and set of goals for the organization. The CoC also needs to be a multi-faceted organization owning a set of capabilities and having a set of goals to achieve with those capabilities. If leveraging this book, the CoC would also be responsible for developing the organizational "Playbook" from the "Plays" presented here, and for understanding and owning the execution of the Plays. These include the following:

- Provide thought leadership for DevOps adoption
- Provide mentorship during a DevOps transformation

- Help project teams follow a *DevOps adoption roadmap*, developed for them, leveraging techniques like *value stream mapping*.
- Facilitate communications within the organization, across teams, and with management.
- Set up a community for DevOps adoption across the organization. This community should have a virtual portal through which best practices, enablement, and other assets can be shared, and practitioners can participate in forums. It should also have local chapters that meet regularly.
- Drive change and enable continuous improvement.
- Provide visibility to the progress and results that the organization is making as it scales its DevOps adoption across the organization.
- Capture and make available measurements and metrics to track success.
- Document and communicate best practices.
- Facilitate or provide common tooling for the DevOps platform.
- Engage the stakeholders across functional silos to drive DevOps adoption.
- Spread and celebrate success stories within the organization to win over skeptics and laggards.
- Be a permanent organization to ensure that DevOps adoption is seen as an ongoing, continuous improvement effort and not a one-time project.
- Provide coaching to project teams through *DevOps coaches*.
- Provide coaching to executive management driving the long-term transformation, to ensure the right level of planning is done, and the right level of investments are made to enable success.

Core CoC Roles

The DevOps CoC needs to have some well-defined roles in order to position it for success:

- *Project managers.* As more and more projects start leveraging the CoC to help drive DevOps adoption, project managers are needed to help manage the resources deployed across the projects and to manage the needs of the various projects.
- *Implementation manager.* This manager drives implementation of assessments, tooling solutions, and measurements across projects adopting DevOps.

- *Infrastructure manager.* This manager sets up and maintains tooling to deliver a DevOps platform to the project teams. The DevOps platform may be owned and managed by the CoC or by a separate tools or environment team.
- *DevOps coach.* I will present more details on this role in the following section.
- *Evangelist.* As the name suggests, the evangelist drives initiative, communicates, and shares DevOps learning and success stories.

The DevOps Coach

COACHING CAN MAKE OR BREAK AN OLYMPIC ATHLETE

What differentiates a superelite from someone who competes at the Olympics but goes home empty-handed? New research suggests it can come down to the coach–athlete relationship. According to findings presented in November at the World Class Performance Conference in London, superelites felt that their coaches fully satisfied their emotional needs by acting as friends, mentors, and unwavering supporters—in addition to providing superb technical support. High-performing athletes who were not medaled did not feel that way. "This turns on its head a long-held view that we must simply pair the best technical and tactical coaches to our best athletes to achieve ultimate performance," says Matthew Barlow, a postdoctoral researcher in sport psychology at Bangor University in Wales, who led the study.

Barlow and his colleagues were commissioned to find out what it takes to win multiple gold medals by the governmental organization UK Sport, which promotes the nation's elite sports and athletic development. The researchers initially identified 43 variables that reliably predicated the probability that someone would become a superelite. One of those factors was the coach–athlete relationship, so UK Sport funded a second in-depth analysis that focused solely on this aspect.

So Barlow and his colleagues recruited 16 male and female superelite athletes, all of whom had won gold at a major championship (such as the Olympics). They also recruited 16 athletes who had competed in such championships but never medaled. The groups were matched in sport, age, and gender. The scientists then conducted in-depth interviews with the athletes as well as their parents and coaches. After analyzing the results they found that all the athletes said they were technically supported by their coaches—but it was the superelites who reported they also enjoyed thorough emotional support. "Superelite athletes perceived their need for emotional and esteem support were met in a way that the elites did not," Barlow says.

Coaches of superelites acted almost as surrogate parents, praising their athletes' efforts, emphasizing unwavering belief in them, providing positive feedback, and taking an interest in personal lives. "A cyclist might come in and the coach says, 'Hey, you're not looking quite right, let's have a coffee and talk about difficulties you might be having at home,'" Barlow says. "They have a bond that goes beyond spreadsheets, power outputs and graphs." Some elite athletes, on the other hand, felt invisible to their coaches or sensed their mentors seemed to expect failure at key moments when they most needed support.

—Nuwer, 2016

While the role of DevOps coach is fairly new in the industry, the concept is not new. It is modeled after the *Agile coach*, which has been a role in Agile adoption for a long time. DevOps coaches bring their knowledge of agility, DevOps practices, and outcome-driven behavior to the projects. DevOps coaches are embedded in one or multiple projects, depending on the project team size, with the goal of transferring their knowledge and experience to leaders in the project team. Their goal is to work themselves out of a job by leaving a self-reliant team that can deliver efficiently leveraging DevOps practices, and that has embarked on a journey of continuous improvement. The team can, of course, continue to receive further guidance even after the assigned coach disengages, through the DevOps CoC. The teams are also expected to give back to the CoC by sharing their own experiences, success, and lessons learned.

A typical role description of a DevOps coach includes the following:

- The DevOps coach works closely with teams and team members to develop and perform activities allowing the development of Lean and DevOps capabilities, with a goal of continuous improvement of their skills.
- The DevOps coach shares her experience and expertise with the teams and ensures that the best practices adopted by the CoC are being used as the organization's DevOps methodology.

- The objective of the DevOps coach is to help teams develop their DevOps capabilities in order to rapidly become self-sufficient and not need the coach in the long term.
- The DevOps coach helps teams adopt the right team model of squads and tribes (which I will introduce later in this chapter) to develop a cross-functional team addressing all their skill requirements.
- DevOps coaches drive communication, collaboration, and group dynamics, and work on increasing trust between team members.
- DevOps coaches need to raise issues and drive change to remove impediments to adoption.
- DevOps coaches need to be the link between multiple projects in the organization, and with the CoC, to ensure uniformity and standardization of DevOps adoption across the organization.
- DevOps coaches need to run experiments within the teams they are coaching to learn which variants of DevOps methods and approaches work best for the team, with which enhancements, if any.
- DevOps coaches own the responsibility of harvesting success stories, lessons learned, and suggested improvements back to the CoC, to share with other teams in the organization.
- DevOps coaches themselves need to have an attitude of continuous improvement for their own capabilities and skills.

Setting Up a CoC

Setting up a CoC requires senior management-level sponsorship. It is a significant investment. In order to get this buy-in, the CoC should begin as a startup. It should operate by developing itself as a minimum viable product, or MVP, with staffing coming from volunteers from various projects to fill the roles. The hypothesis this MVP needs to prove is that a CoC can have an impact on the business results of a project by helping the project adopt DevOps practices. This hypothesis needs to be proven by running it against multiple pilot projects, showing improvement in the projects, and improvement in the CoC itself as it iterates with each pilot project. Once the hypothesis has been proven, and proven as something that can be repeated with similar results, a business case can be made to get sponsorship and funding for the CoC.

The first CoC meeting at a large multinational financial services company was a Friday afternoon brown-bag lunch where I was invited as an external speaker. Today, over three years later, the CoC has over 3,000 members in its global virtual community.

Play: Developing Culture of Innovation at Scale

The most important benefit of DevOps is its ability to drive innovation at scale. The pace of business requires faster software delivery. Instead of taking months to develop and release a new capability, the target should be to introduce innovations in weeks although some businesses demand innovation daily.

No longer do businesses have the luxury of "tweaking" their way towards sustained innovation. They need to reinvent themselves to stay relevant, particularly in the way they deliver software, which is increasingly the lifeblood of market differentiation and innovation.

—Jeff Smith, IBM CIO (Smith, 2015)

As IBM CIO Jeff Smith states here, the eventual goal is to scale a culture of innovation across the organization. While DevOps enables this, changing the culture requires a concerted organization-wide transformation. It requires a transformation that affects how each and every line of business, division, program, project, team, and individual approaches their daily tasks, as well as how they approach delivering the value asked for by the business.

This transformation requires a change in how teams are structured. (The team models have a dedicated play that I discuss later in this chapter.) The transformation requires a change in how teams break down large, complex application development and delivery efforts into *smaller batches* and deliver them and get feedback from the business and users in shorter *cycle times.* Even before you get to the development and delivery phase, the transformation requires that teams—from the line of business to Dev to Ops—ensure they are delivering the right thing. Innovation at its core requires *continuous experimentation* to validate the hypotheses with which the business is striving to deliver business value to its customers.

Let's examine how such a culture can be established—and, more importantly, how such a culture can be established at the scale required for a large, distributed organization. In order to do so, all the stakeholders need to be continuously asking several questions, for example:

- How do I understand *who* the end users are and what *needs* of theirs the organization is looking to fulfill?
- As the users fulfill their needs, how do I determine what *outcomes* the organization is looking for?

- As the users interact with the business via the application or service delivered, what *user experience* do I want them to have?
- What experiments need to be run to ensure that the organization has correctly understood the following:
    - *Who* are the users?
    - What *needs* are we looking to fulfill?
    - What *outcomes* are we looking for?
    - What is the desired *user experience*?
- How can I break these experiments down to *minimal viable products* or *features* that can be delivered with minimal investment to get rapid feedback?
- What *metrics* need to be measured to validate an experiment's success or failure?
- What is the next set of *goals* that need to be delivered to keep moving forward as experiments are run?
- How can the work be *broken down* into components and assigned to small teams while ensuring the teams remain aligned toward the broader delivery roadmap?
- How can teams keep validating their *progress*?
- Who owns the *overall vision* for what needs to be delivered, while the individual teams run experiments at a lower granularity?
- How can I *measure progress* and create an environment where a series of failed experiments is a measure of progress?
- How can I retain the focus on *developing for the user*, as teams grow larger and more distributed?
- How are *duties and responsibilities* distributed across teams and stakeholders?
- How do I *prioritize* work in an experimentation-focused development model?
- How do I *visually communicate* the end goals of a certain user experience that needs to be delivered across all the components being delivered?
- How do I create a culture where anyone on the team can *question* what is being developed and how it is being developed?
- How do I ensure I am asking the *right questions*?
- Regarding the goal of delivering small batches and *getting feedback* in a short cycle time, how do I capture this feedback and communicate it effectively to all stakeholders?

- How do I *consume the feedback* received and make adjustments to what is being developed and delivered?

There are two approaches that introduce this level of thinking and ability to look at every project, every task, and every process through a lens of experimentation in order to innovate:

- Lean startup
- Design thinking

I introduce both of these approaches in Chapter 5. The core themes of *Lean startup* are repeated here, but you can find more detailed descriptions in the section "Lean Startup" in Chapter 5:

- Eliminate uncertainty
- Work smarter, not harder
- Develop a minimum viable product
- Validate learning

The core themes of *design thinking* are also repeated here. Again, you can find more detailed descriptions in the section "Design Thinking" in Chapter 5:

- A focus on user outcomes
- Diverse empowered teams
- Restless reinvention

The synergy and alignment of goals between these approaches is clearly visible. Lean startup provides the core approaches needed to operate like a *startup*—an organization designed to fulfill a business need that is not fully defined, but the business has a "not-yet-validated" hypothesis on how to address it. A startup thus has to run several experiments to validate its multiple unknowns: the business problem, the proposed solution, the existence of a market to monetize, and the ability of the team to deliver the solution.

A startup is a company working to solve a problem where the solution is not obvious and success is not guaranteed.

—Neil Blumenthal, cofounder and co-CEO of Warby Parker

Design thinking, on the other hand, provides a methodology to construct, deliver, and leverage these experiments to progress the organization toward a viable solution that is a match to its users' needs and expectations.

> [Designers] don't try to search for a solution until they have determined the real problem, and even then, instead of solving that problem, they stop to consider a wide range of potential solutions. Only then will they finally converge upon their proposal. This process is called "Design Thinking."
>
> —Don Norman, author, *The Design of Everyday Things*

The goal of design thinking is to understand the users' needs and deliver outcomes continuously. Design thinking achieves this through a continuous *loop* that consists of the following:

- *Observing*—getting to know the users and understanding their needs
- *Reflecting*—forming a point of view upon which to develop plans to address the users' needs
- *Making*—building prototypes to give concrete form to ideas and explore possibilities to deliver real outcomes

Design thinking further provides a mechanism to allow this loop of observe-reflect-make to solve complex problems, leveraging a large number of teams. This mechanism is also made up of three components:

- *Hills.* This is a list of up to three of the most important user outcomes that need to be achieved. *Hills* leverage users' needs into project goals and targets.
- *Playbacks.* This involves bringing the teams together to review and reflect on what has been delivered to date for the hills being worked on, and to get "safe" criticism and feedback.
- *Sponsor users.* These are real users who are the touchpoints between the organization and the real world. They provide the users' perspective through the observe-reflect-make cycle.

The Offering Management Team

Organizations like IBM have adopted Lean startup and design thinking in tandem to develop a culture of innovation across the organization. IBM has done so by creating a new role within IBM called *offering management*.

IBM Offering Management is IBM's point-of-view on markets, users, products, and services. Offering managers decide in which markets IBM will play and how we will differentiate in those markets via unique functionality, great user experiences, digital engagement, and ecosystem partnering.

Offering managers are empowered to act as entrepreneurs to explore new markets of users with new user experiences. They are responsible for leading the co-creation of "whole" offerings that deliver value across all of the six universal experiences.

—IBM Design Thinking Field Guide, 2016

The six *universal experiences* mentioned in the quote that an offering management team needs to focus on are in place to help them view all decisions from a user experience perspective. They are as follows:

1. Discover, try, and buy—How do I get it?
2. Get started—How do I get value?
3. Everyday use—How do I get my job done?
4. Manage and upgrade—How do I keep it running?
5. Leverage and extend—How do I build on it?
6. Support—How do I get unstuck?

It is important to note how the questions for these experiences are worded. You can't read this without feeling like a user. It's not possible to even state them without putting yourself in the shoes of the user. It makes asking the questions a very powerful exercise.

Setting up an offering management team like IBM has done allows organizations to provide holistic ownership of the products and services across their product lifecycle, not just on a transient basis, as has been typically done. As time passes and the market changes, the products and services being offered will change. However, if the organization as a business survives these changes, it does so by evolving what it *offers* to its customer base. It changes its offerings to include new products and services to fulfil the needs of the market. Companies like Apple have gone from having desktops as their primary product, to music players, to laptops, and now to mobile devices. The offering management team leading the company evolved their products as the markets changed and their users' desired experiences changed. And in the case of Apple, they developed entire new markets that users did not even know they wanted (think iPad devices).

Consider a sports franchise offering solutions to address the business need of how fans can engage with their sports team. At the end of the day, their customers are their fans—not the athletes, not the TV networks, and certainly not the sponsors. In the old days, they engaged with them only at the playing field—through selling tickets and concessions. That evolved into selling jerseys and hats and other mementoes. Then came radio and television, which allowed them to engage with fans who did not even need to be geographically close to the franchise's location. This expanded to the web and to mobile apps. Today the focus of fan engagement is all through social media. The team's offering management group owns this evolution and any future evolution that may come. They are responsible for delivering new offerings to allow fans new user experiences by which they can engage with the team. They are responsible for retaining and growing this market and growing the team's business value. The individual products they delivered are transient in nature. Their offering—allowing fans to engage with the team—is permanent, at least as long as the sports team exists.

To summarize, design thinking is technology agnostic. In fact, it is context agnostic. You can use design thinking principles and methods to plan a vacation or design a home. A sports team can use it to develop new plays for the next match. You can (and I did) use it to develop a book. It provides a set of tools to *think*—for example, about *continuous innovations*, and of continuous improvement. It delivers on the core thinking needed to adopt a DevOps culture across an organization of any size.

Play: Developing a Culture of Continuous Improvement

IMPROVING COLLEGE FOOTBALL PLAYS

[If] you were to ask a longtime defensive coach like Manny Diaz where the sport is heading, he'd point you to a signature moment in the most thrilling game in recent memory: Auburn's victory in the 2013 Iron Bowl over mighty Alabama.

But Diaz wasn't as struck by the "Kick Six" touchdown that sealed the deal for the Tigers, nor the budding Saban-vs.-spread rivalry. Instead Diaz zeroes in on a play by Auburn quarterback Nick Marshall, one ending 31 seconds before Chris Davis' 109-yard game-winner.

"It's the most significant thing to happen to college football," the 17-year coaching veteran says. "The most important play of last season was the touchdown that tied the game at 28."

The play in question started out as a standard zone-read play, one Auburn had been running the entire season. It was at this moment that Gus Malzahn's offense brought football's future to the biggest stage.

The workings of the play are standard. It kept with what's become familiar to even NFL fans ... up until the end.

The offensive line started to block for an inside zone play. As far as the linemen knew, they were blocking straight ahead for another Tre Mason run. The fullback, Jay Prosch, arced around the unblocked defensive end to provide a lead block on the edge for Marshall, in case the quarterback got a "keep" read.

The addition of a lead blocker on the edge for the QB has caused enough trouble for college defenses, but that wrinkle is one Alabama already knew was coming. Marshall saw the defensive end stay inside, giving him the sign to keep the ball and follow Prosch's block on the edge.

This is where things got interesting. Marshall made an additional read to determine whether his X receiver, Sammie Coates, was being covered or not. Since both the free safety and corner came up to stop the quarterback keeper, he awkwardly pulled up and tossed a hitch route to Coates.

Touchdown. The Iron Bowl is tied. College football has been changed.

—Boyd, 2014

The *triple option* in (American) football is a play where the quarterback has choices he can make when running the play. There is a "master" play that is called, but the final choice is made by the quarterback—whether to keep the ball and run himself, to pass the ball to the fullback, or to pitch it to the slotback who has moved in place (Davie, 2015). And, of course, as in the 2014 Iron Bowl play described above, to improvise and pass it to a free receiver, after beginning to run with it. A culture of continuous improvement comes from empowering stakeholders to act upon any opportunity for improvement that they may identify in the application delivery pipeline. It is where the stakeholders are empowered so they don't blindly follow the play called but have the option to make, or at least suggest, changes to improve the play. It is what the Toyota Production System in Japan calls *kaizen*.

ACHIEVING *KAIZEN*

The philosophy of *kaizen* is one of Toyota's core values. It means "continuous improvement." No process can ever be declared perfect, but it can always be improved.

Kaizen in practice means that all team members in all parts of the organization are continuously looking for ways to improve operations, and people at every level in the company support this process of improvement.

Kaizen also requires the setting of clear objectives and targets. It is very much a matter of positive attitude, with the focus on what should be done rather than what can be done.

—Toyota Production System

Developing an Adoption Roadmap

I discuss the concept of an adoption roadmap in earlier chapters in this book. An example adoption roadmap is also presented in Appendix A. Such a roadmap has been found to be essential to scaling DevOps adoption in a large enterprise. If a small, isolated team is adopting DevOps, the team can autonomously determine what practices to adopt and in what order and get all the relevant stakeholders engaged. However, when I speak of multiple teams adopting DevOps, in parallel, but not necessarily in a totally synchronized manner, having a master roadmap for each team to follow becomes essential to allow for a structured and organized adoption that does not result in teams adopting practices in a manner that may impact other teams adopting different practices in a negative way.

The adoption roadmap is typically developed at an enterprise, line-of-business, or division level, and rarely at a project level. These levels may vary in name and size, depending on the organization in question and what the boundaries of separation of responsibilities are within the organization: is the IT team shared across the organization, or does each unit or division have its own IT team? The roadmap is thus designed to provide a blueprint that all the projects in the unit or division can leverage, allowing for the adoption to scale. The goal is to ensure that you do not end up with multiple flavors of DevOps being adopted by various teams but that each team adopts DevOps following the master roadmap, with low-level customizations and enhancements for their specific needs.

In addition, the adoption roadmap needs to be a living document and, in the true spirit of *kaizen*, to be *continuously improved* based on feedback from the teams adopting it and based on market, business, technology, and team changes. Market forces may change, requiring a change in the business goals and focus of the organization, as in the following examples:

- An outage may shift focus to quality from speed.
- A competitor posing a new threat with a truly innovative product may require changes to the products being developed.

Changes in technology can trigger the need to update how the roadmap is being adopted, especially in how automation is being implemented, as in the following examples:

- New technology becomes available, which was not available or mature enough before. In recent years, maturing of containers is an example of such a scenario.
- Older technology may become obsolete. For example, a software vendor may stop supporting or developing a version of software being used, leading to its end-of-life.
- The organization may decide to shift platforms or technology vendors, causing significant changes to be made to the DevOps platform.

Lastly, changes to the team may result in a need to change the adoption roadmap, as in the following examples:

- Changes in the team model to new squad-based teams
- Retirements, attrition, or "resource actions" that cause people on the team to leave
- New hires being brought on to the team
- An *outsourcing* service provider being changed

As a result, there needs to be an owner of the adoption roadmap. This owner (or owners) also needs to have a well-defined change management process to update the roadmap. There are two sources of updates to the roadmap:

- Feedback from the teams adopting the roadmap
- Re-running the value stream·mapping exercise to capture changes

Continuous Improvement and Value Stream Mapping

When it comes to leveraging value stream mapping to drive a culture of continuous improvement, there is tremendous value in re-running the value stream mapping exercise—as either a formal workshop or an informal, ad hoc exercise—on a regular basis. This exercise will keep identifying the current *bottlenecks* and sources of waste in the delivery pipeline. However, running a formal exercise is expensive, from both a time and resource-investment perspective. Even running informal sessions requires some expertise with the person running the exercise. Investing in developing this expertise is a good value addition. The DevOps CoC is a good place to have people with value stream mapping skills, for both formal workshops and ad hoc sessions.

That all being said, educating all practitioners about the basic concepts of value stream mapping itself delivers long-term benefits. It enables people to identify sources of waste in any process they encounter. This is invaluable. Ultimately, the goal is continuous improvement. As I mentioned earlier, the way to achieve true continuous improvement is to empower each practitioner to identify and act upon addressing the bottlenecks and sources of waste in the processes they themselves work with. The key here is being able to *identify* the root cause of the waste. Here, knowing how to perform value stream mapping helps.

Let's revisit, from Chapter 2, how you look for sources of waste in a value stream map of the delivery pipeline. In order to identify sources of waste, you need to look at the following:

- Artifacts
- Stakeholders
- Environments
- Processes

The inefficiency and waste can exist in any of these four areas. Let's revisit the list in Chapter 2 of sources of waste in these areas:

- The process is inefficient.
- The process is manual.
- The artifacts are not in the right form.
- Handoffs between stakeholders are inefficient.
- Stakeholders are unable to perform tasks in the processes.

- Stakeholders do not have access to the artifacts they need, when they need them.
- Stakeholders spend time on unnecessary tasks.
- Stakeholders work on unnecessary artifacts.
- Processes are overburdened by governance.

So, how do you develop a culture of continuous improvement? You do so by creating a mentality in each practitioner to always examine the artifacts they work with, the stakeholders they interact with, the environments they work in, and the processes they execute, and examine them to see if any waste exists. Here are some examples of questions they need to ask:

- Is this artifact necessary? Will it add any value to the development delivery process or to the end-user?
- Am I receiving the artifacts in a form that I can consume without unnecessary transformation or work? Is that true for the stakeholders to whom I pass on the artifact?
- Is the operation I am executing on the artifact adding value to it? Who will consume it once I change its state? Am I adding value to that stakeholder?
- Am I making the state changes to the artifact in the most efficient manner?
- Do I have visibility into the entire delivery pipeline for the artifacts I am working on?
- Are my interactions with other stakeholders necessary? Do they add value to my work? Do I add value to their work?
- What artifacts are we exchanging when we interact, and why?
- What processes do we execute, and are both of us needed to execute the processes?
- Is my interaction with the stakeholder efficient, or is one of us having to wait for the other, or a third stakeholder?
- Am I working in the right environments?
- Are the environments configured the way I need them to be, or do I need to spend time and effort to reconfigure them?
- Am I able to efficiently execute the processes I need to, in the environments I need, when I need them?
- Do I need to wait for an unreasonable amount of time to get the environments I need or to get them configured the way I need them?

> Is the process of getting the artifacts and tools I need in and out of the environments an efficient one?

> Am I working on the right development and delivery processes to add value to the processes or to offer value to the end-user?

> Am I executing the processes in the most efficient manner?

> If there are other stakeholders I need to collaborate with to execute the process completely, do I have visibility into what they are working on?

If every stakeholder in the application delivery pipeline can continuously ask these questions as they do their daily work and they are empowered to act on reducing the waste they identify, you are moving toward achieving continuous improvement. True organization-wide continuous improvement will, of course, require such a culture to permeate the entire organization, across all levels—from practitioner to senior executive management.

Play: Team Models for DevOps

How do you develop a scalable team model for DevOps? You need a team of cross-functional stakeholders (as illustrated in Figure 6-1) with the following parameters:

> All the cross-functional skills needed for their work are available to the team, through either dedicated team members or shared resources.

> They can communicate and collaborate without the organizational *silos* disrupting their ability to work together.

> They have visibility into each other's work.

> They are able to pass artifacts back and forth across an integrated toolchain.

> They are small enough to foster the agility and independence needed to operate.

> They are scalable to large, distributed teams by replicating the small team in large numbers.

> These *sets of teams* are able to communicate and collaborate with each other, thus requiring integrated tools and standardized processes.

> There are overarching governance models to manage the teams at scale, while allowing individual teams to operate with autonomous agility.

> The stakeholders in the team are able to report into existing reporting chains and are matrixed into the team.

- Stakeholders with specialized skills are able to share their time across multiple teams. Enterprise architects, security specialists, and networking experts are some examples of stakeholders with such skills.
- Stakeholders with similar skills are able to collaborate and share lessons learnt and best practices, across teams, effectively having overlaid communities of their own. Think: a community of Heat pattern designers.
- The app and system architectures support development and delivery of components by individual teams, which are to be integrated and tested continuously.
- The team models are repeatable to assemble larger teams, and the models allow for geographically distributed teams.

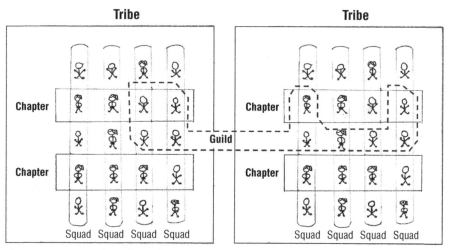

Figure 6-1: Squads, tribes, chapters, and guilds (Image by Shreya Sharma)

The music streaming company Spotify has created exactly such a teaming model, pictured in Figure 6-1. This model, introduced in a paper by Henrik Kniberg and Anders Ivarsson (Ivarsson, 2012), has been adopted, with variations, by several large, distributed organizations like IBM for their own development teams. While the original work on the model referred to it as an approach to develop scalable teams for Agile process adoption, today the model is used at Spotify and elsewhere for DevOps adoption. Here are the core components of the model:

- *Squad.* A *squad* is the smallest unit of a team. It operates like a *mini-startup* that communicates directly with its stakeholders and focuses on developing and delivering one unit of functionality in the overall application being delivered. The squad members own this functionality for a long period of time. Typically, a squad owns a *user story*. A user story is an Agile methodology term used to describe the requirements for a feature from the perspective of how it would be used.

Using a football analogy, a user story is a particular play the team runs in order to move the ball forward. The squad is the players brought on the field by the play callers to execute the play. For example, a dedicated special-plays squad may be called in for a fourth-down play where the team is going for a down, instead of the punting squad.

- *Tribe.* A *tribe* is a set of squads that are working on related functional areas of the app. Together the tribe may own the entire app, or an *epic* or *hill.* An epic is an Agile methodology term used to describe a set of user stories that go together to capture a large set of functionality. Typically the highest-level epic maps to a Design Thinking Hill.

  Squads will have dependencies on other squads within the tribe. They may also have dependencies across tribe boundaries. The tribe should not create impediments or silos to stifle open and free communication and collaboration between squads across multiple tribes.

  To continue the football analogy, an epic is the set of plays the team is working on to get the ball to the end zone. They may not yet know what individual plays they will run as they move the ball forward, but they have a broad plan, given the score, the players they have available, the playbook they have mastered, and the time left on the clock. The offense is a tribe in the team and so is the defense, with special teams as the third tribe.

- *Chapter.* A *chapter* is a team of practitioners working on the same *practice areas* across squads, but within the same tribe. Members of chapters communicate and collaborate to learn from each other by sharing best practices and lessons learned from their individual squads. So, all of the infrastructure in a tribe may meet regularly to discuss IaaS needs, issues, and challenges for the applications being delivered by the tribe.

  Continuing with the football analogy, there are chapters of running backs, receivers, and linebackers on each team. The O-line and D-line are chapters. They have dedicated coaches working with them, and they help each other become better at their specific skills.

- *Guild.* A *guild* is essentially a chapter, but across tribe boundaries. Guilds also include any stakeholder who may be interested in their practice area. Examples would be a testers guild, a security guild, a docker guild, and so on.

If such a thing existed in football, a guild would be a special interest group of running backs, receivers, and linebackers, across team boundaries, for all the teams in the NFL. Punt return specialists would be welcome to the receivers guild. O-line players and D-line players would be welcome to each other's guilds. The parking lot of the quarterback guild meeting would surely be an interesting showcase of performance cars.

Play: Standardization of Tools and Processes

STANDARDIZING GYMNASTICS SCORES

For over 80 years, gymnastics was based on a point scale that ranged from one to ten. A perfect score of 10 was the stuff of legend (as seen with Nadia Comaneci) and the ultimate goal of every gymnast. But after Comaneci and the 1976 Olympics, judges started to become more liberal with their scores and the "10" lost much of its significance.

In the 1984 Los Angeles Olympics, for example, 44 perfect tens were handed out. As a result of score inflation, it became increasingly difficult to differentiate between a good routine (performed well and with high levels of difficulty) and an excellent routine (performed perfectly and with an even higher degree of difficulty).

In the 1990s, the International Federation of Gymnastics (FIG) felt that too many 10s were being awarded and decided to overhaul the entire system. They gave routines start values based on level of difficulty and the succession of tricks in the routine. Any error would deduct from that start value—making it virtually impossible to score a 10.

This scoring system stood throughout the 1990s. However, in 2004 at the Athens games, controversy erupted. American Paul Hamm was awarded the gold medal in the men's all-around competition after winning by only 12/1000s of a point. Later, the bronze medal winner, Yang Tae Young from South Korea, filed a protest claiming that his final score on the parallel bars was inaccurate because it was mistakenly given an incorrect start value. If

continued

continued

the start value for the routine had been correct, Young—not Hamm—would have won the gold.

A huge controversy ensued. Three of the judges were fired, Hamm was asked to give up his medal, then asked to share it, and finally after a lengthy court process, was officially recognized as the winner.

Spurred by this controversy, in 2005 the FIG changed its code of points to reflect a new way of differentiating between gymnast's routines. The perfect 10 was dismissed for a new, more complicated judging procedure that analyzed performances based on starting difficulty and execution. In the current system, a good score is usually in the mid-to-high 16's—not quite the same ring as the perfect 10, but possibly more fair and accurate for the competitors.

—iSport.com

I have discussed the need for people and processes to be fungible across teams and projects and across squads and tribes. I have also discussed how there needs to be *visibility* and *end-to-end traceability* across teams and projects. In order for there to be true measurements of the right metrics, the metrics also need to be standardized across projects and teams. Just like the scoring of two elite gymnasts in the Olympics, you cannot compare the performance improvement of two teams if they are being measured differently.

To achieve all of these—fungible people, and visibility and traceability—a standardized set of integrated tools is required. Standardizing all the applications delivery pipelines in an entire to one tool set is unreasonable. As I have discussed before, organizations are not monolithic. Different business units, divisions, and projects need to use different technology stacks, either because that is what they are standardized and enabled on or because that is the stack their application needs. You cannot switch all applications to Node.js, or deploy them all on the mainframe.[3] However, having tool sprawl leads to chaos when it comes to achieving the goals described here. There needs to be a middle ground, which allows teams to retain their technology stack, while allowing for the standardization, visibility, and traceability goals. The middle ground comes down to limiting the tools to a minimum set of integrated tool

---

[3] My friends from the mainframe world will strongly disagree with this statement, especially with the availability of zLinux and OpenStack for the mainframe.

chains, providing from one to (at the most) two tool chains per technology stack. Integration is the key goal here. That being said, you need tools that are pre-integrated out of the box by the vendor or tool provider. The last thing an organization needs is the overhead of maintaining home-built point integrations between tools.

Standardization of an Integrated DevOps Platform

There are certain tools that are commoditized in the manner in which they are used by practitioners. They have minimal impact on other practitioners and thus do not need to be standardized or integrated. Take, for example, an integrated development environment (IDE). As long as all the developers in a squad use the same IDE, it really does not matter if a squad they interact with uses another IDE. On the other hand, standardizing code repositories is essential as they become the collaboration tool for developers to share code among their peers within and across squads and tribes. The guild of developers should decide what their standard for code repositories is, and as long as all their IDEs can leverage it, it will serve its purpose.

The organization thus needs to determine which tools and platforms need to be standardized and which do not. For the ones that need to be standardized, typically one to two standards should be determined for each technology stack. (There will always be exceptions, and the number will be higher than two for large organizations with complex structures.) Tools that are determined to not need to be standardized should be integrated into the rest of the delivery pipeline. The flow of artifacts across a delivery pipeline, the visibility into work, and end-to-end traceability are all prerequisites for any tool that is selected.

IBM has addressed this need for both standardization and integration by developing an *open toolchain* for their Bluemix PaaS (Brealy, 2016). IBM's open toolchain is pictured in Figure 6-2. In order to allow third-party vendors to add their tools to the tool chain, IBM has also developed a Toolchain SDK. This SDK allows brokers for any tool to be built and made available in the Bluemix PaaS as a service in the tool catalog, which can be added to the tool chain being built by an application development team. The architecture for building a toolchain on IBM Bluemix is shown in Figure 6-3.

Platforms always need to be standardized. While teams will choose the platform that is right for them, the platform should be one that is acceptable to the operations teams, and that can be put within the governance model of the IT organization. Otherwise, you have *shadow IT*.

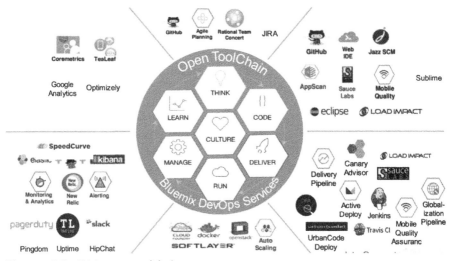

Figure 6-2: IBM open toolchain

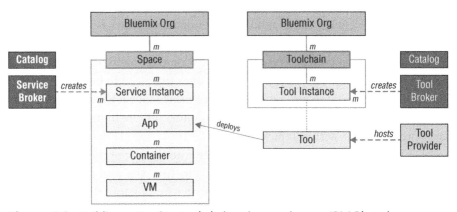

Figure 6-3: Building a DevOps tool chain using services on IBM Bluemix

As I discuss in Chapter 4, for cloud platforms, leveraging technologies like OpenStack, Cloud Foundry, or Docker Containers allows you to standardize on platforms, without limiting the agility the teams need, and thus to deliver *consistency with choice.* For example, one project may choose to deploy on virtualized infrastructure leveraging VMware vCenter; another may choose to leverage the Amazon public cloud; and yet another may prefer a managed bare-metal OpenStack IaaS from IBM Blue Box. All these solutions can be abstracted from the developers by using OpenStack Heat to define the infrastructure as standardized templates or *patterns.*

Play: Security Considerations for DevOps

THE IMPORTANCE OF GOALKEEPING

There is always excitement when you hear the rumors that your team is on the verge of signing that 20-goal striker or the creative genius that will break down even the most stubborn of defenses. That same excitement is not always there when that signing is actually [a] new central defender or an experienced goalkeeper.

In the eyes of the fans, attractive attacking football is always the goal to aspire to. Looking back through the ages, it is always the free-flowing flair of the Brazilians and the pass-and-move of the Barcelonas of this world that appeal to the casual fan. The solid, back-to-the-wall style of the Italians is hardly a style to set the pulse running.

However, one only has to look at the trophies that the Italians have accrued both at club level and international level to suspect that there may be something in this style that breeds success. Their four World Cup titles are behind only Brazil and Germany, while the likes of Internazionale, AC Milan, and Juventus are major players in the European game.

There was an interesting quote from Chelsea's Performance Director, Mike Forde, in a *Financial Times* column by Simon Kuper, where he states that there is a stronger correlation between clean sheets and overall finishing position than there is between goals scored and finishing position.[4]

—DW on Sport, 2012

One of the commonest pushbacks to introducing DevOps in large organizations, especially concepts like *continuous delivery*, and just delivering faster, comes from stakeholders in the security space. From executives to practitioners in the security teams, they all express concerns about the impact on their ability to maintain the security posture desired by the organization.

Security teams, like soccer goalkeepers, are not given the importance by application delivery teams that they deserve. In fact, to most application delivery teams, they are seen as hindering innovation and speed of change. Application delivery teams are motivated to deliver new and innovative capabilities quickly. Security teams are determined to ensure that new systems and capabilities are secure and that security functions are robust. These goals might seem to be at odds.

---

[4] Clean sheet—when no goals are scored against a team in a match.

With regard to business outcomes, however, the goals are not at odds at all. The business outcomes—improved time to value, delivery of innovative business solutions, creation of high-quality products, increased market share—all require both application delivery teams to *continuously deliver* capabilities and security teams to *continuously secure* them. The teams share similar goals but approach them from different angles.

DevOps introduces an approach of continuous delivery and continuous testing of small batches of capabilities being delivered by an application delivery organization. Security teams can take advantage of this delivery approach as a way to reduce security risks. By continuously securing these smaller releases of functionality, they can identify security vulnerabilities early in the lifecycle and mitigate the effects early on.

As security teams scrutinize and secure application delivery processes introduced by DevOps, it is imperative that they also collaborate with the development and operations teams to secure the DevOps delivery pipelines and processes. DevOps is not designed to maximize speed at the expense of security. It is designed to provide rapid feedback from the delivery of smaller batches of capability, with a short cycle time. This rapid delivery and continuous feedback cycle can help to enhance security. Including security in the DevOps lifecycle ensures that securing the applications and systems being delivered is an ongoing process included in the entire delivery lifecycle, rather than a step that is added to the end of the delivery cycle.

Just as Lean manufacturing revolutionized factory automation and product delivery, DevOps transforms application delivery. The advent of factory automation required the development of practices to secure the product delivery assembly line. Incoming components, line workers, automation specialists, assembly processes, and other elements had to be secured and validated. Similarly, security practitioners need to work with the application delivery teams to secure and validate the application delivery practitioners themselves, the processes, and the automation tools. Security needs to become an integral part of DevOps adoption (Elder, 2014).

Managing Security-Related Risks

Businesses fear the risk of residual vulnerabilities in all software that they use. These risks include the following:

- Vulnerabilities related to the supply chain
- Insider attacks from malicious actors

■ Loss or compromise of source code

■ Development process subversions

■ Errors and mistakes in the development project

■ Weaknesses in the design, code, and integration

These risks apply to any style of software development lifecycle or methodology, including waterfall projects, Agile projects, or projects that have adopted a broader DevOps approach. Because of the streamlined nature and advanced automation within DevOps projects, events and conditions related to these risks must be detected and responded to in a continuous manner, throughout the delivery lifecycle.

For each of these risk areas, special considerations are required for DevOps adoption, especially when scaling DevOps adoption across the organization.

Vulnerabilities Related to the Supply Chain

As I describe in Chapter 4, any software project that incorporates software components created outside of the project can be said to have a software development supply chain. The components might be created by suppliers within the company or external to the company or organization that owns or delivers the software project. The security characteristics of the software from the software supply chain have a significant and lasting effect on the security of the software created in the project.

In traditional development projects (including waterfall and iterative projects), it is typical for the development team to evaluate the security characteristics of software from the supply chain. This evaluation involves reviewing component documentation, seeking approval based on licensing and supportability, and performing security scans.

DevOps development teams gain maximum flexibility by making real-time design, coding, and integration decisions throughout the project lifetime. For this reason, the development teams might select supply chain components that advertise greater functionality and ease of integration and that downplay the security and assurance properties of the components.

To mitigate this limitation, it is imperative to build rigorous quality checks into the software delivery process by adopting *continuous testing*. This practice includes testing in every stage of the delivery cycle. The tests need to include security testing of the components and manual and automated code reviews of every component delivered. Because DevOps encourages delivering smaller batches to each component in short cycle times, the result is continuous testing of smaller changes to the components as they are delivered. This approach mitigates the associated risk and speeds up identification of security vulnerabilities.

Insider Attacks from Actors

Although the exact numbers remain unknown, the evidence in the marketplace shows that over the past few years the percentage of all cyber-crimes perpetrated by insiders is statistically significant. These attacks can result in source code loss, source code compromise, or subversion of the development process. These attacks might originate from the direct action of malicious insiders, or as a result of malware infection on networks, workstations, or servers used within the development environment.

To reduce the likelihood of these types of attacks in a traditional development environment, the development infrastructure is typically secured and instrumented for detection and alerting of anomalies. Advanced and streamlined automation within the DevOps platform increases the difficulty of instrumentation and detection of anomalies that might result in source code loss, source code compromise, deployment of malware, or subversion of the development process. This limitation can be mitigated by including security testing—both white box and black box security tests— in the set of testing tasks carried out during the delivery cycle. These security tests, when run in every iteration or sprint, can detect any such malicious attacks.

Virtualized, software-defined infrastructure makes it possible for its configuration to be under change control and thereby auditable. The ability to repeatedly break down and rebuild parts of the DevOps platform helps to minimize the occurrence of persistent malware on those parts.

Errors and Mistakes in the Development Project

Traditional development projects, whether waterfall or iterative, are generally supported by project management and project tracking tools and systems that provide orchestrated workflow and task completion checkpoints. In particular, the release of the finished software product is preceded by a rigorous, extended project review that includes examination of evidence of completion of major tasks and milestones.

Projects that apply an Agile or DevOps approach tend to have shorter delivery cycles in which small components or changes to the software product are delivered more frequently. Although each set of changes might not be delivered to the customer or user, the fast, short cycles can result in less rigorous project reviews and a less careful examination of completion of major tasks and milestones. These shortcuts can make it possible for development project errors and mistakes to slip into the development cycle unchecked. However, the goal of a DevOps project is to deliver smaller components of the software project to the quality assurance team and to the project review processes to reduce the risk of larger project errors and mistakes occurring in the first place. Catching smaller errors early by delivering smaller software component changes more often reduces overall risk.

Weaknesses in the Design, Code, and Integration

If supply chain security is adequately managed and if insider attacks and project errors are under control, the most significant remaining risk in development projects is the introduction of weaknesses that can be exploited after the software has been deployed. These weaknesses might be introduced throughout the development project in design, coding, and integration.

You can minimize the likelihood of software weaknesses using one of these strategies:

- Perform iterative tests and remediation.
- Implement a *Secure by Design* strategy.

Iterative test and remediation strategies can work on small-scale projects in which costs and schedules are not constrained and in which comprehensive testing tools are available. Secure by Design development strategies are maturing at the same time that DevOps projects are emerging. A Secure by Design development strategy as exemplified by the IBM Secure Engineering Framework (Whitmore, 2012) can be applied to DevOps.

Addressing Security for DevOps Processes and Platforms

The adoption of DevOps automation is similar to the transformation of manufacturing systems from being human-intensive to being much more streamlined and automated. A detailed comparison of a software supply chain to a manufacturing supply chain is presented in Chapter 3. Manufacturing processes have evolved from delivering inventory in just the right time and place on a manufacturing floor to positioning the steps on the line, to shifting to controlled, accurate, and high-speed robotic systems, rather than relying on human hands to install, connect, move, and assemble units.

Examples of Vulnerabilities in the Supply Chain

In manufacturing, the existence of multiple suppliers delivering components to the supply chain introduces vulnerabilities. These suppliers can intentionally or unintentionally supply low-quality or defective components. In traditional supply chains, humans notice when something is wrong with the supplied components, and they raise a flag to alert the line. This manual process mitigates risk.

In Lean or DevOps projects in which automation is used extensively, the automated processes may or may not detect an issue with the supply, depending on whether the automated elements contain quality assurance checks to validate the incoming supply.

The mitigation in both cases is to manage and verify the incoming supply chain. For Lean or DevOps projects, this involves adding testing gates to replace the monitoring function performed by humans in the past. For example, a set of automated tests might be implemented to verify that a new level of an open-source toolkit that has just been received is operating within specified tolerances for use by the including application.

Examples of Preventing Insider Attacks from Actors

In manufacturing, line workers can deliberately leave a fitting incorrectly connected, can fail to connect something, can insert foreign objects into the assemblies on the line, or can even sabotage someone else's work and then cover their tracks by wiping clean the device.

In DevOps application-delivery environments, automation takes the place of individual practitioners. However, the programmers of the automation tools (for example, the creators of Chef automation "recipes" or Heat patterns) might also insert behavior into the automation that deploys malware, sabotages a configuration, or otherwise tampers with the system.

The mitigation in both cases is to have checks and balances between workers or, in the case of the automation, to involve multiple checks and balances in the creation of the automation code. Insider attacks are prevented by scope of control, auditing, and a requirement for multiple sign-offs and approvals prior to release. Similar guards and gates can be created as test cases and built into the automation. Consider that the creation of the automation itself can be a possible attack point. The use of software-defined infrastructure under change management control, where every software-defined element is versioned, helps mitigate that attack point.

Examples of Source Code Loss or Compromise

To apply the manufacturing analogy to software development, source code is either the raw materials used to create the assembly on the assembly line or is the blueprints and plans that are followed by the workers to create the assembly. In either case, destruction or removal of the code or plans, or tampering with the code or plans, would affect the resulting assembly on the assembly line.

For DevOps application delivery environments, improper handling of the source code (raw materials or source code used by compilers to build binary components) can result in tampering or compromise. Tampering with design materials or instructions used to develop automation (robotic movements or deployment automation) can cause similar undesired results.

The mitigation on an assembly line is tight control and auditing of both the raw materials and the plans and designs, along with periodic quality assurance testing that the assemblies match the design and that the raw materials have not been tampered with. In the DevOps software delivery model, more automated testing of the assemblies verifies that they conform to the specifications. Furthermore, monitoring, auditing, and enforcing access to design materials, source code, and source code for the automation (robotic behavior of code assembly and deployment) ensure that they do not have any security flaws or vulnerabilities.

Examples of Development Process Subversions

In the analogy of a manufacturing assembly line, the line workers might not follow the assembly line processes and procedures as designed. Every worker in the assembly line has a *standard operating procedure* (SOP) to follow. Departing from these procedures can result in defective products being produced.

In application delivery environments, SOPs exist for the practitioners engaged in software coding, integration, testing, deployment, and similar tasks. Departing from these procedures can result in defective software being delivered. For automation frameworks, errors can be caused by faulty programming of the automation.

In 2012, a trading error at the Knight Capital Group, an international financial services firm, resulted in a US$440 million loss for the firm; it was traced back to a deployment engineer not following the deployment SOP properly

(Popper, 2012). This error went undetected because the firm did not have sufficient quality checks, automated or human, to validate that the deployment was done following the proper processes.

To mitigate the risk on the assembly line, you must implement sufficient training of the line workers on the processes and procedures and institute oversight and quality checks that continuously ensure that workers are following the processes. In the application delivery environment, the processes, the oversight, and the quality checks can be automated using process automation and monitoring tools.

Examples of Development Process Errors and Mistakes

In manufacturing, people make mistakes and errors as they work. Work performed by humans is error-prone. Errors can be introduced by the line workers and by the people designing the processes for the line workers.

In application delivery environments, errors come in various forms: typos in code or scripts, errors in documentation, mistakes in data entry, and similar situations.

To mitigate the risk on the assembly line, you need to implement oversight and quality control and create robust systems that can prevent errors or catch them early. In application delivery systems, methods to reduce errors have been developed over time. Tests can be embedded in code to validate the code and to validate the appropriate use of the code components in the application. This goes back to the discussion in Chapter 5 on *Antifragile systems*, which are the solution here—assume errors will happen and prepare to build automation to mitigate them and recover from them. As I discussed before, some organizations have fully adopted Antifragile systems where if any server instance has an error, it replaces itself with a new instance and de-provisions the instance experiencing the error. No attempt is made to fix the error.

Examples of Weaknesses in Design, Code, and Integration

In manufacturing, handoffs and communication between designers (architects and mechanical engineers), process engineers (industrial engineers and team leaders), and assemblers (machinists and fitters) result in ill-fitting assemblies, changes during manufacturing, bending parts to fit, swapping for other parts in-flight, and other workarounds. This challenge is exacerbated by the reliance on contractors or suppliers who are typically outside firms. One infamous example of a handoff error is the Apollo 13 incident, in which the change of the voltage requirement for a subsystem of the lunar rocket was not communicated to a contractor, resulting in near-disaster during the lunar flight (Christofes, 2014).

In application delivery, such handoff errors occur as teams hand off their code to other teams developing code or to teams responsible for integration, quality assurance, build, and deployment. The challenge is further exacerbated by the need for multiple suppliers and vendors to complete these handoffs across company boundaries.

To mitigate the risk in manufacturing, standards are developed for all vendors to follow. These standards, coupled with extensive documentation and communication about the specifications of components and handoff quality checks, help mitigate these issues. In application development, industry standards for component interfaces have been developed, but teams must still rely on contracts and service level agreements (SLAs) to help mitigate these handoff challenges. Standard tools that provide automation, rather than manual handoffs and deployments, help mitigate the risk that handoffs introduce. Leveraging integrated tool chains across the organization and its suppliers is essential to ensure that risk is mitigated when components are handed from the suppliers to the organization's application delivery team. I will discuss working with suppliers in more detail in the section "Play: DevOps and Outsourcing."

The API Economy and Security

In addition to these security vulnerabilities, the trend toward an *API economy* introduces additional security concerns. As more APIs become available, the risk of security vulnerabilities introduced in the APIs themselves or by rogue users of the APIs can compromise the systems exposed by them. To mitigate the risk, you need to apply strong testing protocols of the APIs and the applications using them.

API providers must ensure that the developed API does not expose them to malicious users who might compromise their systems. These security vulnerabilities might have been intentionally or unintentionally introduced by rogue developers. API consumers must ensure that the data they access or deliver through the API is secure and that the APIs are appropriately used by their applications, without exposing them to any security risks. Both suppliers and providers must use proper authentication and provisioning protocols to ensure only valid use of the API is permitted and no third party is able to misuse the API access provided. API Security is a core component of most API management tools, as shown in Figure 6-4.

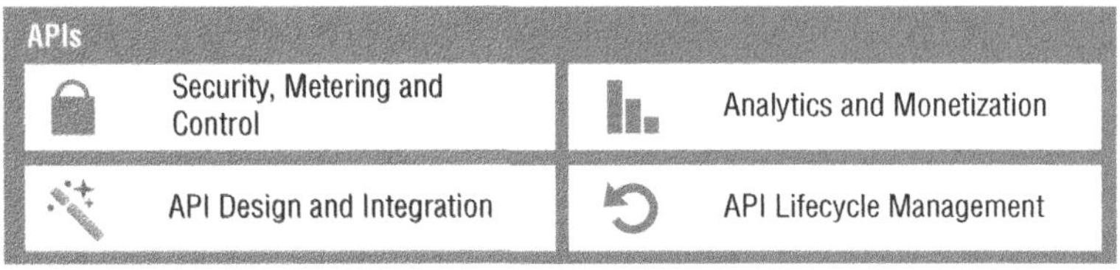

APIs			
🔒	Security, Metering and Control	📊	Analytics and Monetization
✨	API Design and Integration	↺	API Lifecycle Management

Figure 6-4: API security with API management tools

To mitigate this risk with DevOps principles, you must include rigorous security testing on an ongoing basis to ensure the robustness of the API security. Both API providers and consumers must run rigorous automated tests of the API with each new release of the API. They must engage in continuous testing to ensure that any misuse or breach of the API is detected and addressed in a timely manner. These tests must be included in the deployment process of the API itself to ensure continuous security testing of the API and of the deployment processes of all the applications that use the API to ensure that the application is secure. Security testing and security monitoring is a continuum of processing across development, test, and production environments.

In summary, adopting Lean principles on the factory floor and in software development leads to reduction of waste and rework. Similarly, just as factory automation led to a new set of potential security risks and required the adoption of methods to mitigate them, the adoption of DevOps practices can also lead to novel security risks. This chapter describes some of these risks related to DevOps adoption and proposes approaches to mitigate them.

The security risks introduced by adopting DevOps—with its rapid delivery and Agile methods for software development, testing, and delivery—are well identified and easily addressed. They must not be ignored. Just as ignoring security risks related to factory automation can result in serious quality control challenges, not addressing the relevant security risks exposed by DevOps practices can result in severe quality issues as well. As DevOps evolves from a philosophy with a set of guiding principles to a well-defined set of practices with relevant adoption paths, addressing these security risks must become an inherent part of these practices.

Organizations and teams that adopt DevOps can ensure the mitigation of security risks by including the organization's security teams in the DevOps lifecycle. These teams need to become the stakeholders responsible for analyzing and determining which risks are relevant to different projects in the organization and developing strategies to address and mitigate them. Security teams must contribute security-centric quality gates to the DevOps environment as one example point of collaboration.

Play: DevOps and Outsourcing

THE NBA AND OUTSOURCING

It happened years ago. But the tuned out tuning-in to [the 2016] first round of the NBA Draft witnessed a shocker, an überraschen even.

Foreign-born players constituted 14 of the 30 men drafted in the first round. If one adds Domantas Sabonis, who fails to make the list because the birth of the Lithuanian big man occurred in Portland while his Hall of Fame father played for the Trail Blazers, then foreign players constituted half of all first-round selections....

Never in the history of the NBA have so many foreign-born players heard their names said in the first round.

At least one future Hall of Famer who grew up abroad believes players learn to pass, dribble, and play as a team better outside of the United States.

"I just think European players are just way more skillful," Kobe Bryant controversially explained last year. "They are just taught the game the right way at an early age."

Outsourcing also works for NBA bottom lines. Not only did Hakeem Olajuwon, Pau Gasol, and Dirk Nowitzki help teams win championships, they won the league new fans and revenue. Foreigners pay attention because the NBA pays attention to foreigners. The league generates more money per year in their Chinese streaming deal, for instance, than the UFC or MLS makes in its American television contracts. While Americans lament the passing of the good old days when Michael, Magic, or Larry played, international fans see the golden age as now.

—Flynn, 2016

As you look at organizations adopting DevOps, another question that always comes up is regarding outsourcing. Many (read: most) organizations have at least some of their application delivery or IT operations outsourced to an external vendor. This may be the traditional *offshoring* where work is offloaded to an external, offshore, and usually cheaper provider, or a true supply chain model, where external and internal providers deliver components of the application delivery supply chain. Both scenarios have a significantly different impact on DevOps adoption.

Strategic Outsourcing

This is the scenario where an enterprise decides that it is cheaper or, from a business perspective, better to outsource all or part of their application delivery to another provider that excels in that space. This decision to outsource may be made due to cost or to the simple fact that the organization believes that it does not need to have that capability in-house; it is better to hire someone to deliver it. The commonest example would be a company hiring an organization like IBM to run its data centers. The organization chooses to not hire staff to run data centers because it makes sense to let IBM do it. Another example would be a retailer hiring an external vendor to build and deliver its mobile apps. Again, they may have strategically decided that these are capabilities they do not have in-house. Instead of building a new mobile team from scratch, they decide to have it delivered by a company that provides mobile app building as a service.

In the scenario where the entire building and running of an application is outsourced, adopting DevOps is not that much of a challenge. When you outsource an entire application lifecycle, you also outsource the delivery pipeline. If the entire mobile app development and operations are outsourced, the application development and delivery challenges remain limited to ensuring that the mobile app can access the back-end systems it needs to, hopefully through well-defined and managed APIs. Now, in the first scenario I described, if an organization builds an application in-house and delivers it to a production environment managed by an external vendor, the organization needs to do a handoff to the external vendor and receive from the vendor the appropriate feedback to improve continuously. Adopting a continuous delivery model in such a multi-vendor delivery pipeline can be achieved only with the external vendor partnering closely with the organization on standardizing application delivery and feedback practices and tooling between the two.

This does not imply trivializing the planning and collaboration that needs to be done, but if the external vendor is a true partner, this can be achieved. The organization whose application it is still needs to *own* the portfolio management, planning, release management, and governance of the application being delivered. And yes, if the vendor is not willing to partner because the contracts in place do not provide for a DevOps-style model of collaboration, the organization cannot proceed without lawyers getting involved and rene-gotiating the contract.

IT Supply Chain

The DevOps adoption challenge becomes more interesting in a *supply chain* model, where an entire application delivery pipeline is not outsourced, but individual components are being delivered by separate providers in the sup-ply chain. These may not all be external suppliers that the enterprise has outsourced to. More than likely, as shown in Figure 6-5, they will be a com-bination of internal and external providers. Internal providers are easier to deal with. Barring politics and lack of buy-in from senior management, you can apply the DevOps principles to get the suppliers on-board. Best practices, such as creating a central, enterprise-wide artifact repository as a *single source of truth,* or adopting a standardized, integrated tool set to enable end-to-end traceability, go a long way toward getting the required buy-in.

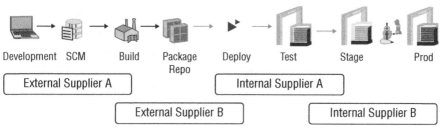

Figure 6-5: Software supply chain

If the organization has external providers, the situation can become tricky. Multiple providers developing and testing individual components leads to many-to-many coordination and collaboration needs. Contracts get in the way. If two providers cannot communicate directly with each other and have to always go through the organization, that is a problem. If every time a busi-ness owner tries to make a change based on feedback (as required for DevOps adoption) the vendor pulls out their contract or charges the organization a change fee, you most certainly have a problem. It is not uncommon to hear horror stories of organizations whose external infrastructure provider for Dev-test environments charged $10,000 for each change to the base VM image. If an organization can't afford to make adjustments to their environments, then *production-like environments* are no longer an option.

The only solution here is to try to get the external providers to see their value in working with the organization and other vendors in the supply chain to adopt DevOps. If they see the value in the efficiencies and reduction of waste DevOps can bring to them and that it allows them to deliver higher-quality software in less time, with fewer resources, that may win them over. If, however, their contracts are written in a way that faster delivery, more efficient delivery, or fewer people needed hurts their bottom line, not much can be done.

Enabling DevOps with Outsourcing

So, is outsourcing the death of DevOps? Or is DevOps the death of outsourcing? Not at all. Organizations cannot have all the IT skills they need in-house. They will need to bring expertise in from external vendors. Outsourcing is here to stay. The advent of DevOps and the need for collaboration, agility, and responsiveness to feedback that is needed to adopt DevOps requires that future contracts will be written with these goals in mind. This is not an unreasonable expectation. Most system integrators are already seeing this in *request for proposals* (RFPs) they are receiving from organizations looking to partner with them on a DevOps journey. This is really not an option. All the external pressures—lowering costs, the need for innovation at speed, and the need to be more agile and responsive to the market—are compelling organizations to adopt DevOps. They are also compelling outsourcing vendors to change how they evolve from suppliers to partners for their clients. DevOps is bringing on the next generation of outsourcing.

Summary

To summarize this chapter, the key to scaling DevOps adoption beyond the isolated, co-located, self-contained team, to enterprise scale projects and programs, is all in culture and teaming. The seven plays introduced in this chapter are as follows:

- DevOps Center of Competency
- Developing Culture of Innovation at Scale
- Developing a Culture of Continuous Improvement
- Team Models for DevOps
- Standardization of Tools and Processes
- Security Considerations for DevOps
- DevOps and Outsourcing

These plays are all about how to adopt the *DevOps Culture* and how to get the necessary teaming in place, including when an outsourcing or a software supply chain model may be in place. In addition, as security is a major inhibitor that prevents wide spread DevOps adoption, ensure that it is addressed as a part of the DevOps transformation.

The themes of this chapter highlight this need for cultural change and for enabling proper communication and collaboration, across function silos, across teams, across stakeholders, and across projects. Namely,

- Organizational Culture
- Standardization of Tools and Practices
- Organized Adoption
- Breaking Down Organizational Silos

Eventually, it all depends upon the ability to overcome the *cultural inertia* your organization has. To transform the existing culture into one of trust—where stakeholders can communicate and collaborate freely, without being burdened by unnecessary governance, arcane policies, disjointed tools, and rigid team structures. To transform to a culture where practitioners can trust the work done by the person working next to them.

CHAPTER 7

Leading DevOps Adoption in the Enterprise

GENERAL MANAGER VERSUS THE COACH

The role of general manager in the NFL is perhaps the most vital position of every team. The GM is mostly forgotten on Sundays in favor of the personnel on the field. Our focus falls on players and coaches, but those players and coaches live and die by their GMs. A bad GM will destroy any team. A good GM can bring you a Super Bowl.

From 2008–10, Scot McCloughan put aside his search for a second "t" in his name and assembled a roster in San Francisco that would put the 49ers into the NFC Championship in 2011 and the Super Bowl in 2012. He did the same for the Seattle Seahawks from 2010–14. The Seahawks did one better than the 49ers and won the Super Bowl in 2013.

—Foss, 2015

Professional American football teams have a critical role in that of a general manager. Where it is done right—and with many teams it is not done right (Breer, 2013)—it can make or break a team. This is because while the general manager is a behind-the-scenes role and it is the players and the coaches on the team who get to play and win or lose games, it is the general manager who is responsible for putting the actual team together in the first place. The general manager also sets morale by managing salaries and, most importantly, by managing the *culture* of the team. Whether the role of the team *executive* is played by the owner (think Jerry Jones and the Dallas Cowboys), the general manager (like it should be), or the coach (think Bill Belichick and the New England Patriots), the responsibility cannot be taken lightly.

The previous chapters were focused on the players and the coaches. In this chapter, I will move up the food chain to the executives who make the decisions to put together, make the business case for, fund, and *lead* a DevOps transformation. They are the ones who own the business results that a DevOps transformation will deliver. They are the decision makers who need to create the vision that a DevOps transformation effort is setting out to deliver. Just like football teams, the titles may vary by organization—CIO, CTO, senior VP, VP, chief digital officer (CDO), or even VP of DevOps—but the goals remain the same.

Above all, it is the executive's role to *lead from the front*. They are the ones who must drive the *cultural* change. They must have the ability to step back and identify the areas of *cultural inertia* that have set in on the organization and thus need to be addressed. They must have a vision of what the target culture needs to look like. They then need to empower their leaders to make the necessary changes to the processes, governance, metrics, and business goals being targeted, which will allow the people on the teams to change how they act. They also need to create a culture of empowerment that goes all the way down to the practitioners, such that the practitioners are able to question the processes, governance, and measurements and suggest changes to move toward improving them. In other words, they need to enable a culture of *continuous improvement*, from the C-suite to the grassroots.

BUILDING A WINNING TEAM

The story of Coach Lad and the Concord, California, De La Salle Spartans is one of the greatest leadership stories ever told because it gets to the heart of building a winning team in sports and in business. Here is an extremely valuable team-building lesson based on the longest-winning streak in sports history.

> Wins are the result of a bigger mission. A great coach knows how to execute game-winning plays, but inspiration is often about the intangibles beyond X's and O's. "De La Salle doesn't win because of anything Bob Ladouceur does. They win because of who he is," says Hayes.

> Coach Lad stands for something bigger than winning games; he stands for commitment, accountability, and pushing the bounds of human achievement. "As a coach you can know who to block and what play to call, but it has no meaning unless the kids know who you are," says Ladouceur. "Our kids aren't fighting for wins. They're fighting for a belief in what we stand for."

Neil Hayes told [interviewer Carmine Gallo] about the moment he realized that Coach Lad's story had to be told. It happened during halftime of a game when his team played poorly. The coach walked into the locker room and his team "looked at their coach, begging for wisdom, his guidance." Lad didn't give them a traditional pep talk. Instead he said, "Why do I always have to be the problem solver? Group problem-solving is a skill you will use your whole life. Figure it out." And with that the most successful high school football coach in history walked out, leaving the players to come up with their own solution. This example is very consistent with Coach Lad's bigger mission to use football as a tool to teach life lessons.

—Gallo, 2014

In this chapter, I present specific *plays* but no *themes* as I did in the other chapters. This is because there is only one theme across all these plays: *leading the DevOps transformation across the organization.*

Play: DevOps as a Transformation Exercise

TRANSFORMING A TECH GIANT

International Business Machines CIO Jeff Smith wants to practice Agile software development and project management at scale, and by scale, he means a company with a headcount that rivals that of Miami.

Mr. Smith arrived at IBM during the middle of 2014, after serving as CEO of Suncorp Business Services, a unit of Australian financial company Suncorp Group. He led a technology transformation at Suncorp and worked on the project with tech vendor IBM, which says the effort produced gains in Suncorp's quality, cycle time, and cost structure. So IBM hired him as its new CIO.

Mr. Smith now leads a 20,000-person global IT team at IBM, which creates tools and services for the IBM workforce of about 380,000 people. Few companies operate at that scale, which is nearly as large as the city of Miami, population 418,000. He immediately embarked on an IT transformation for IBM.

"The mission is to have innovation and the speed of small companies ... and see if we can do that at scale," he said.

continued

continued

> It's a matter of great urgency for IBM, which is in the midst of a painful transition, the WSJ reported on April 21. "Hardware sales continued their slide in the first quarter as IBM exited the commodity server business and focused instead on its more profitable Unix and mainframe computers," the WSJ's Robert McMillan wrote. IBM is betting its future on software and services.
>
> Mr. Smith said his ideas about collaboration and workflow were forged during the financial crisis, during which period, he said, Suncorp was cut off from crucial access to wholesale funding and was days away from going under. He was responsible for leading the development of technology and other business services that helped Suncorp survive a brutal transition.
>
> Now, at IBM, which faces business challenges of its own, he has moved the company away from traditional models of software development. Previously, the company's IT group was divided into two main branches, a transform, or development group, and a run group. "It was more of the classic way that IT shops are structured," he said.
>
> There were pockets of IT that used Agile development and DevOps, which break projects into small units, through which small teams move at top speed.
>
> In February, he replaced the old system with 25 domains, each with its own leader. The domains range from a group that develops a cloud environment to a group in charge of the marketplace where IBM employees can download the tools they need.
>
> "The key piece is how to break big problems and use the wealth of people we have around the world," he said. "The hardest part is to get the raw talent. We have that. The talent and the tooling are there. The way of working is changing. In a nutshell, that is what my mission is."
>
> —Rosenbush, 2015

Organizations are being pressured to change by the market and by competitors. Transformative change always requires a transformative leader. In the context of DevOps, the transformative leader needs to be from the IT organization, like Jeff Smith, as IBM's CIO, has been for leading how IBM has transformed its IT processes and systems to become more Agile. While such transformation already existed in pockets within IBM's IT department, in development and delivery teams within IBM divisions and brands, Jeff drove change across the organization, setting up processes and systems to scale the transformation across the company.

For any organization to adopt transformative change, in addition to the change, it also needs a *trigger* or *catalyst*. It needs a *compelling reason to act* on the transformation effort. Once a reason to act has been identified, the leadership needs to leverage it to act on it. The history of business is littered with the remains of companies that knew they needed to change, but due to poor leadership or their inability to leverage a compelling reason to act, they failed to change and perished. They saw the threat and failed to act, whether the threat was from a market shift (Eastman Kodak missing the move from film to digital photography), from a competitor (Blockbuster missing the threat from Netflix and Redbox), or from legal issues (the entire Napster business model neglecting a minor legal inconvenience called copyright).

Compelling Reasons to Act

Let's examine some compelling reasons to act. Rashik Parmar, VP at IBM, talks of a similar list in the context of driving cloud adoption. However, most of the reasons apply to any transformation effort, especially a DevOps transformation. The commonest compelling reasons to act include:

- *Merger, acquisition, and divestiture.* Mergers, acquisitions, and divestiture are common reasons to act on a DevOps transformation. Mergers and acquisitions bring in new people, applications, systems, tools, and platforms. They also bring in teams with their own processes and, above all, their own culture. These teams need to be integrated and brought to a new standardized state, fit for the new, combined organization. Conversely, divestiture results in the loss of people, applications, systems, tools, and platforms, resulting in an opportunity to revisit the remaining parts and optimize them. Both scenarios bring an excellent opportunity to drive an organization-wide DevOps transformation.
- *Unexpected service interruption.* No one wants to be in the news for an outage. Whether or not it makes the news, the loss of business and reputation can be devastating to your organization. It does not matter if your organization is a bank that has disgruntled customers who could not get to their accounts, a coffee shop that could not process payments from customers, or an airline that had to ground all its planes for hours. When a service interruption, especially one that has a widespread impact, does occur, it usually puts the organization in war footing to first recover from it and then to ensure it never happens again. The latter step is where initiating a DevOps transformation can be leveraged.

- *Launch of an innovation initiative.* Whether the innovation initiative is being launched to counter a competitor, a change in the market, or the arrival of a new externally hired executive, they are all compelling reasons to initiate a DevOps transformation. Such a reason to act can be an opportunity for the sponsoring executives to initiate the development of an *innovation edge* at the organization.
- *Enhancing IT productivity.* While innovation may be the compelling reason to act for some organizations, for others it will be the need to significantly enhance the productivity of the IT organization. This productivity enhancement requires a focus on *optimization,* and adopting DevOps plays for optimization is a necessity.
- *Increasing IT agility.* Any conversation about increasing agility, in today's IT environment, needs to include a conversation about adopting cloud. As I discussed before, the cloud is an enabler for DevOps (and hence agility), and DevOps is an enabler for cloud adoption. If an organization has embarked on a cloud adoption journey, a DevOps conversation needs to occur on how to deploy to the new cloud-hosted platform and how to leverage the cloud-hosted platform to deliver in a manner that maximizes utilization of the benefits and capabilities of cloud services. Thus, a cloud adoption is typically a superset of a DevOps transformation.

Whatever the compelling reason to act may be, it provides a reason and the necessary opportunity to make a business and technical case for a DevOps transformation. Such opportunities are rare in an organization's life. For at least some of these reasons (like service interruption or a merger or acquisition), you hope they are rare. These opportunities, when they do present themselves, should be leveraged as a chance to transform the organization holistically—its applications, processes, tools, platforms, and culture.

DevOps Transformation Anti-patterns

A transformation works only when it is treated like a transformation. While this statement sounds redundant, it is critical. Too many organizations fail to adopt DevOps because their leaders do not manage the transformation with the focus and effort it needs. They fall into common anti-patterns of adoption. Some key *anti-patterns* are listed here:

- *The DevOps "project."* There is no such thing as a DevOps project. Adopting DevOps is not something that is done once and then done with. Adopting DevOps is a transformation that needs to impact everything—processes, automation with tools, platforms, and culture—and this impact needs to be ongoing so that the end result is a culture of continuous improvement.

- *Lack of ownership.* While the executives may own the DevOps transformation itself, having a clear ownership of the individual transformation capabilities, across processes, tools, platforms, and culture, is essential. This ownership must occur all the way down to the grassroots level. You cannot bring about change without clear ownership and responsibility of who is responsible for changing what, with what resources, and by when. You do not transform by edict.

- *A wrong focus on just metrics.* As I describe in earlier chapters, a DevOps transformation requires, as a prerequisite, the identification of the right metrics to focus on improving. However, an overly focused emphasis on rewarding improved metrics can be harmful. If people are measured and rewarded to improve a certain set of metrics and there is no focus on learning, then if and when metrics are not improving, the teams begin to "game" the metrics. This results in a toxic culture.

- *DevOps adoption in islands.* DevOps adoption starts with pilot projects (as I will discuss later in this chapter). However, the goal of the pilot projects is to learn and replicate successful practices and lessons learned in other projects. A common anti-pattern occurs when executives keep this replication isolated to their domain—their own unit, division, or program. If their domain is self-contained and does not interact with the rest of the organization, such an adoption will fail to show desired results. It will certainly not transform the organization as a whole. In the section "Play: Starting with Pilot Projects," I will also discuss the value of selecting the right pilot projects and leveraging the lessons learned from each pilot project.

- *Change of organization reporting structures.* The *squad and tribe* team model that I describe in Chapter 6 results in the creation of cross-functional teams and teams that are small but that can scale to larger structures as *tribes*. There are, however, many common anti-patterns that lead to incorrect organizational restructuring for DevOps:

  - *New leadership roles.* Naming someone *VP of DevOps*, and having the Dev and Ops teams report to her, solves very few problems. Decision making, conflict resolution, budget allocation, and some communication may become easier, but you still have two siloed organizations that did not change and that are no closer to having better communication, collaboration, and trust.

■ *New silos.* The other approach to reorganization that does not work is the creation of new silos. Many organizations redistribute their stakeholders into new reporting structures that do not foster cross-functional collaboration across the required functions but are limited to stakeholders included in the new teams. This only results in old silos being replaced by new ones.

■ *DevOps teams.* There has been a lot of debate on the strengths and weaknesses of creating DevOps teams (Minick, 2015). These DevOps teams typically only have Dev and Ops practitioners. This does not add sufficient value because other practitioners are left out. It is not a true cross-functional *squad.* Furthermore, several organizations make this DevOps team a required stakeholder to every project. That ends up making it no more than another bureaucratic team that now has to *approve* actions by projects.

■ *Outsourcing DevOps adoption.* While consultants, experts, vendors, and contractors are all usually essential to help bring the process, tools, platform, and cultural transformation expertise into an organization, the ownership of the DevOps transformation cannot be outsourced. If the team does not see their own executives taking ownership and leading the transformation, the willingness and urgency to change will not be driven across the entire organization. Cultural inertia cannot be overcome by an outside consultant or by reading this book.

■ *Communication and collaboration.* There needs be true, direct communication and collaboration between stakeholders. Can they really do so, or do they always need to go through their respective reporting chains to communicate? Is collaboration done solely through tickets? Are there *chargeback* requirements that stifle stakeholders working across organizational boundaries? Does a request to a supplier always trigger a formal change-request process?

■ *Contracts.* This becomes a challenge with external vendors and suppliers. If there are rigid contracts in place that require vendors and suppliers to only communicate in a certain manner or that require that every change in the way a process is executed go through a formal change process of the contract, there can be no DevOps.

Addressing these anti-patterns is the responsibility of the executives leading the transformation. This can result in some tough decisions and aggressive changes. New collaboration tools may need to be deployed. Management will need to give up control to allow free communication and collaboration. Collaboration across functional silos that is limited to communicating through tickets alone will need to be eliminated altogether. Self-service catalogs of critical IT services will need to be made available to practitioners. Contracts will need to be renegotiated. Vendors may need to be changed. And (hopefully) lawyers and accountants will need to be fired.

Play: Developing a Culture of Collaboration and Trust

Players need to trust and respect the fact that if I do my job we have the best chance of being successful. I don't have to make every play; I just need to make the plays I'm supposed to make in the gap I'm supposed to make them and trust the guy next to me will do the same.

—Nick Saban, head coach, University of Alabama football team

Why don't Ops teams in large organizations give direct self-service access to the production environments to developers, to deploy continuously, as many startups do? The reason is simple: they don't trust Dev teams to deliver stable, secure, and reliable applications. The reality, of course, is not as simple as just being about a lack of trust. There are several other reasons, including compliance requirements that prevent open access to production environments. Furthermore, some distrust is actually healthy because it puts the Ops team in a mode to question and verify what Dev is delivering. However, a complete lack of trust is not healthy. This lack of trust in large organizations seems to extend beyond just Dev and Ops. Dev does not trust business analysts. Enterprise architecture does not trust Ops. QA does not trust the developers. The audit and compliance team trusts no one. No one trusts management, and so on. This lack of trust results in teams not being able to effectively communicate and collaborate across functional silos. This mistrust is a cultural thing.

In his article "The Simple Math of DevOps" (Reid, 2015), Lee Reid (who was, until recently, a DevOps architect at IBM) proposed a formula to calculate the total *time to delivery*. In his formula, shown here, Lee puts *trust* as the denominator, because it determines the efficiency of the *touchpoints* between the stakeholders and drives the *waste* that may occur with *handoffs* if the stakeholders do not trust the artifacts they are receiving from other stakeholders. To quote Lee from the article:

[A] key factor that will determine the speed to value is TRUST. It's pretty obvious when you draw out the value stream mapping of how work gets done at a given customer site. As members of software delivery teams lose trust in the validity of the work as it flows through the lifecycle … a large amount of rework and waste is introduced. In mathematical terms our equation becomes:

$$T_{DELIVERY} = \frac{T_{PLAN} + T_{DESIGN} + T_{DEVELOP} + T_{BUILD} + T_{DEPLOY} + T_{TEST} + T_{FIX} + T_{RELEASE} + T_{EVALUATE}}{\% \, TRUST (0 - 1)}$$

That is, the Tasks we do in a delivery cycle are impacted by the degree of trust we have in the hand-offs from one to another. If we have zero trust then our $T_{DELIVERY}$ will be infinite (divide by zero). 100% trust and our $T_{DELIVERY}$ will be only limited by how fast each task can be performed.

How can you build an environment and culture of trust? It is certainly not by going through "fall-back-into-the-arms-of-the-person-behind-you" exercises. It comes from building a sense of mission, a sense of team that puts people in a situation where they begin to work with the person next to them with a sense of purpose, and an understanding that the only way to succeed will be by trusting the person next to them. They need to trust that the people they work with understand their roles and believe that they are not only good at what they do but are going to do the best they can. This sense of trust has to be built from the ground up. It has to be established by building small teams by leveraging models like the *spotify squad* model that I introduce in Chapter 6. Those teams need to be empowered to operate across functional silos as one unit with a well-defined mission—a mission they all need to pull together to accomplish. They then need to scale that model across the organization. Ultimately, people trust people they know. They trust people they associate with and have fun with. They trust people who themselves trust the people around them.

Visibility Enables Trust

If there is a factor that can drive an environment and culture of trust, it is visibility across functional silos. And this is something the executives leading a DevOps transformation can ensure the organization makes the right invest-ments in. As stakeholders in the application delivery pipeline work with each other and hand off artifacts to each other, visibility drives trust. If there is no visibility across functional silos and something goes wrong, the stakeholders consuming the artifacts tend to lose trust in the stakeholders they are receiving the artifacts from. For example, if testers receive code from developers that keeps failing basic tests, they will start to distrust any code the developers send them. However, if they have visibility into the various quality checks the developers did before they handed over the code to them, they will start work-ing with the developers to determine why the tests are failing. Furthermore, if the developers know that the testers have visibility into the tasks they per-formed on the code, they will ensure that they do not send un-validated code to the testers. This example can be extended to any set of practitioners who are handing off artifacts to each other.

Visibility also drives trust because it allows practitioners to see who is working on which task in the team, who the right experts are, and who is responsible for the artifact they need. Such visibility also enables better com-munication across the team. Total visibility drives total trust.

It's All about the People

Effective Leaders avoid becoming the weeds that choke the individual passion and overall performance out of their team.

Instead, they become the water bearers who nurture, coach and grow individual passionate seeds into a super star team.

—Ty Howard, former American football player

Ultimately, it is all about the people. The foremost role of the leader is therefore to foster and develop the people. This begins with recruitment, and follows through to putting the right people together on a team, all the way to providing a fun environment where teams thrive and maximize productivity.

If you have the opportunity to visit a startup, one that has moved from the "latte shop" to a real office space, you see a very different workplace from a traditional corporate work environment. There are no isolated cubicles, just open workspaces. There seem to be no titles or even work schedules. People run around in all kinds of attire—and "run around" is not an exaggeration; in fact, it may be on a scooter or skateboard. There are beanbags in conference rooms; in fact, the conference rooms themselves may not have formal tables and chairs. There are whiteboards everywhere. And there is sports equipment all over, from Ping-Pong tables, to foosball, to video game consoles, to pool tables. And yes, there is food and beer—a lot of beer. These are all things that would get both the corporate productivity czars and HR departments up in arms in large organizations. What large organizations consider "inappropriate" is considered essential to developing a fun work environment where people enjoy spending time and working.

Large organizations, on the other hand, have standardized, grayscale cubicles on every floor of every office. There is no sports equipment. Lunch happens from noon to one. And silence is considered golden. Who would not want to leave such a place the moment the clock strikes 5 p.m.?

Developing a fun and engaging work environment is becoming a prerequisite to attracting the best talent. Not everyone expects free massages every afternoon or a keg to be always on tap in the break room, but young, skilled professionals do not want to spend their lives in an environment they do not enjoy. The work/life balance of today's young crowd, especially Millennials, does not just mean having a life outside work but also having a life at work.

Building a team requires having people who want to work with each other, who enjoy and are passionate about their work. It is the executive leadership's responsibility to foster such an environment.

Play: DevOps Thinking for the Line of Business

TEAM OWNERS TRANSFORMING THE NBA

"And the geeks shall inherit the earth" goes the now well-worn appropriation of bible lore referencing the inexorable rise of the tech-minded elite that has come to dominate the business world of the 21st century. No more so is this rise in fortune apparent than in the cut and thrust business of US sport.

Traditionally, when you think of professional sports team ownership in the US, you think of fast-talking business tycoons with larger than life personalities and the bank balance to match. But just as businesses have begun to dance to the tune of a new breed of technologically minded individuals, so too has sport found itself increasingly in the grip of a wealthy cartel of tech industry leaders whose default is to disrupt.

In the NBA in particular, franchise owners like Steve Ballmer (LA Clippers), Mark Cuban (Dallas Mavericks), and Vivek Ranadivé (Sacramento Kings) have played a key role in shaking up their respective teams and the wider league in a bid to make them technologically fit for purpose. Each has brought a very different approach to their ownership, but all are in their natural state when working and thinking digitally and have wasted no time in leveraging technology to gain a competitive and commercial advantage.

—Robbins, 2015

A DevOps transformation needs the *line of business* (LOB) to participate. IT is striving to become better, after all, to deliver their business needs and goals, which they are unable to do in the status quo. The line of business thus needs to be a sponsor of the DevOps transformation, by providing the investment and time, and by participating in the transformation by changing how they engage and interact with IT. They need to become full-fledged stakeholders in the effort. They need to ask questions to help the IT organization identify the gap between their business needs and what they can deliver and then work with IT to help them transform in order to fill the gaps they identified. Three key questions to ask are:

- Can the IT organization rapidly deliver new, innovative applications, leveraging modern architectures?
- Can they modernize existing applications to enable them to achieve faster delivery and innovation?
- Can they adapt culture, tools, and processes to succeed?

Line of Business–IT Engagement

Let's examine the topic of the engagement between the line of business and IT. Typically this engagement is formal and minimal. The line of business identifies some needs, helps to define them, and then disengages while IT builds the solutions to deliver those requirements. It is not an interactive relationship that goes back and forth to help further refine the requirements or to engage with IT as they run experiments to identify the right problems that need to be solved and the right solutions to address them. The LOB can play a critical role. They can represent not just themselves but also the customer and the broader market as IT works on the experiments.

The LOB also needs to be *continuously improving* their own needs and definition of the business value they want to deliver to the customer and to continuously improve their own understanding of the business problems they are trying to solve. They can do so by properly consuming the feedback coming from IT and from the users using the applications in production, both during experimentation and post-release. They can receive and consume feedback on the following:

- *Application usage patterns*. How are the customers using the app? Are their usage patterns in line with the patterns the LOB expected and wanted? Which parts of the application are the customers using and not using?
- *New use cases with customers*. Are the customers using the app in ways it was not designed for? Are the usage patterns leading to new use cases the business had not identified? What else are users doing in conjunction with the app? For example, if they are using another app in parallel, should that external app's feature be included in their app (say, a mapping app the users keep switching to)?
- *User personas*. Are the various user types matching the *personas* that the LOB had identified? Are there new personas to be identified? Are there personas that should be discarded?
- *User sentiment*. What is the user sentiment as they use the application? Are the users happy or frustrated? Are they complaining or becoming fans who are promoting the app?

Using this and other kinds of feedback, the LOB can get into a mode of continuous improvement themselves and work on improving their own understanding of their users and their needs.

In order for the LOB to be able to consume and act on the feedback at this level, the feedback needs to be

- Consumable
- Actionable
- Timely

This is a responsibility of the IT organization to ensure that the feedback is usable by the LOB. Sending them server logs serves no purpose, and neither does usage pattern or user sentiment data for the previous version of the app.

Engaging in the DevOps Transformation

Once a DevOps transformation has been launched and is in progress, in addition to engaging during the application delivery cycle and acting on feedback provided, the LOBs can also engage by helping to actually drive the DevOps adoption with their influence. They need to work with their stakeholders, including the CIO, CTO, or senior application development executive, to do the following:

- Identify education opportunities for development teams in new technologies and platforms in order to quickly react to or innovate faster than the competition
- Prioritize areas for optimization of existing applications, increasing innovation and freeing up resources for innovation
- Sponsor DevOps *value stream mapping* workshops and participate in them

Move Shadow IT out of the Shadows

Lastly, the LOB needs to address *shadow IT*. LOBs create pockets of shadow IT in the organization to help fulfill their IT needs that they believe their own IT organizations cannot deliver. The better approach is to flip the shadow IT model and invest in developing the skills and agility that shadow IT provides, within their own IT.

If an external IT provider does need to be leveraged because there is a specific need that internal IT cannot deliver in a timely manner, then the engagement between the LOB and the external IT provider should be done working with internal IT. This brings shadow IT out of the shadows, and it can be leveraged within the domain of internal IT, utilizing some of its core processes, without being stifled in their ability to innovate. A common example would be a corporate IT utilizing a *private* PaaS like IBM Bluemix, which is managed by IBM, but can exist with the organization's IT-owned firewall, or even in their own datacenter, leveraging the *local* deployment model presented in Chapter 5.

Play: Starting with Pilot Projects

EXPERIMENTING WITH FAN ENGAGEMENT

Matt Higgins, the New York Jets' executive vice president for business operations, believes that the ability to browse has become so engaging that, in a certain sense, watching a single live game from beginning to end cannot compete. At the Jets' new stadium in New Jersey, the team is experimenting with ways to keep fans interested in games by plugging them into the data stream while they are in their seats.

"There's going to be a sense of cognitive dissonance if you don't have access to the comprehensive experience," he said.

One experiment is a partnership with Pre Play Sports, a small technology startup based in New York City. The company designed a game for mobile phones that awards points to fans for predicting the outcome of each play as they watch the game, with more points given for unlikely predictions.

In its initial form, Pre Play Sports allowed fans to predict the outcome only of certain plays. But users quickly demanded the right to guess the length of every kickoff and the result of every coach's challenge, said Andrew Daines, who founded the company last year shortly after graduating from Cornell.

"In order to keep our users engaged we had to offer them much, much more," he said. "We got to 99 percent, and that last 1 percent is what they want most. They want to predict the coin toss."

According to Mr. Daines, the average Pre Play Sports player spends 40 minutes with the app, a monumental period of time by smartphone standards. He thinks the reason it is so easy to persuade people to play is that they are earning a steady stream of positive feedback for doing what they were already doing—putting a small emotional bet on every tiny development in a three-hour football game.

—Brustein, 2011

The only way to validate an idea, and to fine-tune it once validated, is to run experiments. The same is true for adopting specific DevOps capabilities. As a DevOps adoption roadmap is developed, it will define a set of capabilities that need to be adopted in order to address the areas of waste identified (typically by running a value stream mapping exercise). You can adopt these capabilities individually, or you can use the plays documented in this book to adopt sets of capabilities together. The capabilities will impact all areas of DevOps—process, tools, platform, and culture. You should adopt these capabilities by running experiments and leveraging pilot projects.

The ideal approach is to identify one pilot project for each capability being adopted. The goal of each pilot project is to do the following:

- Validate that the capability being adopted is delivering the results being targeted.
- Validate that the investment required to adopt the capability is in line with what was budgeted and is delivering the return on investment expected.
- Validate that the approach and method taken to adopt the capability is the right method.
- Determine what *improvements* can be made to the capability, or the method to adopt it, to make it better for projects that follow.
- Determine the lessons that are learnt from adopting the capability.

These goals will result in an enhanced version of the capability and the method to adopt it that can be leveraged by other projects across the organization.

The main reason why you adopt only one capability per pilot project is to isolate the experiment by capability. If a pilot project adopts more than one capability in parallel, the questions I just listed will get answers that will be difficult to parse between the multiple capabilities being adopted.

For the business goals and technical results that are expected from adopting the capability, it is essential that the right metrics to measure be identified and that the right improvement targets for these metrics be documented up front. Furthermore, it is essential that a baseline of the metrics be taken before the pilot project proceeds, to be used to measure improvement.

As the pilot projects proceed and metrics are measured, there are additional questions to which the leadership of the DevOps transformation needs to find answers:

- Is the capability scalable? Can it be adopted by other projects in the organization?
- What enhancements need to be made to the capability and its adoption method in order to make it reusable across the organization?

Pilot Project Selection

In order to answer these questions, it is important to choose the right pilot project. The pilot project selected should be a good exemplar of a typical project in the organization. It cannot be an outlier in any way. The following is a list of criteria to be considered when selecting the pilot projects:

- *Technology stack*. Is the pilot project using a technology stack that has widespread adoption across the organization, or does it have a unique stack?
- *Platform deployed*. Similarly, is the pilot project deploying to a platform that is unique or an organizational standard?
- *Team location*. Is the team co-located or geographically distributed? What is the norm for the organization?
- *Team composition*. Is the team running the pilot project made up of a typical mix of employees and contractors? Is it a typical mix of veterans and new hires?
- *Team experience*. Is the team's experience in working with the tools, practices, platform, or each other typical for the organization? Or, has the deck been stacked by putting a highly experienced team on the pilot project to ensure its success?
- *Project timing/stage*. Is the capability being adopted at the right time in the project's lifecycle? Is it two weeks to release, making adopting the capability a low priority for the project team?
- *Project importance*. Does the organization care about the project? Is its success critical to the organization? If no one cares about the project, it will not get the attention and resources it needs. In contrast, if it is a mission-critical project, then it will get too much attention and too many resources. Either end of the spectrum makes the project an outlier and not representative of a typical project in the organization.

These are all examples of questions that should be asked when choosing the right pilot projects. It is not uncommon to have to meet with and interview project leads from dozens of projects in order to identify the right projects for each capability being adopted.

Executive Sponsorship

In order to help with the success of these pilot projects, executive sponsorship is essential. The executive sponsor will need to meet several goals:

- Ensure the projects have the right resources and investment, as needed.
- Provide *cover* for the projects to exempt them from any rigid processes and governance oversight that could hamper their ability to adopt the targeted capability.
- Run *interference* to ensure that other executives, business owners, or stakeholders do not pressure the project to abandon the capability or put adoption on hold in order to meet certain project deadlines.
- Allow a pilot project to be delayed, or even fail, without penalty, so that the right lessons can be learnt from their experiences. *Learning* is the primary goal of a pilot project.

Play: Rearing Unicorns on an Aircraft Carrier

FOSTERING MAVERICK ATHLETES

A maverick athlete is one that falls outside the main group and best practice yet delivers winning performances. In athletic pursuits, these individuals understand the current boundaries and consciously or subconsciously develop their own individual strategies/skills to attack those boundaries. Maverick athletes are out there living life on the edge. They excite people because they are different.

In alpine, you have the much celebrated and berated Bode Miller, in cycling there was Graham Obree in the early '90s, in F1 there was Mika Hakkinen, in boxing there was Prince Nasem Hamed in the late '90s, and obviously, Muhammad Ali in the '60/'70s. As mavericks in their sports they generated wins without strictly adhering to current best practice techniques. They were all also agents for change in their respective sports.

continued

continued

> It is important to impress that winning is the key of maverick status. An athlete can develop their own style (technical, skill, tactical, mental), but unless this style allows them to win, dominate, and even decimate the competition, then the athlete is not eligible for maverick status. However, winning is not the only difference; the true maverick generates their performance over the competition by doing things differently. Muhammad Ali defeated almost every top heavyweight in his era; as a maverick in his sport, he was a masterful self-promoter, and his psychological tactics before, during, and after fights became legendary. It was his athleticism and boxing skill, however, that enabled him to scale the heights and sustain his position for so many years.
>
> Several years ago during a Formula One race, an interviewer was talking to a team boss about why they had chosen to contract a new young driver, "Mika Hakkinen," who was quick but erratic. The Team boss responded, "Mika is a very fast driver; we can teach him to be more technical, but we cannot teach him to be fast." The point he was making was that "in his opinion" Mika's skill level/comfort zone for speed was not based on the established best practice techniques for generating fast technical driving. Mika possessed an individual method for FAST driving that the team wanted to exploit.
>
> —Hewitt, 2015

Whether you call them *mavericks* or *Unicorns*, there are always people in every organization who stand out. They are innovative. They truly think outside the box. They are inherent leaders. They can be very easily stifled by corporate structures, policies, hierarchies, and governance. Instead of becoming the most productive contributors and team leaders, they lose their mojo, or leave and take their skills elsewhere.

"If a unicorn is walking east on an aircraft carrier, but the aircraft carrier is headed west, where will the unicorn end up?" Well, either the unicorn will end up in the water, or it will give up on going east and end up going west.

Think of the unicorn as the maverick and the aircraft carrier as the organization. The only way to foster such mavericks is to put them in a unicorn farm and allow them to run free with other unicorns. Building teams that are self-organizing, small (like squads), able to operate freely, and that have fun, is what building unicorn farms is about. A culture of trust and collaboration fosters such farms, where free communication trumps reporting hierarchies.

A culture where innovation and experimentation are not stifled, but rewarded, is the key ingredient. *Learning and discovery* are encouraged even if the actual experiment fails.

The executive team needs to lead the development and fostering of such a culture, and also the maverick attitude. They need to set the example by being mavericks themselves. They need to work the team hard, not to squeeze every ounce of productivity out of them, but to help them develop a culture and attitude of winning.

Fostering Ideas

Early on, all of our movies suck!

—Ed Catmull, Pixar president

Fostering unicorn is not enough. You also need to foster their ideas. The idea may not be impressive, but most ideas aren't in the beginning. They may, however, be the seeds of something great. The executives in leadership positions need to allow such ideas to be experimented with. With the advent of *design thinking* techniques that allow raw ideas to be refined and Lean startup techniques that allow for experimentation with the idea of leveraging *minimum viable products*, the risk and cost associated with validating and refining ideas has become extremely low. The golden rule for fostering ideas is *fail fast, fail often, and fail cheap*. Experimenting with hundreds of such ideas will identify the few that need to be invested in, to launch the even smaller number that will bring about significant business impact.

Introducing the practices of design thinking and Lean startup, and providing a resilient platform to rapidly develop the MVPs for experimentation by establishing an innovation edge, is the responsibility of the executive leadership. They do not need to come up with the ideas. They don't even really need to understand them. They do need to provide the environment for these ideas to be experimented with and for the successful ideas to be developed with proper investment. They need to develop a culture of innovation. They need to let the unicorn take over the aircraft carrier.

To summarize, like a good sports team owner, general manager, and coach, the organization's executive leadership needs to make champions out of amateurs.

COACHING THE 1980 OLYMPICS "MIRACLE ON ICE"

[Herb] Brooks was not a players' coach.

He worked his players relentlessly, wearing on them, making them hate him. It was simply his identity as a coach, and one that he would embrace at all his coaching stops. It's no surprise that Brooks was good friends with Bobby Knight. Like Knight, Brooks was a military-style leader. Players had to do things his way. All the time.

In one famous incident, he was unhappy with the way his team played during an exhibition against the Norwegian national team. He warned his players that if they didn't work during the game, they would work after it. Still unhappy after the final period, Brooks marched the young men onto the ice and forced them to skate suicides as the arena slowly emptied. Finally, as the players were on the brink of collapse, he let them off the ice. His message was clear. Work or go home.

In part, he would tell people later, he wanted the players from the East and the players from the Midwest to hate him more than they hated each other. There was a natural rivalry between the two groups. Fourteen of the players were from either Minnesota or Wisconsin, and 9 of those had played at the University of Minnesota. Four of the players were from in and around the Boston area and had played at Boston University.

In 1976 a vicious fight had broken out between Minnesota and Boston University during the semifinals of the NCAA hockey championship. The fight was so heated that it stopped the game for 30 minutes. Five of the players on that 1980 squad had been on the ice that day, throwing punches at each other.

Brooks had another reason for riding his players, for constantly pushing them to the brink of throwing down their sticks and leaving the team for good. The Soviet team was in awesome physical condition, one of the reasons the Soviets seemed almost super-human to hockey fans. Brooks would drive, exhort, and punish his young collegians until they could skate with the Soviets for three periods. The Americans' conditioning would be their secret weapon.

Brooks the hard-driving disciplinarian had another side. After the Miracle, he left the bench as soon as he could so that his players could have the spotlight to themselves. TV cameras captured only the back of his brown sport coat as he left the bench. "No words necessary, just pictures," Al Michaels intoned as the camera quickly cut back to shots of the players' jubilation on the ice.

> Brooks would later call the year he spent coaching the 1980 Olympic team his loneliest in hockey. He put on the mask of a ruthless tyrant because that was what the team needed. As Mike Eruzione later said, "I firmly believe that he loved our hockey team, but we didn't know it."
>
> —Witnify, 2014

There is one more play that is needed here as it is the responsibility of the executive leading the DevOps Transformation. That is: Building the Business Case for a DevOps Transformation. However, I dedicated the entire Chapter 3 to that very topic. I refer you to that chapter on details on how to build a business case for your organization, using the tools and techniques described in that chapter.

Summary

To summarize, this chapter focused on one theme alone: what does an executive need to do in order to lead a DevOps transformation across her organization. The plays introduced here are the ones that form the playbook for the executive—the coach or General Manager for the organization.

- DevOps as a Transformation Exercise
- Developing a Culture of Collaboration and Trust
- DevOps Thinking for the Line of Business
- Starting with Pilot Projects
- Rearing Unicorns on an Aircraft Carrier
- Building the Business Case for a DevOps Transformation (from Chapter 3)

DevOps is a *transformation exercise*, not a project. It is not something one does one time and moves on. It needs to transform the organization and that takes time and continuous effort. All the automation tools and process improvements in the world are not going to be able to deliver sustained value to the organization, unless accompanied by a shift to a culture of collaboration, communication, and above all *trust*. The cultural inertia in your organization needs to be overcome to achieve transformational change. This requires that the line(s) of business too develop *DevOps thinking* and culture. They too need to transform.

One starts this DevOps transformation through *pilot projects*. These pilots show the value of the DevOps processes, tooling, and organizational change. Furthermore, they help the organization discover how to adapt these processes, tooling, and organizational change based for their needs, maturity, and ability to consume change.

The executives are also responsible for caring for and fostering the mavericks, the change agents in the organization. They are responsible for giving these *unicorns* the freedom to thrive, to allow them to work on their ideas and allow them to lead change.

Finally, to execute the transformation, and in fact even to get it initiated, the executives will also need to build a *business case* for the DevOps transformation. This business case will need to show the value for the investments and the change to the business. The business case will need to show what the return of the investment and the change will be.

APPENDIX

Case Study: Example DevOps Adoption Roadmap

This appendix captures a DevOps adoption roadmap that was developed for a large, multinational financial services organization. Certain details have been modified to make the roadmap more generic and to remove any company-specific references. All names have, of course, been removed, and specific geographical details have been obfuscated to protect the innocent. This particular roadmap was selected because of its broad application to DevOps adoption situations, across a range of industries and organization sizes. Barring the customer-specific situations that have been removed or generalized, this client presented a set of business drivers, their current state of maturity, and constraints—technical, organizational, and financial—that are very common.

The goal here is to present a very broad, relatable, exemplar roadmap that can serve as a template for your organization. Your mileage will vary, because there is not, and never will be, a one-size-fits-all adoption roadmap. Some very important *plays* discussed in this book do not apply here. My recommendation to you is to look at this as a case study of how to start from a *business driver* and *current state* and select the right set of DevOps plays to develop a similar roadmap for your organization to get to the *end state* you want.

Organization Background

The organization in question here, which I have given the fictional name of Massive Bank and Finance Group (MBFG), is a large, multinational financial services organization with traditional banking and financial services:

- Retail banking (branch and digital)
- Commercial banking
- Private banking
- Securities trading

Like most financial services organizations in the wake of the housing bubble crash, MBFG has grown very quickly through acquisitions and mergers. They are multinational, so they face a varied set of ever-changing regulatory requirements from the different markets they operate in. They face an additional challenge of needing to accelerate organic growth by innovating to reach both unbanked millennials in developed markets and unbanked non-millennials in developing markets. Above all, they are facing severe challenges from Financial Technology (FinTech) startups that offer banking (or banking-like) services to these unbanked customers, without being a bank and, thus, without carrying the regulatory constraints that come with having a banking license. They need to reduce the costs of traditional branch-based banking and invest heavily in building a digital presence. And yes, the regulatory environments that they have to comply with keep evolving, from changes in banking and fiduciary laws and regulations to Brexit-like geopolitical events. These ever-accelerating changes and constraints are driving the need for agility, speed, and innovation, while at the same time, MBFG has to maintain quality and manage (lower) costs, just like any other organization in the twenty-first century.

Roadmap Structure

As I describe in detail in Chapter 3, the process of creating a DevOps transformation playbook, or an adoption roadmap, requires three core ingredients:

- To have a clear definition of the *target state* (business goals and drivers)
- To understand the *current state* (current capability and maturity)
- To determine the best path to take, or *plays to run* (risk-value-investment balance)

Let's recap the process of creating a DevOps adoption roadmap:

- The *target state* is determined by understanding and documenting the organization's business drivers and goals. What is the business asking IT to deliver on that IT is unable to deliver without change?
- The *current state* is determined by identifying the organization's current maturity and those factors that inhibit its ability to deliver what the line(s) of business is asking of it. This current state is identified by determining the *bottlenecks* or *inefficiencies* in the delivery pipeline, by conducting a *value stream mapping* exercise.

▓ The roadmap is then developed by identifying the right *plays*; these are the set of DevOps capabilities that need to be adopted in order to address each identified bottleneck. When selecting the plays, you need to take technical, organizational, and financial factors into consideration. I discuss these factors in detail in Chapter 3.

The adoption roadmap that I present in the next section captures all these areas described earlier.

DevOps Optimization and Innovation Workshop

The following roadmap was created as the output of a DevOps Optimization and Innovation Workshop conducted at MBFG. This is a formal half-day workshop run by IBM to help an organization develop a DevOps adoption roadmap and to initiate their DevOps transformation journey. The adoption roadmap is structured in the following five sections:

1. Business drivers
2. Technical initiatives already in play or planned
3. Value stream mapping results
4. Root causes
5. DevOps capabilities (plays)

Each of these sections was created as the output of the five exercises that make up the DevOps Innovation and Optimization Workshop, addressing each of these five areas.

For MBFG, IBM delivered this workshop for their digital banking division, which is a separate line of business that serves their retail banking and commercial banking lines of business, and delivers their web and mobile presence. This division was also leading the charge in transforming the global bank by introducing new technologies, expanding their global footprint through developing innovative applications and business models, and also acquiring FinTechs. They were thus an ideal candidate for DevOps adoption—both on the *innovation edge*[1] side where they primarily operate, and in terms of the services from the *optimized core* of which they are consumers. Because of these factors, they need to be optimized and agile.

---

[1] If you skipped ahead, *innovation edge* and *optimized core* were introduced in Chapter 3.

The workshop was sponsored by the division chief technology officer (CTO). The following technical executives also attended:

- Division chief architect
- Director of application development (including QA)
- Director of enterprise architecture
- Director of digital operations
- Director of service delivery
- Chief operating officer

IBM provided a DevOps subject matter expert (SME) facilitator and an IT specialist with past engagement experience with MBFG to run the workshop. In all, the workshop took around six hours to run, including a one-hour pre-workshop preparatory phone call. The report was prepared in conjunction with MBFG over a two-week period, and then presented to the CTO and the other attendees. It was then handed over to MBFG as a roadmap they now own.

The roadmap is currently being executed. There are regular meetings between MBFG leadership and IBM to review the transformation effort and update the roadmap as needed.

Background and Context

To better appreciate the roadmap, it is important to understand the background information regarding MBFG—and specifically the digital banking division—that the IBM team delivering the workshop knew prior to the workshop. This information created a context for the workshop that would not need to be then discussed during the workshop itself, saving time.

Business Context

This section provides the business and market context in which the DevOps adoption is being considered by MBFG. What were the goals and constraints of the line(s) of business?

- Markets—MBFG in general, and the digital banking division specifically, was targeting two main growth markets:
  - *Millennials* who needed banking services but were not using traditional banks. Here, the main competition included new FinTechs like Venmo and Square.

- *An unbanked growing middle class*, specifically in the growth markets in the developing world. MBFG had acquired several banks around the world in developing nations that had a rapidly growing middle class. Here, the main competition included FinTechs like Novopay (Standard, 2014) in India that were offering banking transactions through corner stores.
- Partner ecosystem—MBFG was looking at additional revenue streams by developing a partner ecosystem. They therefore needed to create an *application programming interface (API) economy* to enable this.
- Regulatory concerns—The regulatory environments that MBFG operates in vary by market. Complying with all of these requirements, and especially new regulations like the Payment Services Directive (PSD2) in Europe, was severely draining IT resources.
- Security concerns—"I never want my name in *The Wall Street Journal*," was how the MBFG chief information security officer (CISO) described their security goals. Recent breaches in large financial institutions had resulted in more investment in security, which reduced investment elsewhere.
- Outages—One of the banks in the MBFG group had had a major outage. MBFG was unable to re-create the outage to determine the root cause. A clear lack of an up-to-date enterprise architecture was the cause of being unable to re-create the outage. Regulators were looking at this inability to even understand how and why the outage occurred very closely because clients were unable to access their accounts for the duration of the outage. MBFG wanted to ensure that any changes were well architected, and all architectural changes well documented, so that a current enterprise architecture could be maintained.

IT Context

This section provides the IT departments context in which the DevOps adoption is being considered by MBFG. What were the goals and constraints of the IT department?

- Hybrid systems—MBFG had grown through acquisitions and mergers and had also been around for several decades. They therefore had a large legacy technology stack, from mainframes, to IBM System i, to Unisys systems, to multiple obsolete versions of middleware that were running older systems, which needed to be upgraded.

- Shadow IT—Shadow IT was rampant, especially outside the digital banking division. Several lines of business had created business applications they were running on public cloud providers like Amazon Web Services (AWS), Rackspace, and SoftLayer. They had hired boutique firms to build these applications.
- Data residency—Data residency was a big issue. Several countries around the world required that their clients' data be stored locally. Because of the acquisitions and mergers, MBFG now had country-specific versions of some applications and systems running in local data centers, managed by them or by external vendors.
- No cloud strategy—Other than the MBFG CIO making statements to the board and the press like, "We are cloud first," in reality, there was no enterprise-wide cloud strategy. Shadow IT usage of multiple cloud vendors was rampant. Experiments were being done by several groups with OpenStack, Docker, and Cloud Foundry. The CIO was still undecided about an official stance on using a public cloud.

Adoption Roadmap

The rest of this chapter documents the adoption roadmap developed for MBFG in its entirety. Of course, several direct references and specific details have been obfuscated and fictionalized to generalize the roadmap.

Business Drivers

The following business drivers for the digital banking division of MBFG were identified in the workshop:

- To manage costs in order to do more.
  - The goal here is not reducing cost but improving productivity to be able to deliver more within the existing budgetary structures.
- To increase pace and throughput of development of new applications and of enhancements to existing applications.
  - The goal is to both innovate faster and improve existing systems at a faster pace.
- To adopt a more product- and customer-centric delivery approach.
  - The goal is to be able to capture customer feedback and develop and enhance applications based on that feedback.

- To increase quality—both of products and software.
  - The goal is to reduce downtime and outages experienced by clients.
- To accommodate regulatory pressures to reduce or eliminate change windows.
  - MBFG, like many FSS organizations, is under regulatory scrutiny in multiple markets to reduce downtime during scheduled change windows, during which clients may be unable to access some account features.

Existing IT Initiatives

MBFG was actively addressing the challenges it faced, even before this workshop. Multiple initiatives are in flight or planned. These initiatives are listed here and have been incorporated into the final adoption roadmap.

- Automation of environment provisioning
  - This initiative refers specifically to full-stack environments that might be deployed. MBFG is currently exploring cloud environment provisioning and orchestration tools.
- Release automation
  - This refers to the automation of application software deployment into production (and by extension dev/test) infrastructures. MBFG has been adopting the IBM UrbanCode tool suite to assist in this challenge.
- Adoption of continuous integration (CI) tooling
  - Several CI tools are in various stages of adoption, across MBFG. The goal is to standardize on a minimal set of tools (one or more) that can create a set of standards and enable any team at MBFG to adopt CI.
- Adoption of service virtualization
  - MBFG has adopted a service virtualization tool and is rapidly expanding its use across the digital banking division.
- QA transformation
  - Work is being assessed to automate testing and to undertake integration testing earlier in the life cycle (shift-left[2]).

---

[2] *Shift-left*, a Lean principle, was introduced in Chapter 1.

- Simplification of application architecture
  - A specific challenge in the digital banking division is the complexity of the existing code-base. They are presently looking at how this might be simplified, by introducing more modularization into the design. This is separate from the enterprise architecture effort.
- Architectural de-layering
  - A further challenge specific to the digital banking division is the apparent over-layering of the architecture, where duplicate and redundant layers can be consolidated. They are presently examining how this can be achieved, along with the associated benefits.
- Pilot of design thinking
  - The digital banking division has been attending a series of workshops to understand how they can leverage design thinking to reduce the highly bureaucratic process of requirements elicitation and documentation. They have identified significant challenges with the existing processes, which require approval from approximately 34 different committees. Initial targets have identified a goal of two weeks to minimum viable product (MVP).
- Extraction of metrics from DevOps tooling
  - Current work extracts metrics for reporting purposes from multiple sources, both commercial and homegrown. Most of the reports provided to management take multiple days to generate, making the data stale in most cases. The MBFG digital banking division is looking at adopting *Hygieia*, an open-source DevOps dashboard developed by Capital One, a U.S. bank.

Bottlenecks

The value stream mapping exercise conducted during the workshop identified the following bottlenecks in the delivery pipeline of the digital banking division at MBFG. The workshop attendees had picked one exemplar pipeline for Java development for the purposes of the value stream mapping exercise.

- Requirements management and design:
  - The *define* phase is excessively costly. Typically, the costs incurred in the define phase are large enough that projects become committed, with very little flexibility.

- The output of the requirements elicitation and design process comprises paper artifacts, rather than artifacts and models that can be iteratively worked on. Documents are long (typically 100+ pages) and often aren't read or fully adhered to by the teams that are intended to consume them.
- The high-level design branches out into different platforms, and as this happens, each team produces a different design that is independent of the higher-level design. This results in no traceability from higher-level to lower-level designs.
- Project governance and management:
  - Project management is too often seen as adopting an observe-and-report mentality, rather than actively driving a project.
  - Project funding can sometimes be inconsistent and intermittent, leading to a start-stop approach that directly impacts consistency. For example, funding may dry up, leading to personnel being released; then, when funding is secured, different people are assigned to the project.
  - It can take a long time for technology decisions to be made through governance.
  - There are processes that tell people what to do, but not how to do it.
- Project teams:
  - The overall philosophy of the organization is to bring work to teams, rather than teams to work. This results in domain knowledge being lost as people on a project team may never have worked in that domain area before, but are assigned because they are available.
  - Cross-functional teams use a ticket-based system to communicate, which is too slow and cumbersome, resulting in long wait times.
- Code and architecture:
  - Code management is currently very inefficient. At T-30 days for a deployment, code from multiple projects is merged into a *business release* code stream.
  - Code lacks any modularization or internal architecture. This lack of application architecture results in a lot of inefficiency and technical debt.
- Application server configuration management:
  - Application server configurations are managed through one large file that contains a very large number of configuration

parameters for multiple applications; this creates configuration management constraints and makes the configuration management very error prone.

- To save costs, early-stage testing uses the *Jetty* app server, despite WebSphere Application Server (WAS) being the production deployment target. This requires every project to dedicate one sprint (iteration) per release cycle to ensure the app runs on WAS before deployment to production.

- Deployment and release management:

  - Deployment is manual, very costly, and time-consuming. Approximately 35 to 40 full-time employees are required to do deployments into dev/test/prod environments.

  - The batch size for a business release is very large; there can be up to 20 projects in a single release, so all these projects need to be coordinated and timed as a single release.

  - There is interlock between multiple projects in a business release at the design phase, and then again at system test, but nothing in between; this results in several integration challenges being identified too late.

Root Causes

The following root causes were identified for the bottlenecks listed in the previous section. These root causes were found by examining each bottleneck individually. The following is a consolidated list that was developed after examining dependencies and duplication.

- Lack of a single application architecture that evolves, rather than a lot of separate designs. Such a model can evolve over the life cycle.

- Having a single, one-size-fits-all governance process creates a desire for projects to bypass the existing governance processes because they are too cumbersome.

- Lack of a product-based single team that has overall ownership of a product through its life cycle. Current ownership shifts from project team to project team, resulting in a lack of end-to-end technical ownership throughout the life cycle and across components of the application.

- Lack of automation, especially release and deployment automation.

- Lack of good application architecture and configuration management practices, especially the need for a microservices-based architecture and loose coupling between services and components.
- Integration testing is done too late in the delivery life cycle.
- A move from a process-focused to a product-focused approach.

DevOps Practices

The following DevOps capabilities were recommended to the MBFG digital banking division to address the bottlenecks in their delivery pipeline and enable them to embark on their DevOps transformation journey.

1. Automation

   Goal

   Introduce automation tools for the following four areas:
   - Deploy
   - Environment-build and maintenance
   - Test
   - Release

   Automation provides the capability to make processes repeatable, reliable, and scalable.

   Business and technical benefits

   During the workshop, several areas of inefficiency were identified that can be addressed by introducing automation. These inefficiencies result in significant business impact by causing waste and increased wait-times:
   - An inefficient ticketing system is used by cross-functional teams to communicate.
   - Manual testing takes multiple days to complete.
   - Regression testing is automated but still requires multiple days and is conducted too late in the delivery life cycle.
   - Deployments for full releases are manual and done in batches with significant wait times, which create overhead costs.
   - Dev-test-prod environments do not use the same middleware and configurations.

   The following recommendations were listed as the first to be adopted because they have the most significant return on investment that can be achieved quickly.

DevOps adoption recommendations

IBM recommended that the MBFG digital banking division adopt automation tools for each of the following four areas to address the inefficiencies that are causing waste and will eventually impact business.

   i. Implement a single collaboration tool that allows all stakeholders across the delivery life cycle to plan, collaborate, and share work items. This will address all collaboration issues by replacing the ticketing systems that are presently used.

  ii. Adopt deployment automation that allows for the automated and reliable deployment of application components, as well as middleware code and configurations, to any environment in the delivery pipeline.

 iii. Continue the adoption and rollout of test virtualization to provide the capability to carry out continuous testing of application components. Continuous testing at all stages of the delivery life cycle allows for the *shifting left* of testing, which results in early identification of defects and architectural flaws, and increases overall quality.

  iv. Adopt a release management tool to provide capabilities to coordinate releases, resource availability, and environment availability. This ensures proper queuing of releases and their components as they flow through the delivery pipelines and integrate across their respective streams.

        It is essential that the right processes be automated, and that they be optimized to achieve maximum efficiency. It is thus recommended by IBM that the MBFG digital banking division work with subject matter experts (SMEs) to examine their existing processes in all four identified areas of automation and embark on a process improvement initiative across these areas. Introducing automation tools also provides the ability to explore alternate efficient processes that are not feasible when carried out manually.

2. Reduction of deliverable batch size

Goal

Make the delivery pipelines as efficient as possible, in order to reduce the cycle time for each iteration, or sprint. Reducing the batch size of each deliverable helps to achieve this objective.

Business and technical benefits

Delivering smaller batches of application functionality changes allows for rapid iterations with enhanced throughput, reduced risk, and improved quality. Enabling the delivery pipeline with automation tools and architecting iterations through the delivery pipeline to be made up of a small number of changes to functionality results in more frequent deployments across the delivery pipeline, more frequent testing of smaller changes to code and configurations, and more frequent integrations for the components. This enables DevOps capabilities like continuous integration, continuous delivery, and continuous testing. Smaller batch sizes also reduce challenges with release planning by reducing competition for available resources in the delivery pipeline and decreasing the length of release cycles that block resources for extended periods of time.

DevOps adoption recommendations

i. Embark on an initiative to reduce their delivery batch sizes. This is not a trivial task because it requires the refactoring of their application and data architecture to ensure that their applications are made up of smaller, loosely coupled components that can be deployed and tested independently. At an application level, adopting a microservices-based architecture would be an ideal approach to address this recommendation.

ii. Use test virtualization allows for more frequent testing of these smaller components, without waiting for other related components to be available. In addition, deployment automation automates frequent and continuous deployments of individual and composite components and applications at higher frequencies.

The MBFG digital banking division would need to get architectural guidance to help them re-architect and refactor their applications to adapt them into a microservices-based architecture.

3. Establishment of offering management teams

Goal

Establish permanent *offering management teams* that have ongoing ownership of the application *products* across the MBFG digital banking division.

Business and technical benefits

Having offering management teams in place that have both programmatic and technical ownership of the application products being delivered provides enhanced resilience in application delivery capabilities, while adhering to the core governance requirements of the MBFG digital banking division. These teams are permanent and retain ownership of products beyond individual projects and across enterprise-wide initiatives. They assemble the requisite teams of subject matter experts and technical practitioners to deliver on individual projects and overall capabilities of the products. They become the teams the *work comes to*, rather than teams that are transient and are assembled to address a unit of work.

DevOps adoption recommendations

i. Identify a minimal set of products that should have their own permanent offering management teams. These teams should have ownership of the architecture, technical design, and long-term vision for the product, and work in conjunction with the lines of business to own the requirements being asked for by the business.

ii. Develop a governance process and standards to manage the identified offering management teams.

iii. Provide the offering management teams the appropriate skilled resources to ensure their long-term viability and success, including product owners, solution architects, and requisite management.

iv. Enable the offering management teams training on *design thinking* techniques to leverage for designing application roadmaps, requirements, and capabilities, based on the desired *user experiences* of a well-defined set of *personas*.

v. Ensure the creation of a *continuous funding* model to ensure continuity for these product teams.

These recommendations are organization-, process-, and governance change-related, and need to be initiated and owned by the MBFG digital banking division senior leadership. IBM shared experiences of their own offering management teams with MBFG, explaining how they are organized and how they operate within the IBM application delivery organization.

4. Application architecture design

Goal

Introduce the capability of application architecture modeling at the MBFG digital banking division to capture the design and architecture of applications and systems as they evolve through the application delivery life cycle.

Business and technical benefits

Having a common set of models that represent the code and the architectures across all the applications and systems is essential to provide a single view, rather than the multiple design artifacts that are used today. Keeping a common set of models also allows for the ability to reuse, as well as for refactoring and better architecture.

DevOps adoption recommendations

i. Start an initiative to capture all the code across multiple components, applications, and systems as well-documented application architectures. The solution architects in each delivery team should take ownership of these architectures as they are created and also take ownership of maintaining them as the application and its dependencies on other applications and services evolve. These solution architects should also be responsible for identifying reuse and refactoring opportunities for the architectures and updating the enterprise architecture.

IBM can provide tool and architectural guidance to the MBFG digital banking division for model and architecture management best practices and enablement for tool usage.

5. Self-service dev-test environment provisioning

Goal

Introduce self-service portals for Dev and Test practitioners to enable them to provision appropriate *production-like* environments, configure them, and deploy the application being developed or tested to the provisioned environment, with the push of a button.

Business and technical benefits

One of the biggest inhibitors to the efficiency and productivity of the development and test practitioners is the lack of access to the *production-like* environments they need. Providing a self-service portal to the practitioners that has preconfigured *full stack* patterns that can be automatically provisioned and made available, without manual intervention required by the operations team, can significantly improve practitioner productivity. Ensuring that these environments are *production like,* so that they resemble the production environments in their topology, configurations, and behavior, can significantly improve the quality of the product being developed and tested.

DevOps adoption recommendations

   i. Start an initiative to create a cloud-based self-service portal. This portal, the patterns available, and the cloud environments on which the dev-test environments are provisioned would be managed by the operations team. The dev-test team would put in a request for new environment patterns, as and when needed.

   ii. Utilize an OpenStack-based cloud, using a cloud management tool that would oversee pattern design, pattern portal, and catalog management, environment provisioning using OpenStack Heat, and orchestration of provisioned environments.

Roadmap Adoption

The adoption roadmap presented in this appendix can appear extremely daunting and a tremendous amount of work for any single organization to undertake. It is important to note that such a roadmap is developed as a guide to undertake a massive organization-wide transformation. An organization like MBFG would not be expected to undertake such a transformation as a "big-bang" approach, but do so through a series of pilot projects to adopt individual recommendations in small, managed projects, as described in earlier chapters. Only upon the successful completion of these pilots and harvesting of lessons learned would one scale broader across the organization. These pilots will need to be staggered to spread out the investment of time, money, and SME resources needed, and allow for the right projects to be in the right phase to allow for introducing significant change to how they develop and deliver applications. This is hence a multi-year transformation roadmap.

Furthermore, in working with MBFG management, prioritization of the recommendations in the roadmap was undertaken to allow them to decide which ones to address first. The investments required, and the expected return on investment for each, was a major consideration for the prioritization effort, as was the time to value needs for certain capabilities, defined by the lines of business goals and market timing needs.

This roadmap should hence be taken as a large-scale DevOps adoption roadmap for an organization-wide transformation. Your roadmaps will vary based on your needs and goals and will hopefully be less complex.

Bibliography

Introduction

Sharma, S. (2016, May 15). *The Ultimate Winning Play?* Retrieved from sportsthrills.wordpress.com: https://sportsthrills.wordpress.com/2016/05/15/the-ultimate-winning-play/

Wikipedia. (2016, September). *DevOps.* Retrieved from wikipedia.org: https://en.wikipedia.org/wiki/DevOps

Chapter 1

Bias, R. (2012, February 16). *Architectures for open and scalable clouds (slide 20).* Retrieved from slideshare.net: http://www.slideshare.net/randybias/architectures-for-open-and-scalable-clouds

Caum, C. (2013, August 28). *@ccaum.* Retrieved from Twitter: https://twitter.com/ccaum/status/372620989257232384

Deming, D. W. (1998, April 27). *Dr. Deming's Management Training.* Retrieved from Dr. Deming's Management Training: http://www.dharma-haven.org/five-havens/deming.htm

Forrester. (2011, July 26). *Water-Scrum-Fall Is The Reality Of Agile For Most Organizations Today.* Retrieved from Forrester.com: https://www.forrester.com/report/WaterScrumFall+Is+The+Reality+Of+Agile+For+Most+Organizations+Today/-/E-RES60109

Garvin, David A., Amy C. Edmondson, and F.G. (2008, March). *Is yours a Learning Organization?* Retrieved from hbr.org: https://hbr.org/2008/03/is-yours-a-learning-organization

Kaz, P. (2013, July 4). *Measurement Myopia.* Retrieved from Drucker Institute: http://www.druckerinstitute.com/2013/07/measurement-myopia/

Kruchten, P. (2002, August 6). *The 4+1 View Model of architecture.* Retrieved from ieee.org: http://ieeexplore.ieee.org/xpl/articleDetails.jsp?arnumber=469759

Lean.org. (2016). *Lean.org*. Retrieved from Lean.org: http://www.lean.org/WhatsLean/History.cfm

McCance, G. (2012, November 19). *CERN Data Centre Evolution (Slide 17)*. Retrieved from Slideshare.net: http://www.slideshare.net/gmccance/cern-data-centre-evolution

Rice, R. (2009). *Achieving Software Quality Using Defect Filters*. Retrieved from Randy Rice's Software Testing Site: http://www.riceconsulting.com/articles/achieving-software-quality-using-defect-filters.htm

Chapter 2

Cantor, M. (2014, July 15). *Flow measurements for software*. Retrieved from IBM DeveloperWorks: http://www.ibm.com/developerworks/library/d-flow-measurements-sw/index.html

Hartman, B. (2009, November 11). *An Introduction to Planning Poker*. Retrieved from dzone.com: https://dzone.com/articles/introduction-planning-poker

Martin, K. (2011, August 11). *Value Stream Mapping in Non-Manufacturing Environments*. Retrieved from Slideshare.net: http://www.slideshare.net/KarenMartinGroup/value-stream-mapping-in-nonmanufacturing-environments/24-Key_Metrics_QualityComplete_and_Accurate

Ohno, T. (2006, March). *Ask 'why' five times about every matter*. Retrieved from toyota-global.com: http://www.toyota-global.com/company/toyota_traditions/quality/mar_apr_2006.html

Poppendieck, M. (2008, October). *Value Stream Mapping*. Retrieved from agiles.org: http://agiles2008.agiles.org/common/pdfs/Poppendieck%20-%20Value%20Stream%20Mapping.pdf

Wagner, B. (2009, January 9). *Notes on Value Stream Mapping*. Retrieved from thebillwagter.com: http://thebillwagner.com/Blog/Item/2009-01-07-NotesfromPoppendieckValueStreamMapping

Wikipedia. (n.d.). *Supply Chain*. Retrieved September 16, 2016, from Wikipedia: https://en.wikipedia.org/wiki/Supply_chain

Wikipedia. (n.d.). *Value Stream Mapping*. Retrieved July 10, 2016, from Value Stream Mapping: https://en.wikipedia.org/wiki/Value_stream_mapping

Chapter 3

Forrester. (2013, July). *Forrester Research Total Economic Impact Study on Service Virtualization and Test Automation Solutions*. Retrieved from ibm.com: `https://www.ibm.com/developerworks/community/blogs/rqtm/entry/forrester_research_total_economic_impact_study_on_service_virtualization_and_test_automation_solutions?lang=en`

Forrester. (2015, August). *The Total Economic Impact Of IBM UrbanCode*. Retrieved from ibm.com: `https://developer.ibm.com/urbancode/docs/the-total-economic-impact-of-ibm-urbancode/`

Osterwalder, Y. P. (2013). *Business Model Generation: A Handbook for Visionaries, Game Changers, and Challengers*. John Wiley and Sons.

Strategyzer. (2013). *Business Model Canvas*. Retrieved from www.businessmodelgeneration.com: `http://www.businessmodelgeneration.com/canvas/bmc`

Vaccaro, A. (2014, Janurary 8). *An Unlikely Case Study in Fast Growth: Major League Soccer*. Retrieved from Inc.com: `http://www.inc.com/adam-vaccaro/mls-commissioner-don-garber.html`

Chapter 4

ASUM, I. (2016, March 1). *Analytics Solutions Unified Method*. Retrieved from IBM Analytics Services: `http://public.dhe.ibm.com/software/data/sw-library/services/ASUM.pdf`

Bradbury, J. (2011, September 26). *A Sports Economist's Thoughts on Moneyball: A Guest Post by J.C. Bradbury*. Retrieved from Freakonomics: `http://freakonomics.com/2011/09/26/a-sports-economists-thoughts-on-moneyball-a-guest-post-by-j-c-bradbury/`

Burke, T. (2016). *This Is Why There Are So Many Ties In Swimming*. Retrieved from deadspin.com: `http://regressing.deadspin.com/this-is-why-there-are-so-many-ties-in-swimming-1785234795`

Capital One GitHub. (2015, July 18). *CapitalOne DevOps Dashboard*. Retrieved from Github.com: `https://github.com/capitalone/Hygieia`

Cheshire, J. (2012, January 9). *Cricket: The Top 10 All-Rounders of All Time*. Retrieved from bleacherreport.com: `http://bleacherreport.com/articles/1017237-the-top-10-all-rounders-of-all-time`

Cockcroft, A. (2012, March 19). *Ops, DevOps and PaaS (NoOps) at Netflix*. Retrieved from Adrian Cockcroft's blog: http://perfcap.blogspot.com/2012/03/ops-devops-and-noops-at-netflix.html

Conway, M. E. (1967). *Conway's Law*. Retrieved from www.melconway.com: http://www.melconway.com/Home/Conways_Law.html

Donato, C. (2016, July 14). *Big Data Analytics are Enhancing Women's Tennis*. Retrieved from ZDNet.com: http://www.zdnet.com/article/big-data-analytics-are-enhancing-womens-tennis/

Harrell, E. (2015, October 30). *How 1% Performance Improvements Led to Olympic Gold*. Retrieved from Harvard Business Review: https://hbr.org/2015/10/how-1-performance-improvements-led-to-olympic-gold

Higdon, H. (2011). *Marathon Training Guide - Introduction*. Retrieved from halhigdon.com: http://halhigdon.com/training/51135/Marathon-Training-Guide/

Hodges, R. (2015). *IT Service Management for DevOps*. Retrieved from IBM DeveloperWorks: https://www.ibm.com/developerworks/community/files/form/anonymous/api/library/42529e82-173a-4f45-805b-93d9eb35ffa6/document/19b71c8c-1675-4727-a3ab-b259ba1d49e6/media/ITSM%20Reference%20Architecture%20-%20DevOps%20-%20Whitepaper.pdf

Judge, L. (2016). *Should power hitters bunt against defensive shifts?* Retrieved from The Kansas City Star: http://www.kansascity.com/sports/spt-columns-blogs/judging-the-royals/article78348842.html#storylink=cpy

Kagan, S. a. (2015). Transforming Application Delivery: Executive Advisory Session. *IBM InterConnect 2015*. IBM.

Kim, G. (2013). *The Three Ways: The Principles Underpinning DevOps*. Retrieved from IT revolution: http://itrevolution.com/the-three-ways-principles-underpinning-devops/

Kniberg, H. (2014, March 27). *Spotify engineering culture*. Retrieved from Spotify Labs: https://labs.spotify.com/2014/03/27/spotify-engineering-culture-part-1/

LinkedIn, Engineering Blog. (2011, October 26). *Continuous Integration for Mobile*. Retrieved from LinkedIn Engineering Blog: https://engineering.linkedin.com/testing/continuous-integration-mobile?cm_mc_uid=92132403740114635134753&cm_mc_sid_50200000=

Medeiros, J. (2014). *The winning formula: data analytics has become the latest tool keeping football teams one step ahead*. Retrieved from wired.co.uk: http://www.wired.co.uk/article/the-winning-formula

Moran, S. S. (2013, September 6). *Test Data Management in the DevOps Lifecycle.* Retrieved from The Invisible Thread: https://www.ibm.com/developerworks/community/blogs/invisiblethread/entry/test_data_management_in_the_devops_lifecycle?lang=en

Pal, T. (2015). *Hygieia Dashboard - Making sense out of your DevOps tools.* Retrieved from capitalone.io: http://www.capitalone.io/blog/hygieia-making-sense-out-of-your-devops-tools/

Pereira, R. (2009). *The Seven Wastes.* Retrieved from iSixSigma Magazine: http://blog.gembaacademy.com/wp-content/uploads/2009/09/7_wastes_isixsigma_magazine_0909.pdf

Peter, U. (2008, August 20). *Tips from a Top Sports Team Coach.* Retrieved from infoq.com: https://www.infoq.com/articles/sport-coaching-and-agile

Pollock, R. (2013, October 17). *Troubled Obamacare website wasn't tested until a week before launch.* Retrieved from Washington Examiner: http://www.washingtonexaminer.com/troubled-obamacare-website-wasnt-tested-until-a-week-before-launch/article/2537381

Powers, J. (2013). *Why pulling the goalie is often worth the risk.* Retrieved from bostonglobe.com: https://www.bostonglobe.com/sports/2013/05/29/pulling-goaltender-may-risky-move-but-bruins-and-other-hockey-teams-have-made-pay-off/u1dbL9XrfejggKHUnxpPUI/story.html

Quirk, T. P. (2004, January 5). *How to quantify downtime.* Retrieved from networkworld.com: http://www.networkworld.com/article/2329877/infrastructure-management/how-to-quantify-downtime.html

Radcliffe, S. S. (2014, July). *Whitepaper: Best practices for a DevOps approach with IBM System z.* Retrieved from IBM Software: https://www14.software.ibm.com/webapp/iwm/web/signup.do?source=swg-rtl-sd-wp&S_PKG=ov26345

Reinertsen, D. G. (2009). *The Principles of Product Development Flow: Second Generation Lean Product Development.* Celeritas.

Roberts, A. (2009, May 14). *How To Build a Championship Basketball Team.* Retrieved from Bleacher Report: http://bleacherreport.com/articles/174989-how-to-build-a-championship-basketball-team

Rosenbaum, M. (n.d.). *Strategies for the 4 x 100 Relay Race.* Retrieved from About.com: http://trackandfield.about.com/od/sprintsandrelays/a/400relaystrat.htm

Sun, J. L. (2013, May 7). *Don't Believe the Myth-information about the Mainframe.* Retrieved from share.org: http://www.share.org/p/bl/et/blogid=2&blogaid=234

Surowiecki, J. (2014). *Better All the Time*. Retrieved from newyorker.com: http://www.newyorker.com/magazine/2014/11/10/better-time

Taylor, B. (2014, April 14). *Why Amazon Is Copying Zappos and Paying Employees to Quit*. Retrieved from Harvard Business Review: https://hbr.org/2014/04/why-amazon-is-copying-zappos-and-paying-employees-to-quit/

UML. (2005). uml.org. Retrieved from What is UML?: http://www.uml.org/what-is-uml.htm

Ward, S. C. (2012, July 23). *The Fastest Baton to the Finish Line*. Retrieved from nytimes.com: http://www.nytimes.com/interactive/2012/07/23/sports/olympics/the-fastest-baton-to-the-finish-line.html?_r=0

Wikipedia. (n.d.). *Daily Standup Meeting*. Retrieved from Wikipedia: https://en.wikipedia.org/wiki/Stand-up_meeting

Williamson, S. S. (2014, May 13). *DevOps for mobile apps challenges and best practices*. Retrieved from IBM DeveloperWorks: https://www.ibm.com/developerworks/library/mo-bestdevops-mobileapps/

Chapter 5

Blue Label Labs. (2016, April 19). *MVPs: Why a Minimum Viable Product Is Your Most Valuable Player*. Retrieved from IdeaToAppster: https://www.bluelabellabs.com/ideatoappster/mvps-why-a-minimum-viable-product-is-your-most-valuable-player/

Bowen, M. (2015, May 21). *What It Takes to Be a Special Teams Demon*. Retrieved from Bleacher Report: http://bleacherreport.com/articles/2470321-what-it-takes-to-be-a-special-teams-demon

Brown, C. (2013, January 25). *Speak My Language*. Retrieved from grantland.com: http://grantland.com/features/how-terminology-erhardt-perkins-system-helped-maintain-dominance-tom-brady-patriots/

Brown, K. (2016). Microservices Architectures for Cloud. *IBM InterConnect 2016*. IBM.

Brown, K. (2016, April 13). *Refactoring to microservices, Part 1 and 2*. Retrieved from IBM DeveloperWorks: https://www.ibm.com/developerworks/cloud/library/cl-refactor-microservices-bluemix-trs-1/index.html

CattleTags.com. (2016). *Year Letter Designations for Beef Cattle Numbering*. Retrieved from CattleTags.com: http://www.cattletags.com/beef-cattle-year-letter-designations

Cavin, J. W. (2014, December 18). *Seattle Sounders Sports Science Weekend: Building the Anti-fragile Athlete: Dave Tenney*. Retrieved from jameswcavin .com: http://www.jameswcavin.com/clinicians-and-coaches/2014/12/18/yiux6yv6ro6feual4j5qelwremc77i

Chase, C. (2015, September 9). *What is Roger Federer's new SABR move?* Retrieved from usatoday.com: http://ftw.usatoday.com/2015/09/what-is-roger-federers-new-sabr-move

Chiara Brandle, e. a. (2014, January 7). *Cloud Computing Patterns of Expertise*. Retrieved from IBm Redpaper: http://www.redbooks.ibm.com/abstracts/redp5040.html?Open

Cloud Native Computing Foundation. (2015, November 6). *CNCF Charter*. Retrieved from CNCF.io: https://cncf.io/about/charter

Edelman, D. M. (2015, October). *How to scale your own digital disruption*. Retrieved from McKinsey.com: http://www.mckinsey.com/business-functions/operations/our-insights/how-to-scale-your-own-digital-disruption

ESPN Developer Center. (2015). *ESPN API Explorer*. Retrieved from ESPN Developer Center: http://www.espn.com/static/apis/devcenter/io-docs.html

Farrell, A. (2008, August 20). *America's Top 10 Olympic Schools*. Retrieved from Forbes: http://www.forbes.com/2008/08/20/olympics-colleges-phelps-biz-sports_cx_af_0820olympics.html

Farres, L. G. (2004, Fall). *Becoming a Better Coach through Reflective Practice*. Retrieved from mindinmotion.ca: http://www.mindinmotion.ca/articles/lgfarres_reflective_practice.pdf

Feinberg, R. (2011, Summer). *Baseball's Newest Farm System*. Retrieved from Americas Quarterly: http://www.americasquarterly.org/node/2752

Fordacell, M. B. (2006, November). *Real Madrid football club: A new model of business organization for sports clubs in Spain*. Retrieved from researchgate.net: https://www.researchgate.net/publication/229478080_Real_Madrid_football_club_A_new_model_of_business_organization_for_sports_clubs_in_Spain

Fowler, J. L. (2014, March 25). *Microservices*. Retrieved from martinfowler.com: http://martinfowler.com/articles/microservices.html

Frederick, S. (2016, February 10). *Which cloud? Any cloud: Getting started with portable HOT documents*. Retrieved from Freddy on Cloudy Stuff: https://sudhakarf.wordpress.com/2016/02/10/which-cloud-any-cloud-designing-portable-hot-documents-with-urbancode/

He, L. (2013, March 29). *Google's Secrets Of Innovation: Empowering Its Employees.* Retrieved from Forbes: `http://www.forbes.com/sites/laurahe/2013/03/29/googles-secrets-of-innovation-empowering-its-employees/`

IBM Design. (2016). *IBM Design Thinking Field Guide.* IBM Design.

IBM Institute for Business Value. (2016). *Digital reinvention in action.* Retrieved from ibm.com: `https://www-01.ibm.com/common/ssi/cgi-bin/ssialias?htmlfid=GBE03752USEN`

Imgur, U. a. (2013, January 28). *Redbox used to be for more than movies. Found this in DC in 2004.* Retrieved from imgur.com: `http://imgur.com/HmQNCwj`

Jenkins, M. (1998). *Overtraining Syndrome .* Retrieved from rice.edu: `http://www.rice.edu/~jenky/sports/overtraining.html`

Joe Loewengruber, K. G. (2016). *High Availability.* Retrieved from IBM Garage Method: `https://www.ibm.com/devops/method/content/manage/practice_high_availability/`

Kalavalapalli, Y. (2016, April 8). *Sony looks to extend IPL broadcasting rights.* Retrieved from Live Mint: `http://www.livemint.com/Companies/NXFJ1Ycguzq1a4vxuv1ruL/Sony-looks-to-extend-IPL-broadcasting-rights.html`

Koffel, W. (2014, January 4). *12-Factor Apps in Plain English.* Retrieved from ClearlyTech: `http://www.clearlytech.com/2014/01/04/12-factor-apps-plain-english/`

Li, C.-S. (2014, March). *Software defined environments: An introduction.* Retrieved from Researchgate: `https://www.researchgate.net/publication/261718883_Software_defined_environments_An_introduction`

Lopez, A. (2014, May 14). *The ESPN Effect – The Evolution of our Sports Consumption.* Retrieved from page2sports: `http://page2sports.com/6038/espn-effect-evolution-sports-consumption-2`

Martin, M. (2014, August 12). *FastCustomer can help get you out of customer service hell.* Retrieved from engadget.com: `https://www.engadget.com/2014/12/08/fastcustomer-can-help-get-you-out-of-customer-service-hell/`

Martinez, C. (2016, August 25). *2016 Rio Olympics: Current NCAA student-athletes competing by school.* Retrieved from NCAA: `http://www.ncaa.com/news/ncaa/article/2016-07-28/2016-rio-olympics-ncaa-olympic-student-athletes-school`

NIST, U.S. Department of Commerce. (2011, September). *The NIST definition of Cloud Computing.* Retrieved from nist.gov: `http://nvlpubs.nist.gov/nistpubs/Legacy/SP/nistspecialpublication800-145.pdf`

Olenski, S. (2015, February 20). *How Pro Sports Teams Are Taking The Customer Experience To The Next Level*. Retrieved from Forbes.com: http://www.forbes.com/sites/steveolenski/2015/02/20/how-pro-sports-teams-are-taking-the-customer-experience-to-the-next-level/2/#4c384afe1c31

OpenStack.org. (2016, September 8). *Networking API v2.0*. Retrieved from OpenStack Documentation: http://developer.openstack.org/api-ref/networking/v2/?expanded=create-network-detail

Peranandam, C. (2012, September 10). *Orchestrating the cloud to simplify and accelerate service delivery*. Retrieved from IBM DeveloperWorks: https://www.ibm.com/developerworks/community/blogs/9e696bfa-94af-4f5a-ab50-c955cca76fd0/entry/orchestrating_the_cloud_to_simplify_and_accelerate_service_delivery1?lang=en

Ries, E. (2011). *The Lean Startup: How Today's Entrepreneurs Use Continuous Innovation to Create Radically Successful Businesses*. Crown Business.

Roettgers, J. (2008, May 3). *Whatever Happened to Red Swoosh?* Retrieved from GigaOm: https://gigaom.com/2008/05/03/whatever-happened-to-red-swoosh/

Spiewak, S. (2016, April 29). *Multi-sport Athletes Dominate First Round of 2016 NFL Draft*. Retrieved from USA Football: http://usafootball.com/blogs/americas-game/post/12009/multi-sport-athletes-dominate-first-round-of-2016-nfl-draft

Taleb, N. N. (2007). *The Black Swan: The Impact of the Highly Improbable*. Random House.

Taleb, N. N. (2012). *Antifragile: Things That Gain from Disorder*. Random House.

The Movie Network. (2014, February 26). *The Rental Revolution: How Redbox Revitalized the Movie Rental Industry*. Retrieved from Themovienetwork.com: http://www.themovienetwork.com/article/rental-revolution-how-redbox-revitalized-movie-rental-industry

Timmons, A. (2008, November 2). *The 10 Greatest Multi-Sport Athletes of All Time*. Retrieved from Bleacher Report: http://bleacherreport.com/articles/76583-the-10-greatest-multi-sport-athletes-of-all-time

Triplett, M. (2014, July 3). *Saints' top plays: 'Ambush' onside kick*. Retrieved from ESPN: http://www.espn.com/blog/nfcsouth/post/_/id/55736/saints-top-play-ambush-onside-kick

Tseitlin, Y. I. (2011, July 19). *The Netflix Simian Army*. Retrieved from The Netflix Tech Blog: http://techblog.netflix.com/2011/07/netflix-simian-army.html

Wilson, J. (2010, April 23). *Business Model Generation: Osterwalder rethinks the publishing industry.* Retrieved from MaRS: https://www.marsdd.com/news-and -insights/business-model-generation-osterwalder-rethinks-the -publishing-industry/

Wolverine, E. (2014, September 4). *Michigan Wolverine Football: Coaches Orchestrating The Big Game.* Retrieved from http://gbmwolverine.com: http:// gbmwolverine.com/2014/09/04/michigan-wolverine-football-coaches -orchestrating-big-game/

Chapter 6

Boyd, I. (2014, August 20). *Evolving the Option.* Retrieved from SB Nation: http://www.sbnation.com/college-football/2014/8/20/6044003/read -option-pass-play-football-xs-os-diagrams

Brealy, C. M. (2016). Adding your tools to IBM Cloud Platform DevOps Toolchains. *IBM InterConnect* (pp. 12, 14). Las Vegas, NV: IBM.

Christofes, M. (2014, April 26). *Engineering Failures: Apollo 13.* Retrieved from Michael Christoffes Engineering Design Blog http://sites .psu.edu/mchristofes/2014/04/26/engineering-failures-apollo-13/

Davie, B. (2015, October 29). *Football 101: Option football.* Retrieved from ESPN .com: http://static.espn.go.com/ncf/columns/davie/1447132.html

DW on Sport. (2012, February 24). *The Importance of Goalkeeping.* Retrieved from DW on Sport: http://www.sportdw.com/2012/02/importance-of -goalkeeping.html

Elder, M. J. (2014, June 1). *Security considerations for DevOps adoption.* Retrieved from IBm DeveloperWorks: https://www.ibm.com/developerworks/ library/d-security-considerations-devops-adoption/

Flynn, D. (2016, June 24). *Outsourced! Foreign Players Constitute Half of NBA Draft's First Round Picks.* Retrieved from www.breitbart.com: http://www.breitbart .com/sports/2016/06/24/outsourced-foreign-players-constitute-half -of-nba-drafts-first-round-picks/

Gartner. (2016). *IT Glossary.* Retrieved from Gartner: http://blogs.gartner.com/ it-glossary/competency-center/

IBM Design Thinking Field Guide. (2016). *IBM Design Thinking Field Guide.* IBM Design.

iSport.com. (n.d.). *History of Gymnastics.* Retrieved from iSport.com Gymnastics: http://gymnastics.isport.com/gymnastics-guides/history -of-gymnastics

Ivarsson, H. K. (2012, October). *Scaling Agile @ Spotify.* Retrieved from Scribd .com: https://www.scribd.com/document/113617905/Scaling-Agile -Spotify

Parcells, B. (2000, November). *The Tough Work of Turning Around a Team.* Retrieved from Harvard Business Review : https://hbr.org/2000/11/the-tough -work-of-turning-around-a-team

Popper, N. (2012, August 2). *Knight Capital Says Trading Glitch Cost It $440 Million.* Retrieved from New York Times: http://dealbook.nytimes.com/2012/08/02/ knight-capital-says-trading-mishap-cost-it-440-million/?_r=0

Smith, J. (2015, June 22). *How "Thinking Like A Developer" Disrupts The Boardroom.* Retrieved from Forbes.com: http://www.forbes.com/sites/ ibm/2015/06/22/how-thinking-like-a-developer-disrupts-the -boardroom/#d9436cb41203

TheSportsCampus. (2016, August 19). *Gopichand, the man behind India's successful women shuttlers.* Retrieved from The Sports Campus: http://www .thesportscampus.com/2016081955475/articles/gopichand-the-man -behind-indias-successful-women-shuttlers

Toyota Production System. (n.d.). *Kaizen.* Retrieved from Toyota Material Handling: http://www.toyota-forklifts.eu/En/company/Toyota-Production -System/Kaizen/Pages/default.aspx

Whitmore, J. T. (2012, August 15). *Security in Development: The IBM Secure Engineering Framework.* Retrieved from IBm DeveloperWorks: https://www .ibm.com/developerworks/library/se-framework/

Chapter 7

Breer, A. (2013, June 10). *Who's really in charge? Power structures vary across NFC East.* Retrieved from NFL.com: http://www.nfl.com/news/story /0ap1000000210494/printable/whos-ireallyi-in-charge-power -structures-vary-across-nfc-east

Brustein, J. (2011, March 12). *A Better Way to Watch Sports.* Retrieved from nytimes.com: http://www.nytimes.com/2011/03/13/weekinreview/ 13watch.html?_r=0

Foss, M. (2015, March 11). *Chip Kelly reminds the NFL that letting a coach also be a GM is stupid.* Retrieved from USA Today: http://ftw.usatoday.com/2015/03/ chip-kelly-reminds-the-nfl-that-letting-a-coach-also-be-gm-is-stupid

Gallo, C. (2014, August 19). *The Coach Behind The Longest Winning Streak In Sports History Shows How To Build A Champion Business Team*. Retrieved from Forbes .com: http://www.forbes.com/sites/carminegallo/2014/08/19/the -coach-behind-the-longest-winning-streak-in-sports-history-shows -how-to-build-a-champion-business-team/#a65422b1e906

Hewitt, J. (2015, June 13). *Why Mavericks are good for Sport ?* Retrieved from InternationalRacer.com: http://www.j3sm.com/index.php/modules-menu/ alpine-ski-racing-academy-coaches-corner/104-fast-or-technical -and-why-mavericks-are-good-for-sport

Minick, E. (2015, April 16). *Building a DevOps Team that Isn't Evil*. Retrieved from IBM DeveloperWorks: https://developer.ibm.com/urbancode/docs/building-a -devops-team-that-isnt-evil/

Reid, L. (2015, June 22). *The Simple Math of DevOps*. Retrieved from DevOps .com: http://devops.com/2015/06/22/the-simple-math-of-devops/

Robbins, B. (2015, January 22). *Meet the technology titans transforming the NBA*. Retrieved from TheGuardian.com: https://www.theguardian.com/sport/ 2015/jan/22/technology-titans-transform-the-nba

Rosenbush, S. (2015, April 27). *IBM CIO Designs New IT Workflow for Tech Giant Under Pressure*. Retrieved from Wall Street Journal: http:// blogs.wsj.com/cio/2015/04/27/ibm-cio-designs-new-it-workflow -for-struggling-tech-giant/

Witnify. (2014, February 11). *The 1980 Miracle On Ice: Herb Brooks*. Retrieved from sbnation.com: http://www.sbnation.com/miracle-on-ice-1980 -us-hockey/2014/2/11/5400156/the-1980-miracle-on-ice-herb-brooks

Appendix

Forrester. (n.d.). *Water-Scrum-Fall Is The Reality Of Agile For Most Organizations Today*. Retrieved from Forrester.com: https://www.forrester .com/report/WaterScrumFall+Is+The+Reality+Of+Agile+For+Most+ Organizations+Today/-/E-RES60109

Garvin, David A., Amy C. Edmondson, and F. G. (n.d.). *Is yours a Learning Organization?* Retrieved from hbr.org: https://hbr.org/2008/03/ is-yours-a-learning-organization

Kaz, P. (n.d.). *Measurement Myopia*. Retrieved from Drucker Institure: http://www.druckerinstitute.com/2013/07/measurement-myopia/

Kruchten, P. (n.d.). *The 4+1 View Model of architecture*. Retrieved from ieee.org: http://ieeexplore.ieee.org/xpl/articleDetails.jsp?arnumber=469759

Lean.org. (n.d.). *Lean.org.* Retrieved from Lean.org: http://www.lean.org/
WhatsLean/History.cfm

Standard, B. (2014, November 4). *Khosla Ventures incubates startup to enable bank transactions via kirana stores.* Retrieved from Business Standard: http://www.business-standard.com/article/companies/khosla-incubates-start-up-to-enable-bank-transcations-via-kirana-stores-114110400013_1.html

Index

Printed and bound by CPI Group (UK) Ltd, Croydon, CR0 4YY

27/10/2024

14580318-0002